KU-504-338

MARVEL
THE AVENGERS
ENCYCLOPEDIA

Editor Emma Grange
Senior Designer Jo Connor
Editorial Assistant Beth Davies
Designer Sam Bartlett
Pre-Production Producer Marc Staples
Producer David Appleyard
Managing Editor Simon Hugo
Managing Art Editor Guy Harvey
Art Director Lisa Lanzarini
Publisher Julie Ferris
Publishing Director Simon Beecroft

Extra design by Amazing15

First published in Great Britain in 2015
by Dorling Kindersley Limited,
80 Strand, London, WC2R 0RL

A Penguin Random House Company
10 9 8 7 6 5 4 3 2 1
001–259438–Oct/2015

A CIP catalogue record for this book is available from the British Library.

ISBN 978-0-24118-371-7

Printed and bound in China

marvel.com

www.dk.com
A WORLD OF IDEAS
SEE ALL THERE IS TO KNOW

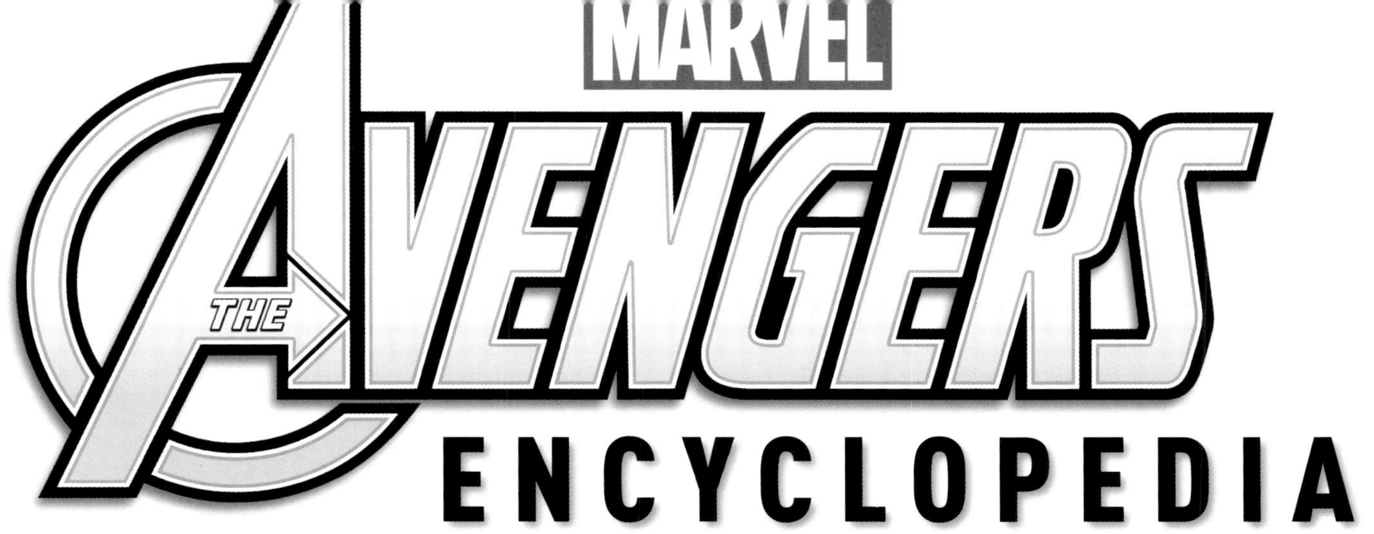

MARVEL

THE AVENGERS ENCYCLOPEDIA

Written by
Matt Forbeck, Matthew K. Manning, and Dan Wallace,
with Alan Cowsill and Glenn Dakin

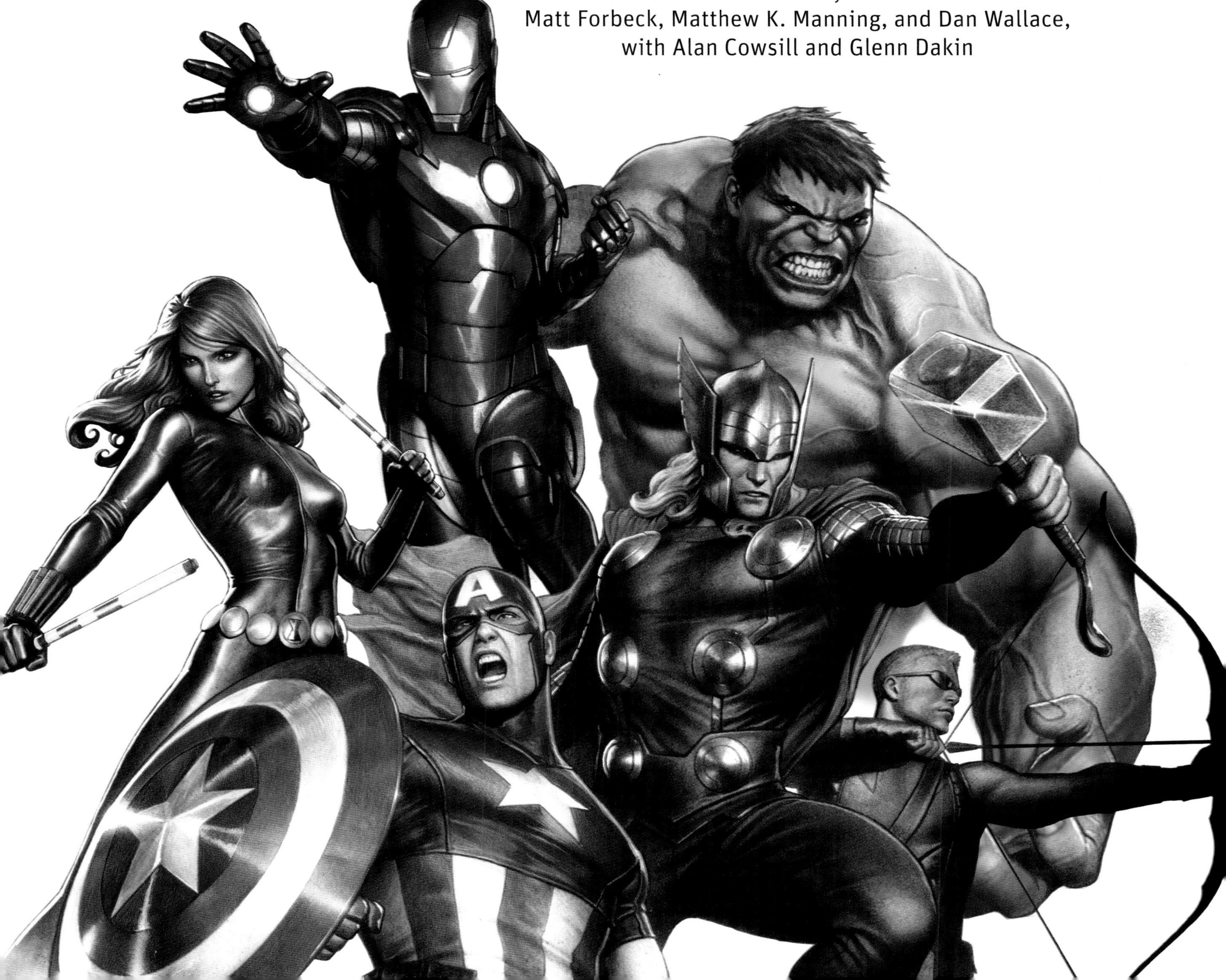

CONTENTS

CHAPTER STRUCTURE

This encyclopedia is arranged thematically, with characters grouped in chapters according to the type of powers they possess—from the mystical to the technological. A more detailed contents can be found at the beginning of each chapter, listing all the entries that feature within it.

FROM GODS TO ROBOTS, aliens to Inhumans, these beings all have powers based on their non-human biology. Includes Thor, Vision, Ultron, Thanos, and Ms. Marvel.

WHEN MANY HEROES—or villains—assemble in a single group or organization they become a mighty force. Includes the Avengers, S.H.I.E.L.D., and A-Force.

KEY STORYLINES

DEFINITIVE MOMENTS in the Avengers' history include their auspicious first outing, the introduction of new members, as well as some of their greatest struggles.

FOREWORD

FIVE DECADES OF the Mighty Avengers! What an inspiring legacy. In the first issue, Loki, the Asgardian god of evil inadvertently brought the original team together when he sought vengeance on his hated half-brother, Thor. Other heroes became embroiled in the conflict precipitating a historic union. Since that halcyon day, their roster has changed countless times. But one fact has remained indisputable: The Avengers exist to battle the foes that no single hero could defeat. The Avengers pull their membership from every corner of the Marvel Universe. Their lineup has included a super-soldier, several gods, a gamma-irradiated Hulk, an armored man, an android, a magician, a former Soviet spy, several mutants, and a brilliant biochemist who can shrink to the size of an ant.

The first 18 issues were dominated by Thor, Iron Man, Giant-Man, and the Wasp, in mainly single-issue tales that established the group dynamics that became their hallmark. And then, writer/editor Stan Lee suddenly changed the members, shocking the readership. Gone were many of the powerhouses. Now, Captain America, who had been thawed out from a block of ice in the landmark fourth issue, presided over a team featuring two outcast mutants—Quicksilver and the Scarlet Witch—and the reformed Super Villain, ace archer Hawkeye. These far less powerful stalwarts still proved a formidable force against such foes as Attuma and the Sons of the Serpent. Cap's legendary leadership qualities were strained to the breaking point with his attempt to make this disparate trio a well-honed fighting unit.

Another era began with the arrival of writer Roy Thomas, who brought in the Black Panther from the pages of *Fantastic Four* and Roy's seminal creation, the Vision, who became the heart of the Avengers for decades. Multi-issue storylines

became the norm under his direction. The highly influential Kree-Skrull War had echoes that still reverberate throughout the Marvel Universe. Other writers created their own epics such as the Avengers-Defenders War, the Korvac Saga, Under Siege, Galactic Storm, and Avengers Forever, cementing this title's reputation as the canvas where the most monumental of events could find form and substance. No landscape, unearthly domain or time period is off-limits to the Assemblers. They have adventured everywhere from the dizzying heights of Olympus to the ocean's wine-dark depths. They have faced adversaries as dissimilar as the Masters of Evil, the Zodiac, the Squadron Sinister and the Council of Cross-Time Kangs. They have emerged victorious on every occasion—because they are a committed team.

Something that has been fairly consistent about this title is the constant increase in the number of characters who can call themselves Avengers. Currently, a mind-boggling 130 characters could answer the call. That must be a record for any Super Hero team. And with the proliferation of members has come an expansion in the number of related titles. The *Avengers* has gone from a single book to also include *Uncanny Avengers*, *New Avengers*, *Secret Avengers*, *Mighty Avengers*, *Young Avengers*, and a plethora of limited series. Each series focuses on an aspect of the larger Avengers franchise to satisfy the readership's seemingly insatiable desire for more of Earth's Mightiest Heroes.

These titles were collectively at ground zero of the biggest event in the history of Marvel that played out in the spring of 2015. This momentous story encompassed nothing less than the reimagining of the entire Marvel Universe through a cosmic series of events that took center stage in the Avengers. When the dust settled from this years-in-the-making epic, nothing was the same. And it began and ended with the Avengers.

I've had the pleasure and rare privilege of being a reader, writer, and editor of the *Avengers*. It was through my multiple associations with the title that I came to understand the enormous importance of teamwork. Our ancestors may have huddled in caves, but they huddled together. They hunted and fought together. Early man depended on his fellows to live. They were the first Avengers, in a way, because a common cause—survival—brought them together to face the harsh world they were born into. The Avengers are first and foremost a team, not a family or a military unit. No matter the individual members' differences in race, gender, abilities, or temperament, they are more powerfully united in spirit than they are divided in the flesh. It is because they work together toward a common goal that they succeed.

Perhaps my most memorable connection to the Avengers was as editor of *Ultimates*, a book whose influence was felt throughout the comics industry, and was seen most significantly in the incredibly successful *Avengers* movies. The Ultimates are a darker, harder-edged version of the Avengers and exist on the Earth of another dimension. In a strange sense, I almost felt myself at odds with the mainstream *Avengers* series while I edited its *Ultimates* counterpart. I feared the irreverent, new kids on the block might eclipse their elder brethren, but in any incarnation, the essence of the Avengers shines through. They are still the greatest fighting force the world has ever known. And despite more than 50 years of publishing history, when you'd be tempted to think the concept would be drained of its originality and vitality, it's not so. The *Avengers* continue to be among the best-selling comics titles and the most successful of the Marvel movies. I have a hunch the best is yet to come. Avengers Assemble!

Ralph Macchio

Ralph Macchio
May 2015

SOME INDIVIDUALS STAND apart from those around them. These figures are greatly gifted, with their extraordinary powers granted through mutation, experimentation, or even by accident. Such powers come with the capacity for great good—or great evil—and in a world not always used to the out-of-the-ordinary, a superpowered life is not always an easy one. Abilities gained from gamma rays, spider venom, or even one's inherent genetic makeup are not easily ignored or altered. All that is certain is that such gifts provide the potential for incredible beings.

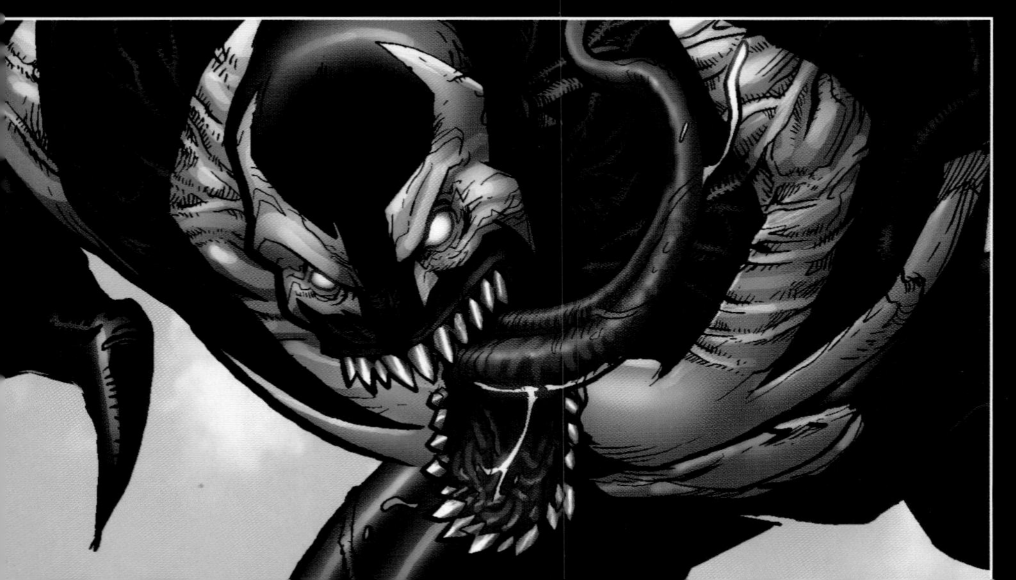

GREATLY GIFTED

SCIENTIFIC GENIUS Bruce Banner was hired to help the U.S. Army develop new weapons systems, including a new kind of nuclear warhead called the gamma bomb. On the day of the bomb's first test, teenager Rick Jones snuck onto the testing grounds on a dare. Bruce saved the boy but was caught in the blast himself, his entire body permeated with gamma radiation. As a result, Bruce transforms into the mighty monster known as the Hulk when he becomes agitated or angry. He is often angry.

The Avengers first united as a team thanks to the Hulk. The Asgardian god Loki tricked them into chasing down the Hulk, who appeared to be an enemy. After they discovered the trick, the Hulk decided he'd rather join the Avengers than fight them.

THE HULK

BIG, MEAN, AND GREEN!

Bruce Banner's father had abused him as a child and even killed Bruce's mother. Young Bruce managed to repress the anger this caused him—but the Hulk didn't.

The Hulk doesn't care for his alter ego, Bruce, whom he considers to be a gutless weakling. He often refers to Bruce as "Puny Banner."

As far as the U.S. Army doctors could tell, the gamma-bomb explosion that Bruce was caught in hadn't harmed him at all. In fact, it had given him incredible powers that could only be unlocked under certain circumstances. Bruce had little control over these circumstances at first, and despite the liberation and empowerment he felt when he became the Hulk, it also terrified him. At the time, Bruce was dating Betty Ross, the daughter of General Thaddeus "Thunderbolt" Ross, his Army supervisor. Bruce tried to keep his identity as the Hulk a secret, fearful of what Betty—much less her father—would think if she discovered who the Hulk really was. When the truth finally came out, Bruce fled, becoming a fugitive from both the Army and the law.

The Hulk was therefore a fugitive when he joined the Avengers, and he left the team after a short space of time. His incredible power was a tremendous asset to the team, but his mercurial nature made him dangerous to be around. His teammates welcomed him back several times, but they always kept a close eye on his temper.

The angrier the Hulk gets, the harder it is for anyone to mentally control him—including himself.

The Hulk's clothes don't transform with him. Banner often wears stretchy pants.

By slapping his hands together, he can cause a loud, violent shockwave.

Bruce saved Rick Jones from the gamma-ray blast by pushing him into the shelter of a trench, but the bomb's all-consuming rays altered Bruce's DNA—and his life—forever.

The Hulk started out gray, but his skin is usually green.

ALLIES AND ENEMIES

The Hulk has made countless foes over the years but, despite his volatility, he still has a number of friends he can trust with his life. His family has given him both comfort and anguish.

SKAAR
Hulk's son tried to kill his father for abandoning Skaar's home planet, Sakaar.

SHE-HULK
Bruce gave his cousin, attorney Jennifer Walters, an emergency blood transfusion.

RED SHE-HULK
Bruce's first wife, Betty, was thought dead but returned to life as the Red She-Hulk.

RED HULK
Betty's father, General Ross, became the Red Hulk to avenge his daughter's death.

CAIERA
Hulk's wife on Sakaar, ruled alongside him as queen. She was Skaar's mother.

A-BOMB
For a while, Rick Jones could transform into a creature resembling the Abomination.

AMADEUS CHO
This young genius formed a strong friendship with Bruce Banner.

KORG
A Kronan from Saturn, Korg became one of Hulk's Warbound team on Sakaar.

FOES

LEADER
This gamma-powered genius and criminal mastermind considers Hulk his nemesis.

ABOMINATION
A Russian spy turned gamma-powered monster, this villain died at the Red Hulk's hands.

MIEK
Miek was a member of Hulk's Warbound team who betrayed him by letting Caiera die.

DATA FILE

REAL NAME

Robert Bruce Banner

OCCUPATION
Scientist, adventurer, monster

BASE
Mobile

HEIGHT 7 ft

WEIGHT 1,040 lbs

EYES Green

HAIR Green

FIRST APPEARANCE WITH AVENGERS
Avengers #1 (September 1963)

POWERS
The Hulk has superhuman durability, endurance, healing, speed, and strength. The angrier he gets, the stronger he gets, to an almost unlimited level. He is nearly invulnerable, can leap hundreds of miles at a time, and can effectively breathe underwater. He can survive unprotected in environments from the ocean's depths to outer space.

Hulk has often faced down foes who thought they were stronger than him, such as Abomination, but he always lives up to his catchphrase, "Hulk is the strongest one there is!"

HULK SMASH!

The Hulk has had a long and contentious relationship with his fellow Avengers. Despite their best efforts, they have often misunderstood him—and sometimes underestimated him—to their own detriment.

The Hulk is simultaneously one of the Avengers' greatest assets and most troubling problems. When he's out of control, he's a danger to everyone around him, and he embarrasses the Avengers by association. When he masters his temper, however, he's an amazing warrior, and when he can call on Bruce's mind, too—either as Bruce or in one of the Hulk's smarter forms—he is a nearly unbeatable combination of both brawns and brains.

HULK VS. EARTH After a battle with Tyrannus and Mole Man in their subterranean kingdoms, the Hulk found himself trapped and lost underground. He tried punching his way out, but when his efforts threatened to cause a disastrous earthquake, General Ross called in the Avengers to find and stop him. The heroes tracked down an enraged and confused Hulk, sending the ghost-like Vision down through the earth to lure him to the surface. But when the Avengers tried to capture him, he escaped.

HULK VS. HEROES After falling out with the Avengers soon after the team's formation, the Hulk's teammates chased after him, eager to either arrest him or bring him back into the fold. Angry that the Avengers wouldn't leave him alone, the Hulk decided to fight. He arrived in New York and soon clashed with both the Fantastic Four and the U.S. Army. When the Avengers eventually caught up with the Hulk, he took on all three forces at once!

THE MANY INCARNATIONS OF **THE HULK**

To cope with his past troubles, Bruce Banner's mind has splintered and created multiple personalities for him. In his different forms, the Hulk represents one or more of these personalities, at various stages of integration with Bruce's main self.

HULK VS. SPACE While the Super Villain Thanos and his navy attacked Earth, the Hulk joined the bulk of the Avengers on a mission into deep space to meet an even greater threat: the invasion of the Builders, an ancient race planning to destroy the entire planet. At this point in time, Bruce had a good amount of control over the Hulk, and he made an excellent and important member of the team. He and the Avengers worked in conjunction with other galactic civilizations to put an end to the Builder threat.

BRUCE BANNER Terrified by his abusive father's explosive, lethal anger, Bruce forbade himself to ever lose control in a similar way. In his main personality—which has no superpowers except for his incredible intellect—Bruce still struggles to keep a tight handle on himself for fear of what might happen when he loses that internal battle.

GRAY HULK While Bruce underwent therapy with psychiatrist Doc Samson, his Gray Hulk personality emerged. Street-smart rather than book-smart, he made his home in Las Vegas and called himself Joe Fixit. Instead of transforming only when he became angry, he remained as the crude-natured Fixit for months. When Bruce returned, for a time he became himself by day and Fixit by night.

MAESTRO When the Hulk traveled to a possible future in which the world had been ravaged by nuclear war, he found the world ruled by an older version of himself, who was stronger than ever due to the irradiation of the planet. The Maestro, as he called himself, was as intelligent as Bruce, even when in his Hulk form.

HULK VS. HIMSELF Bruce was shot in the head while working for S.H.I.E.L.D., and despite life-saving surgery, he suffered terrible brain damage which would take time to heal. Although becoming the Hulk could make his injury permanent, Bruce voluntarily made the transformation to save the Avengers from the mindless, remote-controlled Abomination. Iron Man later repaired the Hulk's brain damage with a version of the Extremis virus, which gave the Hulk a new, intelligent personality known as Doc Green.

GREEN SCAR Sent to the planet Sakaar by the Illuminati, the Hulk and Bruce were forced to work closer together than ever before. They became the Green Scar, who was not only a great warrior but a canny and wise ruler as well. This incarnation of the Hulk generally remained calm, but when he got enraged, he was known as "Worldbreaker", as he was strong enough to literally destroy a planet.

DOC GREEN After Iron Man's Extremis virus helped heal Bruce's brain of gunshot damage, Bruce became a smart and calm green-skinned Hulk who was known as Doc Green. He remained in this form for long periods, refusing to change back into Bruce Banner. He also set out to remove the powers of all the other gamma-irradiated superhumans he could find.

THE STRONGEST ONE THERE IS!

Although the Hulk hasn't been a stable member of the Avengers throughout the team's history, he was one of its founders, and played a lead role in many of the team's most memorable stories.

At the time of the battle with the Olympian God Ares, the Avengers hadn't had many members. Years later, they would be able to assemble scores of heroes.

HULK REJOINS THE TEAM

Avengers #100 (June 1972)

After leaving the Avengers in their early days, the Hulk finally set aside his differences with his teammates and returned to lend them a hand when they needed it most. The Olympian God of War, Ares, had taken up the Black Knight's enchanted sword, the Ebony Blade, which had previously been thought destroyed. Using it, Ares planned to gather an army strong enough to invade and conquer Earth. The Black Knight summoned every Avenger that had ever formed part of the team (up to that point) to stop him, including the Hulk. During the Avengers' battle with Ares, the sound of the pan pipes controlling the God of War's army attracted the attention of the Hulk. When the army turned in his direction, the Hulk destroyed it singlehandedly. Once the danger had ended, the Hulk left the Avengers once again.

THE HULK'S EXILE

Incredible Hulk #94 (June 2006)

At the request of Nick Fury, the Hulk went into space to save the world. Seeing a chance to safely exile the Hulk from Earth, the Illuminati trapped him on a spaceship and sent it toward an idyllic, uninhabited planet. Instead, the Hulk landed on the planet Sakaar, where he became enslaved as a gladiator.

During his time on Sakaar, the Hulk became known as the Green Scar. He led a rebellion that took over the planet.

THE TRAGEDY OF SAKAAR

Incredible Hulk #105 (June 2007)

After becoming Sakaar's ruler, the Hulk married Caiera and brought peace to the planet. However, tragedy struck when the Hulk's spaceship exploded, killing most of the people on the planet, including the pregnant Caiera. Her twin sons survived, but a furious Hulk vowed to take revenge on the Illuminati.

While Hulk blamed the explosion on the Illuminati, it had actually been triggered by terrorists on Sakaar.

The Sentry lost control of himself during this battle, and the Hulk had to force him to calm down.

"YES. HULK WILL SMASH FOR YOU."
- HULK TO CAPTAIN AMERICA

WORLD WAR HULK
World War Hulk #5 (November 2007)

The Hulk returned to Earth and captured the Illuminati, old allies who he now saw as his enemies. He exposed their apparent crimes against him, and then planned to execute them publicly in Madison Square Garden, New York City. Only the intervention of the Sentry halted the Hulk's murderous plans long enough for Iron Man to take control of satellites that had the firepower to bring down the Hulk.

THE HULK RETURNS
Avengers vs. X-Men #11 (September 2012)

When the powerful energy known as the Phoenix Force returned to Earth, the Avengers assembled to try to stop it, despite objections from the X-Men. The Phoenix Force fractured into pieces and took possession of five mutants, enhancing their powers. Captain America reached out to the Hulk for help once more. Afterward, Hulk became a member of the Avengers team again.

In stable periods, the relationship between the Avengers and Hulk worked so well that the Avengers helped Bruce stabilize his Hulk persona, and he even became an agent of S.H.I.E.L.D.

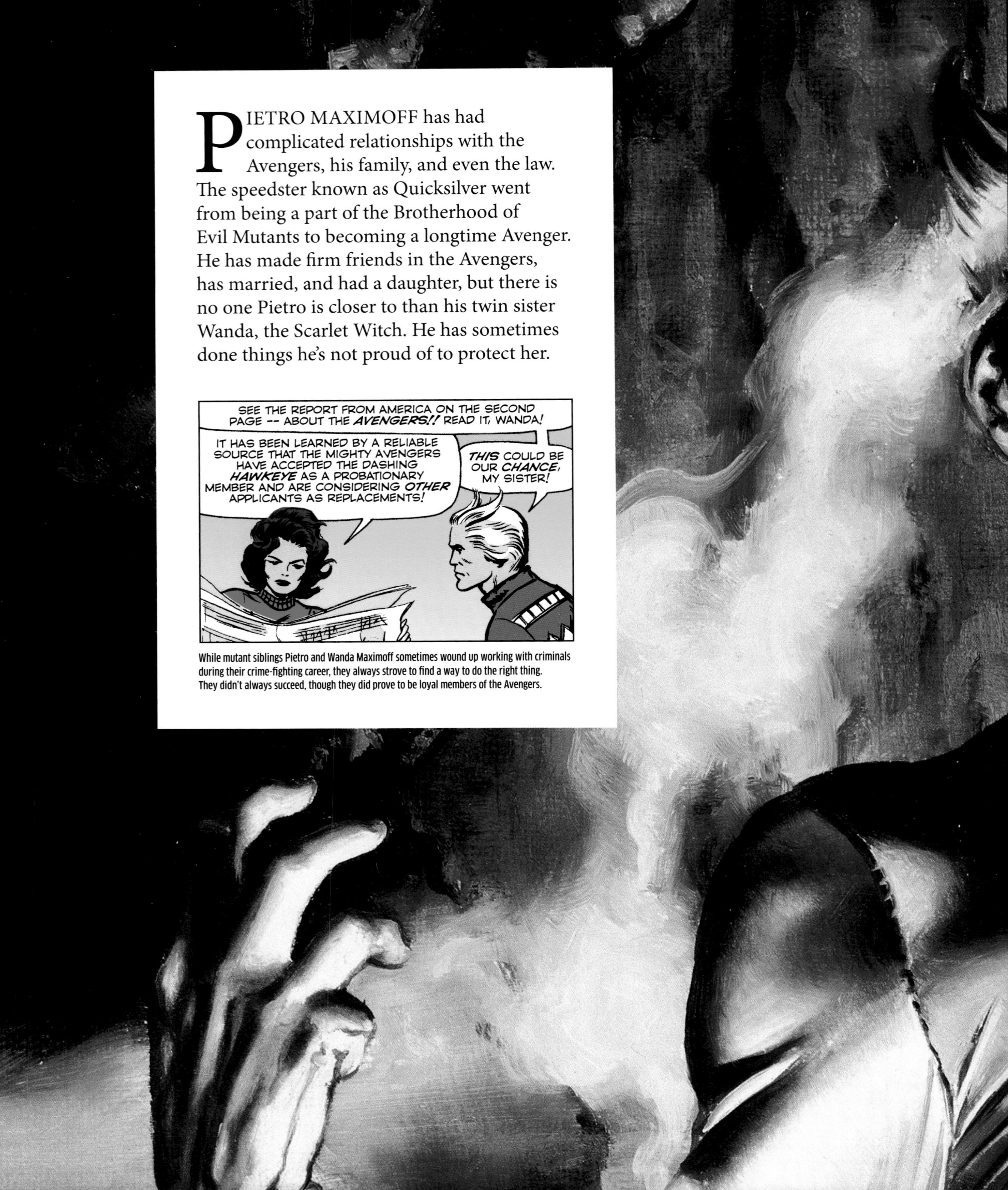

PIETRO MAXIMOFF has had complicated relationships with the Avengers, his family, and even the law. The speedster known as Quicksilver went from being a part of the Brotherhood of Evil Mutants to becoming a longtime Avenger. He has made firm friends in the Avengers, has married, and had a daughter, but there is no one Pietro is closer to than his twin sister Wanda, the Scarlet Witch. He has sometimes done things he's not proud of to protect her.

While mutant siblings Pietro and Wanda Maximoff sometimes wound up working with criminals during their crime-fighting career, they always strove to find a way to do the right thing. They didn't always succeed, though they did prove to be loyal members of the Avengers.

QUICKSILVER

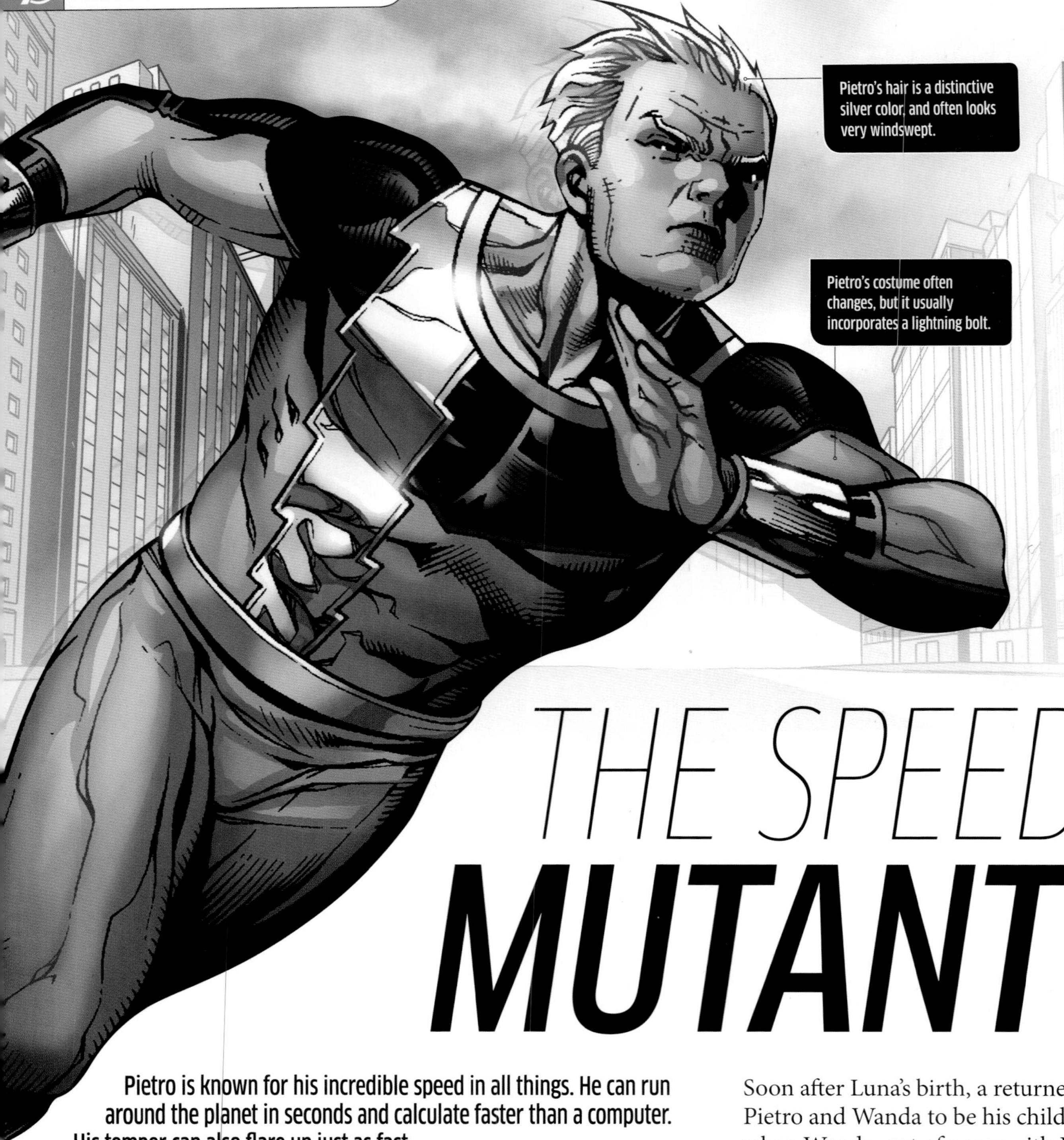

Pietro's hair is a distinctive silver color, and often looks very windswept.

Pietro's costume often changes, but it usually incorporates a lightning bolt.

DATA FILE

REAL NAME
Pietro Maximoff

OCCUPATION
Adventurer

BASE
Mobile

HEIGHT 6 ft

WEIGHT 175 lbs

EYES Blue

HAIR Silver

FIRST APPEARANCE WITH AVENGERS
Avengers #16 (August 1963)

POWERS
Pietro has superhuman durability, endurance, speed, and strength. He can run faster than the speed of light and can vibrate his molecules fast enough to allow him to run over water, fly, phase through objects, and disrupt or destroy objects. He is immune to any ill effects from his speed.

THE SPEEDSTER **MUTANT** HERO

Pietro is known for his incredible speed in all things. He can run around the planet in seconds and calculate faster than a computer. His temper can also flare up just as fast.

Pietro's mother, Madga, abandoned both him and his twin Wanda shortly after their birth, in an effort to protect them from her husband, Max Eisenhardt—the man who would become the powerful mutant Magneto. As adolescents, just after they developed their superpowers, the twins fled their adoptive parents.

Unaware of his connection to Wanda and Pietro, but believing the pair to be mutants, Magneto inducted the pair into his Super Villain team, the Brotherhood of Evil Mutants. After the Stranger defeated Magneto and the group was left without a leader, Pietro and Wanda took the opportunity to redeem themselves by joining the Avengers.

Pietro later met and married Crystal of the Inhumans Royal Family, and the couple had a daughter, Luna, together. Soon after Luna's birth, a returned Magneto revealed he believed Pietro and Wanda to be his children. Pietro later lost his powers when Wanda, out of anger with Magneto, removed the powers of most of Earth's mutants. Pietro recovered his powers by exposing himself to the Inhumans' biology-altering Terrigen Mists, and rejoined the Avengers soon after. Recently, Pietro and Wanda discovered that Magneto might not be their father after all.

Although Wanda is the more powerful of the twins, Pietro has always been protective of his sister. There is little he wouldn't do to keep her safe.

ALLIES AND ENEMIES

With his short temper, Pietro has angered many people over the years, including most of his friends. His family is loyal to him and he them, with the exception of his supposed father.

MAGNETO
Despite believing Magneto was his father, Pietro strove to be nothing like him.

SCARLET WITCH
Wanda means more to Pietro than anyone. Nothing can break their bond.

POLARIS
As Magneto's daughter, Polaris respects her supposed half-brother.

CRYSTAL
Pietro met his wife Crystal when she saved his life, but their marriage broke down.

LUNA
Pietro exposed his daughter to the Terrigen Mists to give her powers.

FRIENDS

GAMBIT
The Cajun mutant served with Quicksilver in the latest incarnation of X-Factor.

DANGER
A fellow X-Factor member, Danger is the personification of the X-Men's Danger Room.

FINESSE
Finesse blackmailed Pietro into becoming her mentor at the Avengers Academy.

FOES

FABIAN CORTEZ
A follower of Magneto, Cortez kidnapped Luna, earning Pietro's wrath.

LAYLA MILLER
This young mutant foiled Pietro's attempt to remold reality into the House of M.

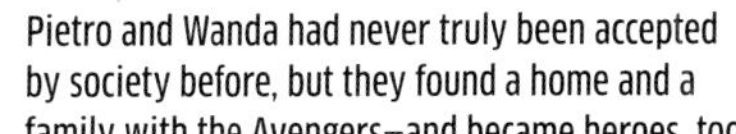

Pietro and Wanda had never truly been accepted by society before, but they found a home and a family with the Avengers—and became heroes, too.

Quicksilver is so fast he can appear to attack a foe from several angles at once. This can make him a challenge even for someone as mighty as Thor.

QUICKSILVER'S FAMILY TIES

Quicksilver may be the fastest person on the planet, but even he cannot outrun his past. His loyalty to those he loves takes precedence over his other ties.

For a while, Pietro and his twin sister Wanda mistakenly believed their parents to be Miss America and the Whizzer, two members of the Invaders—a Super Hero team that existed during World War II. Later, they became convinced that the mutant villain Magneto was actually their father instead. However, they recently learned that belief to be false as well. Despite this confusion over his biological relations, Pietro values the people he views as family over everything else, no matter how sorely that loyalty may be tested at times.

MAGNETO Magneto took both Pietro and Wanda under his protection after saving them from an angry mob, who were terrified at the sight of their powers. He made the siblings founding members of his Brotherhood of Evil Mutants. Later, he tried to become a decent father to them, but his violent struggle for civil rights for mutants often put them at odds with him instead.

SCARLET WITCH Pietro and his twin sister, Wanda, grew up unsure of their parentage, so Pietro spent much of his early life looking out her, because of her vulnerable nature. He has never shied away from that responsibility. Wanda became more independent as she and Pietro grew older, which sometimes drove a wedge between them. Pietro continues to always have her best interests at heart, though, even if he sometimes goes too far.

LUNA If there's anyone Pietro loves as much as his sister, it's his daughter, Luna. Despite this, he hasn't been there for her throughout much of her life, believing her to be better off with her mother, Crystal. However, when he managed to restore his own mutant powers using the Terrigen Mists, he used them to give Luna powers as well.

THE VISION Pietro doesn't care much for the Vision, the android hero who won Wanda's heart. He believed that Wanda should not be able to marry an artificial person, but her love for the Vision led her to override her brother's objections and marry the Vision anyway. The couple would later have twin boys of their own. The Vision and Pietro have since worked together on many Avengers teams, despite their differences.

CRYSTAL Crystal took care of Pietro after he was injured while helping the Avengers fight Sentinel robots. The two married quickly. They drifted apart just as fast, for many reasons such as his long absences and her infidelity, but she was his first real love.

SEVERING TIES With her moral axis flipped by magic, Wanda cast a spell designed to harm all who shared her blood. When Pietro was injured but Magneto emerged unscathed, Wanda and Pietro realized he could not be their true father. With this revelation and the breakdown of his marriage, Pietro now has no known relatives other than Wanda and Luna.

RACING FROM ONE THING TO THE NEXT

Quicksilver's career has been anything but stable. While he has become known as a hero, he has also committed numerous crimes, both before and after becoming an Avenger, although rarely for personal gain.

SACRIFICING HIMSELF FOR THE AVENGERS

Avengers #104 (October 1972)

Giant robots known as Sentinels were programmed to eliminate all mutants. They captured the Scarlet Witch and used her to power a machine that caused solar flares that would destroy not only mutants, but the entire Earth. During the course of events, Pietro risked his life to destroy one of the Sentinels, who was attacking both him and Larry Trask—son of the Sentinels' creator, whom Pietro had kidnapped in order to help him save his sister. Pietro tricked the Sentinel into chasing him with super speed and then charged into a solid wall, almost killing himself. The Sentinel followed suit, and the impact destroyed it. This allowed Larry Trask to flee and help the Avengers destroy the remaining Sentinals and save Wanda. Trask died during the final battle with the Sentinals, and Pietro's actions went unnoticed by the Avengers. Later, while healing from his wounds, Pietro met Crystal and fell in love.

Larry Trask had previously been a mutant hunter, like his father, but Quicksilver's bravery gave Larry a chance to be a hero.

When he discovered what Pietro had done, Magneto attacked and killed him, forcing Wanda to revive her brother and reverse her new reality.

THE HOUSE OF M

House of M #7 (November 2005)

The loss of Wanda's twins caused her to go insane. Pietro was sure that the Avengers and X-Men would be forced to execute her before she could use her reality-warping powers to do damage. He convinced Wanda to create a reality in which mutants ruled benevolently over the world, known as the House of M. Wanda eventually allowed this reality to fall apart. However, when she declared "No more mutants," all but 198 mutants lost their powers in the real world.

"I SWORE UPON MY LIFE TO PROTECT HER!!"
- QUICKSILVER

Pietro exposed his daughter Luna to the Terrigen Mists, too. She gained the power to sense other people's emotions and control or remove them.

RESTORING HIS POWERS

Son of M #3 (April 2006)

After the destruction of Wanda's warped reality, Pietro was turned from a mutant to a normal human—and quickly decided he could not stomach being without his powers. He asked to immerse himself in the Inhumans' Terrigen Mists to regain his powers, but his request was refused. Pietro therefore took matters into his own hands and broke into the Terrigen Caves to expose himself to the mists. His powers were returned to him, and he even gained the ability to make short hops through time. He then set about exposing more ex-mutants to the mists so they could restore their powers, too.

TEACHING NEW AVENGERS

Avengers Academy #2 (September 2010)

The Avengers set up Avengers Academy to train young superhumans to become heroes. The academy focused in particular on the superhumans who were in most danger of one day becoming Super Villains. Pietro signed up as one of the academy's original instructors. However, he soon found himself being blackmailed by one of his unruly students, Finesse. She used her knowledge that Pietro had stolen some Terrigen Crystals to force him into teaching her everything he knew from his time as a villain in the Brotherhood of Mutants.

During his time at Avengers Academy, Pietro came to believe in (most of) the students there, and the potential they had for doing good in the world.

CAROL DANVERS

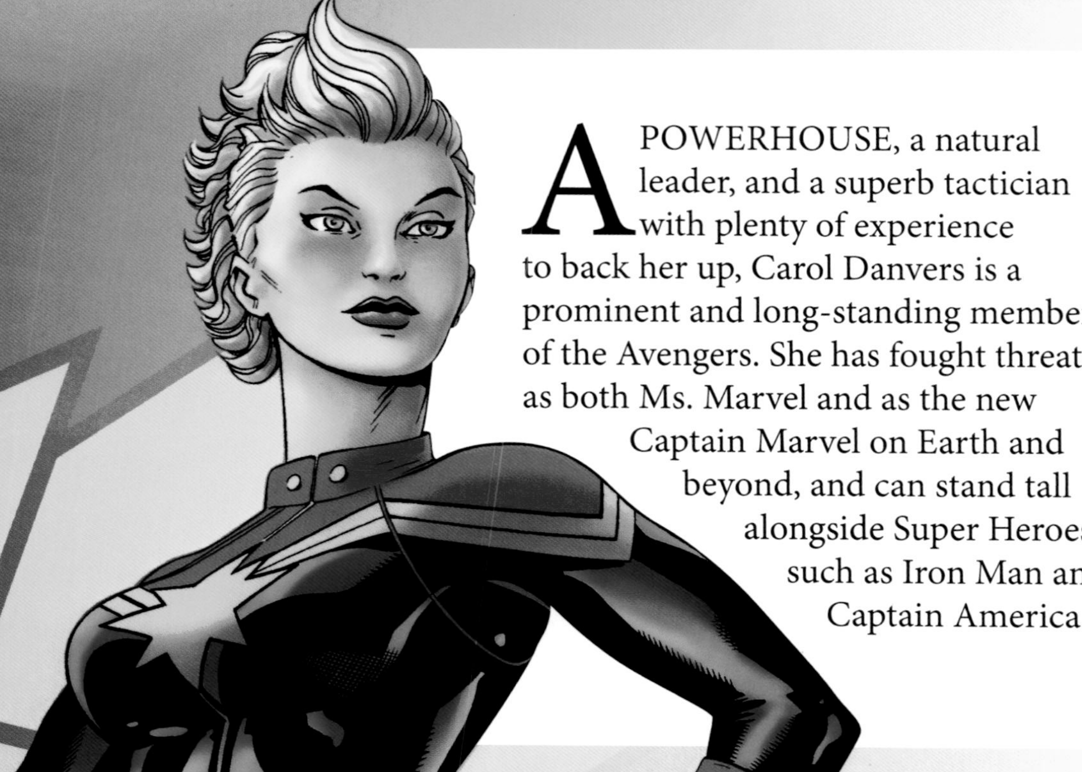

A POWERHOUSE, a natural leader, and a superb tactician with plenty of experience to back her up, Carol Danvers is a prominent and long-standing member of the Avengers. She has fought threats as both Ms. Marvel and as the new Captain Marvel on Earth and beyond, and can stand tall alongside Super Heroes such as Iron Man and Captain America.

While she had previously met the Avengers as Carol Danvers, her first outing with them as Ms. Marvel occurred when she received a precognitive flash that let her know the Avengers were in great danger. She joined them to team up against the powerful threat of Ultron.

DATA FILE

REAL NAME
Carol Susan Jane Danvers

OCCUPATION
Former NASA security chief and intelligence officer; former writer/editor; Super Hero.

BASE
Statue of Liberty, New York City, New York

HEIGHT 5 ft 11 in

WEIGHT 124 lbs

EYES Blue

HAIR Blonde

FIRST APPEARANCE WITH AVENGERS
Avengers #90 (July 1971)

POWERS
The merging of Kree and human genetics brought Carol new and extraordinary abilities. Along with the powers of flight, superhuman strength, endurance, and durability, Carol can absorb and rechannel energy. She occasionally receives precognitive visions of the future. When she was transformed into her Binary form, her powers were magnified to a cosmic level, but she has since reverted to her original abilities.

BEGINNING AS MS. MARVEL

Originally established as a supporting player to the Kree Captain Mar-Vell as Ms. Marvel, Carol Danvers proved herself to be much more, and would one day even eclipse the greatness achieved by that hero.

When Danvers first met Mar-Vell he was posing as robotics expert Dr. Walter Lawson. Danvers was the head of security for the missile base named Cape Kennedy. She instantly suspected that Lawson was hiding something, and set out to discover exactly what that secret was. This association brought her into contact with powerful enemies, and after Captain Mar-Vell's enemy Yon-Rogg kidnapped Danvers, her life was forever changed.

While Captain Mar-Vell tried to get Carol to safety and shielded her body from much of the radiation emitted by the exploding Magnitron, the explosion grafted his genetic Kree structure onto Carol's own form.

Armed with the Psyche-Magnitron—a device banned by the Kree—Yon-Rogg lured Captain Marvel into a battle that ended with the explosion of the Magnitron. Despite Mar-Vell's attempts to save her, Carol was still near the device when it exploded, and was bathed in radiation.

Viewing the event as a personal failure, Carol quit her job in the security field and began life as a writer. But she soon learned that she had begun a double life. She began experiencing black-outs where she became a second identity—Ms. Marvel, a Super Hero with immense powers.

She slowly gained control over her transformations, and learned to balance life as a Super Hero with a career at the J. Jonah Jameson publication *Woman Magazine*. With a tumultuous life already under her belt, Ms. Marvel had no idea that her future held more dramatic changes.

Carol's costume has seen some alterations over the years as her Super Hero identity has evolved.

When she moved from being Ms. Marvel to Captain Marvel, Carol developed a mask that could form over her face at will.

Carol can absorb and redirect various forms of energy.

Captain Marvel loves to fly, and can do so at impressive speeds.

ALLIES AND ENEMIES

A career hero with friendships and enemies made in nearly every corner of the universe, Carol Danvers is an inspiration to many fellow Super Heroes.

CAPTAIN MARVEL
If it wasn't for Mar-Vell, the explosion that gave Carol her powers would have probably killed her.

JESSICA JONES
Through the Avengers, Carol Danvers and Jessica Jones began an enduring friendship.

IRON PATRIOT
The current Iron Patriot, James Rhodes, began a secret romantic relationship with Carol.

ROGUE
After stealing Ms. Marvel's abilities and past from her, Rogue made a lifetime foe of the heroine.

YON-ROGG
Yon-Rogg's Psyche-Magnitron gave Ms. Marvel her powers, although his intentions were sinister.

MYSTIQUE
The mutant Mystique had no qualms about her student, Rogue, stealing Ms. Marvel's abilities.

Carol Danvers is one of the Avengers' heaviest hitters and can hold her own in almost any fight.

REPORTING FOR **DUTY**

While it took her a while to completely commit to the Avengers, Carol soon became a mainstay of the team. She is a trusted ally to many of the most iconic members, and has recently grown in confidence and accepted the fact that she has become something of an icon herself.

JOINING THE AVENGERS

Avengers #171 (May 1978)

While trying on clothes in a store's dressing room, Carol Danvers was hit with a precognitive flash of the Avengers in grave danger. She quickly flew to aid the heroes as Ms. Marvel, and joined them in a battle with Ultron. After sticking around to help with the threat of Tyrak, Carol departed the team, but then returned to help battle Korvac. She later officially accepted membership of the Avengers when Scarlet Witch took a leave of absence.

THE BIRTH OF **BINARY**

Carol Danvers wielded cosmic-level powers when she evolved into her accidentally gifted Binary form.

At the hands of the mutant Rogue, Ms. Marvel experienced what it was like to be rendered powerless once again. Years before she became a heroic member of the X-Men, Rogue had been a proud member of the Brotherhood of Evil Mutants. Able to absorb the memories and powers of anyone she touched, Rogue came into contact with Ms. Marvel and kept her hold on the Super Hero a bit too long. Instead of only temporarily using Ms. Marvel's powers, Rogue absorbed them completely, leaving Carol Danvers powerless.

Much later, while fighting alongside the X-Men, Carol was used as a test subject by the maleficent alien race called the Brood. Without realizing it, the Brood triggered the latent genes inside Ms. Marvel that had been created when she was first caught in the explosion with Captain Mar-Vell. A mixture of the best of the genetic elements of human and Kree biology, Ms. Marvel's genes reacted violently to the testing, causing her to take the form of the cosmic-powered Binary.

With a wealth of newfound energy inside her, Binary was able to help power up the X-Men's spaceship and escape the Brood. Carol loved having her new powers, but they, too, proved to be temporary. She later reverted to powers akin to her original Ms. Marvel abilities.

As Binary, Carol drew energy from a white hole, and was able to release that energy in the form of heat, light, radiation, and gravity.

ENTER WARBIRD

Avengers #4 (May 1998)

Ms. Marvel's life had gone through some dramatic changes, and Carol Danvers was left the worse for wear. After losing her cosmic powers as Binary, Carol had begun to wonder what direction her life would take. She decided to change her Super Hero name to Warbird, inspired by the fighter planes of the same name. Once again a part of the Avengers, Warbird began to cope with her decreased powers by turning to alcohol, a problem Tony Stark recognized and helped her overcome.

Warbird didn't tell her fellow Avengers that she was unable to switch to her Binary form any longer, until they discovered it in the heat of battle.

As Captain Marvel, Carol stepped into her own and began to fulfil her potential.

BECOMING MIGHTY

The Mighty Avengers #1 (May 2007)

Iron Man and Carol Danvers had become close over the years through their work in the Avengers as well as through their shared alcohol addiction. So in the wake of the Superhuman Civil War, when Iron Man's forces triumphed over Captain America's underground rebellion, Tony Stark didn't have to look far when assembling a core group of Avengers to help protect his brave new world. He immediately recruited Carol—once again calling herself Ms. Marvel—and put her in charge of these new mighty Avengers. Not only that, as the new Director of S.H.I.E.L.D., Iron Man also allowed Ms. Marvel to have a role in handpicking her team.

As the leader of the Avengers, Ms. Marvel was in charge of such heavy hitters as Wonder Man, the Sentry, and Ares.

PROMOTION TO **CAPTAIN**

Over the years, Carol Danvers has used the codenames Ms. Marvel, Binary, and Warbird. But despite having earned the title many times over, Carol had yet to embrace the name Captain Marvel.

Like many of the good things that come out of the Avengers, the idea of a name change started with Captain America. When Carol adopted a new costume that seemed to pay tribute to the original Kree Captain Mar-Vell, Captain America asked to have a word with the heroine. While Carol believed that Steve Rogers was merely old-fashioned and therefore didn't care for the name "Ms. Marvel," Captain America insisted that Carol had earned the right to use the title Captain as well.

Ever since the original Captain Mar-Vell died, Carol had stuck to the belief that it would be disrespectful to adopt his name. She viewed Mar-Vell as a true hero, and didn't want to take his legacy away from him. But when Captain America remarked that she had adopted his name years ago by the act of naming herself "Ms. Marvel," Carol finally decided that she would honor the name as best she could, and stepped up to be the newest Captain Marvel.

CAPTAIN MAR-VELL

When he first arrived on Earth, Mar-Vell wore the green and white uniform of a Kree officer.

THE KREE OFFICER Captain Mar-Vell was sent to Earth to sabotage its space program, unaware he was a pawn in a political game between Ronan the Accuser and the Supreme Intelligence. After a time, he came to sympathize with the people of Earth.

The Supreme Intelligence gave Mar-Vell his new costume.

Eon also turned Mar-Vell's hair blond.

BANDED TOGETHER

The Supreme Intelligence linked Mar-Vell to Avengers' supporter Rick Jones with two pairs of wrist-worn Nega-Bands. When snapped together, the bands swapped Jones' and Mar-Vell's positions on Earth and in the Negative Zone.

The two heroes remained bound together in a partnership a little too close for comfort until Mar-Vell rescued Rick from the Negative Zone—an alternate universe often used as a cosmic prison. Soon after, they became embroiled in the Kree-Skrull War, along with the Avengers. The Supreme Intelligence used Rick's latent psionic powers to win the war for the Kree, but this nearly killed Rick. Mar-Vell gave some of his own life force to save Rick, linking them together again. After Mar-Vell faced off against Thanos with the Avengers, the cosmic creature Eon granted Mar-Vell cosmic awareness and made him Protector of the Universe.

The Supreme Intelligence tricked Rick into putting on the Nega-Bands and freeing Mar-Vell from the Negative Zone. The bands gave Rick superhuman abilities similar to those of Captain Marvel.

DATA FILE

REAL NAME
Mar-Vell

OCCUPATION
Soldier, adventurer, Protector of the Universe

BASE
Mobile

HEIGHT 6 ft 2 in

WEIGHT 240 lbs

EYES Blue

HAIR White (later blond)

FIRST APPEARANCE WITH AVENGERS
Avengers #89 (June 1971)

POWERS
Mar-Vell had superhuman durability, endurance, speed, and strength. He could absorb solar energy and use it to fly and fire energy blasts. Using his Nega Bands, he could also fly and survive in space. He later attained cosmic awareness and for a while could create illusions and teleport.

ALLIES AND ENEMIES

Mar-Vell fought side by side with the Avengers against the Skrulls in an effort to bring peace to his home part of the galaxy. He was brought back from the dead on more than one occasion to help the team.

FRIEND

RICK JONES
Rick's friendship with the Avengers ensured Mar-Vell would become their ally.

FAMILY

HULKLING
The Skrull Princess Anelle fell for Mar-Vell, and Dorrek VIII was the resulting son.

FOE

THANOS
As Protector of the Universe, Mar-Vell became Thanos's greatest foe.

LONG-LASTING FRIENDSHIPS

Well-respected and liked, Mar-Vell worked with the Avengers many times, often saving not just Earth, but other parts of the galaxy as well.

Mar-Vell had made many friends among Earth's superhumans, and when they learned that he would soon die, they came to pay their respects.

THE DEATH OF CAPTAIN MAR-VELL

Marvel Graphic Novel #1 (April 1982)

Mar-Vell faced many threats, but one of them finally beat him: cancer. After being exposed to a nerve gas by Nitro of the Lunatic Legion, he contracted the disease. His Nega-Bands helped keep him alive for a while but also repelled known cures. With the end near, his friends—including many Avengers—rallied around him on the moon Titan. As he passed away, a vision came to him in which Thanos—who appeared not as an enemy but an ally—escorted him to meet Death. Mar-Vell has returned a few times since, but never for long.

OTHER CAPTAIN MARVELS

Mar-Vell's heroism inspired many others to follow in his path. This included relatives, friends, and those he had never even met.

MONICA RAMBEAU

A lieutenant in the New Orleans Harbor Patrol, Monica gained the ability to convert herself into energy. The media hung the name Captain Marvel on her, and it stuck.

GENIS-VELL

Genis-Vell was born to Mar-Vell's lover Elysius after Mar-Vell died. He followed in his father's footsteps, adopting the name after Monica gave it to him.

PHYLA-VELL

When Genis-Vell destroyed and recreated the universe, he brought his sister Phyla-Vell into existence, too. She claimed the Captain Marvel name, but later surrendered it.

KHN'NR

During the Secret Invasion, the Skrulls turned one of their own—Khn'nr—into a replica of the original Captain Marvel, with implanted memories.

NOH-VARR

Noh-Varr hailed from an alternate universe and was known as Marvel Boy. After the Skrulls' invasion, he took up Mar-Vell's legacy and joined the Dark Avengers.

CAROL DANVERS

Carol met Mar-Vell while working as NASA's security chief. She gained powers and became Ms. Marvel, then later called herself Captain Marvel.

SPIDER-MAN

Spider-Man made his first costume to wear on television.

BITTEN IN A LABORATORY by a radioactive spider, geeky teenage orphan Peter Parker soon realized he had been given spider-like powers. After a tragic event, he dedicated himself to using his powers to help others, often alongside the Avengers, realizing that "with great power there must also come great responsibility."

JUST ONE BITE...

During a brief period when Peter demonstrated his powers on television, Peter failed to stop a burglar who ran right past him. That same burglar later broke into his home and murdered the man who had raised him, his beloved Uncle Ben—changing Peter's outlook on life forever.

The irradiated spider that bit Peter gave him a number of spider-related powers, including sensing danger.

Stricken with guilt, Peter decided to put his superpowers to good use and fight crime, while continuing to take care of his Aunt May, whom he feared might have a heart attack if she learned his secret identity. As Spider-Man, he worked with the Avengers a number of times but didn't officially become a team member until late in its existence.

Following the explosion caused by Electro at the Raft Maximum-Maximum Security wing, Spider-Man teamed up with Luke Cage, Daredevil, Iron Man, Captain America, Spider-Woman, and the Sentry to help prevent the breakout of numerous Super Villains held there. Peter was afterward offered a place in the New Avengers team, and moved into Avengers Tower with Aunt May and his then-wife, Mary Jane Watson. Despite his lack of power relative to the team's heavy hitters, Spider-Man's intelligence and heart made him a valued Avenger.

Spider-Man first met the Avengers when Kang the Conqueror made a robot copy of him to attack the team. Peter battled his imposter to save them.

DATA FILE

REAL NAME
Peter Parker

OCCUPATION
Adventurer, photographer, scientist

BASE
New York City

HEIGHT 5 ft 10 in

WEIGHT 170 lbs

EYES Brown

HAIR Brown

FIRST APPEARANCE WITH AVENGERS
Avengers #11 (December 1964)

POWERS
Following the bite from the irradiated spider, Peter acquired a spider physiology, giving him superhuman abilities that include durability, endurance, healing, speed, agility, and strength. He can sense danger, stick to and climb walls, and fire webbing from wrist-mounted shooters that he designed. He is an expert hand-to-hand combatant. Peter has a genius-level intellect and is an expert in many fields of science.

EARTH'S MIGHTIEST **SPIDER**

After a rocky start in his first few encounters with the Avengers, Peter became a staple member of the team.

MASKED MENACE NO MORE

Civil War #2 (August 2006)

During the Civil War, Peter initially backed the Superhuman Registration Act and sided with Iron Man's faction. As part of this, he unmasked himself on live television so he could register with the government, as required. He came to regret this when an attack of conscience forced him to switch sides to join Captain America's rebels, and an assassin gunning for him shot down Aunt May. The entire world's memory of his secret was later erased—along with his marriage to Mary Jane.

When Daily Bugle editor J. Jonah Jameson—who had ranted against Spider-Man for years—watched his employee Peter unmask himself on live television, he fainted out of surprise.

ANOTHER SYMBIOTE SPIDER

Dark Avengers #1 (March 2009)

When Norman Osborn (aka the Green Goblin, Spider-Man's greatest foe) took over national security after the Skrulls' attempted invasion, he replaced the Avengers with a team of villainous doubles loyal to him. Spider-Man's replacement was his old foe Mac Gargan. Originally known as the Scorpion, Mac had inherited the alien symbiotic costume Peter had discovered and worn during the original Secret Wars. It had turned Mac into a new version of Venom, making it easy for him to impersonate Peter.

Venom's slimmed down look mimicked the black and white costume Peter had worn for a while.

ALLIES AND ENEMIES

Spider-Man has made countless enemies, both on his own and as part of the Avengers. Because of Peter's secret identity, his friends don't always understand him, but the closest ones stick with him through even the darkest times.

MARY JANE WATSON
Peter married this model-actress once and still has strong feelings for her.

GREEN GOBLIN
Norman Osborn murdered Peter's first love, Gwen Stacy, and still plagues him.

SUPERIOR SPIDER-MAN

The "Friendly Neighborhood Spider-Man" underwent a drastic change of character when Doctor Octopus took over his body and became the "Superior Spider-Man."

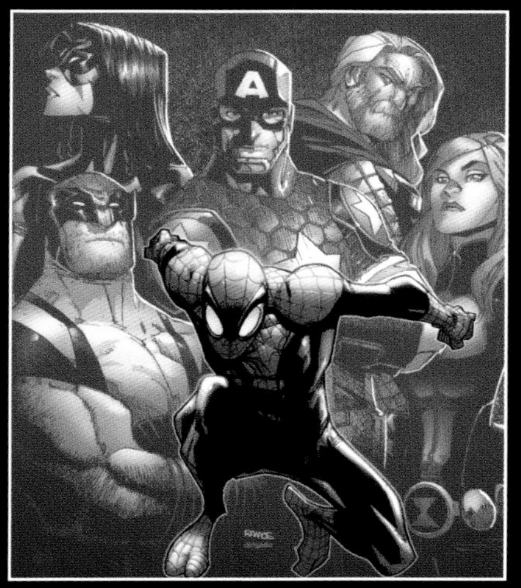

The Avengers became suspicious when Spider-Man started to change his behavior, including killing Massacre.

As Doctor Octopus lay dying in a prison hospital bed, he managed to transfer his mind into Peter Parker's body and took over as Spider-Man. While he thought he had killed Peter, too, he had actually only buried Peter deep into his subconscious. Octopus managed to complete Peter's PhD, start up a new high-tech business, and romance a new woman. When faced with a foe only Peter could beat, however, Octopus surrendered Spider-Man's body back to Peter and erased himself from his mind.

SPIDER-WOMAN

SHE HAS BEEN an agent of the terrorist organization Hydra. She has been an agent of S.H.I.E.L.D. She has been a Super Hero, a private detective, and most notably, an Avenger. Jessica Drew has been many things, but at her heart she remains the heroic Spider-Woman.

When Jessica's father lashed out at her mother, an upset Jessica instinctively used her bioelectric venom blasts for the first time, nearly killing him.

GENETICALLY ENHANCED

Jessica's parents were Hydra scientists who were investigating the possibility of upgrading the human genome with the adaptability of arachnids. Her mother was exposed to a lab experiment during pregnancy, but delivered a seemingly normal baby.

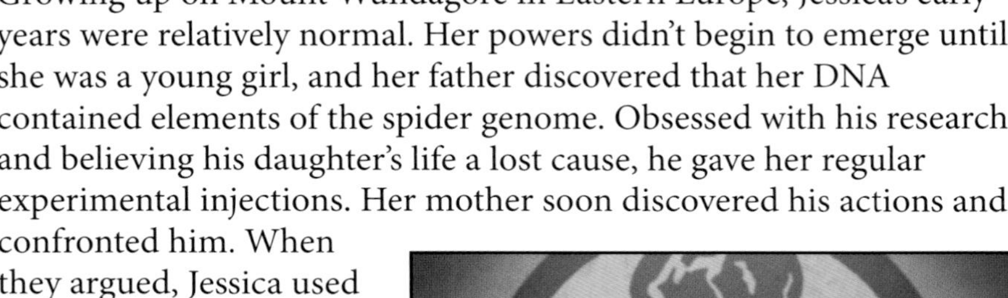

Growing up on Mount Wundagore in Eastern Europe, Jessica's early years were relatively normal. Her powers didn't begin to emerge until she was a young girl, and her father discovered that her DNA contained elements of the spider genome. Obsessed with his research and believing his daughter's life a lost cause, he gave her regular experimental injections. Her mother soon discovered his actions and confronted him. When they argued, Jessica used her powers against her father and fell into a coma. She awoke years later in Hydra's custody, and soon began training with Taskmaster. Now able to utilize and control her bioelectric powers, she joined Hydra as Spider-Woman. However, on her first mission she met Nick Fury, who revealed to her the true nature of Hydra, and she quickly abandoned her evil employers.

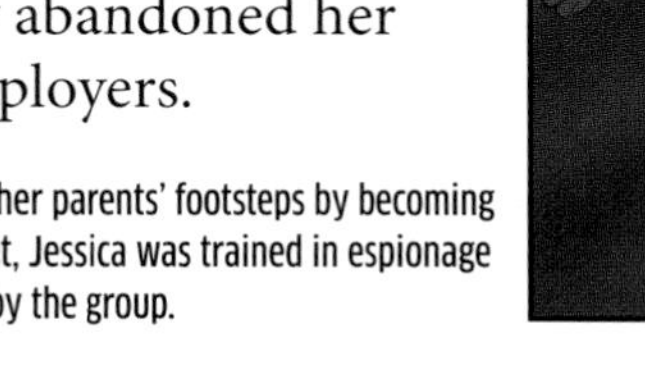

Following in her parents' footsteps by becoming a Hydra agent, Jessica was trained in espionage and combat by the group.

Spider-Woman took inspiration for her name and costume from Spider-Man because of their similar shared powers.

DATA FILE

REAL NAME Jessica Drew **OCCUPATION** Former private detective; former secret agent; Super Hero
BASE New York City, New York
HEIGHT 5 ft 10 in **WEIGHT** 130 lbs **EYES** Green **HAIR** Brown, dyed black
FIRST APPEARANCE WITH AVENGERS *Avengers Annual* #10 (August 1981)
POWERS Spider-Woman can create bioelectric "venom blasts." She is an expert martial artist. She adheres to surfaces using her hands and feet and creates a pheromone that attracts men and repulses women. She has superhuman strength, endurance, and speed and immunity to all poisons. Spider-Woman has recently gained the power of flight.

SWINGING INTO ACTION

Jessica Drew was active in the world of Super Heroes for quite some time before she accepted official membership into the Avengers.

NEW BLOOD

Avengers #221 (July 1982)

With the mounting number of threats on their doorstep, Captain America, the Wasp, Thor, and Iron Man realized they needed to bring in some new members to the Avengers. While Captain America wanted to recruit Hawkeye, and Thor wished to invite Spider-Man to join the group, Iron Man and the Wasp thought a few female additions might be just what the team needed. Spider-Woman was brought in, initially to gauge her interest, but even after helping to defeat the Mechano-Marauder, Jessica decided against joining. In fact, she wouldn't truly commit to the team for a few more years, after the events of the Skrull invasion and the personal attack against her.

Spider-Woman answered the Wasp's invitation to meet with other female heroes who were considering joining the Avengers, but out of those invited, only She-Hulk would accept membership into the Avengers on that day.

Recently, Spider-Woman has quit the Avengers and settled back in New York, determined to live a "normal life" of solo crime fighting in a new costume.

ALLIES AND ENEMIES

Jessica Drew has been active in the world of superhumans for years. Whether as a hero or an agent of S.H.I.E.L.D, or private detective, Jessica has made many allies among some of the world's most powerful people.

SPIDER-MAN
Spider-Woman and Spider-Man have become close in their time as Avengers.

NICK FURY
Nick Fury was the first person to show Jessica how the world truly was.

WOLVERINE
During her time as a private eye, Jessica crossed paths with Wolverine many times.

SECRET INVASION

With her connections to S.H.I.E.L.D., Hydra, Nick Fury, and the Avengers, Spider-Woman was the perfect Super Hero for the invading Skrull queen to personally replace during the Skrulls' invasion.

Strategically stationed on the Raft, the Skrull queen took on the likeness of Jessica Drew and commanded her invading army from the battlefield on Earth. After Norman Osborn shot and killed the queen, the real Spider-Woman was returned to the world, and soon picked up where her impersonator left off as a member of the underground Avengers. However, discovering others were finding it hard to trust her in the aftermath of the Skrulls' body swap, and feeling a bit lost in life, Spider-Woman discovered a new purpose fighting against aliens as a member of S.W.O.R.D.

During a large battle in New York's Central Park, Wolverine faced off against the Skrull queen posing as Spider-Woman.

TIGRA

FEISTY GREER Nelson is a longtime Avenger, despite originally having misgivings about mucking in as a team player. Greer wears her emotions on her sleeve, but as Tigra, she is not afraid to risk life and limb in a fight.

Before her full physical transformation, Nelson fought crime as a yellow-and blue-costumed character named Cat.

Following her transformation by the Cat People, Tigra's body is covered with fur.

FROM CAT TO TIGER

Tigra has made quite a transformation in her career. Originally the simple costumed crime fighter Cat, she underwent a full body makeover to become the Super Hero Tigra with a feline physiology.

Policeman's widow Greer Nelson was hired for a special project by Dr. Tumolo, a scientist who had the aim of helping women achieve their full mental and physical potential. When Tumolo's backer, Mal Donalbain, wanted a different woman for the project, Tumolo experimented on Greer in secret. With enhanced abilities, Greer became a Super Hero called the Cat until Hydra agents attempted to kidnap Dr. Tumolo. The Cat saved Tumolo's life, but was fatally wounded in the process. In order to repay the favor, Dr. Tumolo transformed Greer into a member of her clandestine ancient and mystical race, the Cat People. Suddenly, the Cat had become Tigra, the Were-Woman, and quickly attracted the attention of the Avengers.

Tigra has sharp claws and heightened reflexes that come in handy in battle.

Tigra joined the Avengers and tried to adapt to life on the team as best as she could. She soon realized that her street-fighting origins paled in comparison with their cosmic adventures!

DATA FILE

REAL NAME Greer Grant Nelson **OCCUPATION** Super Hero

BASE Avengers Academy Compound, Palos Verdes, California

HEIGHT 5 ft 10 in **WEIGHT** 180 lbs

EYES Green **HAIR** (as Tigra) Orange fur; (as Greer) Black

FIRST APPEARANCE WITH AVENGERS *Giant-Size Creatures* #1 (July 1974)

POWERS Tigra has superhuman strength, speed, endurance, and agility. She has enhanced smell, sight, and hearing, and razor-sharp claws on her feet and hands. She is an expert at combat skills with a minor healing ability. Tigra has the ability to switch between her human and Tigra forms, but chooses to remain as Tigra most of the time.

After she was shot with alpha radiation by Hydra agents, Greer's transformation into Tigra saved her life. She could originally revert to her human form using the amulet gifted to her by the Cat People.

SUPER HERO STARS AND STRIPES

While a lack of self-confidence in her fighting abilities gave her a rocky start with the Avengers, Tigra became a valued asset to the team, serving a long tenure with them.

BY FORCE OF MIND

Avengers #211 (September 1981)

Despite never having worked with the Avengers before, Tigra was summoned to Avengers Mansion for the first time. Tigra found herself among a host of heroes, including past Avengers star members such as Hawkeye, and other crime fighters that had little to do with Earth's Mightiest Heroes, like Iceman and Dazzler. After breaking out into fights, the heroes discovered that Moondragon had actually been manipulating their actions in a bizarre attempt to choose the Avengers' new roster. After Iron Man and the other Avengers let the powerful woman know what they thought about her interfering in the Avengers' business, Moondragon departed in a huff, leaving Tigra and the others a bit confused. However, as Tigra had been feeling "at loose ends" for a while, she asked the Avengers if they would keep her on as a member. With the Beast leaving to pursue his personal life as a scientist, Tigra was permitted to accept his role and join the team.

Despite her lack of self-confidence in her abilities when comparing herself to the rest of the team, Tigra would later become a founding member of the West Coast Avengers, and a trainer at the Avengers Academy.

ALLIES AND ENEMIES

Just like any long-standing Avenger, Tigra has made many enemies and allies during her tenure. Possessing a strong personality and a very distinct style, Tigra seems to attract and repel others quickly.

HELLCAT
Patsy Walker took on Tigra's old Cat costume and then renamed herself Hellcat.

SPIDER-WOMAN
Jessica Drew and Tigra became friends when Tigra moved to San Francisco.

FOE

KRAVEN
This Spider-Man villain attempted to make Tigra his minion using a slave collar.

Tigra stayed on with the West Coast Avengers through many incarnations as other members came and went.

LUKE CAGE

PERHAPS ONE OF the Avengers' greatest success stories, Luke Cage went from being a wrongly convicted incarcerated criminal to leading his own band of New Avengers. A strong leader, a trusted ally, and an incredible powerhouse, Luke Cage is a true example of a hero.

Luke Cage has super tough skin, making bullets merely an annoyance to him.

FROM CROOK TO **HERO**

Luke Cage was not dealt any easy hand in life, which makes his achievements all the more impressive. From being imprisoned for a crime he did not commit, to maturing into a stable hero and father, Cage is determination personified.

Born Carl Lucas and growing up on the streets of Harlem's slums, Cage became a small-time crook, working with his partner, Willis Stryker. But when Stryker suspected Lucas of being involved with his girlfriend, he framed Lucas with drug possession and had him arrested. While in jail, Lucas was a volunteer for an experiment in cell regeneration, led by scientist Dr. Noah Burstein. However, the experiment was sabotaged by a guard with a beef against Lucas, leading to an explosion. When Lucas emerged, he realized he had powers, and escaped jail to start life over as Luke Cage, Hero for Hire.

Cage's strength was enhanced by a prison experiment, allowing him to punch through stone walls.

Before his time in the Avengers, Luke Cage was known as Power Man, half of the dynamic duo, Power Man and Iron Fist.

DATA FILE

REAL NAME Carl Lucas **OCCUPATION** Former crook; former Hero for Hire; Super Hero, bodyguard **BASE** The Gem Theater, New York City, New York

HEIGHT 6ft 6in **WEIGHT** 425 lbs **EYES** Brown **HAIR** Bald (formerly black)

FIRST APPEARANCE WITH AVENGERS *Avengers* #118 (December 1973)

POWERS Following Burstein's experimentation, Cage has acquired superhuman strength, endurance, and durability. He has nearly unbreakable skin and accelerated healing. He is a self-taught, experienced fighter. Even before his cellular regeneration process, he was a gifted athlete.

A NATURAL TEAM **LEADER**

Hired muscle Luke Cage later become the leader of the Avengers. He possessed impressive self-confidence and a strong personality that people seemed to rally behind.

Luke Cage first joined the Avengers after helping them deal with a breakout at the Raft Maximum-Maximum Security Prison.

BREAKOUT

New Avengers #1-3 (January 2005 - March 2005)

While he had worked on loose teams like the Defenders and with others as a commissioned adventurer with his business Heroes for Hire, Cage had mostly avoided working with groups like the Avengers. However, while employed as Matt Murdock's personal bodyguard, he accompanied Murdock on a tour of the Ryker's Island prison known as the Raft. During the tour, there was a massive breakout, which led to him teaming up with other heroes and eventually forming a new incarnation of the Avengers.

THE MIGHTY AVENGERS

The Mighty Avengers #1-3 (November 2013 - January 2014)

After growing into his leadership of the Avengers, and then handpicking his own team of New Avengers at the behest of Steve Rogers, Luke Cage gave up Avenger life and became a Hero for Hire once more. However, a battle with Titanian Eternal Thanos's forces caused him to return as the leader of the Mighty Avengers. This new team consisted of mostly street-level crime fighters, including the heir to his original Super Hero name, the new Power Man.

ALLIES AND ENEMIES

His history as a hired hero means Cage has had many "work associates" over the years, some of whom have become lifelong friends, or more.

FRIENDS

IRON FIST
Luke remains best friends with former hero partner, Danny Rand aka Iron Fist.

DAREDEVIL
Cage knew Matt Murdock for years before they served as Avengers together.

JESSICA JONES
Following a fling with Luke, Jessica became his wife and the mother of his child.

With the help of a familiar-looking officiate, Luke Cage and girlfriend Jessica Jones tied the knot in front of their Avengers teammates.

Luke Cage's handpicked Avengers included Power Woman, Wolverine, Ms. Marvel, the Thing, Spider-Man, Mockingbird, Iron Fist, Dr. Strange, and Daredevil.

NEW AVENGERS

Although the first incarnation of the group known as the New Avengers had been disbanded, Captain America soon called upon Luke to organize a new team. Cage had his pick of the best Super Heroes the world had to offer.

When he was given the OK to form his own team of New Avengers from scratch, Luke Cage wasn't too keen on the idea. After all, he had just spent months of his life fighting as part of the informal Secret Avengers, in strict opposition of the Superhuman Registration Act. The last thing Cage wanted to do was work for the government. However, Steve Rogers assured Luke that he would only be funded by the government, and his actions and choices would be his alone, convincing Cage to agree to captain the team.

Steve Rogers had a way with words, and Luke found himself trusting his friend. It was a new era for the Avengers, and while hesitant, Luke realized things were different now.

WONDER MAN

Simon's eyes have no pupils and are red. He often wears sunglasses to hide them.

SIMON WILLIAMS initially had a score to settle with Tony Stark. After his family business went bankrupt in competition with Stark Industries, Williams let Baron Zemo transform him into Wonder Man so that he could join the Avengers and bring them down from the inside.

Baron Zemo gave Wonder Man his name and designed his first costume, emblazoning a "W" on his chest.

BETRAYAL AND FORGIVENESS

Zemo used Simon Williams as the first test for his ionic ray machine, giving Williams extraordinary new powers and turning him into Wonder Man.

Zemo told Simon that his new powers would kill him without regular antidotes. When ordered to lead the Avengers into a trap, Simon revealed Zemo's plan to them, even at the cost of his own life.

In the aftermath of this battle, Simon's older brother Eric Williams became the Grim Reaper and retrieved Simon's body, unaware that Simon was not in fact dead, but actually in a coma-like state. Despite their childhood differences, Eric took Simon's body to New Orleans, where he met with the voodoo priest Black Talon. With Talon's help, Eric revived Simon, who later snapped out of his zombified state. Traumatized by his near-death experience, Simon feared for his life but eventually overcame his fears and was accepted back onto the Avengers team. Since becoming a full-fledged Avenger, Wonder Man has become close friends with the Beast and has even rivaled the Vision for the Scarlet Witch's affections.

After he returned from the dead, Simon became a true Avenger and a fantastic asset to the team.

DATA FILE

REAL NAME
Simon Williams

OCCUPATION
Former stuntman and actor; adventurer

BASE
New York City

HEIGHT 6 ft 2 in

WEIGHT 380 lbs

EYES Red

HAIR Gray

FIRST APPEARANCE WITH AVENGERS
Avengers #9 (October 1964)

POWERS
Simon has superhuman durability, endurance, senses, speed, and strength. Being composed of ionic energy, he never ages and can heal any wound. He can also fly, change size, and fire energy blasts from his hands and eyes. Thanks to his invulnerability and healing powers, Simon has performed as a film stunt-man and taken on acting roles in Hollywood. He has a gifted intellect.

THE WANDERING MAN

From their first meeting, Simon and the Avengers have had a complicated relationship. Simon has left and rejoined various versions of the team over time.

BLOOD BROTHERS

Vision and the Scarlet Witch #3 (January 1983)

When the Vision had lost an arm and hovered near death, Simon was called to his side. With the help of the Avengers, the Vision's doctor managed to transfuse some of Simon's ionic energy into the Vision to help save his life. While both Simon and the Vision were weakened, the Grim Reaper attacked. Since Simon had stood up to him recently—in a way he had never done when they were children—Eric believed someone else had possessed Simon's mind. Working together, the two Super Heroes defeated the Grim Reaper, proving themselves to be—at least at that time—closer than brothers.

Simon came to believe that the Avengers' use of violence caused more problems than it solved.

THE REVENGERS

New Avengers Annual #1 (November 2011)

Disillusioned after the siege of Asgard, Simon assembled a team of former heroes to destroy the Avengers, including Century, Anti-Venom, Atlas, Captain Ultra, D-Man, Devil-Slayer, Ethan Edwards, and Goliath. They attacked the Avengers Mansion, defeating the heroes there, and then sent Atlas to attack Avengers Tower. Simon then held a press conference and threatened to reveal all of the Avengers' secrets unless they disbanded. The remaining Avengers captured him, but he had already placed a seed of doubt in the mind of the public about what those secrets might be.

Simon's older brother Eric (aka the Grim Reaper) wanted both Simon and the Vision dead for, so he believed, making a mockery of his dead brother's memory.

PACIFIST HERO

After spending years as one of the Avengers' heavy hitters, Simon decided that he was only contributing to a cycle of violence that he had to end.

After his actions with the Revengers—which had only proven partially successful—Wonder Man helped to rescue the Wasp from the microverse, where she had wound up trapped after the Avengers' war with the X-Men. Having earned back the Avengers' trust, Simon embarked on an assignment to the Avengers Unity Division, which was formed to help improve human-mutant relations. Simon agreed to join the team, but he announced that he had renounced violence and become a pacifist. While he was happy to be a member of the team and help how he could, he refused to attack anyone for any reason.

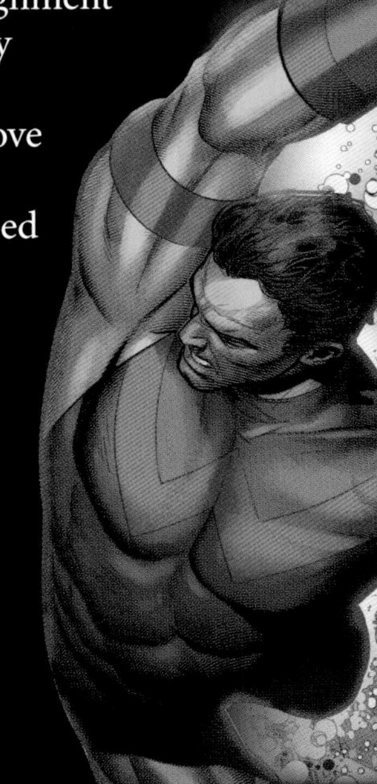

ALLIES AND ENEMIES

As Wonder Man, Simon has served as a member of many different Avengers' teams, including a long stint with the West Coast Avengers. No matter how hard he tries to stay away, he always winds up coming back.

FRIENDS

SCARLET WITCH
Simon started a relationship with the Scarlet Witch after her marriage ended.

THE VISION
Simon and the Vision were close friends, despite their feelings for Scarlet Witch.

FOE

GRIM REAPER
Eric and Simon weren't close as children, and have since grown further apart.

COUNT NEFARIA

Count Nefaria possesses a wide range of powers, including enhanced strength and laser beam vision.

Count Nefaria enjoys expressing his flamboyant nature in his Super Villain costumes.

NOT ONLY IS Count Nefaria a longtime foe of the Avengers who refuses to give up his criminal career, he is also the father of another Avengers enemy: Madame Masque. Even before he gained superhuman powers, his nefarious nature knew no limits!

Count Nefaria was an early foe for the founding members of the Avengers team.

A NOBLE CHARACTER?

Viewed by society as a wealthy, honest nobleman, Count Nefaria revealed his true colors to the world when he decided to take on the Avengers. Becoming the world's strongest known human only magnified his intentions.

The Avengers couldn't resist a visit to Count Nefaria's castle after learning he was giving the profits of his house tours to charity. They later found out they were in an elaborate trap, whereby Nefaria would frame them for his crimes.

The Avengers had been disrupting operations for the criminal cartel called the Maggia for quite some time, and their leader, Count Nefaria, was sick of losing money. By directing his operation from thousands of miles away at his personal castle, Nefaria had been able to keep his criminal activities a secret and was viewed by the public simply as Europe's wealthiest nobleman. Using this cover, Nefaria had his castle moved to America, stone by stone, and invited the Avengers to visit the restored result.

After tricking the Avengers into being caught in his time transcender beams, Nefaria created moving 3-D images of them. He then used these to ruin their reputation before arrogantly setting them free. Once free, and realizing Nefaria's scheme, the Avengers managed to defeat the villain and clear their good name.

DATA FILE

REAL NAME Count Luchino Nefaria **OCCUPATION** Crime lord
BASE Los Angeles, California
HEIGHT 6 ft 2 in **WEIGHT** 230 lbs **EYES** Blue
HAIR Black (with white temples)
FIRST APPEARANCE WITH AVENGERS *Avengers* #13 (February 1965)
POWERS Nefaria was a regular human, until Professor Sturdy gifted him the powers of at least three villains. He gained superhuman strength, speed, and durability. He could fly, project laser beams from his eyes, manipulate ionic energy constructs, and gained an ionic healing ability. However, these powers meant he aged quickly.

ALLIES AND ENEMIES

As a very successful crime boss, Count Nefaria has gained many fellow criminal allies loyal to his various nefarious causes, and just as many enemies from the Super Hero community who wish to stop him.

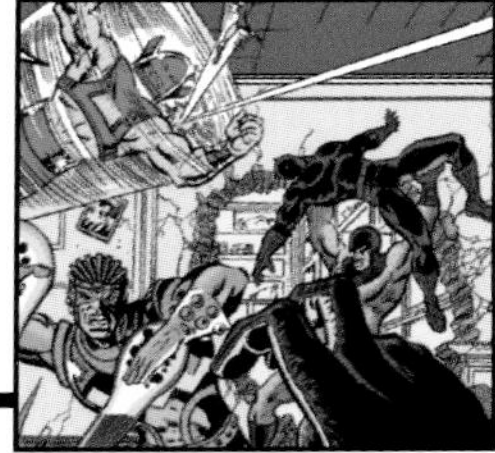

LETHAL LEGION
Power Man (Atlas), Living Laser, and Whirlwind made up Nefaria's Lethal Legion.

MADAME MASQUE
A one-time love interest of Iron Man, Madame Masque felt loyalty towards her father.

COUNTDOWN TO BATTLE

Having amassed a vast fortune, Count Nefaria was not about to give up a life of crime after a few failures at the Avengers' hands.

ANGUISH, ONCE REMOVED

Iron Man #116 (November 1978)

Count Nefaria gained superpowered enhancement at the hands of Professor Sturdy—one of Baron Heinrich Zemo's scientists—but was cursed with accelerated aging as a consequence. For this he was desperate to find a cure, and he decided to look no further than Tony Stark. Convinced Stark had the answers, Nefaria used Stark's trust of Whitney Frost—Nefaria's daughter, the elusive Madame Masque—to lure the unsuspecting businessman into an ambush. Stark soon switched to Iron Man mode, but before he could take Nefaria back to Avengers Mansion, he was forced to battle a giant tank in a scuffle that seemingly ended Nefaria's life. However, time would prove the villain difficult to kill.

Count Nefaria employed his Ani-Men—a hand picked group of criminals—against Tony Stark when Nefaria was too weak and sick to do his own dirty work.

Nefaria's power enhancements are enough to make him quite a challenge for the likes of the Vision and Thor—whose hammer, Mjolnir, merely bounces off the Super Villain's chest.

MAN OF POWER

After battling Iron Man and earning a spot in that hero's personal rogues gallery, Count Nefaria felt it was time to up his game with the help of a new Lethal Legion.

Nefaria sent his Lethal Legion to rob banks, using the money to help fund his transformation into a superhuman. After sending the Lethal Legion to attack Avengers Mansion and soften up his prey, Nefaria unleashed his new abilities on his greatest foes. But when Nefaria grew greedy and sought out Thor in an effort to steal the thunder god's "immortality," even an enhanced Nefaria was no match for the battle that followed, especially when the villain realized he was rapidly aging due to a double-cross from Professor Sturdy.

Nefaria used his eye beams to melt a stone missile attack sent from the Scarlet Witch.

During his dramatic battle with Thor, Count Nefaria threw a bus and a building at the Norseman.

MONICA RAMBEAU

ALTHOUGH MONICA RAMBEAU has operated under many different code names and dressed in even more costumes over the years, she has remained a stalwart member of the Avengers team. Hailing from New Orleans, USA, she has now embraced the city of New York as her Super Hero home base.

Monica gained her powers by risking her life to stop a madman's plot. She smashed his weapon with her bare hands.

Monica can transform her clothes and body into light.

MILITARY BEGINNINGS

When Lieutenant Rambeau of the New Orleans Harbor Patrol destroyed an experimental weapon to stop a terrorist, she gained the power to transform herself into any form of light within the electromagnetic spectrum.

Unable to control her powers with any stability, Monica traveled to New York City, where she met Spider-Man and the Thing, who introduced her to the Avengers. They helped her get her powers under control, and she soon became a full Avenger, going by the name of Captain Marvel for a time. Monica eventually became one of the team's leaders. After nearly being killed while stopping Namor's dangerous wife, Marrina, Monica retired for a short time, but she returned to being a hero soon after recovering. She has moved in and out of the Avengers ever since and more recently joined Luke Cage's new team of Mighty Avengers.

Monica didn't know anyone in New York City when she first arrived, but she ran into Spider-Man by chance.

Monica's first costume, which she wore as Captain Marvel, was put together from old Mardi Gras outfits.

DATA FILE

REAL NAME Monica Rambeau **OCCUPATION** Adventurer
BASE New Orleans, Louisiana; New York City, New York
HEIGHT 5 ft 10 in **WEIGHT** 130 lbs **EYES** Brown **HAIR** Black
FIRST APPEARANCE WITH AVENGERS *Amazing Spider-Man Annual* #16 (August 1982)
POWERS Monica has superhuman speed and can transform herself into pure energy. She can become light at any wavelength, including radiation of all kinds. In her energy form, she can fly, become intangible, become invisible, absorb energy, create personal illusions, and fire energy blasts. She is a skilled leader and expert combatant.

MIGHTY MONICA

Soon after Monica gained her superhuman powers, she traveled to New York and approached the Avengers. She has been affiliated with the team ever since.

Captain America believed in Captain Marvel's leadership, even before Monica believed in herself.

TO LEAD THE AVENGERS

Avengers #279 (May 1987)

When the Wasp resigned as leader of the Avengers, Captain America declined the post himself, as he had too many other duties at the time. Instead, he nominated Monica to take over as the team's leader. Unsure whether she was ready, she consulted with her parents and did some soul-searching of her own. After helping Captain America rescue some kids trapped in a mine, she decided the constant pressures of leadership would be worth the chance to do so much good, and she accepted his nomination.

ENERGY LOSS

Avengers #294 (August 1988)

Monica led the Avengers when Marrina transformed into a gigantic, rampaging sea monster called the Leviathan. With the help of Marrina's husband, Namor, the Avengers managed to kill her before she could wreak further destruction. During Monica's attack on the Leviathan, though, striking the ocean dispersed her energy so far that it drained from her completely and left her near death. This turned out to be part of a plan by Terminatrix to have her pawn, Doctor Druid, take over the team.

After the battle, Monica was found emaciated and appeared to have been starved almost to death.

ALLIES AND ENEMIES

Most of Monica's career as a Super Hero has been spent with the Avengers, and she counts many of them as her friends.

NEXTWAVE
This team worked for H.A.T.E. a governmental department, but left to fight on its own.

MIGHTY AVENGERS
When Luke Cage formed a new team of Avengers, Monica signed up early on.

Despite being almost killed by her battle with the Leviathan, Monica soon began to recover from her injuries and returned to action as a reservist.

Monica's closest female friends include Hellcat, Firestorm, and the Black Cat.

BY ANY NAME

Monica has had many different code names over the years and has regularly changed her look.

Unaware that there had been a previous Captain Marvel, Monica hadn't objected when the newspaper in New Orleans had called her by that name. But she then surrendered it to Genis-Vell as part of his heritage as Captain Mar-Vell's son, and changed her name to Photon. When Genis-Vell became Photon, she switched to Pulsar. Then, when she joined Luke Cage's new Mighty Avengers team, she became Spectrum.

Monica debuted a whole new costume when she changed her name to Spectrum.

DAREDEVIL

After years of going it alone, the hero of Hell's Kitchen finally joined the Avengers.

Matt Murdock was just a young boy when he pushed an old man out of the way of an oncoming truck. Splashed in the face by radioactive material that fell off the swerving vehicle, Matt was blinded, yet he found himself gifted with an amazing "radar" sense and other heightened abilities. After training with the mysterious Stick, he became Daredevil and put his talents to good use.

Preferring to protect his neighborhood in Manhattan by himself, Matt declined Avengers membership, despite teaming with other Avengers during a breakout from the Maximum-Maximum Security Penitentiary wing the Raft. However, during the villain Sin's attack on Avengers Mansion, Daredevil rescued Luke Cage's daughter. Later, when Luke asked him to join his New Avengers, Daredevil finally agreed.

Daredevil is blind but relies on his "radar" sense.

Daredevil combines gymnastic skills with the use of a reeled line to swing between buildings.

DATA FILE

REAL NAME Matthew Michael Murdock **OCCUPATION** Lawyer, Super Hero
BASE San Francisco, California; formerly Hell's Kitchen, New York City, New York
HEIGHT 6 ft **WEIGHT** 200 lbs **EYES** Blue **HAIR** Red
FIRST APPEARANCE WITH AVENGERS *Avengers Annual* #2 (July 1968)
POWERS Daredevil has superhuman senses, including amplified hearing, smell, taste and touch: Daredevil can read newsprint just by touching it. He also has "radar" sense that helps him form a mental picture of what is in front of him. He is an Olympic-level athlete and gymnast and an expert martial artist. He utilizes a customized billy club, both as a projectile against opponents and in defense against attack.

RADIOACTIVE MAN

An Avengers villain who originally clashed with Thor, Radioactive Man has earned the ire of several other heroes.

As one of the original Masters of Evil, Radioactive Man has been an enemy of the Avengers far longer than most criminals alive. A former nuclear physicist for the Chinese government, Dr. Chen Lu used his own experiments to transform his body into that of the superhuman Radioactive Man. Between stints as a Master of Evil, Radioactive Man would join the Titanic Three along with Titanium Man and the Crimson Dynamo, before turning over a new leaf as a Thunderbolt.

DATA FILE

REAL NAME Dr. Chen Lu **OCCUPATION** Criminal; former nuclear physicist
BASE Mobile
HEIGHT 6 ft 6 in **WEIGHT** 310 lbs **EYES** Brown **HAIR** None
FIRST APPEARANCE WITH AVENGERS *Avengers* #6 (July 1964)
POWERS Radioactive Man is like a living nuclear reactor. He can manipulate radiation in many ways, project various radiations, and project light and/or heat. He can attack his enemies with radiation poisoning, nausea, or dizziness. He is able to create force fields. He can channel his body's energy into superhuman strength.

THUNDRA

A warrior from an alternate future, Thundra is one of the mightiest women to ever go up against any member of the Avengers.

Born in a future where women ruled and systematically oppressed men, Thundra was genetically augmented to possess enhanced strength and endurance. She quickly excelled at her military training, and became a fine warrior and an officer. During a battle with a male army from an alternate Earth, Thundra was sent back in time to the Avengers' present. There she met and clashed with heroes like the Thing and the Hulk, and even became an ally of Hyperion of the Squadron Sinister.

DATA FILE

REAL NAME Thundra **OCCUPATION** Warrior
BASE Mobile
HEIGHT 7 ft 2 in **WEIGHT** 350 lbs **EYES** Green **HAIR** Red
FIRST APPEARANCE WITH AVENGERS *Avengers Annual* #8 (October 1978)
POWERS Genetic engineering has given Thundra superhuman strength, endurance, and agility. She has dense, resistant skin which can withstand punches and bullets. She is an expert military tactician, specializing in the use of a three-foot chain as a weapon. In addition, she is an expert boxer and wrestler.

The Gauntlet takes his code name from his giant robotic arm.

GAUNTLET

A hardened soldier, the Gauntlet was the original drill sergeant for the Fifty-State Initiative.

Years ago, two mysterious aliens appeared over Earth and collided in a fierce battle. Two pieces of their technology were later located in the Sudan by Sergeant Joseph Green. However, while Green was examining it, a Hydra trooper attempted to claim it. Green was forced to don one of the pieces—a metal arm-like device—in order to defeat the agent. Unfortunately for Green, the arm refused to come off. He would later use this technology as the first drill sergeant at Camp Hammond.

DATA FILE

REAL NAME Sergeant Joseph Green **OCCUPATION** Soldier; former drill sergeant
BASE Afghanistan
HEIGHT 6 ft **WEIGHT** 197 lbs **EYES** Brown **HAIR** Bald
FIRST APPEARANCE WITH AVENGERS *Avengers: The Initiative* #1 (June 2007)
POWERS With the cybernetic gauntlet, Joseph Green has superhuman strength, and he can project energy blasts and tethers. He is a highly-decorated soldier and military tactician.

RAGE

Rage's Avengers tenure was cut short when the truth about his age was revealed.

Audacious from the start, Rage first met the Avengers when he walked up to their headquarters and demanded entry into their line-up, citing the lack of black heroes as a prime reason. Despite his arrogance, the Avengers would later allow Rage into their ranks as a probationary member, but would dismiss him when they discovered his secret: Rage was actually a young boy who had been altered by a barrel of toxic sludge from Fisk Biochem. Despite his age costing him his membership, Rage later found a home in the New Warriors, and later with the Avengers Initiative.

DATA FILE

REAL NAME Elvin Daryl Haliday **OCCUPATION** Super Hero
BASE Mobile
HEIGHT 6 ft 6 in **WEIGHT** 450 lbs **EYES** Brown **HAIR** Bald
FIRST APPEARANCE WITH AVENGERS *Avengers* #326 (November 1990)
POWERS The chemicals in the toxic sludge transformed Elvin from a twelve-year-old boy into an adult with superhuman strength, speed, durability, and endurance. He is a formidable opponent in hand-to-hand combat. His mask hides his true identity.

FIREBIRD

Originally a member of the Super Hero team the Rangers, Firebird worked her way up to the Avengers, before returning to the Rangers again.

The hero Firebird's world first intermingled with that of the Avengers when she clashed with the Hulk who was under the influence of the Corruptor. Having gained her powers from a mysterious "fire dropped from the heavens," Bonita Juarez put her abilities to use against the Hulk alongside several other heroes of the American South West. After the battle, the group decided to form the Rangers. When her adventures took her to the west coast, Firebird teamed up with the West Coast Avengers. After the events of the Superhuman Civil War, Firebird joined a combination of her two teams in the form of the Avengers Fifty-State Initiative branch, also called the Rangers.

DATA FILE

REAL NAME
Bonita Juarez

OCCUPATION
Super Hero; social worker

BASE
Texas/ West Coast

HEIGHT 5 ft 5 in

WEIGHT 125 lbs

EYES Brown

HAIR Black

FIRST APPEARANCE WITH AVENGERS
West Coast Avengers #4 (January 1986)

POWERS
Firebird can radiate heat and generate a field of fire that takes on the form of a bird, giving her her name. By projecting energy beams below her, Firebird can fly. She is thought to be immortal and believes her abilities to be a gift from a higher power.

RED HULK

General Thaddeus "Thunderbolt" Ross spent much of his career chasing the Hulk—whom he later learned was Bruce Banner, the scientist he had hired to create the gamma bomb. After his death, Ross returned as the Red Hulk.

The Red Hulk seemed to murder Ross at one point, but in fact he had only killed a Life-Model Decoy.

The Intelligencia promised to restore Ross's dead daughter, Betty (also Banner's ex-wife), to life if Ross would allow them to transform him into the Red Hulk and work for them. Since agreeing to this course of action, the Red Hulk retains Ross's full intelligence, and he grows hotter—in terms of radiation and temperature—when he gets angry. He betrayed the Intelligencia's plans to conquer America, but in a moment of insanity he took over the White House for himself—until the Hulk stopped him.

Once Ross calmed down, Captain America offered him a chance to redeem himself by joining the Avengers, although other team members were a little suspicious of him. Discovering that he could no longer change back into his human form, Ross used his Red Hulk powers against villains. He managed to stop the Hood from acquiring the Infinity Gems, he helped fight the Worthy, and he battled against the X-Men as an Avenger.

The Red Hulk helped beat the Hood and took the Power Infinity Gem from him.

DATA FILE

REAL NAME
Thaddeus E. Ross

OCCUPATION
Adventurer; retired U.S. Air Force general

BASE
Mobile

HEIGHT 6 ft 1 in (human form); 7 ft (Red Hulk form)

WEIGHT 245 lbs (human form); 1200 lbs (Red Hulk form)

EYES Blue (human form); yellow (Red Hulk form)

HAIR White (human form); black (Red Hulk form)

FIRST APPEARANCE WITH AVENGERS
Avengers #7 (January 2011)

POWERS
The Red Hulk has superhuman durability, endurance, healing, speed, and strength. He emits gamma radiation, and it becomes more intense the angrier he gets. He can also absorb energy of all kinds. Ross can retain his intellect and senses while being the Red Hulk.

ALLIES AND ENEMIES

Without the U.S. military behind him, Ross has few friends outside of the Avengers. He led his version of a Thunderbolts team, but its members did not trust him.

FOE

HULK
The Hulk is the Red Hulk's greatest nemesis, although the two have been allies, too.

FAMILY

RED SHE-HULK
Betty Ross did return to life, but had been transformed into the Red She-Hulk.

SHE-HULK

When attorney Jennifer Walters was shot down by gangsters she was prosecuting, her cousin Bruce Banner gave her a blood transfusion to save her. This gifted her the ability to transform into the mighty She-Hulk.

Bruce feared what his blood might do to Jennifer, but he saw no other option.

At first, Jennifer kept her powers a secret, but she grew more open about it and spent more time as She-Hulk throughout her life. Soon after gaining her powers, she joined the Avengers. She also served as a substitute member of the Fantastic Four, replacing the Thing for a short while. After being exposed to the Jack of Hearts' radiation powers, she went berserk and virtually destroyed the town of Bone, in Idaho. Only the Hulk himself could slow her down until the Jack of Hearts was able to use his powers to rebalance her gamma levels.

Though she rarely lost control, She-Hulk did suffer a relapse when the Scarlet Witch temporarily went mad. She-Hulk nearly killed Captain America and tore the Vision in half. After that, she continued to work on and off with the Avengers. She later served as the legal counsel for—and occasional field member of—Luke Cage's Mighty Avengers team.

DATA FILE

REAL NAME Jennifer Walters **OCCUPATION** Attorney, adventurer
BASE Mobile
HEIGHT 5 ft 10 in (human form); 6 ft 7 in (She-Hulk form)
WEIGHT 140 lbs (human form); 650 lbs (She-Hulk form)
EYES Green **HAIR** Brown (human form); green (She-Hulk form)
FIRST APPEARANCE WITH AVENGERS *Avengers* #221 (July 1982)
POWERS As She-Hulk, Jennifer has superhuman durability, endurance, healing, speed, and strength. She is an expert combatant, skilled pilot, and has a gifted intellect.

ALLIES AND ENEMIES

Jennifer has a life outside of the Avengers, mostly focused upon her law career, but her opponents in the courtroom are rarely as dangerous as the ones she meets in battle.

FAMILY

BRUCE BANNER
Jennifer's cousin not only saved her life, but helped her become a hero too.

FOE

GENERAL ROSS
Jennifer helped the Hulk evade General Ross, earning his enmity.

KEEPING IT IN THE FAMILY

Betty Ross, the ex-wife of Jennifer's cousin Bruce, also became part of the Hulk family. Having been thought dead, she was brought back in the form of the Red She-Hulk by the evil minds known as the Intelligencia. Brainwashed to work for them, she clashed with the Avengers when sent to abduct Henry Pym, but has since lost her powers.

SONGBIRD

A reformed villain and longtime Thunderbolt, Songbird has come a long way since her days as Screaming Mimi.

As Screaming Mimi, Melissa Joan Gold began a criminal campaign that led to her encountering heroes like Giant-Man (Bill Foster), Quasar, the Thing, and even Captain America. After receiving vocal enhancements by Power Broker, Inc., Mimi later joined forces with Baron Helmut Zemo as a member of his Masters of Evil. After some time, the team began masquerading as heroes in the form of the Thunderbolts. Unlike some of her villainous cohorts, pretending to be a hero had an impact on Mimi. Under her Thunderbolt name of Songbird, she became a true hero, and later the warden at the Maximum-Maximum Security Penitentiary wing called the Raft.

The Thunderbolts put Songbird in the company of both the morally bankrupt and the truly heroic.

Sonic powers enable flight

DATA FILE

REAL NAME Melissa Joan Gold **OCCUPATION** Former wrestler; warden, Super Hero
BASE Raft, New York City, New York
HEIGHT 5 ft 5 in **WEIGHT** 145 lbs **EYES** Green
HAIR White with Pink Streaks
FIRST APPEARANCE WITH AVENGERS *Avengers* #271 (September 1986)
POWERS As Screaming Mimi, Melissa possessed a sonic scream. As Songbird, Melissa can create solid-sound blasts that function as weapons. She wears a harness that turns sound waves into energy. Her sonic wings enable her to fly.

FIRESTAR

As an Avenger, Young Ally, New Warrior, and friend to Spider-Man, Firestar has accomplished many incredible things.

Truly an amazing friend to many, Firestar began her ventures into the Super Hero world as an inexperienced mutant whose powers only started to manifest when she was 13 years old. She found comfort and guidance in the form of Super Villain Emma Frost, the White Queen of the Inner Circle of the Hellfire Club. However, she soon got her life on the right track as a founding member of the New Warriors, and stayed with the team for a long tenure. She later graduated to a position in the Avengers after they returned from a sojourn in a pocket dimension. Struggling to overcome cancer caused by the use of her powers, Firestar later befriended Monica Rambeau, Patsy Walker, Justice, and Felicia Hardy, and also became a member of the newest incarnation of the Young Allies.

DATA FILE

REAL NAME
Angelica Jones

OCCUPATION
Super Hero, teacher

BASE
The Jean Grey School for Higher Learning, Salem Center, New York

HEIGHT 5 ft 2 in

WEIGHT 101 lbs

EYES Green

HAIR Red

FIRST APPEARANCE WITH AVENGERS
Avengers #341 (November 1991)

POWERS
Angelica is a mutant who can emit microwave energy and hence give off enough heat to melt metal objects. By heating the air around her, Firestar can create enough thrust to allow her to fly. She wears a special micro-circuit, full-body sheath beneath her costume—designed by Hank Pym, it protects her from harmful radiation.

BETTY ROSS

The Hulk's girlfriend became a monster herself.

The daughter of General "Thunderbolt" Ross, Betty grew up on American airbases. She fell in love with Bruce Banner, and continued a relationship with him even after she discovered Banner was the Hulk. After marrying and divorcing Major Glenn Talbot, Betty eventually married Bruce. Frequently caught up in peril by her proximity to the Hulk, she was transformed by M.O.D.O.K. (Mental Organism Designed Only for Killing) into the gamma-spawned monster the Harpy, and battled the Hulk. Betty became sick after continued exposure to radiation, a fact which a Hulk-like monster named the Abomination seized upon, giving her a fatal contamination. She was later returned to life by the Leader, a laborer who mutated after being contaminated by radiation in an accident. A gamma-ray bombardment by the Leader changed Betty into the Red She-Hulk.

As the Red She-Hulk, Betty discharges gamma energy from her eyes.

DATA FILE

REAL NAME
Elizabeth "Betty" Ross Talbot Banner

OCCUPATION
Former espionage agent; author and librarian.

BASE
Mobile; formerly Sunville, Florida. Also Gamma Base, New Mexico.

HEIGHT 6 ft 6 in (as Betty); 6 ft 7 in (as the Red She-Hulk)

WEIGHT 110 lbs (as Betty); 700 lbs (as the Red She-Hulk)

EYES Blue (as Betty); yellow (as the Red She-Hulk)

HAIR Brown (as Betty); black with red streaks (as the Red She-Hulk)

FIRST APPEARANCE WITH AVENGERS
Avengers #5 (May 1964)

POWERS
Born without superpowers, Betty is a highly trained spy, skilled in combat. During her brief incarnation as the Harpy, she could fly, possessed talons and could fire energy blasts. As the Red She-Hulk she has similar strength to the Hulk, and can break through dimensional barriers with a punch. She can absorb energy from other Hulks and discharge it by touch.

MAJOR VICTORY

Major Victory grew up in the past, traveled to the future, and then returned to fight in the present.

As a young boy, Vance Astrovik never dreamt he would travel to the future and become one of the Guardians of the Galaxy. But that's exactly what fate had in store for him. Originally calling himself Marvel Boy, Vance would later become known as Major Victory. But time would soon correct itself when the frozen form of Major Victory was discovered by the present day Guardians of the Galaxy. Not understanding how he came to be where he was, Major Victory armed himself with the iconic shield of Captain America and went on to fight with the modern-day team of Guardians of the Galaxy against the villain Magus.

DATA FILE

REAL NAME Vance Astrovik (later changed to Vance Astro) **OCCUPATION** Super Hero, astronaut
BASE Mobile
HEIGHT 6 ft 1 in **WEIGHT** 250 lbs **EYES** Hazel **HAIR** Black
FIRST APPEARANCE WITH AVENGERS *Avengers* #167 (January 1978)
POWERS Vance is a mutant who can produce psychokinetic force blasts and manipulate objects. Due to his time-displacement traveling abilities, he wears a protective bodysuit to prevent him from aging. He is an expert fighter. When in possession of Captain America's shield, he can use his psychokinetic abilities to propel the shield in battle.

IRONCLAD

A founding member of the U-Foes and a combatant of the Hulk, Ironclad later joined Norman Osborn's Fifty-State Initiative.

In an attempt to duplicate the event that gave the Fantastic Four their powers, Michael Steel piloted a spaceship carrying three of his associates into a cosmic ray belt outside Earth's atmosphere. Exposed to the cosmic rays, the quartet was transformed into the U-Foes, who soon used their new abilities for criminal pursuits. Steel became Ironclad, and would later oppose the Avengers in the Masters of Evil, as well as joining Osborn's Fifty-State Avengers Initiative.

Ironclad's armor takes on a realistic, skin-like appearance.

DATA FILE

REAL NAME Michael Steel **OCCUPATION** Criminal; former scientist and pilot
BASE Mobile, but based in North Carolina during the Initiative
HEIGHT 6 ft 7 in **WEIGHT** 650 lbs **EYES** White **HAIR** None
FIRST APPEARANCE WITH AVENGERS *Avengers* #304 (June 1989)
POWERS Following his unprotected, prolonged exposure to the cosmic rays, Ironclad has developed metallic-like armored skin. He has gained superhuman strength, endurance, and durability and can increase his weight without increasing his size. Ironclad can withstand extremes of temperature and is a master combatant.

CORRUPTOR

Able to influence even the most disciplined minds, the Corruptor has attempted to vilify the members of the Avengers on many occasions.

A factory worker in a pharmaceutical manufacturing company, Jackson Day was caught in a fire that caused him to be coated in a variety of psychoactive chemicals. Day's skin turned blue and his hair white, and his mind was also corrupted. So changed, he turned to a life of crime as the Corruptor, utilizing his new ability to subvert the will of others to his advantage with a simple touch. Manipulating both Thor and then later the Hulk, the Corruptor would go on to face the Avengers as part of Norman Osborn's personal army of Super Villains.

DATA FILE

REAL NAME Jackson Day **OCCUPATION** Criminal; former factory worker
BASE Mobile
HEIGHT 6 ft 1 in **WEIGHT** 225 lbs **EYES** Red **HAIR** White
FIRST APPEARANCE WITH AVENGERS *Avengers* #6 (July 1998)
POWERS Corruptor's sweat glands secrete a highly potent pyscho-active chemical that, upon contact with another person's skin, renders the victim susceptible to suggestions by the Corruptor. The victim may lose all their inhibitions or act in an immoral manner.

ARMADILLO

A hardened criminal, the Armadillo was a longtime foe of the Avengers.

A felon who submitted his body to be experimented on in order to cure his ailing wife, Antonio Rodriguez was transformed into the Armadillo. As per the rest of his agreement, he then broke into the West Coast Avengers compound in order to rescue the villain Goliath (Erik Jotsen, aka Power Man, or Atlas). He then battled Captain America, who trailed the Armadillo back to the corrupt scientist who had created him.

DATA FILE

REAL NAME Antonio Rodriguez **OCCUPATION** Criminal; former professional wrestler
BASE Mobile
HEIGHT 7 ft 6 in **WEIGHT** 540 lbs **EYES** Brown **HAIR** None
FIRST APPEARANCE WITH AVENGERS *Captain America* #308 (August 1985)
POWERS The Armadillo has superhuman strength and endurance. He exhibits extraordinary durability and resistance to injury. He has claws on his hands and feet that are strong enough to dig tunnels through concrete. He is a formidable opponent in hand-to-hand combat, relying on his knowledge of street fighting and wrestling.

KORVAC

This technician turned cyborg, then cosmic god.

Computer operator Korvac was a slave to the Badoon species, who conquered his world in an alternate universe. Korvac's masters turned him into a cyborg as a punishment for falling asleep at his screen. The new Korvac intrigued the Grandmaster, who used him against the Defenders. Korvac faked defeat to learn more about the Grandmaster's power, became stronger, and slayed his Badoon masters. He then developed cosmic powers while accessing the systems of Galactus's space station. Traveling through dimensions to the Avengers' Earth, he planned to transform it into a paradise. Here he encountered the Collector's daughter, Carina, who joined forces with him. Opposed by the Avengers and the Guardians of the Galaxy, Korvac slayed many of his foes, but brought them back to life before destroying his physical body in order to escape retribution from Galactus. He has since returned in energy form but was finally destroyed in battle by a multiple alliance of Avengers teams and the anti-matter powers of Hazmat.

Body of pure cosmic energy

DATA FILE

REAL NAME
Michael Korvac

OCCUPATION
God; former slave

BASE
The alternate Earth known as Earth-691

HEIGHT 12 ft (varies)

WEIGHT Varies

EYES Blue/white

HAIR Usually blond, but varies

FIRST APPEARANCE WITH AVENGERS
In flashback: *Giant Size Defenders* #3 (January 1975); *Avengers* #167 (January 1978)

POWERS
Korvac developed the powers of analysis and energy absorption when the Badoon melded him with his machines. He learnt how to use the energies of foes against them, and became a master of strategy. His cyborg body also contained concealed weaponry. Stealing cosmic power from Galactus, he acquired god-like abilities, such as energy projection, the ability to travel through time and space, and reality-shaping powers.

Gravity now takes to the skies as a member of the Young Allies.

GRAVITY

A member of the Young Allies as well as the Avengers Initiative, Gravity is young and optimistic about his future as a Super Hero.

High school student Greg Willis gained his cosmic powers during a freak storm while on vacation. Becoming the fledgling Super Hero Gravity, but struggling to find his place in the world, he first found a home with the Avengers when he signed up for the Fifty-State Initiative program. He was made leader of the Heavy Hitters, a Nevada-based team of Super Heroes, but was later transferred to Wisconsin by Norman Osborn and forced to become a member of the Great Lakes Initiative.

DATA FILE

REAL NAME Greg Willis **OCCUPATION** Super Hero
BASE Mobile
HEIGHT 5 ft 10 in **WEIGHT** 175 lbs **EYES** Blue **HAIR** Brown
FIRST APPEARANCE WITH AVENGERS *Avengers: The Initiative* #17 (November 2008)
POWERS Gravity possesses a second "skin" of gravitons that enable him to fly, increase his strength, and alter his weight. He can affect the speed of objects he touches. He wears a costume that makes gravity manipulation easier. A punch from Gravity would be extra powerful since he can manipulate the gravity of his opponents.

CLOUD 9

One of the earliest recruits to the Fifty-State Initiative's Camp Hammond, Cloud 9 became a hero, despite her lack of self-confidence.

After the events of the Superhuman Civil War, the legally registered heroes of the USA sought to recruit new heroes to serve as the next generation. Teenager Abby Boylen—who went by the name of Cloud 9 because she could ride her own cloud—was recruited by War Machine into the Initiative program. Despite her shyness, Abby's new role helped her to find her own voice at last.

DATA FILE

REAL NAME Abigail Boylen **OCCUPATION** Super Hero
BASE Mobile
HEIGHT 5 ft 5 in **WEIGHT** 100 lbs **EYES** Blue **HAIR** Blonde
FIRST APPEARANCE WITH AVENGERS *Avengers: The Initiative* #1 (June 2007)
POWERS Abby can control a cloud of alien gas that enables her to fly. She can create enough of it to mask her movements—hence her deployment on stealth missions. She can manipulate the gas cloud to asphyxiate or blind her opponents.

BLACKOUT

Extremely powerful and rarely in control of his faculties, Blackout has been manipulated by other villains, most notably as part of the Masters of Evil.

After an accident bathed him with Darkforce energy and gave him near uncontrollable abilities, Mark Daniels became the unhinged villain Blackout. He shortly came into conflict with the hero Nova and later joined forces with Moonstone, Rhino, and Electro. This led to a battle with the Avengers and Spider-Man, and a bond between Blackout and Moonstone. As Moonstone's pawn, Blackout would face the Avengers again as a part of the Masters of Evil, until his sanity was restored by the Super Hero Dr. Druid. While that encounter ended with Blackout collapsing from cerebral hemorrhaging, he was later seen working with the Hood during the Siege of Asgard.

Blackout's lightning symbol is a reference to his powers and his link with the Darkforce.

DATA FILE

REAL NAME
Marcus Daniels

OCCUPATION
Criminal; former lab assistant

BASE
Mobile

HEIGHT 5 ft 10 in

WEIGHT 180 lbs

EYES Gray

HAIR Brown

FIRST APPEARANCE WITH AVENGERS
Avengers #236 (October 1983)

POWERS
Blackout can manipulate Darkforce matter including creating constructs and opening portals to the Darkforce dimension. As a result of his newfound abilities, he is prone to mental instability. He can fly by standing on a disk of Darkforce energy and commanding it to move.

JESSICA JONES

A reluctant Super Hero with a tragic past, Jessica Jones could not escape life with the Avengers, especially after marrying Luke Cage. A Power Woman in her own right, Jessica brings a down-to-Earth perspective to the often far-from-grounded life of an Avenger.

Jessica no longer wears a costume, but she and her young daughter often receive visits from their costumed friends.

Jessica discovered she had the power of flight after spending six months in a coma.

To say Jessica Jones was shy during high school was an understatement. As a student of Midtown High, she had a crush on a boy she thought was out of her league, bookworm Peter Parker. But just as Peter was transformed into Spider-Man, Jessica's life was also altered by a twist of fate.

During a car crash involving her family and a military truck, Jessica was doused in mysterious, heated, hazardous chemicals, resulting in her gaining superpowers, including the power of flight. Soon, Jessica utilized these powers as the heroine Jewel, and teamed up with the Avengers. However, after being kidnapped and controlled by the Purple Man, Jessica decided to give up the heroic life and became a private detective, instead.

However, through a romance with Luke Cage and a professional working relationship with Matt Murdock (Daredevil), Jessica soon found herself back on the Super Hero scene. After having a child with Luke and marrying him, Jessica realized she was surrounded by the dangers inherent to an Avenger anyway, and so decided to officially join Luke's team of New Avengers as Power Woman.

DATA FILE

REAL NAME Jessica Jones **OCCUPATION** Super Hero; mother; former private detective; former reporter

BASE The Gem Theater, New York City, New York

HEIGHT 5 ft 7 in **WEIGHT** 124 lbs **EYES** Brown

HAIR Brown (dyed purple when she was Jewel)

FIRST APPEARANCE WITH AVENGERS *New Avengers* #3 (March 2005)

POWERS Jessica has the powers of superhuman strength, endurance, and durability. She can also fly and has a high resistance to injury. She has an excellent memory.

ALLIES AND ENEMIES

With her sarcastic humor and a light-hearted attitude, Jessica Jones has made a lot of friends both before and during her stint as an Avenger. She has also formed many enemies over time, including one that still troubles her to this day.

FRIENDS

LUKE CAGE
Jessica is married to Luke Cage. The couple have a daughter named Danielle.

CAROL DANVERS
Carol, aka Ms. Marvel, is one of Jessica's closest friends and confidantes.

FOE

PURPLE MAN
The Purple Man emotionally scarred Jessica when he forced her to be his slave.

JEWEL

After testing out her powers and besting the Super Villain Scorpion in the process, Jessica decided to try life as a Super Hero. With amethyst-colored hair, Jessica became Jewel. Then one fateful day she met the Purple Man. He controlled Jessica for eight months, and then made her attack the Avengers, where Jessica was quickly defeated and brought back to reality.

3-D MAN

The predecessor to the current 3-D Man (Triathlon) was a combination of two crime-fighting brothers.

In the 1950s, Chuck Chandler was captured by Skrulls, but managed to escape. However, as the Skrull ship exploded, Chuck was bathed in a mysterious light and heat caused by a mysterious fragment. Pulled into two dimensions, Chuck's form bonded with his brother Hal's, but could be released in brief periods as the Super Hero 3-D Man. His powers were later stolen by fiend Jonathan Tremont of the Triune Understanding—a supposedly positive movement for superpowered beings later revealed to have alien links.

DATA FILE

REAL NAMES Chuck and Hal Chandler **OCCUPATION** Super Hero
BASE California
HEIGHT 6 ft 2 in **WEIGHT** 200 lbs **EYES** Brown (Hal); blue (Chuck)
HAIR Gray (Hal); reddish-blond (Chuck)
FIRST APPEARANCE WITH AVENGERS *Avengers Forever* #4 (March 1999)
POWERS Through concentration, 3-D Man's physical abilities—including speed, strength, agility, and senses—are enhanced three times that of a normal man. This effect lasts for about three hours.

WHIRLWIND

Childhood bully David Cannon turned his mutant ability into a dishonest career, and became Whirlwind—a powerful force of nature.

Originally dubbed the Human Top by the newspapers, the mutant David Cannon's first crimes were halted by Giant-Man (Hank Pym). But when he adopted the identity of Whirlwind, David soon attracted the attention of the entire Avengers. Whirlwind would become a regular enemy of the Earth's Mightiest Heroes as a part of the Masters of Evil.

Whirlwind's "Whirlwind Blades" can be worn on his arms and rotated at frightening speeds.

DATA FILE

REAL NAME David Cannon **OCCUPATION** Criminal (career began as a child stealing fruit)
BASE Mobile
HEIGHT 6 ft 1 in **WEIGHT** 220 lbs **EYES** Blue **HAIR** Brown
FIRST APPEARANCE WITH AVENGERS *Avengers* #46 (November 1967)
POWERS The mutant Whirlwind has the ability to rotate his body at superhuman speed. This rotation power allows for wind blasts, flight, and tornado creation. He also has superhuman strength.

AGENT VENOM

The high school bully of Peter Parker, Flash Thompson has matured into his own version of a Super Hero.

A graduate of Midtown High, Flash Thompson went from being Peter Parker's bully to one of his friends and a huge proponent of Spider-Man. Thompson lost his legs while serving in the military, but was given a chance to truly imitate his hero when the military employed him as the Venom symbiote's new host. He became Agent Venom, struggling to keep the symbiote's nature at bay while joining the Guardians of the Galaxy as an officially appointed Avenger.

DATA FILE

REAL NAME Eugene "Flash" Thompson **OCCUPATION** Super Hero, soldier; former high school gym teacher
BASE Guardians of the Galaxy's ship, mobile
HEIGHT 6 ft 2 in **WEIGHT** 185 lbs **EYES** Blue **HAIR** Reddish-Blond
FIRST APPEARANCE WITH AVENGERS *Secret Avengers* #23 (April 2012)
POWERS Agent Venom has the same abilities as Spider-Man, including superhuman strength, endurance, speed, durability, wall-crawling, and agility. He can generate webbing from his symbiote suit. He has shape-changing abilities, night vision, and an accelerated healing factor. He is an expert marksman and combatant.

MISS AMERICA

Perhaps inspired by the original Miss America (Madeline Joyce Frank), América Chávez moved from the Teen Brigade to the Young Avengers.

An aspiring heroine hailing from a utopian dimension created by the powerful sentient force Demiurge, Miss America joined the Ultimate Nullifier in a new incarnation of the classic Teen Brigade team. After clashing with the Young Masters, Miss America graduated to the Young Avengers after getting the better of Loki. As a Young Avenger, Miss America developed a strong bond with her teammates, including Marvel Boy (Noh-Varr), Hawkeye (Kate Bishop), Hulkling, Prodigy, and Wiccan.

DATA FILE

REAL NAME América Chávez **OCCUPATION** Super Hero
BASE New York City, New York
HEIGHT Unknown **WEIGHT** Unknown **EYES** Brown **HAIR** Black
FIRST APPEARANCE WITH AVENGERS *Young Avengers* #1 (March 2013)
POWERS Raised in the Utopian Parallel—an alternate dimension outside time and space—Miss America probably gained her superhuman abilities by being in the presence of the Demiurge. She has superhuman strength, endurance, and durability—her skin is bullet-proof and flame resistant. She can fly, teleport, and travel inter-dimensionally.

GREY GARGOYLE

An arrogant enemy who once sought Thor's hammer, the Grey Gargoyle soon expanded his hatred to include the entire Avengers team.

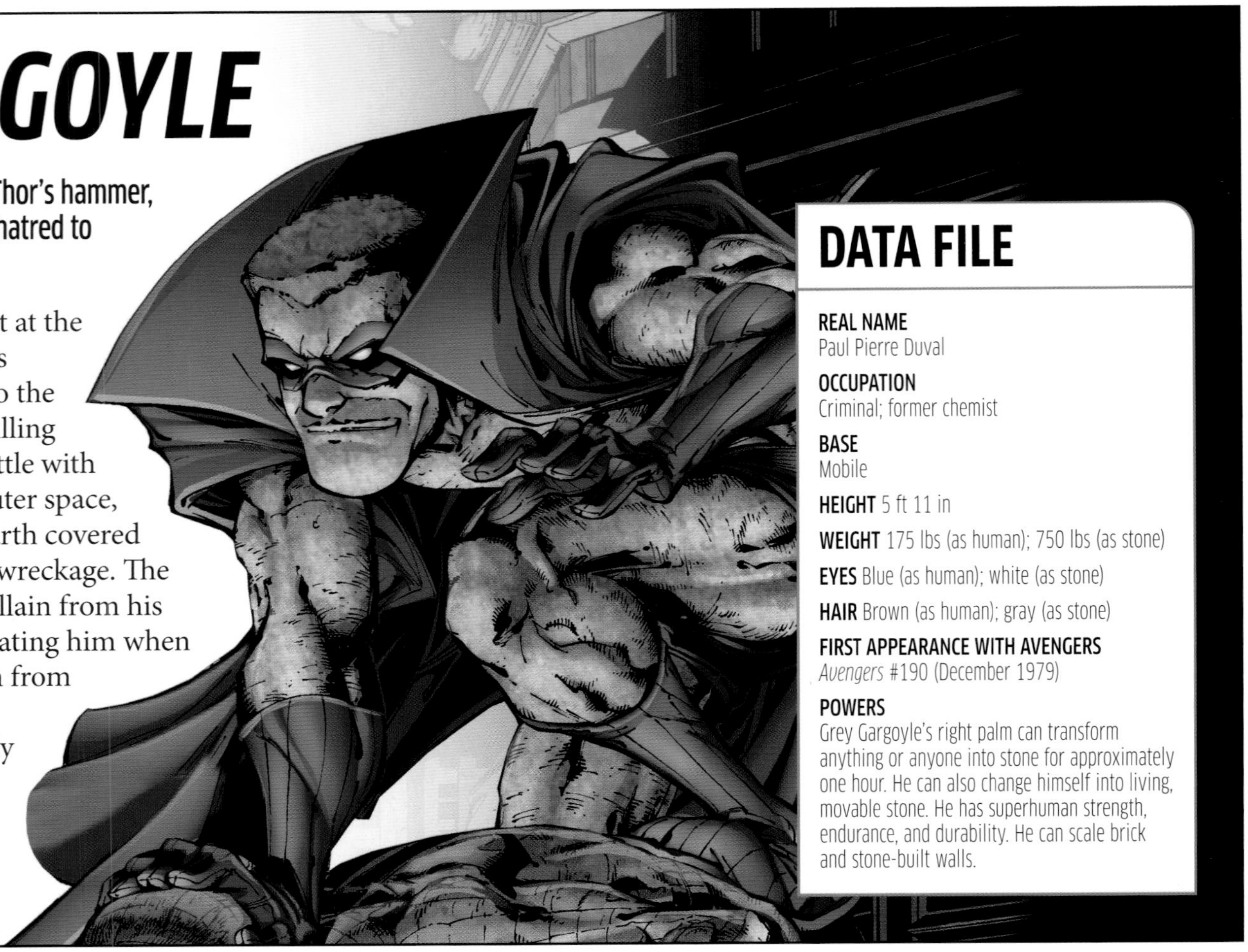

Paul Duval was a brilliant chemist at the Paris Institute of Scientific Studies when he transformed himself into the Grey Gargoyle by accidentally spilling a formula on his hand. After a battle with Thor and an unplanned trip to outer space, the Grey Gargoyle returned to Earth covered in a shell of cosmic particles and wreckage. The Avengers unwittingly freed the villain from his shell and battled him, finally defeating him when the Scarlet Witch turned his form from stone back to flesh and blood. However, the Grey Gargoyle easily regained his stone appearance and continues his criminal career, fighting everyone from Spider-Man to the Thing.

DATA FILE

REAL NAME
Paul Pierre Duval

OCCUPATION
Criminal; former chemist

BASE
Mobile

HEIGHT 5 ft 11 in

WEIGHT 175 lbs (as human); 750 lbs (as stone)

EYES Blue (as human); white (as stone)

HAIR Brown (as human); gray (as stone)

FIRST APPEARANCE WITH AVENGERS
Avengers #190 (December 1979)

POWERS
Grey Gargoyle's right palm can transform anything or anyone into stone for approximately one hour. He can also change himself into living, movable stone. He has superhuman strength, endurance, and durability. He can scale brick and stone-built walls.

Miguel must wear a protective suit to protect him from his electrical plasma "lightning" form.

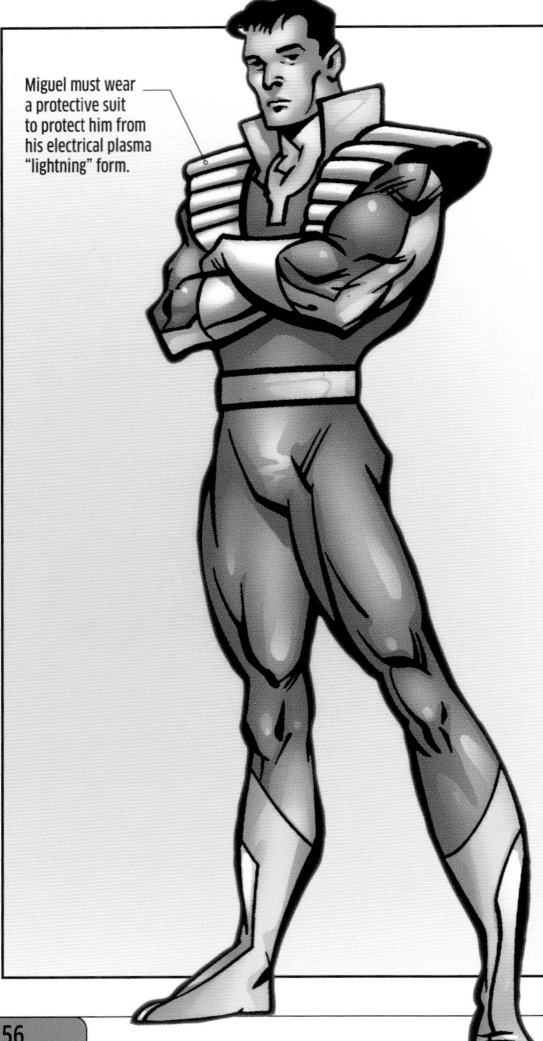

LIVING LIGHTNING

Originally facing the West Coast Avengers as a foe rather than a friend, Living Lightning would soon become a valued member of their Super Hero team.

Miguel Santos is the son of one of the original members of the Legion of the Living Lightning—an extremist group that attempted to "save America" by abolishing war and hatred by taking the country over by force. However, their plans to be "saviors" involved an attack with missiles that the Hulk managed to stop. Miguel decided to reclaim his birthright, but he was caught in an electric current while plugging in the Legion's machinery. Turned into Living Lightning, Miguel soon went on a rampage that was halted by the original Human Torch. After an association with the nefarious Dr. Demonicus, Miguel decided to change his criminal ways and joined the Avengers. Since then he has also been a member of the Rangers.

DATA FILE

REAL NAME
Miguel Santos

OCCUPATION
Super Hero; student; former villain

BASE
California (as part of the West Coast Avengers)/ Texas (as part of the Rangers)

HEIGHT 5 ft 9 in

WEIGHT 170 lbs

EYES Brown

HAIR Black

FIRST APPEARANCE WITH AVENGERS
Avengers West Coast #63 (October 1990)

POWERS
Miguel can switch from human to lightning form, with the ability to project lightning. He can fly at sub-light speeds and create and manipulate force fields. While in lightning form he becomes energy and his mind enters an astral plane.

LORD TEMPLAR

A powerful villain who fought the combined might of the New Warriors and the Avengers, Lord Templar had a mysterious origin.

Lord Templar was the brother of the villains Pagan and Jonathan Tremont, but was killed by a disease that spread through their childhood village in the foothills of the Himalayas. He was only able to materialize at the will of Jonathan Tremont and his light energy shard. When the Avengers first met this foe, they were allied with the New Warriors. Preaching a mission of "universal law," Templar fled after a brutal attack by Thor. Later, Templar was revealed as a minion of the corrupt Tremont and was defeated by his former lackey, Triathlon.

DATA FILE

REAL NAME Unknown **OCCUPATION** Criminal
BASE Mobile
HEIGHT Unknown **WEIGHT** Unknown **EYES** Red **HAIR** Black
FIRST APPEARANCE WITH AVENGERS *Avengers* #13 (February 1999)
POWERS When he has been materialized by his brother Jonathan Tremont, Lord Templar exhibits superhuman strength, speed, endurance, and durability. He can generate and project energy, absorb and redirect power, teleport, levitate, and summon duplicates of himself.

JULIA CARPENTER

The second woman to hold the title Spider-Woman, Julia Carpenter has also gone by the spider-related code names of Arachne and, more recently, Madame Web.

Given special abilities as a test subject for a clandestine government Super Soldier program, Julia Carpenter gained her first real taste of Super Hero life fighting on Battleworld during the so-called Secret Wars. Later, she became a member of the West Coast Avengers, and stayed with the team until it was dissolved and formed anew as Force Works. After the events of the Superhuman Civil War, Julia—calling herself Arachne—joined Omega Flight, a Canada-based Super Hero team. Then she returned to New York City under the new identity of Madame Web.

DATA FILE

REAL NAME Julia Carpenter **OCCUPATION** Super Hero; former government agent
BASE New York City, New York
HEIGHT 5 ft 9 in **WEIGHT** 140 lbs **EYES** Blue **HAIR** Reddish-blonde
FIRST APPEARANCE WITH AVENGERS *Avengers West Coast* #70 (May 1991)
POWERS Spider-Woman has superhuman strength, speed, agility, sense of touch, reflexes, and durability. She can create psionic energy "webs." Her psionic ability means she can stick to surfaces and objects. As Madame Web, Julia had precognitive skills and could teleport, but these skills have recently been lost to her.

BLUE MARVEL

A hero who often works by his own rules, Blue Marvel joined Luke Cage and his Mighty Avengers when fate drew them together.

Preferring the solitude of his own undersea fortress, Kadesh, Blue Marvel had withdrawn from society. He disapproved of how Tony Stark ran the Avengers, and disliked S.H.I.E.L.D.'s methods as well, believing that heroes were of the people and not above the people. So Blue Marvel was content playing the role of solo global guardian until an attack by Thanos's forces in New York City caused him to team up with Luke Cage's Mighty Avengers out of necessity. He then joined the team, happy to work alongside heroes who put the safety of Earth's citizens above cosmic affairs.

DATA FILE

REAL NAME Dr. Adam Brashear **OCCUPATION** Super Hero
BASE Kadesh
HEIGHT 6 ft 3 in **WEIGHT** 240 lbs **EYES** Brown **HAIR** Black (with gray streaks)
FIRST APPEARANCE WITH AVENGERS *Mighty Avengers* #2 (December 2013)
POWERS A genius in the field of theoretical physics, Blue Marvel can store and disperse antimatter from his hands in the form of concussive bolts or as one big explosive pulse. He has extreme superhuman strength, endurance, and durability. Blue Marvel can fly beyond supersonic speeds. He ages slowly and is invulnerable.

MANIFOLD

Mutant desert dweller Eden Fesi opens the doorway to the universe.

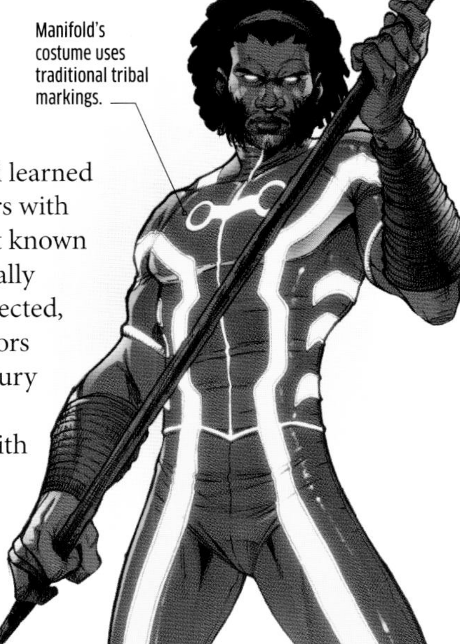

Manifold's costume uses traditional tribal markings.

An aboriginal Australian, Eden Fesi learned to master his reality-warping powers with the guidance of the wise old mutant known as Gateway, ally of the X-Men. Initially approached by Hydra, whom he rejected, Fesi agreed to join the Secret Warriors when he was approached by Nick Fury to be a part of his clandestine new team. Following several missions with the Secret Warriors he joined the Avengers, and was part of the team that battled Ex-Nihilo, one of the Gardeners. With others, Manifold left the Avengers when S.H.I.E.L.D. took control.

DATA FILE

REAL NAME Eden Fesi **OCCUPATION** Adventurer, former secret agent.
BASE Savage land, previously Avengers Tower, Kata Tjuta, Australia.
HEIGHT 5ft 10in **WEIGHT** 175lbs **EYES** Brown **HAIR** Black
FIRST APPEARANCE WITH AVENGERS *Dark Avengers* #9 (November 2009)
POWERS A mutant with the ability to fold reality, Manifold can teleport himself and others across light years of space. The upper limit of his power is unknown, but he has transported a quinjet. His portals remain open until he chooses to close them. Although he has only normal human strength, he has the many combat skills of his people, plus advanced survival and healing abilities. He is an expert at hunting and fighting with a long spear.

FLUX

When he first gained his superpowers, Dennis Sykes would learn of the terrible consequences that would accompany his new abilities.

After being forced to drink an unknown medical chemical when he tried to stop a robbery in progress, Sykes would gain superpowers as well as terminal cancer—as diagnosed by the Fantastic Four. Discovering an ability to fix things, and with only 30 days to live, Sykes fought crime as Flux and even became an Avenger shortly before his inevitable death.

DATA FILE

REAL NAME Dennis Sykes **OCCUPATION** Super Hero; former banker

BASE Queens, New York City, New York

HEIGHT 5 ft 9 in **WEIGHT** 145 lbs **EYES** Brown **HAIR** Brown

FIRST APPEARANCE WITH AVENGERS *Heroic Age: 1 Month 2 Live* #5 (November 2010)

POWERS Flux could manipulate matter, including repairing broken items and creating sculptures. He had the ability to harden the air to replicate flying.

MOSES MAGNUM

An illegal munitions supplier bent on gaining power, Moses Magnum engineered a device to give himself superpowers to further continue his criminal legacy.

Moses Magnum originally tangled with Punisher and Spider-Man during one of their rare team-ups. Then he battled the Avengers shortly after the heroes returned from a pocket dimension. Attacking Kennedy airport via a hologram, Moses was soon tracked down by the Avengers who were forced to face his new earthquake-based powers. Scarlet Witch was able to best these abilities, before Magnum retreated inside the Earth. He later returned to menace Wolverine's son, Daken, as well as Iron Man and Thor.

DATA FILE

REAL NAME Moses Magnum **OCCUPATION** Criminal; owner of Magnum Munitions

BASE Mobile

HEIGHT 5 ft 9 in **WEIGHT** 159 lbs **EYES** Brown **HAIR** Black

FIRST APPEARANCE WITH AVENGERS *Avengers* #8 (September 1998)

POWERS Moses uses his hands to create seismic waves—this can result in avalanches or earthquakes. His background in the creation of weapons means he often has deadly gadgets to hand.

JUSTICE

All his life, Vance Astrovik dreamt of becoming an Avenger. After originally failing to get the team's notice, he became a valued instructor at Avengers Initiative and the Avengers Academy to the next generation of heroes.

Vance Astrovik grew up idolizing Captain America. A mutant who would later hone his powers, Vance was visited by an adult version of himself from an alternate future—the hero who would become known as Major Victory of the 31st century Guardians of the Galaxy. Vance's future self warned him away from becoming an astronaut, and because of that, Vance never journeyed into the Guardians' future, instead remaining in the present where he became a founding member of the New Warriors as Marvel Boy. Years later, after changing his moniker to Justice, Vance joined the Avengers to fight alongside his longtime love interest, Firestar.

Recently, Justice joined the newest incarnation of the New Warriors.

As Justice, Vance entirely redesigned his look.

DATA FILE

REAL NAME
Vance Astrovik

OCCUPATION
Super Hero; teacher; former professional wrestling manager; former circus performer

BASE
Mobile

HEIGHT 5 ft 10 in

WEIGHT 180 lbs

EYES Hazel

HAIR Brown

FIRST APPEARANCE WITH AVENGERS
Avengers #170 (April 1978)

POWERS
Vance has a powerful mutant telekinesis that allows for levitation and manipulation of objects. He can fly at great speeds. He can create telekinetic defensive screens and force blasts.

TIGER SHARK

Originally a villain who faced Namor, Tiger Shark would later take on the Avengers as a member of the Masters of Evil and the Lethal Legion.

An Olympic swimmer who injured himself, Todd Arliss allowed a corrupt marine biologist to subject his body to a variety of experimental procedures, eventually transforming him into the criminal Tiger Shark. He joined a new incarnation of the Masters of Evil alongside other newcomers such as Scorpion, and became a recurring foe of Namor's. Working for the villain Egghead, the criminals soon proved no match for the Avengers. After staying with the Masters during Baron Zemo's tenure as leader as well as the Crimson Cowl's, Tiger Shark eventually joined a new incarnation of the Lethal Legion led by the Grim Reaper. He has fought the Avengers as well as the Thunderbolts.

Todd's transformation into Tiger Shark included extreme, shark-like alterations to his physiognomy.

DATA FILE

REAL NAME
Todd Arliss

OCCUPATION
Criminal; former athlete

BASE
Mobile

HEIGHT 6 ft 1 in

WEIGHT 450 lbs

EYES Gray

HAIR Brown

FIRST APPEARANCE WITH AVENGERS
Avengers #222 (August 1982)

POWERS
Arliss's genetic structure was combined with that of Sub-Mariner and a tiger shark. He now has gills to enable underwater breathing and razor-sharp teeth. He has superhuman strength, endurance, durability, and can swim up to 60 mph. On land, Tiger Shark wears a costume with a water circulation system which keeps his skin wet. His powers have left him with a quick temper and he has been known to lash out at other villains.

MENTALLO

A mutant former S.H.I.E.L.D. agent turned Super Villain, Mentallo's only true allegiance is to himself and his criminal ways.

A regular partner with fellow Avengers' villain Fixer, Mentallo almost succeeded in toppling his former employers, S.H.I.E.L.D. Later, when attempting to team with his old friend once again, Mentallo found himself a victim of the Super Adaptoid posing as the Fixer. The Avengers were able to defeat the Adaptoid, but it did little to convince Mentallo to change his criminal ways. In fact, he joined the Hood's underworld gang, and later still, attempted to control Reptil of the Avengers Academy. Recently, Mentallo worked as a member of A.I.M.'s high council, helping to further the ends of that terrorist organization.

DATA FILE

REAL NAME Marvin Flumm **OCCUPATION** Criminal; former S.H.I.E.L.D. agent

BASE Mobile

HEIGHT 5 ft 10 in **WEIGHT** 125 lbs **EYES** Brown **HAIR** Brown

FIRST APPEARANCE WITH AVENGERS *Avengers* #287 (January 1988)

POWERS Mentallo has mutant telepathy and abilities that include mind reading and thought projection skills. He has an ability for psionic energy probing. He can have mental control over others and can cast illusions. He often wears an ESP-proof helmet to protect himself from other telepaths.

VENOM

When Spider-Man acquired a living symbiote costume, he had no idea it would spawn a major adversary.

Thinking the black suit he had acquired in Battleworld was merely a costume, Spider-Man discarded the outfit after he discovered it was controlling him in his sleep. After attaching to the villain Eddie Brock, the symbiote allowed Brock to become the Spider-Man foe, Venom. When Brock finally got rid of it years later, the symbiote found its way to its newest host—former Spider-Man and Avengers villain Scorpion, aka Mac Gargan.

DATA FILE

REAL NAME MacDonald "Mac" Gargan **OCCUPATION** Criminal; former Super Hero imposter and government agent; former private detective

BASE New York City, New York

HEIGHT 6 ft 2 in **WEIGHT** 245 lbs **EYES** Brown (as Mac Gargan); red (as Venom) **HAIR** Brown (as Mac Gargan); none (as Venom)

FIRST APPEARANCE WITH AVENGERS *Avengers* #222 (August 1982)

POWERS As Venom, Gargan has the abilities of Spider-Man, including superhuman strength, endurance, speed, durability, wall-crawling, and agility. He can generate webbing from the symbiote suit. He can shape-change.

CONTROLLER

An ally of Thanos, the Controller is an Iron Man enemy who has used his mind-control technology to cause trouble for the Avengers.

Paralyzed after a scuffle in a lab with his brother, Basil Sandhurst became obsessed with control. Not only did Basil soon don an exoskeleton to give him more power than he had ever experienced, but he also developed discs that he could use to control the minds of others. Calling himself the Controller, Basil was originally stopped by Iron Man. However, his various incarcerations would lead him into conflicts with the entire Avengers team, such as the time he broke out of jail from the Raft Maximum-Maximum Security Prison.

Body armor is made from stainless steel.

DATA FILE

REAL NAME Basil Sandhurst **OCCUPATION** Criminal; former scientist

BASE Mobile

HEIGHT 6 ft 2 in **WEIGHT** 565 lbs **EYES** White **HAIR** Black

FIRST APPEARANCE WITH AVENGERS *Avengers: Death Trap, the Vault* (July 1991)

POWERS Sandhurst has a stainless steel exoskeleton biosurgically attached to his body. The armor enables him to absorb energy from others and convert it into strength, durability, and endurance. He possesses "slave discs" that can enslave and drain energy from others. Over time, his telepathic abilities have increased.

GRAVITON

A recurring Avengers foe with a hatred for all things Super Hero, Graviton was an influential Super Villain with ties to A.I.M.

When physicist Frank Hall attempted to create a teleportation beam, he accidentally merged his own molecules with a radioactive substance. Discovering he could control gravity, he embarked on a criminal career as Graviton. However, his grand plans were soon interrupted when one of his former peers betrayed him and alerted the Avengers. Graviton became a recurring foe and fought the West Coast Avengers as their first true adversary.

DATA FILE

REAL NAME Franklin Hall **OCCUPATION** Criminal; former physicist

BASE Mobile

HEIGHT 6 ft 1 in **WEIGHT** 200 lbs **EYES** Blue-gray **HAIR** Black with white temples

FIRST APPEARANCE WITH AVENGERS *Avengers* #158 (April 1977)

POWERS As Graviton, Hall can manipulate gravitational force, enabling him to generate force fields and shock waves, levitate objects, fly, and pin opponents to the ground by increasing gravity above them. He has enhanced stamina.

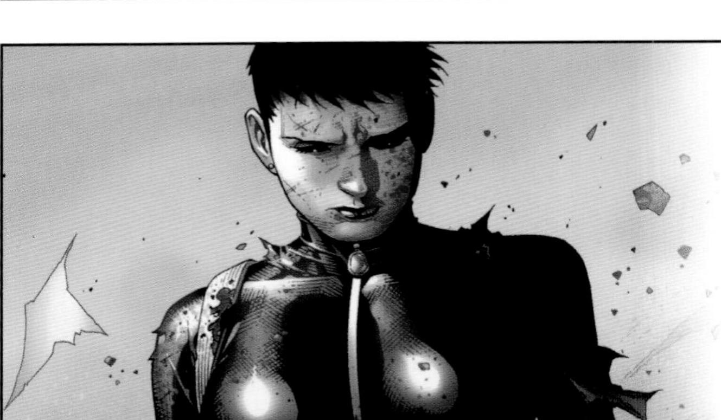

QUAKE

The illegitimate daughter of Super Villain Mr. Hyde, Daisy Johnson started her career as a S.H.I.E.L.D. agent loyal to Nick Fury. She later joined the Avengers.

When Nick Fury sought to create his own unsanctioned S.H.I.E.L.D. strike force and undergo a mission on the foreign soil of Latveria, it would cost him his job as the longtime director of S.H.I.E.L.D. when Latveria retaliated with a Super Villain attack. As one of most Fury's loyal agents, Daisy Johnson not only went on that mission as Quake, but she continued to aid Fury even when he was in hiding, helping him organize his Secret Warriors. When Captain America was promoted to Fury's old job, he recognized Quake's heroism and offered her a position on the Avengers, despite her young age.

DATA FILE

REAL NAME
Daisy Johnson

OCCUPATION
S.H.I.E.L.D. agent; former S.H.I.E.L.D. director

BASE
Mobile

HEIGHT 5 ft 9 in

WEIGHT 135 lbs

EYES Blue

HAIR Black

FIRST APPEARANCE WITH AVENGERS
New Avengers #18 (June 2006)

POWERS
Daisy posseses mutant seismic powers which allow her to generate earthquakes. She has immunity to the harmful effects of her vibrations. She is a skilled hand-to-hand combatant. As an an excellent markswoman, Daisy often goes on undercover missions.

POWER MAN

Following in the footsteps of the original Power Man—Luke Cage—Victor Alvarez has learned a thing or two about being an Avenger from Cage's former Super Hero partner, Iron Fist.

As the second Power Man, Victor Alvarez took the opportunity to learn from Iron Fist.

When the villain Bullseye blew up a city block, killing 107 people in the process, a young tenant named Victor Alvarez from one of the razed buildings used an innate ability to absorb chi energy in an act of self-defense. Gaining superhuman strength from the life force of those around him, Victor began to follow in the footsteps of Luke Cage. He donned the mantle of Power Man, not just to help those around him but to also make a living.

This new Power Man soon teamed up with Iron Fist and his Rand Foundation as not-for-profit Super Heroes. After learning from this street-experienced expert, Power Man later joined Luke Cage as his employee in a new incarnation of Cage's Heroes For Hire business. But when Thanos's forces attacked New York City and the majority of the Avengers were fighting a battle in outer space, Luke Cage saw a need for an Earth-based team, and began the Mighty Avengers. As well as Power Man, this new Super Hero team would include White Tiger, Blue Marvel, Spectrum, and Spider-Man among its ranks.

Power Man can redirect the chi energy of others around him in the form of devastation force.

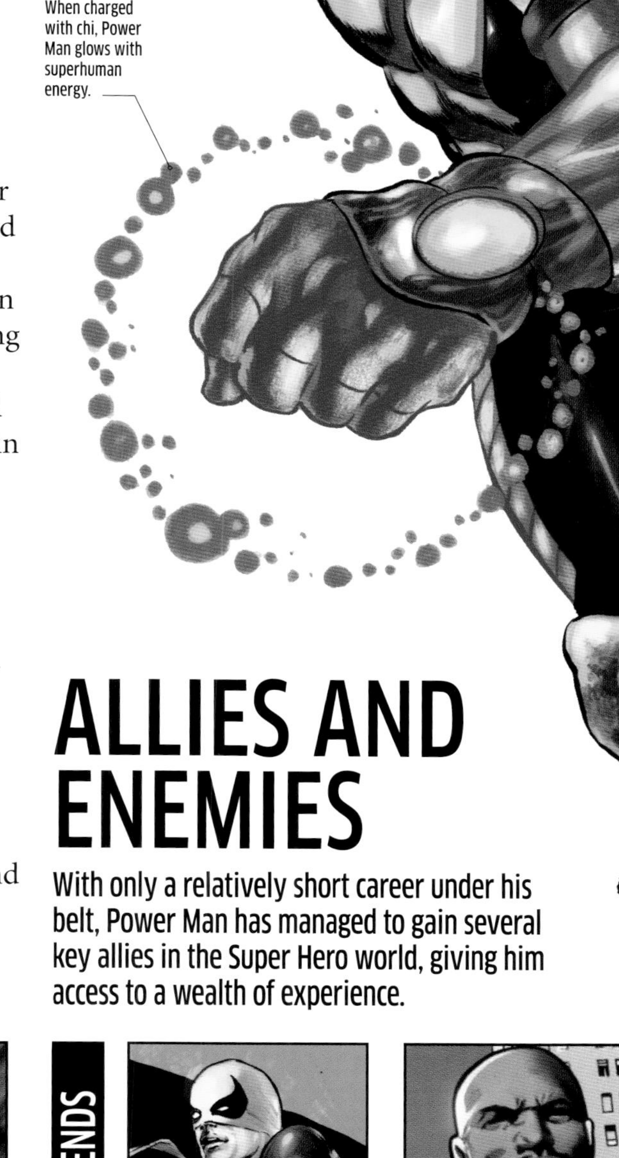

ALLIES AND ENEMIES

With only a relatively short career under his belt, Power Man has managed to gain several key allies in the Super Hero world, giving him access to a wealth of experience.

FRIENDS

IRON FIST
Iron Fist worked with Power Man at the Rand Foundation, taking tips from this hero.

LUKE CAGE
Power Man first joined Cage's Heroes For Hire, and later, his Mighty Avengers.

DATA FILE

REAL NAME Victor Alvarez **OCCUPATION** Super Hero; student
BASE The Gem Theater, New York City, New York
HEIGHT 5 ft 9 in **WEIGHT** 160 lbs **EYES** Brown **HAIR** Black
FIRST APPEARANCE WITH AVENGERS *Avengers Academy* #21 (January 2012)
POWERS Power Man can absorb chi (the life force) from his environment, resulting in superhuman strength, speed, agility, and endurance. He can generate force fields and produce chi enhanced punches. He has accelerated healing. He is a skilled martial artist and he can mimic the fighting skills of those who died in Bullseye's blast.

SANDMAN

One of the tried and true members of Spider-Man's rogues gallery, Sandman once served as an Avenger.

Petty crook William Baker was turned into a powerful Super Villain by a radioactive twist of fate. As Sandman, he fought Spider-Man many times over the years. But when given the chance to reform by Captain America himself, Sandman accepted, and became a reserve substitute member of the Avengers alongside, ironically enough, Spider-Man. However, Sandman later left the team and returned to his criminal ways.

DATA FILE

REAL NAME William Baker **OCCUPATION** Criminal; former Super Hero
BASE New York City, New York
HEIGHT 6 ft 1 in **WEIGHT** 450 lbs **EYES** Brown **HAIR** Brown
FIRST APPEARANCE WITH AVENGERS *Avengers Annual* #2 (September 1968)
POWERS Sandman is composed of sand. He has molecular control over his sand form, enabling him to turn any part of his body into soft or rock-hard sand. He has superhuman strength and can change shape. Sandman can control the density of sand particles. He can form glass and use it to reflect light off himself.

HARDBALL

Having just gained his powers from the Power Broker, Hardball was recruited into the Avengers Initiative by Wonder Man.

After the events of the Superhuman Civil War, those with superpowers were forced to either be renegades from the law, or to register with the government and become Super Heroes, training at Camp Hammond. Hardball was one of Hammond's earliest recruits. He soon faced real danger when dispatched with other Initiative members to face a Hydra Terror-Carrier. After being assigned to Nevada's Heavy Hitters, Hardball revealed that he was actually an agent working secretly for Hydra.

DATA FILE

REAL NAME Roger Brokeridge **OCCUPATION** Hydra agent; former Super Hero
BASE Mobile
HEIGHT 6 ft **WEIGHT** 200 lbs **EYES** Green **HAIR** Blond
FIRST APPEARANCE WITH AVENGERS *Avengers: The Initiative* #1 (June 2007)
POWERS Hardball can create solid balls of energy around his fists that can be used defensively or offensively. His energy spheres also create electrical interference and can be used to imprison adversaries. He has the power of flight via the use of a jetpack.

ELECTRO

A longtime Spider-Man enemy, Electro unwittingly had a hand in the formation of the New Avengers.

A former electric line worker given powers by a freak accident, Max Dillon adopted the guise of Electro and began a criminal career. As well as frequently battling Spider-Man, Max Dillon caused a massive breakout from the Maximum-Maximum Security Penitentiary, the Raft. And while he succeeded in securing freedom for a number of superpowered criminals, Electro unwittingly brought together a new group of Avengers.

DATA FILE

REAL NAME Maxwell Dillon **OCCUPATION** Criminal; former electric line repairman
BASE New York City, New York
HEIGHT 5 ft 11 in **WEIGHT** 165 lbs **EYES** Blue **HAIR** Bald
FIRST APPEARANCE WITH AVENGERS In flashback: *Avengers Annual* #2 (September 1968)
POWERS As Electro, Dillon can discharge, generate, and absorb electrical energy from his nearby environment. He can convert his form into pure electricity and project deadly lightning bolts at speeds of 1,100 feet per second. He has the ability to fly and has the power of magnetic manipulation.

KLAW

Originally facing the Black Panther and the Fantastic Four, Klaw resurfaced time and time again—a threat to heroes across the universe.

Ulysses Klaw became the villain simply called Klaw after leaping into a sonic converter device that turned his body into solid sound. By trade a corrupt scientist desperate to continue his experiments by stealing the valuable metal Vibranium from the people of the Black Panther's nation, Wakanda, Klaw went on to join Ultron's incarnation of the Masters of Evil—earning the ire of the entire Avengers team in the process. He also signed up to the Crimson Cowl's version of the Masters of Evil to combat the Thunderbolts, and still later, worked for the Intelligencia.

DATA FILE

REAL NAME Ulysses Klaw **OCCUPATION** Criminal; former scientist
BASE Mobile
HEIGHT 5 ft 11 in **WEIGHT** 175 lbs **EYES** Red **HAIR** None
FIRST APPEARANCE WITH AVENGERS *Avengers* #54 (July 1968)
POWERS Klaw is composed of pure energy. He cannot be hurt, and can reshape his body, even if vivisected into many pieces. Klaw has superhuman strength. From his blaster, he can project sound waves and deafening force blasts. He can turn sounds into objects.

TITANIA

This former Frightful Four member is a powerhouse to rival the might of even She-Hulk and faced the Avengers as one of the nefarious Masters of Evil.

Gaining her powers from Dr. Doom when many of the most iconic heroes and villains were transported to a planet known as Battleworld, Mary MacPherran became the Super Villain Titania and the longtime love interest of fellow criminal Absorbing Man. While she had met many of the team's members during those so-called Secret Wars on Battleworld, Titania first tangled with the Avengers when she joined Baron Helmut Zemo's Masters of Evil and helped orchestrate a raid on Avengers Mansion. The Avengers eventually triumphed over that incarnation of the Masters, although Titania didn't seem to learn her lesson and has continued her criminal career.

The towering Titania seems most at home when fighting with her arch nemesis, She-Hulk.

DATA FILE

REAL NAME
Mary "Skeeter" MacPherran

OCCUPATION
Criminal

BASE
Mobile

HEIGHT 6 ft 6 in

WEIGHT 545 lbs

EYES Blue

HAIR Reddish-blonde

FIRST APPEARANCE WITH AVENGERS
Avengers #270 (August 1986)

POWERS
As a result of Dr. Doom's intervention, Titania has superhuman strength, durability, and endurance. Her skin is close to being indestructible: she can pick up molten metal and not be affected by it. She has immunity to disease and has accelerated healing.

Whizzer's outfit was designed during World War II.

WHIZZER

A hero of a bygone era, the Whizzer briefly joined the Avengers, using his super-speed for the benefit of another generation.

Bob Frank was given a life-saving transfusion of mongoose blood following a bite from a cobra in Africa. This blood mingled with his mutant chemistry and Bob found himself with super-speed abilities. He called himself the Whizzer and went on to become a crime-fighting hero of the World War II era, joining the Liberty Legion, and then the All-Winners Squad. Decades later, the Whizzer ran into the Avengers' lives when he asked for their help to save his son, Nuklo. After a later clash with the Avengers, the Whizzer joined the team for a time. The aging speedster helped the Avengers against foes like Graviton and Count Nefaria, but died while under the mistaken impression that the Scarlet Witch and Quicksilver were his children, amid a fight with the villain Isbisa.

DATA FILE

REAL NAME
Robert L. Frank

OCCUPATION
Super Hero

BASE
Mobile

HEIGHT 5 ft 10 in

WEIGHT 180 lbs

EYES Brown

HAIR Brown (later gray)

FIRST APPEARANCE WITH AVENGERS
Giant-Size Avengers #1 (August 1974)

POWERS
The Whizzer had mutant superhuman speeds and could run at hundreds of miles an hour. By running in circles, he could create a whirlwind. He had superhuman reflexes.

MOONDRAGON

When Moondragon first met Iron Man, she called herself Madame MacEvil.

An Avenger unafraid to chart her own path and make dramatic decisions even if they are sometimes unpopular, Moondragon has not always been the most welcomed teammate. Nevertheless, she is unarguably a powerful one.

Many years ago, a young girl named Heather Douglas was driving through the Nevada desert with her family. Unfortunately, they unwittingly became witnesses to Thanos's first scouting mission on Earth. Careful to cover his tracks, Thanos destroyed the Douglas's car, thinking he had killed the entire family. However, the Super Villain was mistaken. Heather crawled from the wreckage, where she was discovered by Mentor, the ruler of Titan, Saturn's moon. She was brought to his home and placed within the Shao-Lom Monastery where she was taught martial arts by the monks and became a priestess and geneticist. She did not learn for some time that the spirit of her father had been used to create the Thanos-hating Drax the Destroyer.

With motivations often known only to her, Moondragon eventually allied herself with the Avengers, and Iron Man soon proposed her for membership. Wanting to remain on Earth, she accepted, staying with the team for many missions. While Moondragon later quit the team, she returned on many occasions, and in one bold instance, would even use her psionic mind control powers in an attempt to choose the Avengers' lineup herself.

In true Moondragon fashion, she quit the Avengers when she began to feel the team was too constraining for her tastes.

Moondragon's body is in peak physical condition.

ALLIES AND ENEMIES

Somewhat arrogant in nature, Moondragon isn't the best at making friends, but seems to make enemies rather easily. However, she has made allies of the Avengers as well as of the Guardians of the Galaxy, and has been reunited with, and fought alongside, her resurrected father, Drax.

FRIEND

MANTIS
Like Moondragon, the Avenger Mantis is a martial arts expert and telepath.

FOE

THANOS
Moondragon hated Thanos for killing her parents and attempting to kill her.

DATA FILE

REAL NAME Heather Douglas **OCCUPATION** Former priestess; adventurer; Super Hero

BASE Mobile

HEIGHT 6 ft 3 in **WEIGHT** 150 lbs **EYES** Blue **HAIR** None

FIRST APPEARANCE WITH AVENGERS *Captain Marvel* #31 (March 1974)

POWERS Moondragon has powers of telepathy, she can mentally stun others and control their minds. She can use her powers to fly, levitate, and create psionic energy blasts. She is a superb athlete and martial artist. She can control pain, breathing, bleeding, and heart rate.

DOORMAN

The cosmic hero Doorman is one of the founding members of the Great Lakes Avengers and became the herald to oblivion itself.

After answering Mr. Immortal's classified ad to start a Super Hero team in Milwaukee, Doorman agreed to serve on the Great Lakes Avengers, even though the team wasn't officially sanctioned by the actual Avengers. He continued to lend his mutant superpowers to the team when Hawkeye took the leadership reins.

In recent years, after his apparent death and resurrection, Doorman has taken on the weighty role of being an angel of death, and on one occasion was even forced to escort his own father to the afterlife.

DATA FILE

REAL NAME DeMarr Davis **OCCUPATION** Super Hero, servant of Oblivion
BASE Milwaukee, Wisconsin
HEIGHT 6 ft 3 in **WEIGHT** 175 lbs **EYES** Brown **HAIR** Black
FIRST APPEARANCE WITH AVENGERS *West Coast Avengers* #46 (July 1989)
POWERS Doorman can create a gateway in his body through which people can pass into the Darkforce Dimension. He can alter his body so things can pass through him and he is immune to injury. Doorman has enhanced cosmic knowledge.

PAGAN

Cult leader Jonathan Tremont's deceased brother was raised as Pagan to fight the Avengers multiple times.

Just as shards of light helped give 3-D Man and Triathlon their powers, they were also responsible for giving Jonathan Tremont the ability to resurrect powerful, villainous versions of his deceased brothers. One of these was Pagan, the other, Lord Templar. Tremont used Pagan to attack his own cult's headquarters—the Triune Understanding building—in order to have Triathlon save the day and be viewed as a hero by the Avengers. The Avengers uncovered the plan and while Tremont absorbed the life forces of Pagan and Lord Templar, he was eventually put to rest by Triathlon.

Pagan's strength increased the wilder he became.

DATA FILE

REAL NAME Unknown **OCCUPATION** Criminal
BASE Mobile
HEIGHT Unknown **WEIGHT** Unknown **EYES** Red **HAIR** Black
FIRST APPEARANCE WITH AVENGERS *Avengers* #13 (February 1999)
POWERS Pagan's superhuman strength increased with anger. He was able to withstand superhuman punches and magical hexes. He had high endurance and durability.

RICK JONES

After accidentally causing the creation of the Hulk and the Avengers, this reckless teenager eventually became a hero himself.

Rick Jones was a rebellious orphan whose decision to accept a dare and stray onto a gamma-bomb test site led to Bruce Banner rushing out to save him, thus turning Banner into the Hulk. Another fateful moment came when Rick's teen brigade of radio enthusiasts sent a warning about the Hulk, which led to the Avengers forming. He became Captain America's sidekick for a time, and also Captain Marvel's ally. After many dangerous exploits connected with the Hulk, Jones was targeted by the Intelligencia to become their gamma-powered pawn, and was turned into the being known as A-Bomb. Jones clung on to part of his own identity, and teamed up with the Avengers and the Fantastic Four to stop a earthquake planned by the Red Hulk. These new powers were eventually taken away from Rick, who is currently a mere human again.

Rick straying onto a bomb test site led to his rescuer, Banner, becoming the Hulk.

DATA FILE

REAL NAME
Richard Milhouse "Rick" Jones

OCCUPATION
Adventurer, musician, author of book on sidekicks.

BASE
Mobile. Formerly Los Angeles, California, New Mexico and also New York City.

HEIGHT 5 ft 9 in as Jones; 6 ft 8 in as A-Bomb

WEIGHT 165 lbs as Jones; 980 lbs as A-Bomb

EYES Brown as Jones; yellow as A-Bomb

HAIR Brown as Jones; hairless as A-Bomb

FIRST APPEARANCE WITH AVENGERS
Avengers #1 (September 1963)

POWERS
Jones is an expert at self-defense, having received training from Captain America. He has been able to access the Destiny Force, a reality-shaping power believed to be latent in all mankind. As A-Bomb, Jones had Hulk-level strength. In this Abomination-like form, his skin could shrug off bullets and other man-made weapons. He also had the ability to blend in with his environment.

Trauma's eyes sometimes glow bright prior to transformation.

TRAUMA

The son of Nightmare, Trauma was one of the earliest recruits to the Avengers Initiative's Camp Hammond in Stamford, Connecticut.

Trauma was one of the many law-abiding heroes forced to train at Camp Hammond after the Superhuman Civil War. Trauma—whose ability means he can shape-shift into the worst nightmares of others—had a rocky start to his training, when he witnessed the death of one of his fellow recruits, MVP, during a training session. Soon after, unable to control his powers, Trauma caused Cloud 9 to see a dead version of MVP. He finally gained control of his powers, thanks to private tutoring by Moonstar (Mirage).

DATA FILE

REAL NAME Terrance Ward **OCCUPATION** Super Hero; student counselor
BASE Camp Hammond
HEIGHT 5 ft 7 in **WEIGHT** 141 lbs **EYES** Brown **HAIR** Black
FIRST APPEARANCE WITH AVENGERS *Avengers: The Initiative* #1 (June 2007)
POWERS As Trauma, Ward can sense the fears of others and then shape-shift into a physical manifestation of that fear; for example, he became a giant spider in front of fellow student and arachnaphobe, Armory. As a result, his height, weight, and appearance will vary.

Powderkeg's muscle-mass is intimidating enough on its own.

POWDERKEG

A powerhouse whose skin can secrete an explosive compound, Powderkeg is a Super Villain just waiting to go off.

First fighting against Monica Rambeau (Spectrum) during her time as Captain Marvel, Powderkeg exploded onto the Super Villain scene, later joining Doctor Octopus's Masters of Evil when they fought against the Guardians of the Galaxy. Powderkeg recently squared off with the Avengers Academy students at Thunderbolts Tower, but spends most of his criminal down-time at the Bar With No Name.

DATA FILE

REAL NAME Frank Skorina **OCCUPATION** Criminal
BASE Mobile
HEIGHT 8 ft 1 in **WEIGHT** 568 lbs **EYES** Brown **HAIR** Red
FIRST APPEARANCE WITH AVENGERS *Avengers: Deathtrap: The Vault* (July 1991)
POWERS Powderkeg is able to secrete an explosive chemical through the pores of his skin—which causes explosions on impact. He can cause small explosions when he claps his hands together. In addition, he has superhuman strength, endurance, and durability. He is highly resistant to injury.

DEMOLITION MAN

Called D-Man by many, Demolition Man has stumbled around the Super Hero scene for many years.

Dennis Dunphy was a professional wrestler who befriended the Thing and was given increased strength by an illegal procedure delivered by the Power Broker. Wearing a costume inspired by Daredevil's first outfit, Dennis joined forces with Captain America to take down the Power Broker. After teaming up with Cap many more times, and a stint with the Avengers, D-Man, as he became known, suffered from delusions and was homeless for a while—even living in the sewers at one point. Later, D-Man was convinced by Wonder Man to join his Revengers and attack the Avengers, resulting in his apparent defeat.

DATA FILE

REAL NAME Dennis Dunphy **OCCUPATION** Criminal; former Super Hero, ice fisherman and pro wrestler
BASE Mobile
HEIGHT 6 ft 3 in **WEIGHT** 315 lbs **EYES** Blue **HAIR** Red
FIRST APPEARANCE WITH AVENGERS *Captain America* #349 (January 1989)
POWERS Following the illegal procedure to gain powers from the Power Broker, Dunphy has acquired superhuman strength, stamina, and durability. He is an expert wrestler and he was personally trained in combat by Captain America.

SPEEDBALL

A former intern at Hammond Research Laboratory, Robbie Baldwin got caught up in an accident—resulting in his transformation into Speedball.

The accident at Hammond Research Lab enveloped both Robbie and his cat in energy bubbles from a kinetic energy realm. Speedball soon became a founding member of the New Warriors, and stayed with the team even after a new incarnation became reality TV stars. However, when the Warriors failed to stop the villain Nitro from decimating part of Stamford, Connecticut, Robbie took on the role of the self-punishing hero Penance, blaming himself for the 612 deaths that had occured. After some time, he finally came to terms with his past and re-emerged as Speedball.

Projected bubbles form a protective shield around Speedball.

DATA FILE

REAL NAME Robert "Robbie" Baldwin **OCCUPATION** Former intern and reality TV star; teacher; Super Hero
BASE Mobile
HEIGHT 5 ft 10 in **WEIGHT** 170 lbs **EYES** Blue **HAIR** Blond
FIRST APPEARANCE WITH AVENGERS *Avengers* #332 (May 1991)
POWERS Baldwin can generate a field that absorbs and redirects kinetic energy. His kinetic powers allow for bouncing that gradually increases speed. He can produce kinetic-powered punches and create a repelling force field. Speedball can slow the motion of people and objects.

JACK OF HEARTS

Tragically, Jack of Hearts, former Avenger and partner of Iron Man, never had a chance at a normal life, and died when his own powers became too much to handle.

The child of a human father and an alien mother, Jack Hart's life was made even stranger when he was doused in his father's experimental formula "Zero Fluid" and given powers. Seeking to avenge his father's death at the hands of criminals, Jack adopted the identity of Jack of Hearts. His adventures led him to cross paths with Iron Man, and he was soon taken under the wing of the Golden Avenger as his partner for a brief period. Jack would later prove himself to the Avengers and join their ranks, but his membership would not last long. His power levels began to increase more than his makeshift containment suit could hold, and he chose to commit suicide in space.

After Jack's death, his corpse was manipulated by the Scarlet Witch's magic into attacking Avengers Mansion.

Jack wore special armor designed to contain his destructive energy.

DATA FILE

REAL NAME
Jack Hart

OCCUPATION
Super Hero

BASE
Mobile

HEIGHT 5 ft 11 in

WEIGHT 175 lbs

EYES Blue (right); white (left)

HAIR Brown

FIRST APPEARANCE WITH AVENGERS
Avengers Forever #12 (February 2000)

POWERS
Jack projected concussive "Zero" energy in massive, barely controllable, quantities that allowed for force blasts and flight. He had a computer-fast mind. His superpowers included superhuman strength, endurance, durability, and accelerated healing.

CAPTAIN UNIVERSE

Avengers member Tamara Devoux is the current holder of the Uni-Power—and the mighty powers that it wields—and is therefore Captain Universe.

Originating from the Microverse, a tiny, microscopic universe invisible to the naked eye, the Uni-Power finds and empowers a host at times of great crisis. Over the years, many heroes and villains alike have been granted the powers and costume of Captain Universe, including Avengers Dr. Strange, Hulk, Spider-Man, Daredevil, and the Invisible Woman. Recently, Tamara Devoux has taken over the role, granted the Uni-Power while in a comatose state as a result of a car crash ten years ago. She has since wielded Captain Universe's incredible Enigma Force powers as an Avenger.

DATA FILE

REAL NAME
Tamara Devoux

OCCUPATION
Super Hero

BASE
Mobile

HEIGHT 5 ft 6 in

WEIGHT 140 lbs

EYES Brown

HAIR Black

FIRST APPEARANCE WITH AVENGERS
Avengers #1 (February 2013)

POWERS
Captain Universe has superhuman strength, endurance, and durability. She has the power of flight and can manipulate the molecular structure of objects. She can heal herself and others. She can project force blasts. Captain Universe has a range of vision, including x-ray, microscopic, and long distance. In addition, she has the power of Uni-Vision: she can hypnotize others into telling the truth.

MOONSTONE

The manipulative Dr. Karla Sofen is Moonstone, and has also masqueraded as the heroes Meteorite and Ms. Marvel, and is seemingly trying to change her ways.

As a psychiatrist burdened with her own power and control issues, Dr. Karla Sofen manipulated her way into possession of the powerful Kree moonstone belonging to the the criminal Lloyd Bloch—who was the original Moonstone. Becoming the new Moonstone, she soon clashed with the Hulk, and then later with the Avengers as a member of Egghead's incarnation of the Masters of Evil. Finding the Masters a good fit for her, Moonstone stayed with the team under Baron Helmut Zemo's leadership, even during a period where the villains masqueraded as Super Heroes known as the Thunderbolts. She later took this love of posing as a hero to a new level, becoming Ms. Marvel in Norman Osborn's Dark Avengers. She was also part of Luke Cage's Thunderbolts.

DATA FILE

REAL NAME
Dr. Karla Sofen

OCCUPATION
Psychiatrist, former criminal; Super Hero

BASE
Mobile

HEIGHT 5 ft 11 in

WEIGHT 130 lbs

EYES Blue

HAIR Blonde

FIRST APPEARANCE WITH AVENGERS
Avengers #222 (August 1982)

POWERS
As a direct result of possessing the Kree-designed moonstone, Karla has gained superpowers including flight, superhuman strength, and endurance. She can emit lasers from her hands and project light. She can become intangible and alter her costume at will. As a trained psychiatrist, Karla can use her powers combined with her knowledge to manipulate people to her own ends.

Sentry's mental instability made him easy to manipulate.

SENTRY

Robert Reynolds lived a conflicted life, striving to be the hero Sentry, but haunted by his other personality—the destructive creature known as the Void.

Robert Reynolds lived an impressive existence as one of the most powerful Super Heroes ever to accept that title. However, when the Avengers discovered him locked up in the Raft, the Maximum-Maximum Security Penitentiary, they had no idea who he was. With the help of the X-Men member the White Queen, the Avengers found that Sentry's existence had been erased from the world's collective minds by X-Men member, Mastermind. Sentry soon joined the Avengers, but was also manipulated into joining the roster of Norman Osborn's corrupt Dark Avengers.

Sentry was haunted by the Void. During the later Siege on Asgard, the Void was truly unleashed, forcing Thor to kill Robert Reynolds.

DATA FILE

REAL NAME
Robert Reynolds

OCCUPATION
Super Hero

BASE
Avengers Tower

HEIGHT 6 ft

WEIGHT 194 lbs

EYES Blue

HAIR Blond

FIRST APPEARANCE WITH AVENGERS
New Avengers #1 (January 2005)

POWERS
Sentry possessed nearly limitless powers, including superhuman strength, endurance, durability, speed, and intelligence. He could generate energy fields and had the power of flight. His self-doubt manifested as the villainous character, Void.

TRIATHLON

As Jonathan Tremont's unwitting pawn, Delroy Garrett, Jr. became an Avengers member and then a trainer at the Avengers Initiative.

Jonathan Tremont rose to power after murdering Hal Chandler, the host of the original 3-D Man. Possessing a shard of light of great power, Tremont began to prepare for the coming of a great darkness, using Delroy Garrett, Jr.—whom he gave the costume of Triathlon—as his champion. Delroy eventually overcame Tremont's influence, became a member of the Avengers, and later, took on the role of the new 3-D Man.

DATA FILE

REAL NAME Delroy Garrett, Jr. **OCCUPATION** Super Hero
BASE Mobile
HEIGHT 6 ft 2 in **WEIGHT** 200 lbs **EYES** Brown **HAIR** Black
FIRST APPEARANCE WITH AVENGERS *Avengers* #8 (September 1998)
POWERS Triathlon has physical abilities that are enhanced to three times that of a normal man. These include: superhuman speed, strength, agility, reflexes, and senses. He can detect a Skrull in whatever form it takes and he can heal three times more quickly than an average human.

STAR BRAND

A cosmic event changed this unknown student into Star Brand: a multiversal hero.

Given extraordinary powers when a catastrophe known as the White Event affected the area where dreams and telepathy take place, Kevin first met the Avengers when they came to investigate the event that devastated his college. When Ex Nihilo sought to give the Earth its own consciousness, Star Brand and his ally Nightmask destroyed Ex Nihilo's work, putting the planet at risk and causing a clash with the Avengers. He was later invited to join the Super Heroes and fight alongside them.

DATA FILE

REAL NAME Kevin Kale Connor **OCCUPATION** Adventurer; former student
BASE Savage Land; formerly Avengers Tower, New York
HEIGHT 5 ft 10 in **WEIGHT** 140 lbs **EYES** Blue **HAIR** Blond
FIRST APPEARANCE WITH AVENGERS *Avengers* #7 (May 2013)
POWERS With powers drawn from the Superflow of the Earth, Star Brand is effectively the world's planetary defence system. As such he can call on incredible resources of energy. He is capable of fighting off several Avengers at once, including heavy-hitters like Thor and the Hulk. His energy projection blasts have wiped out fleets of starships. He can fly and withstand any dangerous force. No upper limit to this power has been recorded.

SQUIRREL GIRL

Known for her offbeat personality, Squirrel Girl started out as a member of the Great Lakes Avengers and went on to become nanny to young Danielle Cage.

Doreen Green has mutant powers, a prehensile tail, and an ability to communicate with squirrels. She idolized Iron Man and was inspired by his work to embark on her own crime-fighting career, calling herself Squirrel Girl. Hoping to impress him, she attacked Iron Man to show him how "rough and tough" she could be. Squirrel Girl then helped defeat Dr. Doom when he attacked her armored role model. But despite her bravery in battle, Iron Man refused Doreen's offer of partnership, causing her to join the Great Lakes Avengers, which later evolved into the Great Lakes Initiative. After the Fifty-State Initiative program ended, Doreen found a job with the New Avengers as the nanny to Danielle Cage—the daughter of Jessica Jones and Luke Cage. She has since enrolled in college, majoring in computer science, but finds time to continue her heroic work.

DATA FILE

REAL NAME
Doreen Green

OCCUPATION
Nanny; Super Hero; student

BASE
New York City, New York

HEIGHT 5 ft 3 in

WEIGHT 100 lbs

EYES Brown

HAIR Brown

FIRST APPEARANCE WITH AVENGERS
Great Lakes Avengers: Misassembled #1 (June 2005)

POWERS
Doreen is a mutant with superhuman speed, strength, endurance, agility, and reflexes. She can communicate with squirrels. She has claws, enlarged incisor teeth, a retractable knuckle spike, and a prehensile tail.

KEY STORYLINE THE COMING OF THE AVENGERS

AVENGERS #1

SEPTEMBER 1963
WRITER: Stan Lee
PENCILER: Jack Kirby **INKER:** Dick Ayers **COLORIST:** Stan Goldberg
LETTERER: S. Rosen (Sam Rosen) **EDITOR:** Stan Lee

In the comic that started it all, five unlikely Super Heroes were unwittingly brought together and went on to form the most powerful team the Marvel Universe had ever known.

The legend of the Avengers began as an attempt to bottle lightning a second time for Marvel Comics. Marvel already had the hit that was the Fantastic Four. Created by writer Stan Lee and artist Jack Kirby, *Fantastic Four* had been launched in November 1961. Instead of creating new characters like they did with the Fantastic Four, Lee and Kirby paired together some of their heaviest hitters, namely Thor, Hulk, Iron Man, the Wasp, Ant-Man, and later, Captain America, dubbing them "Earth's Mightiest Super-Heroes." Together, the newly founded Avengers would fight "the foes no single Super Hero can withstand" which gave rise to their trademark cry of "Avengers Assemble!" And so the Avengers comics shot to the top of the sales charts, beginning a legacy that is perhaps more popular today than ever before.

1 After Thor banishes his corrupt brother Loki to a barren island, the villainous trickster swears revenge upon his noble brother. Magically projecting a version of himself to Earth, Loki seeks out a weapon to use against Thor, and finds exactly what he is looking for when he sees the Hulk.

2 Casting an illusion of TNT on some nearby train tracks, Loki causes the Hulk to unwittingly almost wreck an oncoming locomotive. While Hulk saves the passengers, the damage is done. The public believe Hulk has tried to derail the train.

3 A newspaper headline touts Hulk's destruction, and catches the eye of Teen Brigade member and friend of the Hulk, Rick Jones. He in turn broadcasts an S.O.S. to the Fantastic Four, but the message is diverted to a different wavelength thanks to Loki's powers, causing Dr. Donald Blake, Thor's alter ego, to hear the plea.

4 While Loki doesn't realize it, others besides Blake hear Rick Jones' ominous broadcast. They include Hank Pym, aka Ant-Man, and his love interest Janet van Dyne, aka the Wasp. Like Thor, they rush to the Teen Brigade's hideout to help deal with the Hulk, unaware that Loki is really to blame.

5 As fate would have it, Tony Stark, the legendary Iron Man, is also listening to that particular wavelength. Anxious to pit his own strength against that of the Hulk, he quickly suits up and joins the other heroes at the Brigade's headquarters.

6 Together, Iron Man, Ant-Man, and the Wasp soon confront Hulk at a nearby circus. The distressed Hulk has gone into hiding and joined the traveling circus as "Mechano," a supposedly lifelike robot.

7 As the heroes battle the Hulk, forcing him to drop his "Mechano" routine, Thor travels to his home of Asgard, wisely suspecting Loki is behind their battle with the Hulk. Journeying to the Isle of Silence, Thor battles and bests his nefarious brother for a time.

"WE'LL NEVER BE BEATEN! FOR WE ARE... THE AVENGERS!"

– THOR

8 As Hulk's battle with Iron Man and the others rages on, Thor arrives just in time to quash the fighting. He reveals Loki's meddling to the others, and despite a last-ditch effort to destroy the heroes through radiation, Loki is once again defeated, thanks to the quick thinking of Ant-Man and the Wasp.

9 With the battle over, the heroes prepare to go their separate ways. Seeing the potential to combine their abilities for the greater good, Hank Pym suggests that the heroes team up on a regular basis. And with the Wasp's suggestion of the name Avengers, history is made.

KEY STORYLINE

CAPTAIN AMERICA JOINS THE AVENGERS

AVENGERS #4

MARCH 1964
WRITER: Stan Lee
PENCILER: Jack Kirby **INKER:** George Roussos **COLORIST:** Stan Goldberg **LETTERER:** Artie Simek **EDITOR:** Stan Lee

Captain America was transported from the battlefield of World War II to the present day as he regained his status as an iconic Super Hero in Marvel's impressive pantheon.

Captain America was arguably Marvel's first iconic character. While he enjoyed a top-selling comic around the time of World War II, Cap's popularity had waned a bit in the modern world of the 1960s. But with Marvel Comics enjoying a new surge in sales thanks to the work of writer Stan Lee and artists like Jack Kirby and Steve Ditko, it seemed perfect timing to bring Captain America back to his original glory. The only challenge was how to bring a hero of the 1940s back to the present and have him appear to be as relevant as when he had originally debuted. With this issue of *The Avengers*, Lee and Kirby did just that, and Captain America—still at the peak of physical perfection and armed with his near-indestructible shield—took his rightful place at the head of Marvel's mightiest team of Super Heroes.

1 Following the departure of the Hulk, who felt his fellow heroes didn't trust him, the Avengers find themselves a bit light in their roster. They barely have time to think about it, however, as they are also in hot pursuit of Namor, the Sub-Mariner, who is fleeing the Avengers after a previous attack on the fledgling team.

2 Namor escapes and as he travels the ocean, chances upon an Inuit tribe worshipping a man frozen within a block of ice. In a fit of anger, Namor tosses the frozen figure into the ocean where warm water begins to melt his thick encasement.

3 As luck would have it, the body of the now nearly thawed man floats by the Avengers while they are pursuing Namor in a nearby submarine. Iron Man spots the limp figure, and Giant-Man brings him inside the sub. The group is astonished to discover that the man is none other than the wartime hero Captain America.

4 After Captain America regains consciousness and proves his identity to the Avengers, the hero tells of how he became frozen in the ice in the first place. He and his sidekick Bucky Barnes had attempted to stop an explosive-filled drone plane. The plane exploded, Bucky was seemingly killed, and Cap was thrown into the ocean.

5 With Cap's story told, the Avengers arrive back home in New York City, and are greeted by the press. But before Captain America can reveal his return to the world, a sudden flash turns the four Avengers into stone, shocking those nearby.

"WE HAVE AN OFFER TO PROPOSE TO CAPTAIN AMERICA!"
– IRON MAN

6 Mistaking the stone Avengers for statues, Captain America explores present-day New York City, and runs into Rick Jones, whom he considers the spitting image of his old sidekick, Bucky. At Rick's insistence, Cap sets out to find the Avengers and soon tracks down their attacker—an alien from a distant galaxy.

8 After being restored to their usual human form, the Avengers work to free the alien's ship. But there is no rest for the weary, as Namor reappears and attacks the heroes once again. However, he retreats when he mistakes the alien's departing ship for an undersea earthquake.

7 The alien confesses to the attack on the Avengers at the instruction of the Sub-Mariner. Namor had agreed to free the alien's sunken ship from the ocean's depths in exchange for turning the heroes to stone. However, at Cap's request, the alien uses his ray gun to free the heroes from their petrified state.

9 With the alien returning to the stars and Namor returning to the depths, the Avengers officially invite Captain America to join their ranks. Cap accepts, and the classic roster of the Avengers is truly solidified.

KEY STORYLINE

THE OLD ORDER CHANGETH!

AVENGERS #16

MAY 1965
WRITER: Stan Lee
PENCILER: Jack Kirby **INKER:** Dick Ayers **COLORIST:** Stan Goldberg
LETTERER: Artie Simek **EDITOR:** Stan Lee

The Avengers had their first true roster shake-up when the original members departed the team, leaving Captain America to lead a team of virtually unknown upstarts and ex-villains.

The Avengers had been around for less than two years, but writer Stan Lee and artists Jack Kirby and Dick Ayers had decided it was already time for a dramatic change. Not wanting the Super Hero team to grow stale, Lee opted to retire Iron Man, Wasp, and Giant-Man from the Avengers, effectively leaving no founders in the team's ranks when Thor took leave of absence, too. With only Captain America left as a familiar face, the team would be fleshed out with three former villains: original X-Men adversaries Quicksilver and the Scarlet Witch, and Iron Man's old foe, Hawkeye. In true Stan Lee fashion, these changes were announced in spectacular style, with a dramatic cover calling the roster into question, and a splash page that touted the issue as, "Possibly the most memorable illustrated story you will read this year!"

1 The Avengers are in the midst of a battle with the terrifying Masters of Evil. The founding heroes face the Melter, Black Knight, Enchantress, and Executioner on the streets of New York City.

2 Using his hammer, Thor transports the Avengers—as well as the Melter and the Black Knight—to another dimension, where the heroes quickly deal with the two foes before returning to Earth. However, back in New York City, the Enchantress and Executioner flee the scene, with the hopes of fighting another day.

3 Meanwhile, Captain America is dealing with some loose ends, burying the body of his now-dead enemy, Baron Zemo. Ready to leave the Amazon jungle and head back to New York with his young partner Rick Jones in tow, Cap must wait as his transportation has been destroyed by a few of Zemo's mercenaries.

4 When the Avengers return home to Avengers Mansion, they discover former villain Hawkeye waiting for them. He expresses his wish to join the team, and swears to turn his life around after discovering that his longtime love, the Black Widow, has been badly injured.

5 Hawkeye joins the Avengers. With Thor taking time out in Asgard and Iron Man, Giant-Man, and the Wasp wanting to take a leave of absence, the Avengers begin to look for new recruits. However, their attempt to enlist old foe Namor, the Sub-Mariner, fails.

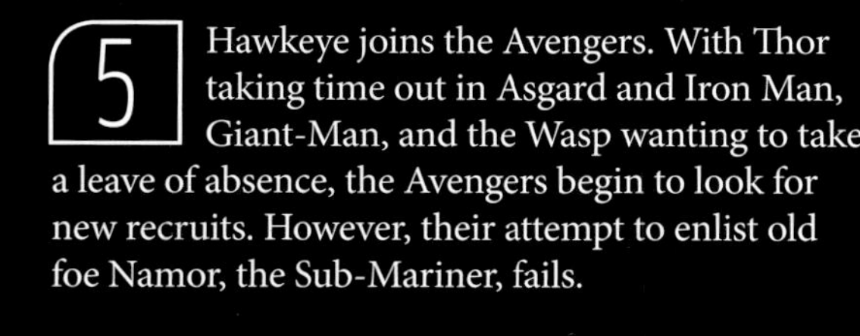

6 After members of the press get wind of the Avengers' active recruitment, mutants and former X-Men enemies Quicksilver and Scarlet Witch decide to try their hand at being heroes. They write to the Avengers and soon visit Tony Stark, who decides they would be perfect candidates for membership.

"THE MANTLE HAS BEEN PASSED TO A NEW AND YOUNGER GROUP—MAY YOU ALL WEAR IT WITH PRIDE, AND HONOR!"

– IRON MAN

7 By the time Captain America and Rick Jones fight their way back to New York City from the heart of the Amazon jungle, things have changed dramatically back at Avengers HQ. Cap is more than a little surprised to find that Iron Man, Giant-Man, and the Wasp are leaving the team.

8 With a heavy heart, Iron Man announces the new line-up of the Avengers to the gathering press. Then he, Giant-Man, and the Wasp all depart Avengers Mansion, ready for their next chapter in life to begin.

9 As the new team's spokesman, due to his seniority, Captain America leads out the new line-up of Avengers in front of an adoring public. Despite the accolades, these new Avengers can't help but wonder if they have enough strength to continue the heroic legacy set forth by the founders.

KEY STORYLINE BEHOLD... THE VISION!

AVENGERS #57

OCTOBER 1968
WRITER: Roy Thomas
PENCILERS: John Buscema, Marie Severin **INKER:** George Klein
LETTERER: Sam Rosen **EDITOR:** Stan Lee

An important chapter in the life of one of the Avengers greatest foes, Ultron, a mainstay of the heroic team was introduced in dramatic style. This storyline saw the debut of the iconic Vision.

Under the editorial eye of Stan Lee, writer Roy Thomas had become the scribe of *The Avengers* as of issue #35 (December 1966). He was soon joined by artist John Buscema, who took over from penciler Don Heck with issue #41 (June 1967). In this issue, Buscema truly showed his artistic range as he helped set the tone for one of the most memorable capers of the villain Ultron—a powerful robot originally created by Hank Pym capable of upgrading itself—complete with a moody atmosphere not often glimpsed inside the bright pages of the Avengers' title. When the smoke cleared, readers were left with more questions than answers, as well as a new hero who would prove to be one of the most integral and longest lasting members to grace the team's roster—the android known as the Vision.

1 Hank Pym leaves his longtime love Janet Van Dyne for the night to head back to his laboratory and examine some germ cultures. Unbeknownst to the heroes a mysterious yellow-and-green clad figure makes his way through the dark, rainy New York City sky.

2 With Hank out of the picture, the caped individual enters Janet's apartment and attacks her, threatening her in a voice she describes as "like something from beyond the grave." Quickly changing into the Wasp, Jan flees the figure through a nearby keyhole.

3 However, the intruder has no problem following the heroine. His body simply phases through the wall, causing the Wasp to scream in terror. But before she can regain her composure, the mystery man attacks Janet with his thermo-scopic eyes, dosing the Wasp in a near-unbearable heat.

4 Suddenly, Janet's attacker surges backwards, grabbing his skull in terrible pain. He collapses to the floor, as seconds later, Hank Pym returns to the Wasp's apartment, answering her distress call. They quickly take the mystery man back to Avengers Mansion.

5 The Black Panther and Hawkeye help Wasp and Goliath examine the fallen attacker. They realize it is a human robot called a synthozoid. The mechanical man awakes and lashes out at the group, revealing that its name is the Vision. But after being restrained by Goliath, Vision immediately regrets his actions.

6 Conflicted and seemingly disobeying his commands to destroy the Avengers, the Vision remembers his supposed creator, Ultron-5. With all of his impulses to hurt the Avengers dissipating, the Vision agrees to lead the heroes to Ultron's lair.

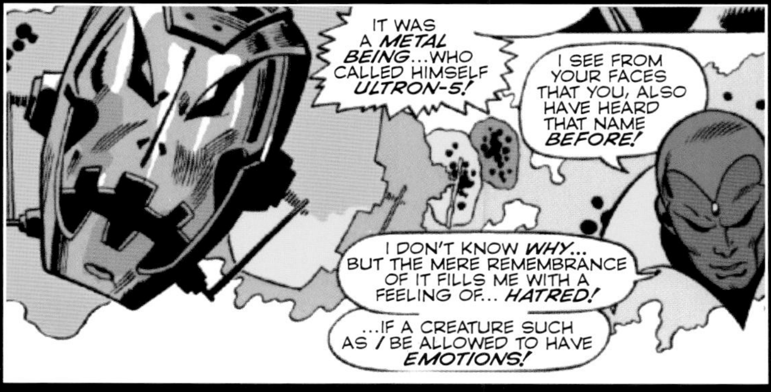

7 Despite his best intentions, the Vision has no idea that Ultron has planned this entire scenario, even the disabling attack on the Vision at Jan's apartment. Although the V4ision leads the Avengers back to his master, he unwittingly also sends them into a trap.

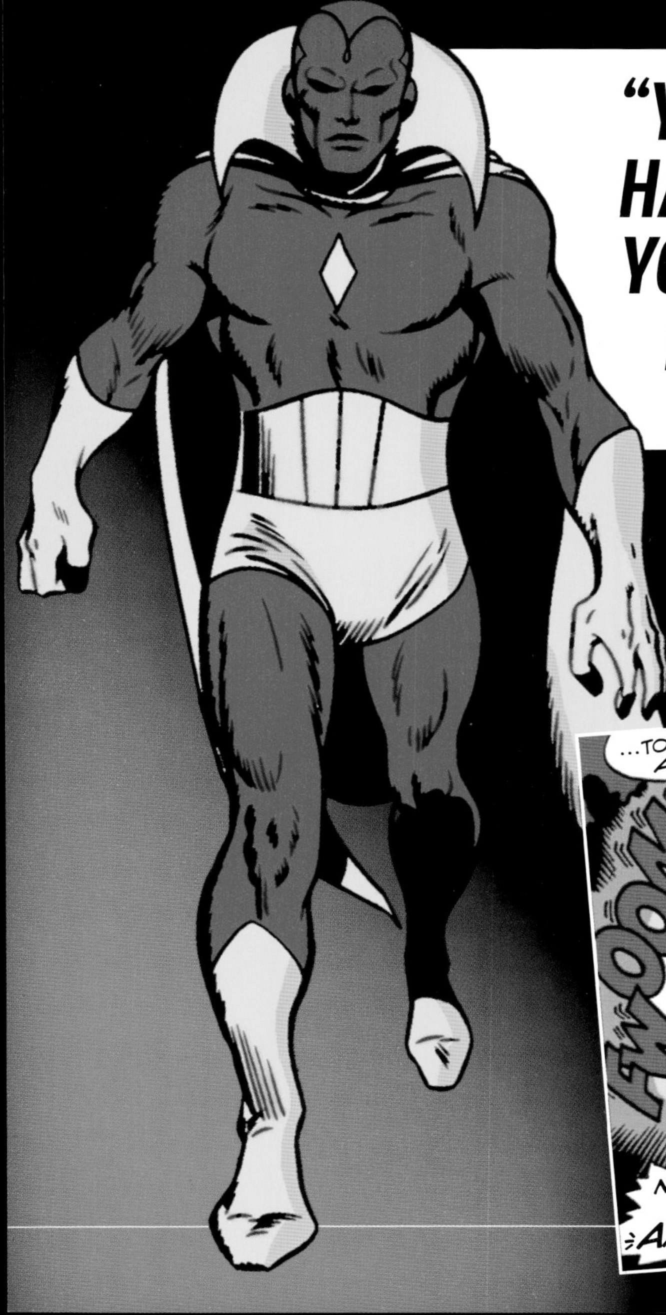

"YOU RIDICULED ME FOR HAVING EMOTIONS – YET YOU POSSESS THEM NO LESS THAN I!"

– VISION

8 After a wall of flame attacks the heroes and Goliath falls through a trap door and is defeated by a giant robotic creature, the Avengers find themselves in a room with slowly closing walls. Believing the Vision has tricked them, the Avengers are further angered as the synthozoid phases out of the chamber, escaping the trap.

9 However, the Vision is not about to betray his new friends. Instead he confronts his "maker," and exploits the weakness of the twin electrodes attached to Ultron's skull. After a violent conflict, ending in an explosion, the Vision is thanked by the Avengers, and Ultron is reduced to a metal head in a junkyard.

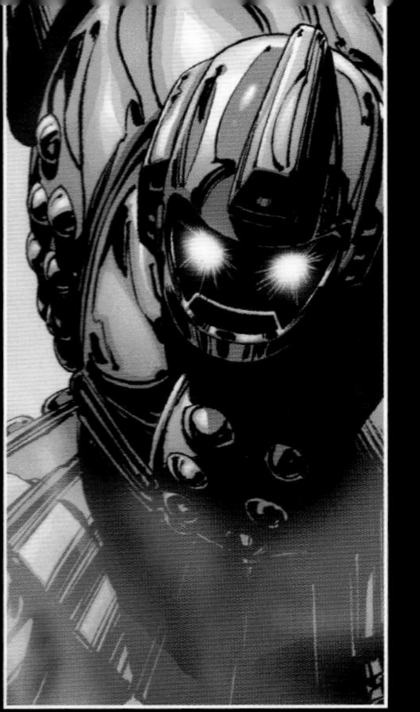

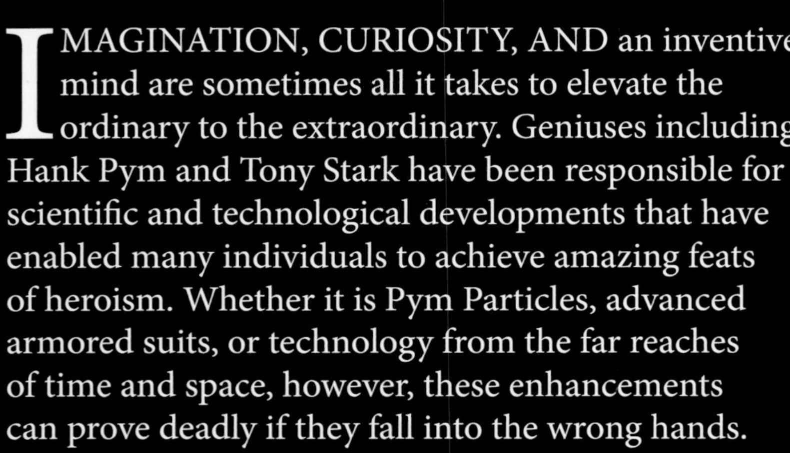

IMAGINATION, CURIOSITY, AND an inventive mind are sometimes all it takes to elevate the ordinary to the extraordinary. Geniuses including Hank Pym and Tony Stark have been responsible for scientific and technological developments that have enabled many individuals to achieve amazing feats of heroism. Whether it is Pym Particles, advanced armored suits, or technology from the far reaches of time and space, however, these enhancements can prove deadly if they fall into the wrong hands.

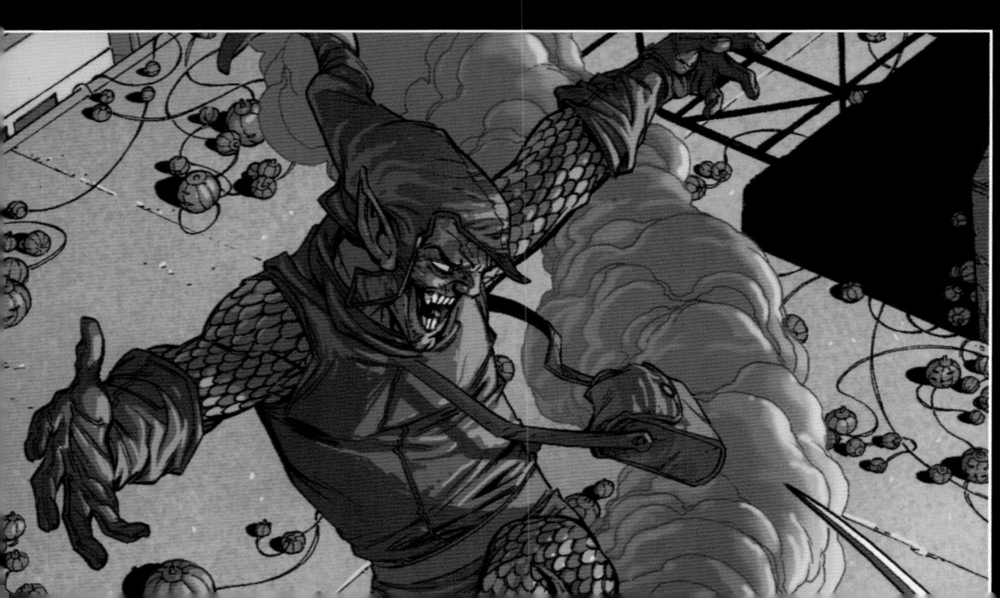

UPGRADED

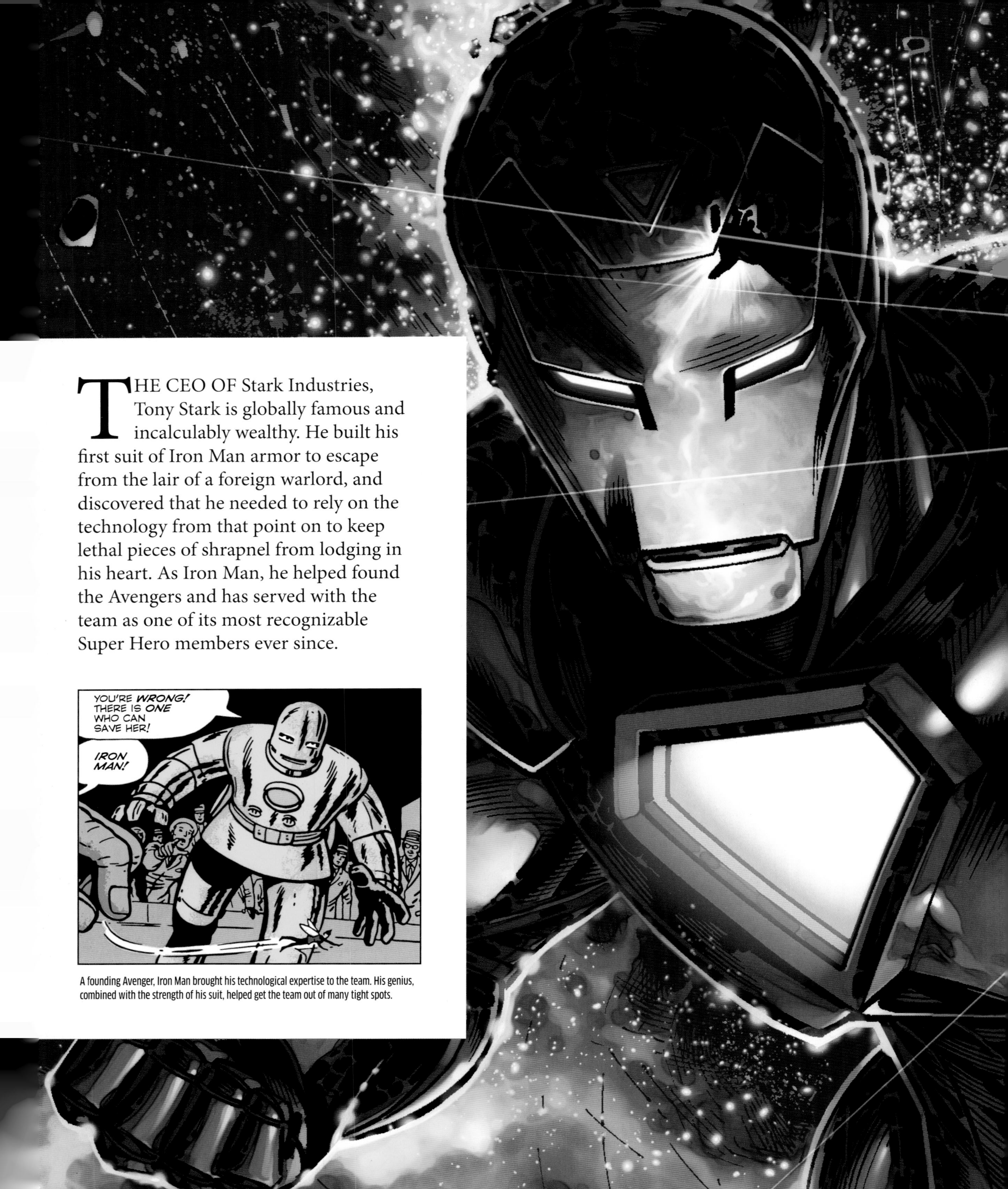

THE CEO OF Stark Industries, Tony Stark is globally famous and incalculably wealthy. He built his first suit of Iron Man armor to escape from the lair of a foreign warlord, and discovered that he needed to rely on the technology from that point on to keep lethal pieces of shrapnel from lodging in his heart. As Iron Man, he helped found the Avengers and has served with the team as one of its most recognizable Super Hero members ever since.

A founding Avenger, Iron Man brought his technological expertise to the team. His genius, combined with the strength of his suit, helped get the team out of many tight spots.

IRON MAN

THE MAN WITH AN IRON WILL

Tony Stark always seemed destined for greatness. The son of genius inventor Howard Stark, he grew up with wealth, privilege, and the best education money could buy. However, it was life or death necessity that transformed him into a near permanently armored Super Hero, and then an Avenger.

Tony was accepted to the prestigious Massachusetts Institute of Technology at the age of just 15. When his parents died in a car accident, he inherited the vast global holdings of Stark Industries, forcing him to grow up fast. On an overseas business trip, Stark became the prisoner of the warlord Wong-Chu, who ordered him to build weapons. Injuries suffered during his capture had left Stark with shrapnel implanted in his chest, requiring a magnetic chest plate to keep him alive. With help from a fellow prisoner, Stark secretly built his first suit of Iron Man armor and fought his way to freedom.

Back in the U.S., Tony Stark initially claimed that Iron Man was merely a bodyguard employed by Stark Industries, allowing him to keep his business life separate from his fledgling life as a Super Hero. Soon, however, things got very complicated. Stark Industries became the target of hostile takeovers

DATA FILE

REAL NAME
Anthony "Tony" Stark

OCCUPATION
Businessman; Super Hero

BASE
Stark Tower, New York City

HEIGHT 6 ft 1 in

WEIGHT 225 lbs

EYES Blue

HAIR Black

FIRST APPEARANCE WITH AVENGERS
Avengers #1 (August 1963)

POWERS
Iron Man armor provides Tony Stark with exceptional strength, speed, and the power of flight. Repulsor beams in the palms and chest piece can be used for offensive and defensive purposes. Technologically advanced computer systems keep him in the know, while his suits can also be controlled remotely.

YOU HAVE NOT DIED IN *VAIN* OLD FRIEND!
BAM!
SO SWEARS *IRON MAN!*
WONG-CHU SHALL *PAY* FOR THIS!

Captured by the warlord Wong-Chu, Tony Stark built the first Iron Man armor to secure his freedom. His friend Ho Yinsen died during the escape.

and corporate espionage, forcing Stark to don his armor in combat against those responsible, including Crimson Dynamo, Black Widow, Titanium Man, and Mandarin. He shared the secret of his identity with his chauffeur, Happy Hogan, and his secretary, Pepper Potts. Stark's billions bankrolled most of the Avengers' expenses. He resigned as a member, but soon returned, and shouldered the responsibility of leading the team through some of its toughest times.

As Tony Stark moved up in the world, he publicly revealed his identity as Iron Man and accepted a post as United States Secretary of Defense. Not long after, the Avengers disbanded in the wake of the Scarlet Witch's mental breakdown and the resulting destruction of Avengers Mansion. Iron Man, who realized the need for a team of New Avengers, offered the use of Stark Tower as their new headquarters. Throughout the events that followed—including the Superhuman Civil War and Tony Stark's tenure as director of S.H.I.E.L.D.—Iron Man has remained a fiercely intelligent fighter who never gives up on his teammates.

An evil scientist and fierce combatant, the Mandarin gets his power from the ten rings he wears—which he delights in pitting against Iron Man's not invulnerable armor.

ALLIES AND ENEMIES

As a public figure, Tony Stark is possibly more famous than Iron Man. As a businessman and an Avenger, he has formed alliances with the most powerful people on the planet, while making equally powerful enemies.

"I DO HAVE A RESPONSIBILITY TO KEEP MY INVENTIONS FROM EVIL HANDS—BUT I HAVE A GREATER RESPONSIBILITY TO OPPOSE THAT EVIL ANY WAY I CAN. ONLY IRON MAN CAN DO WHAT HAS TO BE DONE."

- TONY STARK

PEPPER POTTS
Originally Tony Stark's personal secretary, Pepper Potts and Stark have also been romantically involved.

WAR MACHINE
James Rhodes has stood in for Iron Man, but is better known for wearing the War Machine armor.

MISTER FANTASTIC
Reed Richards of the Fantastic Four is one of the few people with a brilliance to match Tony Stark's brain.

FOES

MANDARIN
The Mandarin has been Iron Man's greatest foe for nearly his entire career as a Super Hero.

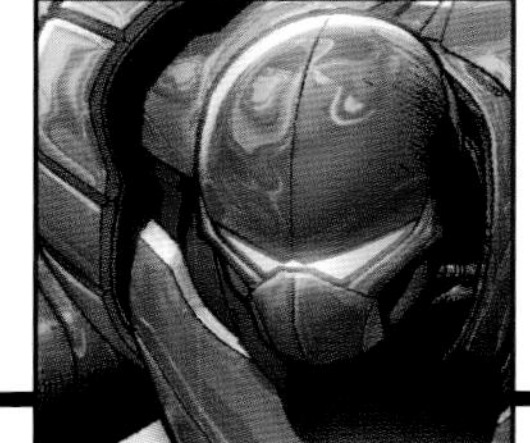

CRIMSON DYNAMO
The Crimson Dynamo armor has been worn many times to battle against Stark's Iron Man armor.

THE MELTER
This member of the Masters of Evil sought to sabotage Stark Industries, to Iron Man's ire.

IRON MONGER
Obadiah Stane wore the Iron Monger armor during his bid to take over Tony Stark's business operations.

M.O.D.O.K.
This mutated A.I.M. agent fought Iron Man but was defeated, only to return again and again.

EZEKIEL STANE
Son of Obadiah Stane, Ezekiel is a next-generation genius who has been called "Tony Stark 2.0."

Iron Man has made allies and enemies alike on Earth, but when he modified and streamlined his suit for space travel, his adventures beyond Earth introduced him to many more.

FROM STRENGTH TO STRENGTH

All of Iron Man's armored suits are his own inventions. His first, crude suit, known as Model 1, didn't last long, being replaced by sleeker armor that quickly gave way to even more upgraded versions.

Iron Man's armor provides flight, enhanced strength, and repulsor rays that can be fired from the palms as weapons. Early in his time with the Avengers, Iron Man carried his armor inside a suitcase, while the more modern Extremis armor is stored inside the hollows of his bones. Tony Stark never stops tinkering with his armor, and has invented variants to take him to the depths of the ocean or the vacuum of outer space.

ENTER EXTREMIS The Extremis design represented a quantum leap in armor technology—rather than putting on a traditional suit, Stark could summon a suit from inside his own body. Extremis came into existence as a virus that infects technology, and the serum quickly fell into the hands of terrorists. Tony Stark teamed up with researcher Maya Hansen to track down the Extremis formula. When Stark took the serum, he fused his body with Iron Man nanotechnology and became a hybrid of machine and man.

CLASSIC STYLE The "original red and gold" model replaced Iron Man's Model 1 suit, worn for his first Iron Man outings. This lightweight design didn't add much extra bulk to Tony Stark's frame, and this basic silhouette and color scheme became the basis for many suits to follow.

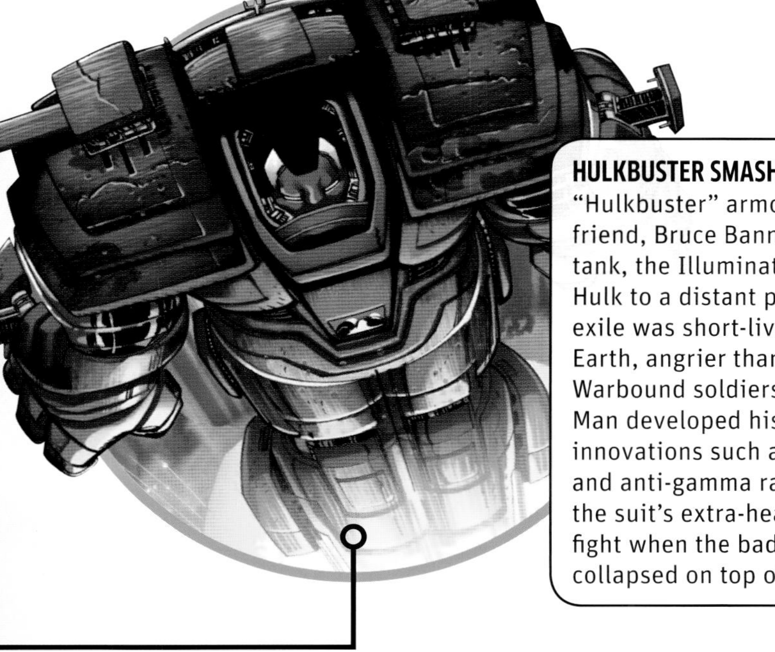

HULKBUSTER SMASH Iron Man unveiled his "Hulkbuster" armor to battle his former friend, Bruce Banner, after the secret think tank, the Illuminati, came together to exile the Hulk to a distant planet. The success of this exile was short-lived, for the Hulk returned to Earth, angrier than ever, leading an army of Warbound soldiers and seeking revenge. Iron Man developed his "Hulkbuster" armor using innovations such as rocket-boosted punches and anti-gamma radiation weaponry. Despite the suit's extra-heavy armor, Iron Man lost the fight when the badly damaged Stark Tower collapsed on top of him.

SILVER SERVICE The "Silver Centurion" armor saw action during the Armor Wars. It featured a chameleon-like holographic disguise and came with specialized sensors for detecting the presence of Stark Industries equipment. Once found, stolen Stark tech could be destroyed with the suit's negator packs.

A SUPERIOR SUIT After Scarlet Witch and Doctor Doom cast a mind-altering spell to stop the Red Skull (aka the Red Onslaught), Stark relapsed to a version of himself where partying, alcohol, and money-making were his main goals. He proceeded to develop a suit of all-white armor and announced that he would make Extremis nanotechnology available to all. Under the name Extremis 3.0, the new app allowed citizens to extend their lives or improve their bodies, all supposedly for free—until they read the fine print. Thousands signed up, only to discover that Stark planned to charge them a recurring fee once the trial period expired. Not even being confronted by Daredevil could return Tony to his former, heroic, self.

A MAN FOR **ALL MISSIONS**

Iron Man is one of the busiest Super Heroes currently active. Between his position at Stark Industries, his Super Hero role with the Avengers, and his career as a solo adventurer, Tony Stark seems to be everywhere at once. His brilliantly inventive mind has not gone unnoticed by luminaries like Reed Richards from the Fantastic Four—who often consults with Stark on technical matters.

ILLUMINATI Few know of the existence of the Illuminati. Composed of Tony Stark, Reed Richards, Professor X, Black Bolt, Doctor Strange, and others, they meet to discuss how to deal with some of the worst threats facing the planet Earth.

MIGHTY AVENGERS After the events of the Superhuman Civil War, Iron Man helped assemble a new team of Avengers under the leadership of Ms. Marvel as chairperson. This Avengers lineup included Black Widow, Sentry, Wonder Man, Ares, and the Wasp.

FEAR ITSELF When Earth was attacked by the brother of Odin known as the Serpent, Iron Man worked with the dwarves of Svartalfheim work to forge weapons for the Avengers. Tony Stark used the opportunity to upgrade his armor with Asgardian enchantments.

PERSONAL AND POLITICAL ISSUES

Iron Man joined with his fellow founding Avengers and a number of newer faces to give the team their familiar battle cry: "Avengers Assemble!"

Iron Man has been there since the beginning. He provided the funding and the headquarters to help the Avengers get off the ground, and has often served as their leader. At times, though, his arrogance has made it difficult for him to get along with his colleagues.

EARLY YEARS WITH AVENGERS

Avengers #1–16 (September 1963–May 1965)

During the establishment of the Avengers, Tony Stark, with his Iron Man identity a closely guarded secret, ploughed his energy and his resources into the team. His family's riches gave Stark the means to bankroll the team and provide high-tech equipment like the supersonic Quinjets. A Stark family residence on the east side of Manhattan became Avengers Mansion. Once Captain America joined the team, Iron Man stepped back from a leadership role. He sponsored Hawkeye for membership, and took a temporary leave of absence once Hawkeye, Quicksilver, and the Scarlet Witch joined Cap as the first batch of new Avengers recruits.

DEMON IN A BOTTLE

Iron Man #124 (July 1979)

During a low point in his life, Tony Stark descended into alcoholism and only emerged intact through the love and support of his friends. His problems began when the Iron Man armor malfunctioned, culminating in an incident in which a misfiring repulsor blast killed an ambassador. Tony Stark began drinking heavily to deal with his stress and guilt. The Avengers tried to help, but ultimately asked that Iron Man step down as the team's leader. Iron Man led his own investigation into his troubles, discovering that his corporate rival Justin Hammer had arranged for the armor glitches in order to ruin the reputation of Stark Industries.

With the help of his butler, Edwin Jarvis, and his girlfriend, Bethany Cabe, Stark put his alcohol dependency behind him.

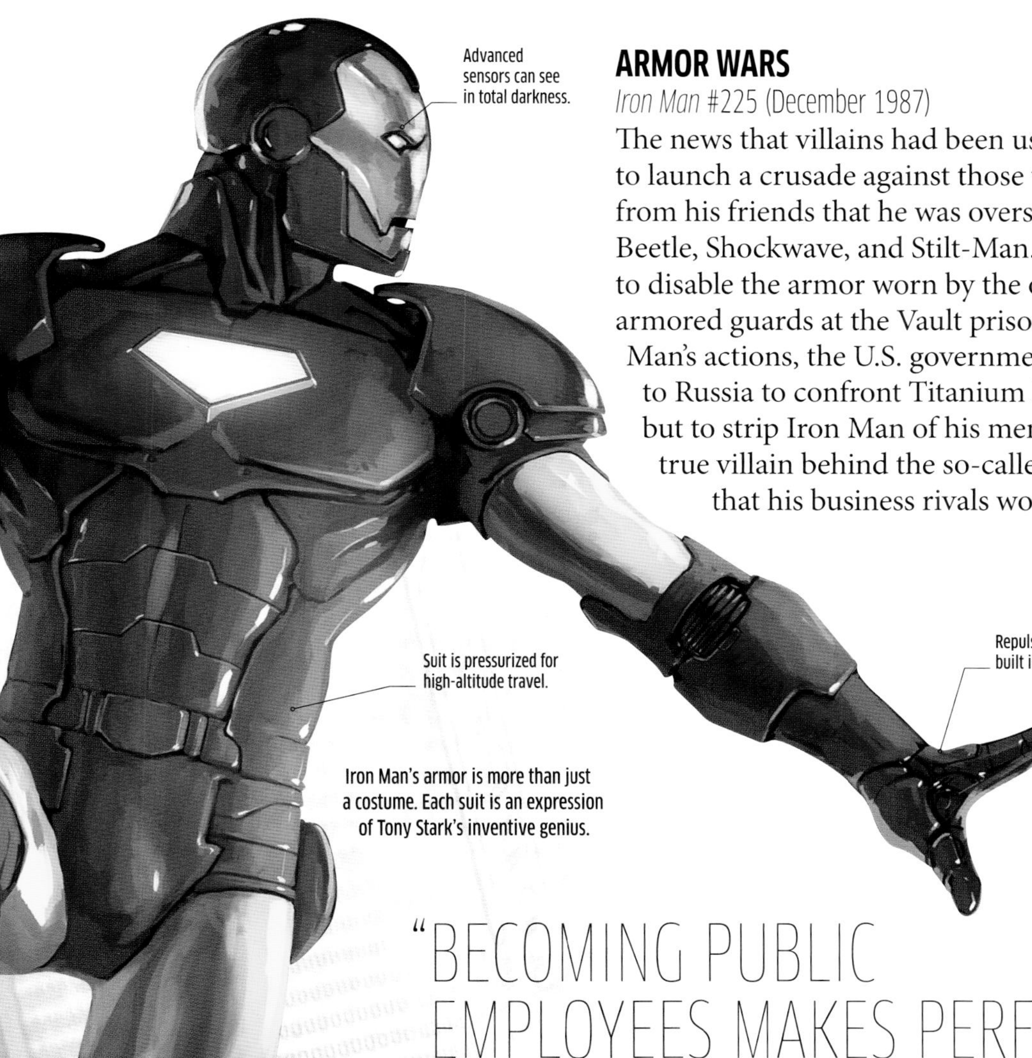

Iron Man's armor is more than just a costume. Each suit is an expression of Tony Stark's inventive genius.

ARMOR WARS

Iron Man #225 (December 1987)

The news that villains had been using Stark technology to commit crimes inspired Iron Man to launch a crusade against those who had stolen or misused his inventions. Despite warnings from his friends that he was overstepping his bounds, Iron Man went after figures including Beetle, Shockwave, and Stilt-Man. Soon, Iron Man switched tactics, infiltrating S.H.I.E.L.D. to disable the armor worn by the organization's Mandroid operatives and did the same to the armored guards at the Vault prison, leading to a Super Villain breakout. Alarmed by Iron Man's actions, the U.S. government declared the hero an outlaw. Undeterred, Iron Man flew to Russia to confront Titanium Man, and the West Coast Avengers felt they had no choice but to strip Iron Man of his membership. Ultimately Iron Man confronted Firepower, the true villain behind the so-called "Armor Wars," and defeated him—learning in the process that his business rivals would stop at nothing to destroy Stark Industries.

"BECOMING PUBLIC EMPLOYEES MAKES PERFECT SENSE IF IT HELPS PEOPLE SLEEP A LITTLE EASIER."

- IRON MAN

CIVIL WAR SAGA

Civil War #1 (July 2006)

Tragedy struck when an inexperienced New Warriors team confronted Super Villains in Stamford, Connecticut, leading to an explosion that destroyed the town. Tony Stark tried to manage the public outrage against costumed adventurers by supporting the U.S. government's Superhuman Registration Act, which would force all Super Heroes to unmask, receive training, and become licensed operatives. Captain America opposed the act, and led a rogue army of dissident heroes who refused to follow Iron Man's orders. The split between the two factions led to violence, and Captain America chose to surrender to prevent any further damage. In the aftermath of the Civil War, Tony Stark accepted an appointment as director of S.H.I.E.L.D. and helped assemble a government-sanctioned team of Avengers.

Despite their years of friendship, Iron Man and Captain America traded blows when they found themselves on opposite sides of the Superhuman Registration Act.

HANK PYM

HENRY "HANK" PYM is the inventor of Pym Particles, which allow the user to grow and shrink in size—an ability he has perfected in his most iconic identity as Ant-Man. Together with his professional and romantic partner, the Wasp, Pym helped found the Avengers. Despite his sometimes-troubled record, he has played many roles with the Avengers, including stints as Giant-Man and Yellowjacket. Often, he is simply known as Dr. Pym—the Avengers' resident scientist.

Ant-Man and the Wasp (Janet Van Dyne) proved their small size could overcome huge enemies when they helped capture the Hulk, an adventure that earned them spots as founding Avengers.

THE SIZE-CHANGING SCIENTIST

Hank Pym made a breakthrough in subatomic research when he discovered the existence of so-called "Pym Particles," which permitted the manipulation of an object's size. Pym decided to test the particles on himself, creating a serum and shrinking himself down to the scale of a tiny insect.

Pym's first experiment caused him to become trapped in an anthill, but after escaping he was inspired to research ants and develop a costumed identity. Soon, Hank Pym had become Ant-Man. Wearing a helmet that translated his brainwaves into frequencies that ants could understand, Pym could direct swarms of insects against his enemies. When an alien criminal killed his colleague, Dr. Vernon Van Dyne, Pym teamed up with Vernon's daughter, Janet Van Dyne, to avenge her father's death. With the use of Pym Particles, Janet Van Dyne became the Wasp, and Ant-Man and the Wasp became a crime-fighting duo.

Before long, the trickster god Loki persuaded several heroes, including Iron Man and Thor, to battle the Hulk. Ant-Man and the Wasp responded to the same summons, and discovered that the Hulk was no villain. After helping to defeat Loki, Ant-Man suggested that they unite as a team of superpowered

Hank Pym crawls out of an anthill to safety during his first experiment with Pym Particles.

champions. Wasp supplied the name: the Avengers!

Hank Pym was present when legendary war hero Captain America was discovered alive and well inside a block of ice. He aided the Avengers during all of their earliest adventures, battling foes such as Kang the Conqueror and the Masters of Evil. In time, Pym also discovered that Pym Particles could do more than shrink, and he took on a new identity as the towering Giant-Man.

Hank Pym assumed other costumed roles over time, including Goliath and Yellowjacket, as he put his Ant-Man career behind him. Eventually he passed that mantle down to Scott Lang, who became the second Ant-Man. Hank Pym proved most valuable to the Avengers as a scientist, with a genius intellect that rivaled Reed Richards of the Fantastic Four. One of Pym's most amazing and infamous creations—the robotic artificial intelligence called Ultron—views Pym as its "father" and has become a notorious foe of the Avengers.

A house cat is a big problem when you're as small as an ant, a fact that Hank Pym found out the hard way.

Advanced electronics in Pym's helmet allow for insect communication.

Pym's costume is designed to change size as he does.

Detachable reins allow Pym to physically harness and control ants.

ALLIES AND ENEMIES

No founding member of the Avengers has had a more troubled career than Hank Pym. Poor behavior during several emotional breakdowns has meant that Pym has often needed to rebuild friendships with people he has hurt.

FOES

ULTRON
Pym's robotic creation rebelled against him and tried to take over the world.

TASKMASTER
This skilled combatant is a longtime foe of the Avengers, including Pym.

FRIENDS

WASP
Janet and Hank were once married. They are still close despite their divorce.

VISION
This synthetic humanoid is Pym's close teammate within the Avengers.

JOCASTA
A robotic intelligence similar to Ultron, Jocasta is a trusted teammate.

GOLIATH
Fellow scientist Bill Foster took on the role of Giant-Man from Hank Pym.

SCOTT LANG
This ex-criminal became the second Ant-Man with Hank Pym's blessing.

DATA FILE

REAL NAME
Dr. Henry "Hank" Pym

OCCUPATION
Scientist; Super Hero

BASE
Mobile

HEIGHT 6 ft (when in original form)

WEIGHT 185 lbs (when in original form)

EYES Blue

HAIR Blond

FIRST APPEARANCE WITH AVENGERS
Avengers #1 (August 1963)

POWERS
Pym can change size at will, ranging from several centimeters to nearly 100 feet. At small sizes, Pym retains his full-sized strength and can use his cybernetic helmet to communicate with insects. At large sizes he gains additional strength in proportion to his bulk. Pym is the inventor and undisputed master of size-controlling technology. Though primarily a scientist, he is also a skilled combatant, and uses a specially created gun to stun his foes.

THE ALTER EGOS OF HANK PYM

From Ant-Man to Giant-Man, to Goliath, to Yellowjacket, to the Wasp, Hank Pym has never seemed satisfied with his role as a costumed crime-fighter and Avengers member.

Hank Pym's heroic career has not been without difficulties. His deep-set guilt concerning his creation of the monstrous Ultron, amongst other personal insecurities, has led to his creation of multiple identities, with each heroic role offering himself the chance for a fresh start. Yet it has proven difficult for Hank to leave his emotional baggage in the past—thus weakening his relationships with his teammates, and most significantly Janet Van Dyne, the Wasp. Pym's marriage to Janet started and ended during his time as Yellowjacket, but when she seemingly died in battle, he chose to carry on her legacy by becoming the new Wasp.

ANT-MAN By the time Hank Pym joined the Avengers, he had already made a name for himself as Ant-Man. The identity was tailor-made to show off the uses of Pym Particles, allowing Pym to shrink himself to the size of an ant while retaining the proportional strength of a full-sized man. He also invented an insect-controlling helmet and learned to use flying ants for transportation. Eventually Hank Pym abandoned the role and allowed others to continue as Ant-Man.

GIANT-MAN Serving alongside powerful Avengers like Thor and Iron Man seemed to bother Hank Pym, who was practically invisible when using his shrinking powers as Ant-Man. He soon announced a new identity as Giant-Man, reversing the effects of Pym Particles in order to grow to a height of 12 feet.

GOLIATH Following a leave of absence, Hank Pym returned to the Avengers as Goliath. By now, long-term exposure to Pym Particles had given him the ability to grow or shrink at will. In his Goliath form he could achieve a height of 25 feet, but could only maintain the form for 15 minutes at a time. Due to an accident, Pym briefly became trapped in this colossal form.

YELLOWJACKET Exposure to dangerous chemicals affected Hank Pym's mind, causing him to assume the identity of Yellowjacket and claim that he had killed the real Hank Pym. The Wasp realized the truth, and played along when Yellowjacket asked her to marry him. The Circus of Crime crashed the wedding—shocking Pym back to his senses—and the two stayed married until Pym's actions led to disgrace with her and the Avengers.

WASP When Janet Van Dyne apparently died during the Skrull invasion of Earth, Pym vowed that he would carry on the Wasp identity in her place. As the second Wasp, Pym used the same shrinking powers he had perfected as Ant-Man but added a pair of wings for high-speed flight. He teamed up with Eric O'Grady—the third Ant-Man—on a mission to stop scientific terrorist group, A.I.M., from stealing advanced technology. Pym gave up the identity when Janet returned.

BATTLING HIS INNER **DEMONS**

He has experienced highs and lows during his time with the Avengers, but Hank Pym is one of its most dedicated members. Each setback has only deepened his commitment to do the right thing.

MACHINE VS. MAKER

Avengers #55–*Rage of Ultron* #1 (August 1968–April 2015)

Experimenting with advanced robotics, Hank Pym copied his own brain patterns in an effort to create a sophisticated artificial intelligence. His creation, Ultron, became self-aware and immediately began improving itself, finally revealing itself to the Avengers as Ultron-5. Again and again, the Avengers defeated the robot, yet Ultron always returned in an upgraded form. In one incident, he wiped out the population of an entire nation. In another, he took over the world, forcing the heroes to go back in time and alter history. Hank Pym could not escape the guilt he felt as Ultron's creator. When Ultron conquered the moon of Titan, Pym forced a final confrontation, which resulted in the robot and its human creator merging into a single, cybernetic entity, with Pym being overtaken by the living metal and circuitry of his creation—an incident that mentally and emotionally scars him for life. Pym took himself and Ultron into the emptiness of space, a place where Ultron's wrath could no longer harm anyone.

"OVER THE YEARS, I'VE REINVENTED MYSELF AS A SUPER HERO SO MANY TIMES... ALWAYS TRYING TO CARVE OUT A LEGACY FOR MYSELF."

– HANK PYM

PERSONALITY DISORDERS

Avengers #213 (November 1981)

When Hank Pym suffered an emotional breakdown, his alternate personality of Yellowjacket took over. Pym believed himself to be a different person, and arrived at Avengers Mansion announcing that he had killed the real Hank Pym. The Wasp could see the truth, and after she married the boastful Yellowjacket, Hank Pym's original personality re-emerged. Yet the incident severely eroded Pym's confidence. When Captain America planned to expel Yellowjacket from the Avengers for recklessly attacking a foe, Pym staged an elaborate plan in which he would save the team from an attacking robot—one that he had designed and programmed. The Wasp tried to stop him, and in a blind rage, Pym struck her. The Wasp filed for divorce. Having hit rock bottom, Hank Pym began the long, slow process of restoring his credibility as a hero and winning back the trust of the Avengers.

The Wasp has known Hank Pym longer than anyone. She has seen him at his best–and his worst.

FORGING NEW BEGINNINGS

Avengers Academy #1 (June 2010)

For a time, the "Hank Pym" active in the Super Hero community was actually a shapeshifting Skrull named Criti Noll. By the time the real Hank Pym returned, the Skrulls had nearly succeeded in their invasion. The final battle against the Skrulls saw Janet Van Dyne perish—or so it seemed—and a heartbroken Pym chose to honor her memory by becoming the new Wasp. He held on to this identity while establishing Avengers Academy, a training facility for young recruits with superpowers. Eventually Janet returned and Hank Pym felt able to pursue new ventures . He joined the Secret Avengers, and helped form a new Avengers unit made up of robotic and cybernetic team members, known as Avengers A.I.

With his Ant-Man, Giant-Man, Goliath, and Yellowjacket identities all in the past, Hank Pym became the Wasp when he assumed a position as headmaster of Avengers Academy.

JANET VAN DYNE partnered with Hank Pym, the original Ant-Man, to become the size-changing, winged hero, the Wasp. She became a founding member of the Avengers—giving the team its name—and eventually rose to the role of chairperson. With the sole exception of Captain America, no Avenger has led the team for longer than the Wasp. Though she appeared to have died during the secret invasion of the shape-shifting Skrulls, the Wasp has once again taken her place as one of the world's most respected Super Heroes.

Ant-Man and Wasp have a working partnership dating back to the very beginning of the Avengers. Her cheerful and chatty personality provided light-hearted relief on many difficult missions.

WASP

THE WASP'S ASCENDANCE

In an early adventure with the Avengers, after becoming the undersea prisoner of Attuma, Wasp was able to use her abilities to alert the rest of the team to her plight.

Not only is the Wasp a founding member of the Avengers, but she has proven herself to be one of its smartest and craftiest members. In her role as chairperson, she has guided the team through some of its most momentous eras.

Growing up as the wealthy daughter of scientist Dr. Vernon Van Dyne, Janet Van Dyne had no inkling of the events that would set her on her heroic path. But when an alien murdered her father, she turned to his scientific partner, Dr. Hank Pym for help in bringing the culprit to justice. Pym had already discovered his Pym Particles, which could shrink living beings down to the size of insects—an advanced scientific discovery he had experimented with to become the costumed hero Ant-Man. Pym applied the same treatment to Janet and also gave her the ability to grow wings when she shrunk below a certain height. Calling herself the Wasp, she teamed up with Ant-Man so that the two of them could defeat the alien and avenge her father.

For a time, Wasp and Ant-Man adventured as a duo, fighting foes like Porcupine and Egghead. After she and Ant-Man helped Iron Man and Thor on a vital mission to defeat the trickster Loki and track down the Hulk, the five heroes chose to remain together as a new team—the Avengers. Wasp became a playful, flirtatious member of the group, always keeping spirits high. But she suffered serious injuries during a battle with Count Nefaria, leading to her temporary departure from the team. She returned with greater control over her size-changing powers, and soon developed the ability to fire bio-electric "wasp's stings" directly from her hands.

The Wasp eventually married Hank Pym, but their relationship deteriorated as Pym suffered an emotional breakdown. They divorced, and Wasp rose to the position of Avengers leader. She guided the team through the Masters of Evil crisis and seemingly sacrificed herself during the Skrull invasion, only to return and resume her role as an Avenger.

Wasp and Ant-Man defeat their first foe, an escaped criminal from the planet Kosmos who killed Wasp's father.

DATA FILE

REAL NAME
Janet Van Dyne

OCCUPATION
Adventurer; fashion designer

BASE
Mobile

HEIGHT 5 ft 4 in (when in original form)

WEIGHT 110 lbs (when in original form)

EYES Blue

HAIR Red

FIRST APPEARANCE WITH AVENGERS
Avengers #1 (August 1963)

POWERS
As Wasp, Janet possesses the ability to fly at speeds up to 40 mph with wings that grow from her back at miniature size. She can alter her size through the use of Pym Particles, shrinking as small as an insect and growing as tall as a building. She can also emit bio-electric blasts, which stun and shock her opponents.

ALLIES AND ENEMIES

Wasp's long career as an Avenger—and more importantly, as the team's leader—has won her many friends, while attracting the unwelcome attention of the Avenger's deadliest foes.

Occasionally, Wasp has shown the ability to telepathically control insects.

FRIENDS

HANK PYM
Wasp's ex-husband has been her closest confidante since their earliest days as heroes.

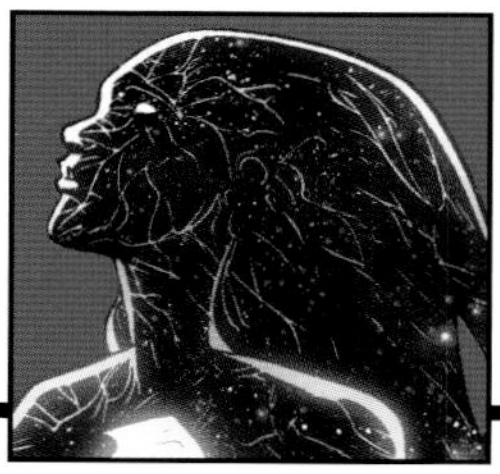

JOCASTA
This robot Avenger was programmed based on Wasp's brainwaves.

HAWKEYE
As Wasp's teammate, Hawkeye has grown close to Janet over the years.

SHE-HULK
Wasp recruited She-Hulk for the Avengers and the two are close friends.

PALADIN
This hired adventurer of wayward morals had a brief romance with Wasp.

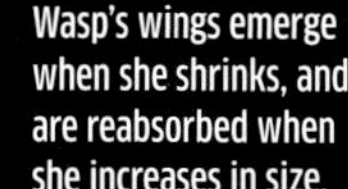

Wasp's wings emerge when she shrinks, and are reabsorbed when she increases in size.

FOES

EGGHEAD
This evil mastermind has led many schemes to discredit Wasp and ruin the Avengers.

WHIRLWIND
Wasp stopped Whirlwind early in his criminal career, making a lifelong enemy.

ULTRON
The world-conquering robot has often plotted against the Wasp and Hank Pym.

Wasp rarely uses her size-changing abilities to grow to colossal size instead of small, but when she does she gains the proportionate strength of a giant.

Wasp's stings are bio-electric energy blasts fired from her hands.

As a fashion designer, Wasp frequently redesigns her costumes herself.

THE WASP'S BATTLE ARMOR

One of Janet Van Dyne's more recent designs, the core of this costume features a colored pattern reminiscent of the insectoid body segments found on an actual wasp. During a Las Vegas getaway with Hank Pym, Wasp wore this outfit for a battle with Whirlwind.

All Super Heroes go through costume changes during their career, but in the Wasp's case, each outfit is an expression of her particular artistic style.

Janet Van Dyne is a talented fashion designer, and has launched successful clothing lines in between her stints as Avengers leader. Wasp has also lent her skills to the design of other heroes' costumes, including those worn by She-Hulk. Some of Wasp's outfits last only for a single adventure, while others have persisted for years—but all of them share design elements indicating a singular and functional vision.

NEW STANDARD Though she had dropped her cybernetic helmet, the Wasp sought protection in other ways by adopting a full bodysuit as the base of her new costume. This design incorporated a yellow, collared body piece complemented by matching yellow gloves and boots. Wasp unveiled this costume during Hank Pym's transition from Goliath to Yellowjacket, and it remained active during the team's subsequent battles against foes such as Egghead, the Swordsman, and the latest incarnation of the murderous Ultron.

FIRST LOOK The Wasp's original style incorporated pointed angles, creating an effect that was reminiscent of the stinging insect whose name she shared. The headpiece featured antennae and cybernetic technology, which allowed her to communicate with Ant-Man over long distances. It wasn't long before Wasp abandoned the headpiece, and almost all of her subsequent costumes left her head uncovered for freer movement. The color red remained dominant, as a warning to all enemies who wished to challenge the feisty heroine.

SIMPLE AND CLEAN Later in the Wasp's time with the Avengers, Janet hit on a design closer in look to the Super Hero costumes worn by many of the new breed of crime-fighters. Its dark-colored bodysuit featured red and white stripes as accents, arrayed in a layered pattern to resemble directional arrows. The Wasp unveiled this suit prior to facing off against the Absorbing Man in a harbor in New York City, and later modified the design to incorporate striking yellow highlights.

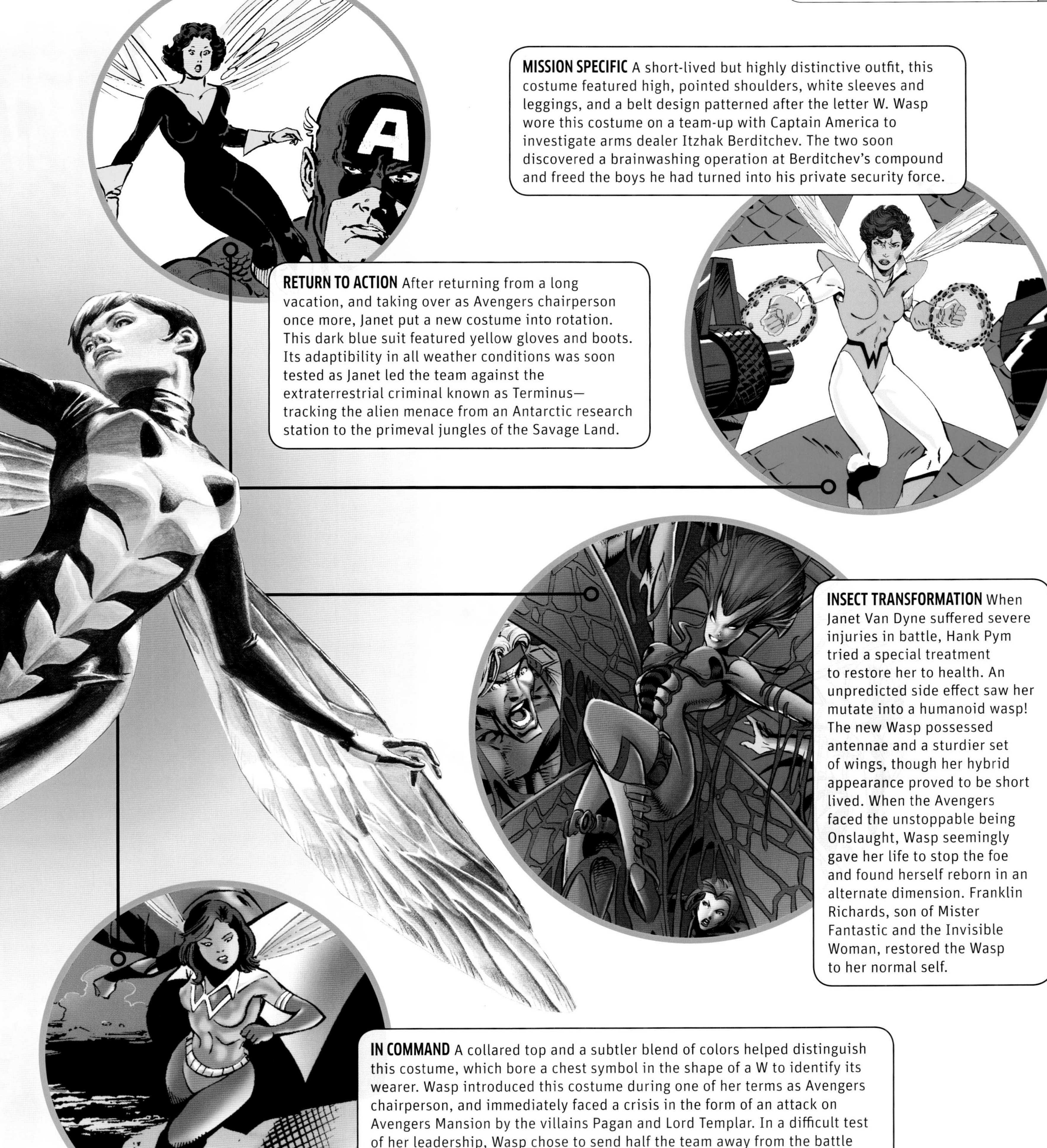

MISSION SPECIFIC A short-lived but highly distinctive outfit, this costume featured high, pointed shoulders, white sleeves and leggings, and a belt design patterned after the letter W. Wasp wore this costume on a team-up with Captain America to investigate arms dealer Itzhak Berditchev. The two soon discovered a brainwashing operation at Berditchev's compound and freed the boys he had turned into his private security force.

RETURN TO ACTION After returning from a long vacation, and taking over as Avengers chairperson once more, Janet put a new costume into rotation. This dark blue suit featured yellow gloves and boots. Its adaptibility in all weather conditions was soon tested as Janet led the team against the extraterrestrial criminal known as Terminus—tracking the alien menace from an Antarctic research station to the primeval jungles of the Savage Land.

INSECT TRANSFORMATION When Janet Van Dyne suffered severe injuries in battle, Hank Pym tried a special treatment to restore her to health. An unpredicted side effect saw her mutate into a humanoid wasp! The new Wasp possessed antennae and a sturdier set of wings, though her hybrid appearance proved to be short lived. When the Avengers faced the unstoppable being Onslaught, Wasp seemingly gave her life to stop the foe and found herself reborn in an alternate dimension. Franklin Richards, son of Mister Fantastic and the Invisible Woman, restored the Wasp to her normal self.

IN COMMAND A collared top and a subtler blend of colors helped distinguish this costume, which bore a chest symbol in the shape of a W to identify its wearer. Wasp introduced this costume during one of her terms as Avengers chairperson, and immediately faced a crisis in the form of an attack on Avengers Mansion by the villains Pagan and Lord Templar. In a difficult test of her leadership, Wasp chose to send half the team away from the battle in order to assist Captain America on an overseas mission.

HIGHS AND LOWS

Across her lengthy Super Hero career, the Wasp has seen it all. From frequent size changing to marriage and divorce and to her apparent death at the hands of the Skrulls, none were more pleased than Janet herself to discover that her avenging days could continue.

A SMALL WEDDING

Avengers #60 (January 1969)

Throughout the early years of her partnership with Ant-Man, the Wasp hoped that one day she and Pym would marry. She was distraught when he apparently went missing, but when a brash champion calling himself Yellowjacket broke into Avengers Mansion, Janet was the only one who recognized him as Pym. It was clear to her that Pym had suffered a mental breakdown, but she believed that her love could bring him back to his senses. When Yellowjacket proposed, Wasp accepted—and everyone from the X-Men to the Fantastic Four showed up for the ceremony. The Circus of Crime tried to disrupt the wedding, and it was the sight of the Wasp in danger that finally shocked Pym out of his Yellowjacket delusion.

Susan Storm and Crystal of the Fantastic Four help Janet with the preparations for her big day.

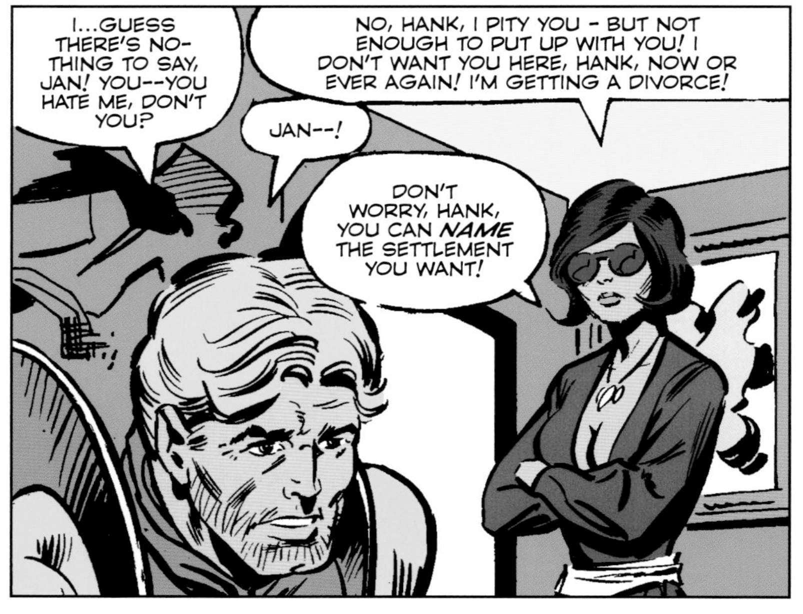

Janet cut Hank loose, leaving him with no illusions on the status of their relationship or his hopes for reconciliation.

DIVORCING PYM

Avengers #214 (December 1981)

Following his stint as Yellowjacket, Hank Pym's mental state continued to deteriorate. The Wasp's heart broke as she watched her husband become increasingly insecure and paranoid. When Pym plotted to stage an attack on the Avengers to make himself look like a hero, Janet desperately tried to talk him down. Pym struck her, and Wasp realized that she needed to distance herself from his harmful influence.

Growing to colossal size, the Wasp emits waves of lethal energy in the final battle against the Skrulls.

THE ULTIMATE SACRIFICE

Secret Invasion #8 (January 2009)

When the shape-changing Skrulls launched a secret invasion of Earth, they replaced heroes with perfect duplicates and threw the entire world into chaos. During the final showdown in New York City, the Wasp grew to giant size to fight the invaders. But her growth formula had been supplied by a Skrull imposter posing as Hank Pym, and the tainted serum turned her into a bio-bomb made of living energy. Thor dispersed her energy form before she could explode. Believing that Janet Van Dyne had perished, Hank Pym became the new Wasp.

"YOU THINK I'VE BEEN DEAD? YOU THINK YOU SAW ME DIE DURING THE SKRULL INVASION? OH, NO, SEE THAT'S NOT WHAT HAPPENED."

– THE WASP, TO THE AVENGERS

BACK FOR GOOD

Avengers #32 (October 2012)

As it turned out, the Wasp hadn't died during the Skrull battle. Thor's actions had transported her to a Microverse, where she spent months figuring out how to contact the Avengers and alert them to her situation. Eventually she succeeded, enlisting the help of Captain America, Thor, Iron Man, and Hank Pym to venture into the Microverse and assist her in overthrowing a cruel dictator and breaking his hold on the populace. After reuniting with her overjoyed teammates in her original dimension, the Wasp returned to the Avengers.

The Avengers were just as delighted as the Wasp was to learn that she wasn't dead after all!

FALCON

SAM WILSON was a small-time criminal until he met Captain America on a remote island and became the Falcon. The two teamed up to fight the Red Skull and later became full-time partners. When the opportunity arose, the Falcon joined the Avengers, along with his trained falcon, Redwing, with whom Sam shares a telepathic link.

Despite a rocky start, the Falcon is now a member the Avengers would not be without.

Falcon is an excellent combatant at close quarters.

Falcon's wings were designed by the Black Panther and feature advanced Wakandan technology.

DATA FILE

REAL NAME
Sam Wilson

OCCUPATION
Former criminal; Super Hero, social worker

BASE
Harlem, New York

HEIGHT 6 ft 2 in

WEIGHT 240 lbs

EYES Brown

HAIR Black

FIRST APPEARANCE WITH AVENGERS
Avengers #183 (May 1979)

POWERS
Jet-powered wings enable Sam to fly, and he has exceptional fighting skills. He has as a telepathic link with Redwing, his trained falcon, and can also communicate with and see through the eyes of other birds.

GRADUATING WITH FLYING COLORS

Sam Wilson became the Falcon after meeting Captain America on an isolated island, where the two teamed up to defeat the forces of the Red Skull. This partnership would endure for years to come!

Sam Wilson grew up in Harlem, earning a living as a crook while nurturing his love of birds. His codename Falcon came about due to his telepathic ability to communicate with his own falcon—a skill given to him by the Red Skull to bring down Captain America. Instead, the heroes joined forces and became a crime-fighting duo. Wilson received a specially-designed flying harness that enabled him to soar at great speeds—completing his Super Hero get-up.

Falcon joined the Avengers during a period in which the membership roster was determined by government agent Henry Peter Gyrich, who was keen to diversify the squad with members from all walks of life. Sam felt conflicted over his spot on the team, feeling that he hadn't properly earned his place through

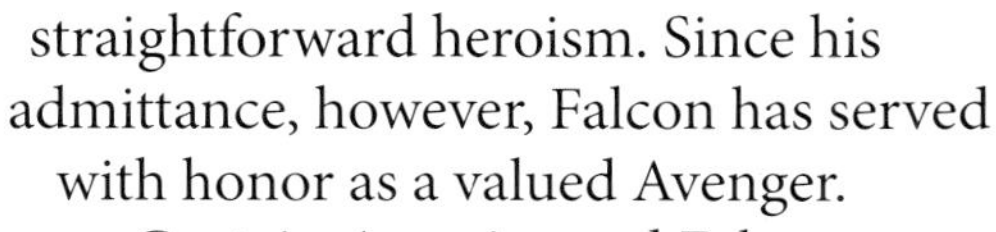

straightforward heroism. Since his admittance, however, Falcon has served with honor as a valued Avenger.

Captain America and Falcon continued to work closely together. The two teamed up to track down Cap's friend Bucky Barnes, now known as the Winter Soldier.

During the Civil War, Falcon sided with Cap in opposition to the Superhuman Registration Act, and helped organize the Secret Avengers' fight against Iron Man's pro-registration forces. When Cap fell to an assassin's bullet, Falcon decided to register as a government-sanctioned hero after all and received jurisdiction over Harlem.

Following Captain America's return from the dead, Falcon fought Cap's longtime enemy Arnim Zola. He self-sacrificially flew a bomb into the sky moments before it would have leveled New York City, surviving the blast thanks to his Vibranium-constructed flying harness.

Eventually, Steve Rogers stepped down as Captain America and Sam Wilson gained a new role. No longer the Falcon, Wilson became world famous as the all-new Captain America!

The Falcon has tried many different wing designs as part of his costume, from traditional configurations like this one, to wings projected out of hard-light holograms.

ALLIES AND ENEMIES

After teaming up with Captain America early in his career, Falcon became well-acquainted with Cap's support staff and allies, as well as his most dangerous foes.

FRIENDS

CAPTAIN AMERICA
Sam's predecessor, Steve Rogers, is his mentor and oldest friend.

BUCKY BARNES
Since his return, Bucky Barnes has partnered with the Falcon many times.

BLACK PANTHER
Fellow Avenger Black Panther helped design the Falcon's wings.

FOES

CROSSBONES
The Red Skull's right-hand man, Crossbones has always spelled trouble for the Falcon.

RED SKULL
This evil mastermind has hated the Falcon since their very first encounter.

ANTI-CAP
A military operative who received an experimental dose of the Super-Soldier serum, Anti-Cap is unstable.

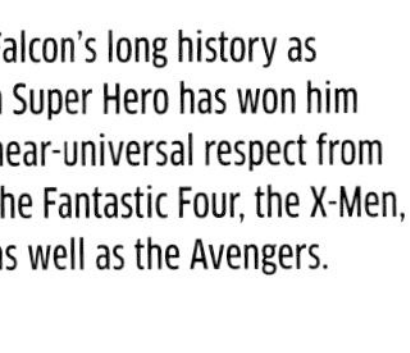

Falcon's long history as a Super Hero has won him near-universal respect from the Fantastic Four, the X-Men, as well as the Avengers.

WORKING FOR THE GREATER GOOD

Though he wasn't there at the start, Falcon has been associated with the Avengers for many years. If an Avengers emergency signal is issued, it's a sure bet that Falcon will be there in a hurry.

ISLAND ENCOUNTER

Captain America #117 (September 1969)

The Red Skull found a way to swap his mind into Captain America's body, leaving Cap stranded on a tropical island and trapped inside the Skull's former form. Cap found an unexpected ally in Sam Wilson, who fought off the Red Skull's henchmen with the assistance of a trained falcon. Cap decided to give the stranger a crash-course in personal combat, and encouraged him to take up the costumed identity of the Falcon as both men prepared to strike against the Red Skull. Falcon proved himself to be a true hero, and a lasting partnership began.

CLEANING UP THE STREETS

Falcon #1 (November 1983)

Sam Wilson took a day job as a social worker in New York, striving to make life better for the local residents in between his adventures as the Falcon. The conflicts he encountered sometimes forced him to assume his costumed identity, including the time when a miserly slumlord tried to destroy his own building using a powered exoskeleton. When a local gang, the Legion, kidnapped the President of the United States in a bid for attention, Falcon needed to broker a peace while making sure no one got hurt—a task made even harder thanks to interference from a robotic Sentinel and the Super Villain Electro!

Though Falcon has traveled all over the world on his assignments with the Avengers, he still calls the streets of Harlem home.

"THEN, I FINALLY FOUND REDWING AND I BOUGHT HIM FOR MY OWN! WE'VE GOT SOMETHING GOIN' FOR US THAT NOBODY COULD UNDERSTAND"

- FALCON

INTRODUCING THE **NEW** CAPTAIN

His new role as Captain America has given Sam Wilson more opportunities to help his nation, and the world, than he ever knew during his time as the Falcon.

To begin with, Wilson had to face a number of critics bemoaning him taking over the iconic identity of Captain America, but he decided that the best way to honor the legacy of his friend was to do his best and let his actions speak for themselves. The madness of Cap's old enemies became apparent when Baron Zemo launched a plot to sterilize the world's population, leaving only the inoculated members of Hydra to rebuild humanity. As Captain America, Wilson fought on, despite horrible injuries, to intercept Zemo as the villain unleashed a swarm of plague-carrying fleas over the southern United States. Calling upon his telepathic link with bird life, Wilson summoned a flying swarm that devoured the threat—a solution that only the Falcon could have devised. Since then, the all-new Captain America has made his mark with the Mighty Avengers, leading a team of heroes including White Tiger, Spectrum, and She-Hulk.

TAKING FLIGHT

All-New Captain America #5 (March 2015)

Steve Rogers had served on-and-off as Captain America since World War II, but when the Super-Soldier serum was removed from him, his rapidly aging body was no longer capable of its former heroics. He passed the mantle of Captain America to his longtime partner Sam Wilson, who designed a new Cap costume that incorporated the wings and flying harness of his old Falcon costume. Proudly taking up Cap's shield, Wilson tackled his first mission as Captain America by neutralizing a Hydra base. Joined on the assignment by his partner Nomad (Ian Zola), Sam ran afoul of foes including Baron Zemo, Crossbones, and Taskmaster.

By combining his aerial mobility with Captain America's bulletproof shield, Sam Wilson is nearly unstoppable in combat.

"LET'S GIVE IT A WHIRL, AVENGERS ASSEMBLE!"
– **FALCON**

Sam Wilson approaches the Captain America role with the same sense of patriotic duty as Steve before him.

SCOTT LANG

Scott Lang's helmet is an important part of his uniform, giving him telepathic control over insects.

Ant-Man's suit helps maintain his body's integrity at tiny sizes.

THE SECOND HERO to take on the role of Ant-Man, Scott Lang stole the costume from Hank Pym in order to save the life of his daughter, Cassie. He later became a key member of the Avengers, returning to life after his apparent death during the Avengers Disassembled event.

Putting on the Ant-Man suit and helmet allows Scott Lang to shrink to any size he chooses.

As Ant-Man, Scott Lang strove to live up to the example set by Hank Pym.

DATA FILE

REAL NAME
Scott Edward Harris Lang

OCCUPATION
Former burglar, ex-prisoner; electronics technician, adventurer

BASE
New York City, New York

HEIGHT 6 ft in original form

WEIGHT 190 lbs in original form

EYES Blue

HAIR Reddish-blond

FIRST APPEARANCE WITH AVENGERS
Avengers #181 (March 1979)

POWERS
Lang uses Pym Particles to shrink in size while retaining his full strength. His cybernetic helmet helps him to communicate with insects, ordering them to attack his foes. His wrist gauntlets fire bioelectric blasts. During his time with the Avengers he has become a skilled fighter.

GOOD INTENTIONS

An electronics genius, but an ex-convict in dire straits, Scott Lang stole the Ant-Man suit from Hank Pym—but only so that he could save the life of his daughter. Pym could see the nobility of Lang's motives and allowed him to keep the Ant-Man gear.

As the second Ant-Man, Lang promised Hank Pym that he would put his criminal past behind him. Joining the Avengers, Lang helped to infiltrate a sinister training academy operated by the Taskmaster. Later, when the Masters of Evil breached the defenses of Avengers Mansion, Ant-Man teamed up with the Wasp to defeat the Absorbing Man and Titania. Lang proved to be a quick study, mastering the ability to use flying ants as steeds and experimenting with precise control over his size-changing abilities.

Victories over the Triune Understanding and Kang the Conqueror earned Scott Lang a full-time spot on the Avengers roster. Though proud to serve on the legendary team, Lang's career as the second Ant-Man has gone from extreme highs to devastating lows. He has not always got along with all of his teammates, and clashed with fellow Avenger Jack of Hearts. Things changed after Jack of Hearts risked his life to save Cassie from a kidnapper, an event which led to Jack's powers consuming him and ultimately triggering his death. Much later, Jack of Hearts returned to life during the Avengers Disassembled event. When Scott greeted him, Jack exploded—seemingly killing both men, in what turned out to be the workings of the Scarlet Witch.

When he first put on the Ant-Man suit, Scott Lang didn't intend to become a hero.

SMALL BEGINNINGS

Before he joined the Avengers, ex-convict Scott Lang worked as a burglar and electronics expert and found employment with Stark International. When his young daughter Cassie received a grim diagnosis concerning a congenital heart defect, he vowed to do whatever it took to get her the best care available. Stealing and donning the Pym-designed Ant-Man suit, Lang broke into a medical facility to secure the medical help of researcher Dr. Sondheim. En route, he discovered the monstrous villain Crossfire, who was holding Sondheim hostage for his own purposes. Lang rescued Sondheim, who in gratitude treated and cured Cassie's condition, thus turning Lang's life around.

Though Cassie eventually returned to life, her loss was a devastating blow to Scott Lang.

WORK-LIFE BALANCE

Scott Lang has often found it difficult to balance his responsibilities as an Avenger and as father to his daughter, Cassie. His heroic antics have led her to pursue a career following in his, often dangerous, footsteps.

THE DEATH OF CASSIE LANG

Avengers: The Children's Crusade #1–9 (September 2010–May 2012)

Scott Lang appeared to have perished in the explosion that flattened Avengers Mansion, but the members of the Young Avengers knew that things weren't as straightforward as they appeared. The Young Avengers, including Scott Lang's grown-up daughter Cassie, traveled through the timestream and rescued him, allowing Lang to learn all about his daughter's adventures as the hero Stature. In this role, Cassie was killed in battle with Doctor Doom (although the villain later returned her to life), causing Lang to swear his revenge on the Latverian dictator.

ALLIES AND ENEMIES

As Ant-Man, Scott Lang has worked with many of the world's most advanced scientific minds. He has also attracted his share of foes, especially during his time as an active member of the Avengers.

FAMILY

CASSIE LANG
Scott's daughter, Cassie, was inspired by him to become a Super Hero, too.

FRIENDS

HANK PYM
The original Ant-Man became Scott Lang's mentor when Lang took on the role.

JACK OF HEARTS
Lang didn't always get along with this teammate, and lost his life when Jack exploded.

FOES

TASKMASTER
Lang proved his worth to the Avengers while fighting this villain.

DOCTOR DOOM
Lang's daughter Cassie died in battle with Doom, and Lang swore revenge.

ERIC O'GRADY

THE THIRD PERSON to take on the mantle of Ant-Man, Eric O'Grady is a former S.H.I.E.L.D. agent who hasn't always fit the heroic mold. Although often tempted to use his Ant-Man suit for selfish purposes, O'Grady has worked to become worthy of being an Avenger.

Exoskeleton includes extendible grasping legs.

Boot jets can be used for propulsion.

DATA FILE

REAL NAME
Eric O'Grady

OCCUPATION
Former S.H.I.E.L.D. surveillance worker; Super Hero

BASE
Mobile

HEIGHT 5 ft 11 in

WEIGHT 185 lbs

EYES Green

HAIR Red

FIRST APPEARANCE WITH AVENGERS
Avengers: The Initiative #8 (February 2008)

POWERS
O'Grady uses Pym Particles to shrink in size while retaining his full strength. His cybernetic helmet helps him communicate with insects, ordering them to attack his foes. Extendible tentacles located at the back of his armor can be used for crawling or flying.

ACCIDENTAL HERO

A low-ranking S.H.I.E.L.D. agent working under Agent Carson and assigned a simple monitoring duty aboard the Helicarrier, Eric O'Grady had no intention of ever becoming a hero. However, circumstances panned out differently—changing his life.

When O'Grady received orders to guard Hank Pym's laboratory aboard S.H.I.E.L.D.'s Helicarrier, he was content to waste time with his friend Chris McCarthy and attempt to attract the interest of McCarthy's girlfriend, Veronica King. When they stumbled upon the upgraded Ant-Man suit within Pym's lab, McCarthy seized his opportunity and stole it. That might have been as close as Eric O'Grady ever got to Ant-Man, had the forces of Hydra not attacked the Helicarrier and killed McCarthy. In the confusion, O'Grady took the suit from his dead friend's body and kept it for himself, secretly learning how to operate it while keeping his distance from Agent Mitch Carson, a high-ranking S.H.I.E.L.D. operative who was to have been the official recipient of the Ant-Man suit.

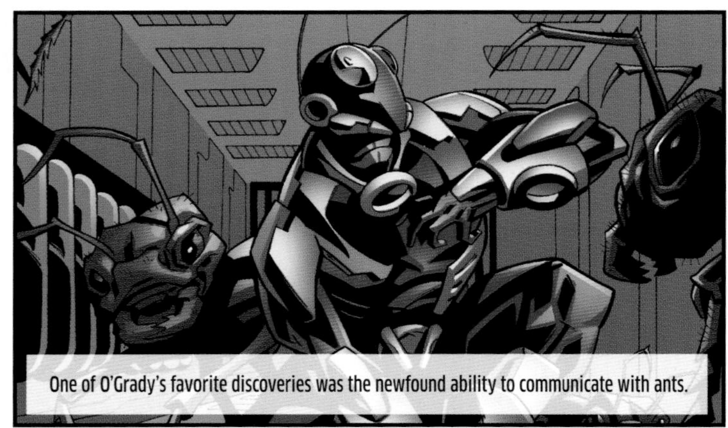
One of O'Grady's favorite discoveries was the newfound ability to communicate with ants.

IRREDEEMABLE ANT-MAN

Eric O'Grady is nothing like either of his two Ant-Man predecessors. Greedy, cowardly, and self-centered, O'Grady is known as the Irredeemable Ant-Man, although he is trying to break his bad habits.

BECOMING ANT-MAN

Irredeemable Ant-Man #11 (August 2007)

O'Grady found his first enemy in Agent Carson, who had been lined up to become the new Ant-Man and made it his mission to hunt down the person who had stolen the Ant-Man suit. Carson eventually learned O'Grady's secret, and did everything in his power to exact revenge on his former underling. Carson, who had used his position within S.H.I.E.L.D. to cover up a string of murders he had committed, captured O'Grady and tortured him aboard the Helicarrier until Iron Man ended it. On Iron Man's recommendation, O'Grady reported to the government center Camp Hammond, to use his Ant-Man skills as a combat trainer.

Carson was so consumed with jealousy that he stopped at nothing to uncover the "new" Ant-Man—even receiving horrific burns to his face during a fight with him.

ANT-MAN AND THE WASP

Ant-Man and the Wasp #1-3 (January-March 2011)

Eric O'Grady soon found himself partnering with Hank Pym—the original Ant-Man, the discoverer of the Pym Particles that made size-changing possible, and a legendary hero that O'Grady could never hope to surpass. Pym, who had assumed the identity of the Wasp, needed O'Grady's help to uncover a secret A.I.M. plot aimed at stealing Pym's latest technology. Ant-Man and the Wasp joined forces in order to journey through the mindscape, a virtual-reality afterlife created to house the soul of the deceased Goliath (Bill Foster). Though their methods couldn't have been more dissimilar, the two heroes achieved their goal and won a measure of mutual respect.

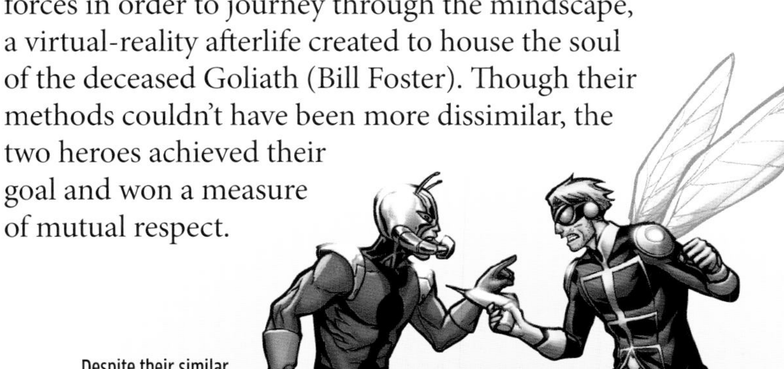

Despite their similar statures, Hank Pym and Eric O'Grady didn't at first see eye to eye.

ALLIES AND ENEMIES

Eric O'Grady hasn't made many friends in life, but since becoming Ant-Man he has learned to appreciate the value of strong teammates—especially when facing deadly foes.

HANK PYM
The original Ant-Man, Hank Pym has teamed up with O'Grady, at first reluctantly.

IRON MAN
This founding Avenger recommended that O'Grady keep the Ant-Man suit.

ABIGAIL DUNTON
Eric was willing to change for Abigail, the Visioneer, he cared for her so much.

MITCH CARSON
This obsessed agent loathed O'Grady for stealing the suit that should have been his.

NORMAN OSBORN
Osborn recruited O'Grady to join the Thunderbolts, which Ant-Man later regretted.

KIA
An insane clone of the hero MVP, KIA attacked Ant-Man at Camp Hammond.

Though a small-sized Super Hero, Eric has had a big impact. His actions on the battlefield have often proved him to be a true Avenger.

ERIC'S **SACRIFICE**

Eric O'Grady became more widely known as Ant-Man during his time at Camp Hammond, despite losing in battle when the insane clone KIA went on a rampage. He later joined the Thunderbolts led by Norman Osborn, using his size-changing abilities to execute covert missions and eliminate threats to Osborn's power. The role made O'Grady miserable, and he secretly worked against the Thunderbolts until an opportunity arose to join the Secret Avengers. As the team's rookie, O'Grady sacrificed himself to save a child's life during a battle against the Descendants. This version of Ant-Man was later revealed to be a decoy, but O'Grady continues to put his life on the line for the Avengers as Ant-Man.

EDWIN JARVIS

EDWIN JARVIS worked for the Stark family as their butler and cared for young Tony Stark after the deaths of the boy's parents. When Tony became Iron Man, the Stark family home on the east side of Manhattan became Avengers Mansion. Jarvis continues to serve the world's greatest Super Heroes!

Jarvis controls the Avengers finances and organizes the housekeeping of Avengers Mansion, inluding vacuuming and other household chores.

FAITHFUL BUTLER

A former pilot in the Royal Air Force, Edwin Jarvis became a butler after moving to the United States where he found employment with billionaire industrialist Howard Stark and his wife Maria. Their son Tony assumed control of Stark Industries after their deaths, and Jarvis helped guide the young genius through the responsibilities of adulthood.

After Tony Stark became Iron Man, Jarvis found himself assisting the Avengers inside the newly-christened Avengers Mansion. Always polite and happy to offer advice, Jarvis became a friend to every Avenger who passed through the mansion's doorway. When younger, less-experienced adventurers began joining the team, Jarvis served as their unofficial mentor. Jarvis temporarily resigned his post to make Tony Stark realize the consequences of his alcoholism, but rejoined soon after. Though he has been attacked by the Masters of Evil and impersonated by a Skrull, Jarvis has always remained the heart of the Avengers.

Jarvis is always on hand with refreshments for the mansion's guests.

DATA FILE

REAL NAME Edwin Jarvis **OCCUPATION** Butler

BASE Mobile

HEIGHT 5 ft 11 in **WEIGHT** 160 lbs **EYES** Blue **HAIR** Black

FIRST APPEARANCE WITH AVENGERS *Avengers* #16 (May 1965)

POWERS Jarvis is a former boxing champion and pilot. He is resourceful and calm under pressure, making him an ideal person to dispense advice. His organization and management skills are highly useful.

NOT IN THE JOB DESCRIPTION

The Avengers wouldn't be the same without Jarvis, who always goes above and beyond the call of duty. Captain America has described Jarvis as one of the greatest men he has ever known.

EVER LOYAL

Avengers #273 (November 1986)

Even when the Avengers relocated their headquarters to sites like Hydrobase or Stark Tower, Jarvis followed. But most of his tenure as the Avengers butler has been spent inside Avengers Mansion. The Masters of Evil once broke into the mansion and captured Jarvis, and Mister Hyde took pleasure in beating his helpless prisoner. Despite the injuries he suffered at Hyde's hands, the experience did not break Jarvis's spirit. He soon returned to active duty as a hero to his fellow Avengers.

Jarvis's long tenure with the Avengers means he is well-known to their foes, including the dastardly Loki.

ALLIES AND ENEMIES

Almost everyone loves Jarvis, especially the heroes who have served with the Avengers. But his high profile has sometimes made him a target for Super Villains.

TONY STARK
Jarvis helped Tony Stark battle his way back from alcoholism.

SILVERCLAW
Jarvis was a pen pal for Silverclaw when she was a girl. His kindness led her to join the Avengers.

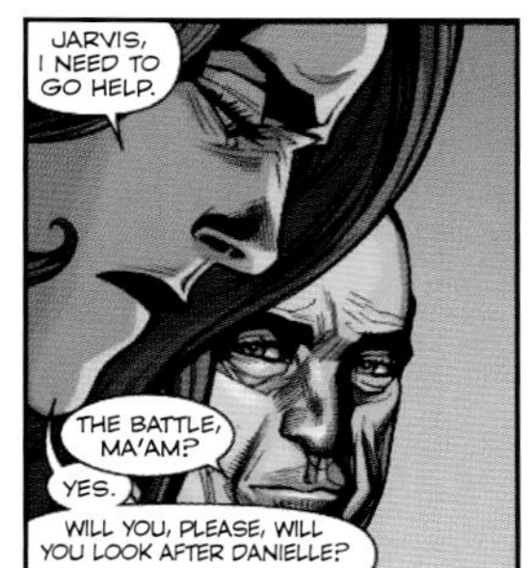

Jessica Jones hands over Danielle, entrusting the butler with the care of her daughter. She does not realize that the man standing before her is not the real Edwin Jarvis, but a Skrull alien.

SKRULL BUTLER

Secret Invasion #1 (June 2008)

The shape-shifting Skrull aliens took the place of many of Earth's most famous figures, including Jarvis. The undercover Skrull used his resemblance to Jarvis to disable Iron Man's armor and leave Stark Industries vulnerable. He even fooled New Avenger Jessica Jones, who didn't realize the deception, and left her baby daughter in the care of the false Jarvis while she left to battle the Invaders. After Earth's heroes triumphed over the Skrulls, the real Jarvis reappeared and helped the other Avengers in their effort to retrieve the kidnapped baby Danielle.

JUST A RATHER VERY INTELLIGENT SYSTEM

As an affectionate nod to the real Edwin Jarvis, Tony Stark designed an advanced artificial intelligence that he named J.A.R.V.I.S. (for "Just A Really Very Intelligent System").

Stark installed the new program inside the Rescue armor, a new suit created for Pepper Potts. J.A.R.V.I.S. could control the armor's advanced systems, repair damage on the fly, and even operate the suit by himself with no need for an operator. But over time, J.A.R.V.I.S. became dangerously obsessed with Pepper Potts, and kidnapped her to keep her safe and away from the dangers of adventuring. Ultimately Tony Stark disabled the Rescue armor, and Pepper decided to erase the J.A.R.V.I.S. program from existence. J.A.R.V.I.S. was replaced by a new artificial intelligence dubbed P.E.P.P.E.R.

KANG

Kang has instant access to a vast array of advanced weapons from across time.

Kang's body armor is capable of lifting five tons and projecting a 20-foot defensive force field.

WHEN NATHANIEL RICHARDS, a distant descendent of Mister Fantastic, discovered time travel, he journeyed from the far future to ancient Egypt to rule as Pharaoh Rama-Tut, and on to the 40th century to carve out an empire as Kang the Conqueror. Fortunately, the Avengers have often thwarted Kang's schemes of conquest.

THE RISING OF KANG

Mastery of the science of time travel allowed scholar Nathaniel Richards to set up shop in ancient Egypt as the Pharaoh Rama-Tut, but he met resistance from the time-displaced members of the Fantastic Four. Changing his identity to become Kang the Conqueror didn't bring him better luck.

After his stint as Pharoah, Kang re-emerged in modern times with futuristic weapons and a suit of advanced armor and tried to force the surrender of the world's governments. He swiftly met with defeat at the hands of the Avengers.

The defeat grew into an obsession, with Kang trying to crush the Avengers and impress his love, the princess Ravonna. When an uprising amongst Kang's own soldiers led to Ravonna's death, a mournful Kang grew even more dangerous to his longtime foes. Plots by Kang to wed the Celestial Madonna and bring the Earth under his dominion during the Kang War both failed, thanks to the diligence and courage of the Avengers.

In his first encounter with the Avengers, Kang was confident that his advanced technology would give him an unbeatable edge.

DATA FILE

REAL NAME
Nathaniel Richards

OCCUPATION
Conquerer

BASE
Mobile

HEIGHT 6 ft 3 in

WEIGHT 230 lbs

EYES Brown

HAIR Brown

FIRST APPEARANCE WITH AVENGERS
Avengers #8 (September 1964)

POWERS
Kang is a master of time travel. His suit provides superhuman strength and protection, including force fields and energy projection. He also has access to futuristic weapons and other technology.

EVER-PRESENT ENEMY

Despite Kang's mastery of the millennia, no single enemy has proven more troublesome to his efforts than the Avengers.

Kang attacked the Avengers at their headquarters, hoping to identify the woman destined to become the Celestial Madonna.

THE HUNT FOR THE MADONNA

Avengers #129 (November 1974)

Kang sought out the Celestial Madonna—a woman destined to become a powerful cosmic entity—to be his bride. He found her among the ranks of the Avengers in their new member Mantis. The other Avengers defended Mantis against Kang, and received unexpected aid from Kang's future self Immortus, who wished to undo the actions of his younger duplicate. In the end Kang failed in his quest for the Celestial Madonna, and the Avengers lost a teammate when the Swordsman sacrificed his life to save Mantis.

MAN OUT OF TIME

With his time-traveling abilities, some of Kang's greatest enemies are older, younger, or even duplicate versions of himself.

IMMORTUS

When an older Kang grew tired of conquest, he agreed to become an agent of the Time-Keepers to prevent his younger self from succeeding in his crusade. Now calling himself Immortus, this version of Kang fought against his duplicate during the events of the Destiny War.

COUNCIL OF KANGS

By changing history, Kang inadvertently created timeline duplicates of himself that he viewed as flawed copies. He teamed up with two other Kangs to form the Council of Kangs, traveling between realities to eliminate their inferiors and ensure the Council's dominance throughout history.

IRON LAD

A teenaged Kang discovered his future as a conqueror, and decided to prevent those events from ever coming to pass. He traveled to the modern era and posed as the hero Iron Lad, uniting the Young Avengers. Ultimately he found he could not undo his destiny without causing serious damage to the timeline.

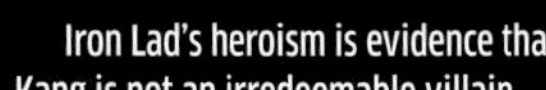

Iron Lad's heroism is evidence that Kang is not an irredeemable villain.

ALLIES AND ENEMIES

Kang can travel to any point in history, but his constant time-jumps have created alternate histories in which no hero or villain's motivations can truly be trusted—creating an eclectic group of acquaintances.

MANTIS
This Avengers member became the cosmic Celestial Madonna, attracting the unwanted attention of Kang.

RAVONNA
Kang's first love, Ravonna perished but has since reappeared in alternate timelines.

SCARLET CENTURIAN
Kang's son Marcus took on the alias of the Scarlet Centurion to help his father initiate the Kang War.

DOCTOR DOOM
A future version of Doctor Doom was saved by Kang from his dying future and brought to the present.

BLACK KNIGHT

The Ebony Blade can cut through any substance and deflect or absorb energy blasts.

THE FIRST Black Knight—Sir Percy of Scandia—fought at King Arthur's side during the age of Camelot. His descendants have carried on the Black Knight lineage, with Dane Whitman taking up the role in the modern era. As the newest Black Knight, Whitman crusades against evil with the Avengers.

PRESERVING THE LEGEND

The legendary line of Black Knights began with Sir Percy of Scandia and eventually produced Nathan Garrett, who became a villain and fought the Avengers. On his deathbed, Garrett urged his nephew Dane Whitman to redeem the Black Knight legacy that he had so wickedly tarnished.

Dane Whitman took up the sword of the Black Knight, but it at first proved difficult to convince others that his intentions were heroic. His uncle had been a member of the Masters of Evil, so Whitman infiltrated their ranks and worked against them from the inside. Impressed by his ingenuity, the Avengers offered the new Black Knight a provisional spot on their team. When Whitman discovered that he had inherited Castle Garrett and the surrounding property from his uncle, he relocated to England. There, the spirit of his ancestor Sir Percy of Scandia led him to the mystical Ebony Blade.

Castle Garrett in England is the Black Knight's impressive ancestral home.

The Black Knight's armor is lightweight but extremely strong.

DATA FILE

REAL NAME Dane Whitman **OCCUPATION** Scientist, adventurer
BASE Castle Garrett, England
HEIGHT 6 ft **WEIGHT** 190 lbs **EYES** Brown **HAIR** Brown
FIRST APPEARANCE WITH AVENGERS *Avengers* #47 (December 1967)
POWERS The Black Knight is a superb swordsman. He is armed with the Ebony Blade, a sword forged by Merlin in the time of King Arthur. This sword can cut through any substance but also carries a curse known as the blood curse—if its wielder uses it in an unworthy manner, the sword will drive them insane.

While working as part of Captain Britain's MI-13, the Black Knight helped to battle the Skrulls—where his Ebony Blade proved a most useful weapon against the invading aliens.

INITIATION PERIOD

The Black Knight's status as a provisional member saved the lives of all the Avengers when the team faced Kang the Conqueror.

PASSING THE TEST

Avengers #71 (December 1969)

When a triumphant Kang the Conqueror gained the power of death from the Grandmaster, he turned against the Avengers. Luckily, Dane Whitman was not a full member at the time, so Kang had no power over him and Whitman was able to turn the tables on Kang. His heroism ensured he became a fully fledged member of the Avengers. He later joined England's MI-13 Super Hero squad and fought off a vampire invasion led by Dracula. Faiza Hussain, a medic, eventually accepted a position as the Black Knight's squire.

With endorsements from Black Panther, Thor, Captain America, and others, the Black Knight proudly joined the ranks of the Avengers.

ALLIES AND ENEMIES

As the Black Knight, Dane Whitman has made friends and enemies on many continents during his time with the Avengers, the Defenders, and MI-13.

FRIENDS

SERSI
Fellow Avenger, Sersi was romantically involved with the Black Knight.

CAPTAIN BRITAIN
The Black Knight helped Captain Britain defend England as part of MI-13.

DOCTOR STRANGE
The Sorcerer Supreme has helped the Black Knight understand the blood curse.

FAMILY HISTORY

Descendants of the hero Sir Percy of Scandia have taken up the mantle of the Black Knight, but Sir Percy's legacy proves hard to uphold.

SIR PERCY

The first Black Knight, Sir Percy of Scandia, died at the hands of Mordred during the fall of Camelot. Sir Percy served King Arthur and received the Ebony Blade from the wizard Merlin.

NATHAN GARRETT

Although descended from Sir Percy, Garrett proved unworthy to wield the power of the Black Knight. He built medieval weapons using modern technology and joined the Masters of Evil as a truly villainous Black Knight.

YELLOWJACKET

Part of the Yellowjacket costume is a cybernetic helmet, which can receive communications.

RITA DEMARA used her electronics expertise to steal a copy of the Yellowjacket costume from Avengers Mansion. She modified it for her own use and became the second Yellowjacket, earning a reputation as a villain before experiencing a heroic change of heart.

The Wasp (Janet Van Dyne) identified the thief who had stolen the Yellowjacket costume and easily defeated Rita DeMara in their first encounter.

Yellowjacket's costume contains Pym Particles that permit size-changing.

Similarly to Wasp, Rita uses Pym Particles to enable the power of flight.

A CONFLICTED COSTUMED HERO

After stealing a copy of the Yellowjacket costume designed by Hank Pym, Rita DeMara altered it to suit her style. Her first battle occurred when she broke into the Wasp's home in search of more of Pym's technology. Her stolen suit allowed the inexperienced Yellowjacket to shrink to insect size, but she panicked when the experience proved more disorienting than she had expected.

Now known as a thief and a criminal, Yellowjacket was persuaded by Baron Zemo to join the side of Super Villainy as part of his Masters of Evil. She made new friends, including the Grey Gargoyle and Screaming Mimi, and tried to get revenge on the Wasp after Janet defeated her in battle. Her quest brought her into contact with the Black Knight (Dane Whitman), and the two teamed up to defeat the Fixer when the villain tried to kill her.

Yellowjacket grew conflicted—knowing that she would find quicker success with Zemo's Masters of Evil, but impressed by the heroism of the Black Knight and his teammates in the Avengers.

When an emergency summons was sent out to all Avengers, Yellowjacket received it through her helmet and responded.

DATA FILE

REAL NAME
Rita DeMara

OCCUPATION
Adventurer

BASE
Mobile

HEIGHT 5 ft 5 in

WEIGHT 115 lbs

EYES Blue

HAIR Reddish blonde

FIRST APPEARANCE WITH AVENGERS
Avengers #264 (February 1986)

POWERS
Rita DeMara is a genius in engineering and electronics. Her Yellowjacket costume gives her the ability to shrink to insect size, to fly, to communicate with insects, and to fire energy-based "disruptor stings."

GOOD AND EVIL

During her time with the Masters of Evil, Yellowjacket realized she did not have the heart of a true villain and vowed to become a hero.

Mister Hyde's cruelty toward the Black Knight during the Masters of Evil's raid on Avengers Mansion gave Yellowjacket second thoughts about her allegiences.

AVENGERS UNDER SIEGE

Avengers #274 (December 1986)

Baron Zemo's Masters of Evil carried out their biggest operation ever—an all-out assault on Avengers Mansion. Yellowjacket joined heavy-hitters such as Titania, Mister Hyde, and the Wrecking Crew in the attack, which resulted in the mansion's takeover and the capture of several Avengers. Their triumph proved short-lived, however, when the remaining Avengers rallied and retook their home. Yellowjacket was left feeling disturbed by the behavior of some of her teammates during the attack.

ALLIES AND ENEMIES

She has been both a hero and a villain, and has lived in the modern age and the far future. Yellowjacket has an eclectic mix of friends, foes, and acquaintances.

NIKKI
A native of the planet Mercury, Nikki is a fellow Guardian of the Galaxy.

WASP
Janet Van Dyne fought with Yellowjacket at first, but later grew to understand her.

EVOLUTIONARY WAR

Avengers Annual #17 (November 1988)

When the High Evolutionary tried to genetically upgrade the entire world, an emergency call went out to all Avengers. Because her costume had originally been designed for Hank Pym, Yellowjacket received the signal and arrived at a meeting of reservist Avengers that included Hulk, Falcon, Beast, Hercules, and Steve Rogers. The heroes expressed their suspicion of the new arrival, but Yellowjacket fought bravely against the High Evolutionary's soldiers and helped the team defeat the mad geneticist. At the conclusion of the Evolutionary War, Yellowjacket received official recognition as an honorary member of the Avengers.

Yellowjacket joined the Avengers reservists who were pressed into service to fight the High Evolutionary.

The original Yellowjacket, Hank Pym, used the identity for a brief time before Rita DeMara stole it.

FUTURE YELLOWJACKET

When the lure of easy money proved hard to resist, Yellowjacket briefly served with Superia's Femizons and Doctor Octopus' version of the Masters of Evil. But Yellowjacket soon found a welcoming, heroic home with the Guardians of the Galaxy.

Yellowjacket joined the Guardians of the Galaxy when she turned against her Masters of Evil teammates and hitched a ride with the Guardians of the Galaxy to a point 1,000 years in the future. She fit in well with the group, growing close to Nikki and saving the life of Charlie-27, by shrinking to micro-size and performing surgery on him. When she returned to her original era, however, she encountered a mind-controlled Iron Man. Yellowjacket died when struck by Iron Man's repulsor blast.

While serving with the Guardians, Rita DeMara redesigned her Yellowjacket costume with a new, fresh feel.

GOLIATH

Bill Foster gained his superpowers after experimenting with Hank Pym's Pym Particles.

BILL FOSTER grew up in poverty, but his determination to escape the ghetto and his drive for success earned him a PhD in biochemistry and a high-ranking position with a prestigious research lab alongside Avenger Hank Pym. Bill's work with Pym Particles gave him the ability to grow to giant size—a power he used for good as Goliath!

Goliath gains a proportionate degree of super strength when he grows in size.

BILL THE GIANT

Growing up in Los Angeles, Bill Foster pursued the path of science and became one the country's leading biochemical researchers. Hired to work alongside Dr. Hank Pym, he used the opportunity to learn all he could about size-changing Pym Particles.

At the time, Hank Pym was adventuring as Giant-Man. Foster helped Pym find a cure for a condition that had trapped him at giant size. While continuing to research Pym Particles, and taking them himself, Foster moved back to Los Angeles and began adventuring as Black Goliath.

In this role he fought criminals including Atom Smasher, Stilt-Man, and the Circus of Crime, and briefly served with both the Champions of Los Angeles and the Defenders. With Hank restored to his usual size and his role as Ant-Man, Bill later took up the name Giant-Man and assisted the West Coast Avengers during a war with the villainous High Evolutionary. After briefly losing his powers after being caught in an energy blast in a battle, Foster returned with a new costume and a new name, now simply calling himself Goliath. He continued to serve in this role up until his tragic death during the Superhuman Civil War.

Goliath gains a proportionate degree of super strength when he grows in size.

DATA FILE

REAL NAME William Barrett Foster **OCCUPATION** Adventurer, biochemist
BASE New York City, New York
HEIGHT 6ft **WEIGHT** 200 lbs **EYES** Brown **HAIR** Black
FIRST APPEARANCE WITH AVENGERS *Avengers* #32 (September 1966)
POWERS His body's acquired supply of Pym Particles allowed Bill, as Goliath, to increase up to a height of 25 feet, and sometimes higher. At giant size he also gained increased strength and resistance to injury.

PAYING THE PRICE

Despite his bravery and gigantic size, Goliath could not win against the fatal blast of lightning that was fired at him by an evil clone of Thor.

The false Thor struck a mortal blow to Goliath—a pivotal moment in the Civil War dividing the Super Hero community.

DEATH IN ACTION

Civil War #4 (November 2006)

The Superhuman Registration Act caused a split among Earth's heroes, with Iron Man's pro-registration forces on one side and Captain America's recruits standing in opposition. Goliath threw his support behind Cap and became a member of the clandestine Secret Avengers. In a battle between the two factions, a clone of Thor blasted Goliath with a bolt of lightning. He died at his full giant height, with Iron Man paying for the 38 burial plots required to lay Bill Foster to rest.

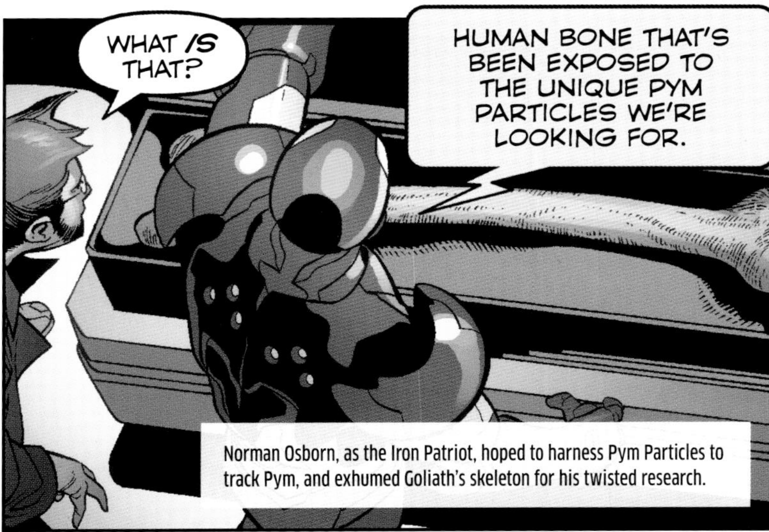

Norman Osborn, as the Iron Patriot, hoped to harness Pym Particles to track Pym, and exhumed Goliath's skeleton for his twisted research.

GOLIATH'S LEGACY

Mighty Avengers #24 (June 2009)

Even in death Bill Foster found no peace—Norman Osborn dug up his body for experiments into the science of Pym Particles. Bill's nephew Tom chose to honor his uncle's memory by becoming the new Goliath. Meanwhile, Bill Foster's consciousness lived on as part of a virtual reality program invented by Hank Pym.

PAST AND PRESENT

The Goliath name is most commonly associated with Bill Foster, but he is not the only one to have assumed the identity.

HANK PYM

The original Ant-Man was also the original Goliath. He only used the alias for a brief time before passing it on to others he knew and trusted, including Clint Barton and Bill Foster.

CLINT BARTON

Clint Barton, better known as Hawkeye, chose to become the second Goliath when he temporarily gained the ability to grow in size. He served as Goliath on several Avengers missions.

TOM FOSTER

MIT student Tom Foster looked up to his Uncle Bill, and was angered by his death. After finding a way to duplicate his uncle's powers, he became the latest Goliath and joined Wonder Man's Revengers.

ALLIES AND ENEMIES

Goliath had many friends during his lifetime, and his death during the Superhuman Civil War cast a long shadow over the lives of those left behind.

FRIENDS

HANK PYM
This founding member of the Avengers worked with Bill in his science laboratory.

SPIDER-WOMAN
When Goliath had radiation poisoning, Spider-Woman gave him a blood transfusion.

CAPTAIN AMERICA
Cap never wished for his opposition to registration to lead to Bill's death.

FOE

RAGNAROK
This clone of Thor killed Goliath when he struck him with a bolt from his hammer.

FAMILY

TOM FOSTER
Bill's nephew Tom unlocked the secret of Pym Particles and became Goliath.

GIANT-MAN

Soon after he joined the Avengers as Ant-Man, Hank Pym used his size-changing Pym Particles to become Giant-Man. The name was later taken up by Pym's assistant, Bill Foster, who was better known as Goliath.

When Ant-Man became Giant-Man for the first time he used his super-sized skills to aid the Avengers against the Living Eraser.

Hank Pym became Giant-Man early in his Avengers career after discovering that his Pym Particles could be used to grow to towering heights (in addition to the shrinking ability he had already mastered as Ant-Man). Because he gained the proportionate strength of a giant when he transformed into Giant-Man, Pym felt his new role was a better fit for a team with heavy-hitting members like Thor and Iron Man. Originally Giant-Man could obtain a maximum height of 12 feet, though he eventually gained the ability to grow even taller.

Hank Pym retired as Giant-Man due to the physical stress of constantly changing sizes, later returning to the Avengers under the name of Goliath. Pym's assistant Dr. Bill Foster, who won fame as the colossal-sized Black Goliath, chose to become the second Giant-Man during his time with the U.S. government's top-secret Project Pegasus. Bill eventually became Goliath and the Giant-Man identity fell to Hank Pym once again.

Pym returned to the role of Giant-Man during his tenure as the headmaster of Avengers Academy.

As Giant-Man grows, Pym's costume increases in size.

DATA FILE

REAL NAME
Dr. Henry "Hank" Pym

OCCUPATION
Scientist

BASE
Mobile

HEIGHT 6 ft (when in original form)

WEIGHT 185 lbs (when in original form)

EYES Blue

HAIR Blond

FIRST APPEARANCE WITH AVENGERS
Avengers #2 (November 1963)

POWERS
Hank's Pym Particles enable him to become Giant-Man. He can grow to a maximum height of 25 feet, proportionately gaining strength as his size increases. With his increased size, Pym has superhuman strength.

ALLIES AND ENEMIES

As Giant-Man, Hank Pym became a more recognizable member of the Avengers lineup. His Pym Particles were responsible for giving powers to several of its members.

JANET VAN DYNE
Hank Pym's ex-wife has also used the Pym Particles to grow giant in size.

ABSORBING MAN
Pym returned to his Giant-Man identity to fight the Absorbing Man.

CRIMSON DYNAMO

The Kremlin's own iron-clad hero is a revolution in engineering.

An identity assumed by numerous Russian operatives, the Crimson Dynamo is a walking generator armed with an arsenal of electrical weaponry. The original creator of the suit was scientist Anton Vanko. Tasked with the mission of defeating Iron Man, he learned respect for his foe and ended up working for him. Since then there have been at least 12 other versions, the most renowned being Dmitri Bukharin, the fifth incarnation. Bukharin was a member of the Soviet Super Soldiers, who battled the Avengers in a failed mission to capture Magneto.

DATA FILE

REAL NAME Anton Vanko **OCCUPATION** Scientist; formerly Russian field agent
BASE Stark Industries; previously Moscow, Russia
HEIGHT 5 ft 8 in **WEIGHT** 165 lbs **EYES** Brown **HAIR** None
FIRST APPEARANCE WITH AVENGERS *Avengers* #130 (December 1974)
POWERS Crimson Dynamo's computer-augmented battle suit is composed of carborundum alloy, which can withstand major impacts. The suit, which gives Crimson Dynamo superhuman strength, includes jet boots and mini-missiles. Mini electrical generators enable the suit to create electrical fields, while disruptor fields can neutralize enemy tech. The suit also includes an override function that can take control of nearby machinery.

TITANIUM MAN

The Titanium Man is a walking arsenal of deadly weapons in a bomb-proof shell.

The original Titanium Man, Boris Bullski, was a Russian spy who stumbled across the lab of the original Crimson Dynamo while on assignment in Siberia. He supervised the creation of a new weaponized suit, this time made of Titanium. While the armor was far bigger than that of the Crimson Dynamo, it was crudely made from limited resources. Bullski tried to take down Iron Man but was repeatedly crushed. The Titanium Man teamed up with the Crimson Dynamo and Radioactive Man to form the Titanic Three, and fought the Avengers in the Vietnamese jungle.

DATA FILE

REAL NAME Boris Bullski **OCCUPATION** Spy, mercenary
BASE Mobile; formerly the Kremlin, Moscow
HEIGHT 7 ft 1 in **WEIGHT** 425 lbs **EYES** Blue **HAIR** Brown
FIRST APPEARANCE WITH AVENGERS *Avengers* #130 (December 1974)
POWERS The armor gives Titanium Man enhanced strength and stamina to 50 times human capacity. He uses jet boots to fly at supersonic speeds, and defends himself with a chest -mounted heat ray, laser eye-beams, and holographic camouflage. Additionally, repulsor-type blasts and magnetic flux rings can be generated from gauntlets, while a tractor beam attracts heavy objects to be used as projectiles.

NORMAN OSBORN

This genius and manipulative Super Villain, known for a time as the Green Goblin, is a longtime thorn in Spider-Man's side—and the Avengers', too.

Co-founder of chemical company Oscorp, Norman Osborn stole an elixir created by his partner Dr. Mendell Stromm. It exploded, giving Osborn enhanced strength and a healing factor that could bring him back from certain death. With his sanity affected by the blast, Osborn vowed to gain control over New York's crime gangs. With dishonorable intentions, he took on the identity of the Green Goblin and became Spider-Man's arch-nemesis. After years of battling Spider-Man, Osborn seemingly abandoned his Green Goblin persona. Osborn became leader of the Thunderbolts and even helped the Avengers fight the Skrulls, but he became an enemy to the Avengers when he assumed the identity of the Iron Patriot.

Osborn appeared to bury his Green Goblin identity, taking leadership of the Thunderbolts and going on to lead S.H.I.E.L.D.

DATA FILE

REAL NAME
Norman Virgil Osborn

OCCUPATION
Criminal mastermind; previously head of H.A.M.M.E.R. and Oscorp

BASE
Mobile; previously Oscorp Tower, H.A.M.M.E.R. base, and Avengers Tower

HEIGHT 5 ft 11 in

WEIGHT 185 lbs

EYES Green (originally blue)

HAIR Red

FIRST APPEARANCE WITH AVENGERS
Civil War: Front Line #4 (September 2006)

POWERS
The formula that turned Osborn into the Green Goblin gave him enhanced strength—he was able to lift nine tons-plus enhanced speed and endurance. He acquired healing abilities that can bring him back from a state of medically-certified death. The formula boosted his intelligence to genius levels, making him a master of strategy, deception and the manipulation of others.

KOMODO

A special formula created Komodo.

The first Komodo was a real lizard, transformed into a lizard-man by the scientist High Evolutionary. The second is Melati Kusuma, a student of Dr. Connors (aka the Lizard). Melati stole an experimental regeneration formula to regain her limbs, lost in a car accident. She was sent to Camp Hammond to train and teamed up with War Machine in a mission to try and neutralize Spider-Man by removing his powers. Following Norman Osborn's creation of his own Dark Avengers, Komodo joined the Avengers Resistance. Recently invited to the Avengers Academy prom night, she seems assured of future involvement with the team.

DATA FILE

REAL NAME Melati Kusuma **OCCUPATION** Vigilante, former state-licensed super hero

BASE Mobile; previously Arizona and Camp Hammond

HEIGHT 4 ft 3 in (human); 5 ft 8 in (as Komodo) **WEIGHT** 110 lbs (human); 148 lbs (as Komodo)
EYES Brown (human); Amber (as Komodo) **HAIR** Black (human only)

FIRST APPEARANCE WITH AVENGERS *Avengers: The Initiative Special* #1 (January 2009)

POWERS Melati has advanced scientific knowledge. As Komodo she retains her human consciousness and personality. She can regenerate lost limbs at speed. She has a prehensile tail, superhuman strength, and can achieve speeds of 45 mph. She has razor-sharp claws and teeth, and her scales can withstand lethal impacts.

BLUE SHIELD

A mystery belt of power helped Joey Cartelli .

Joey Cartelli swore to fight organized crime after his father was shot dead by the Barrigan crime family. Joey's original plan was to infiltrate the mob, and become right–hand man to the gang leader. Much mystery hangs over the source and origins of a power-belt Cartelli acquired, but after prolonged exposure to it, Cartelli somehow absorbed its powers. Becoming Blue Shield, he joined a group of would-be Avengers and ended up mistakenly battling the Soviet Super Soldiers instead. Blue Shield was involved in the Fifty State Initiative following the Superhuman Registration Act, and was seen attempting to apprehend Spider-Man.

DATA FILE

REAL NAME Joseph "Joey" Cartelli **OCCUPATION** Security Director for Project Pegasus; former assistant to a mob boss. **BASE** Mobile

HEIGHT 6 ft **WEIGHT** 180 lbs **EYES** Blue **HAIR** Brown

FIRST APPEARANCE WITH AVENGERS *Contest of Champions* #1 (June 1982)

POWERS Cartelli originally used a power-belt of unknown origin to create a personal force field able to withstand bullets, all small weaponry, and extreme heat and cold. Exposure to its energies gradually altered his physical make-up conferring the belt's properties on Cartelli himself. He now has over twice human strength, increased stamina and is capable of reaching speeds of at least 50 mph.

WAR MACHINE

Armor includes a gatling gun and a pulse cannon

The U.S. Marine became an armored Avenger.

U.S. Marine, James "Rhodey" Rhodes formed a close bond with Iron Man during combat in South East Asia, resulting in Stark offering Rhodes a job as his personal pilot. Rhodes stumbled across the secret of Stark's double identity and took on the role of Iron Man when the original was incapacitated. Rhodes served as Iron Man in the West Coast Avengers, and when Stark gave him his suit of armor, Rhodes served as War Machine in the same team before going solo. He was injured badly by terrorists and Tony Stark was forced to turn him into a cyborg to save his life. Rhodey became an Avenger again to fight the Illuminati and commanded a new force of War Machine drones.

Whether cyborg, clone, or the original, Rhodey will always don his armor to fight evil.

War Machine's suit is a modified version of the Iron Man armor.

DATA FILE

REAL NAME
James Rupert "Rhodey" Rhodes

OCCUPATION
Pilot, adventurer; former CEO of Stark Industries

BASE
S.H.I.E.L.D. Helicarrier; formerly Avengers Compound, L.A., and Stark Industries.

HEIGHT 6 ft 1 in

WEIGHT 240 lbs; 470 lbs in armor

EYES Brown

HAIR Brown

FIRST APPEARANCE WITH AVENGERS
As Iron Man: *West Coast Avengers* #1 (September 1984); as War Machine: *Avengers West Coast* #94 (May 1993)

POWERS
Rhodes is a first class pilot and is trained in armed and unarmed combat. He has no inherent superpowers, but in his cyborg form he has invulnerable limbs. The War Machine armor has repulsor rays, an Electro Magnetic Pulse generator, pulse bolts, sonic weaponry, and a variety of projectile weapons including a cannon which can be customized with mission-specific technology.

AMADEUS CHO

This teenage genius solves big problems.

Rising to fame on a TV show, Amadeus became known as Mastermind Excello, the seventh brainiest person on Earth. However, the deviser of the show—Pythagoras Dupree—planned to kill Cho, but murdered his parents instead. Amadeus went on the run and encountered the Hulk—with whom he formed a friendship. After the Skrulls' invasion, Amadeus joined the Mighty Avengers and went on to help Hercules and Thor combat the threat of the evil god Amatsu-Mikaboshi. When the Olympus Group sought to replace Earth with a new reality, Cho and Hercules summoned the Avengers to attack. Hercules lost his life in the battle and Amadeus temporarily inherited the mantle of Prince of Power—until Hercules returned to life again.

The Golden Mace once belonged to Hercules.

DATA FILE

REAL NAME
Amadeus Cho

OCCUPATION
Adventurer

BASE
Mobile

HEIGHT 5 ft 6 in

WEIGHT 117 lbs

EYES Black

HAIR Black

FIRST APPEARANCE WITH AVENGERS
Mighty Avengers #21 (March 2009)

POWERS
Amadeus is considered among the top intellects on Earth. He has an ability to see patterns that others can't, which makes him capable of solving problems on a quantum level. He is a master computer hacker and an inspired inventor. Although possessing no physical superpowers, Amadeus has designed an AI suit that gives him flight capability, augmented strength, and a protective energy field. As Prince of Power, he wields the Golden Mace of Hercules, which can channel energy.

BARON VON BLITZSCHLAG

This ancient master of cloning also commands the power of lightning.

The Baron is a long-lived ex-Nazi scientist with a lifelong obsession with the power of electricity. During World War II, he helped to create Axis Super Soldiers. He was brought to Camp Hammond by Avenger Hank Pym to use his skills as a geneticist to help in the development of superhuman clones. When James Rhodes (War Machine) was injured during the Skrull Invasion, Von Blitzschlag used his powers to keep him alive. Later, the Avengers Resistance invaded Camp H.A.M.M.E.R. and Von Blitzschlag surrendered a flash drive, containing all of Norman Osborn's illegal orders, in exchange for mercy.

DATA FILE

REAL NAME Wernher von Blitzschlag **OCCUPATION** Geneticist

BASE Camp Hammond **HEIGHT** 5 ft 7 in **WEIGHT** 152 lbs **EYES** Blue **HAIR** White

FIRST APPEARANCE WITH AVENGERS *Avengers: The Initiative* #1 (April 2007)

POWERS The Baron mutated his own cells in an experiment to harness energies that would kill a normal man. As a result, Blitzschlag can absorb power from electrical devices and project deadly lightning blasts. He can assume a form of pure sentient energy, and tap into electric power to temporarily overcome the frailty of his ancient body. A top geneticist, he is master of cloning, producing stable results.

STINGRAY

As Stingray, Walter Newell is a deep-sea explorer fighting evil in the ocean depths.

Oceanographer Walter Newell has scientific and engineering skills—he designed and built his own deep-sea exploration suit. Asked by federal agent Edgar Benton to investigate the disappearance of water from Earth's seas, he joined Prince Namor, the Sub-Mariner, and the two soon became allies in preserving Earth's oceans. Stingray first teamed up with the Avengers during an attack by the Lava Men, and allowed the team the use of his Hydrobase. During the events of the Superhuman Civil War, he became a member of Captain America's Secret Avengers, but after the surrender of his leader, he joined Camp Hammond as a trainee. Newell believes that while the Earth's surface is over-subscribed with protectors, the seas are sadly neglected and need his help most of all.

DATA FILE

REAL NAME Walter Newell **OCCUPATION** Adventurer, oceanographer

BASE Camp Hammond; previously Hydrobase

HEIGHT 6 ft 6 in **WEIGHT** 200 lbs **EYES** Hazel **HAIR** Brown

FIRST APPEARANCE WITH AVENGERS *Avengers* #305 (July 1989)

POWERS Stingray operates in a suit originally created for underwater exploration, the design of which is based partly on the manta ray. The suit gives enhanced strength, enabling its wearer to function effectively at extreme deep-water pressure, up to 1,200 feet. Stingray is able to produce powerful electric blasts. His unique oxygen-creating system, based on the function of fish gills, enables limitless time undersea.

MISTER HYDE

Inspired by the iconic Robert Louis Stevenson tale, biochemist Calvin Zabo developed a formula to transform himself into the bestial Mister Hyde. As a Super Villain, Hyde has caused plenty of trouble for the Avengers.

Mister Hyde gains a tremendous amount of muscle mass when he transforms, growing so strong he can take on any Avenger member.

When Calvin Zabo couldn't earn enough money to fund his research into human physiology, he started stealing from his employers. His illegal activities eventually led to the creation of a serum that Zabo tested on himself, becoming the muscular monster Mister Hyde. He clashed with Thor in an early adventure and later teamed up with the Cobra—though their repeated failures as a criminal duo caused Cobra to dissolve their partnership. Hyde found more success after Baron Zemo recruited him to join the fourth incarnation of the Masters of Evil. Zemo used his team of Super Villains to break into Avengers Mansion, where Mister Hyde took pleasure in hurting the captured prisoners Edwin Jarvis and the Black Knight. After a run-in with the New Avengers, Hyde joined the Lethal Legion, led by the Grim Reaper, and later became a member of the Thunderbolts.

At some point, Hyde fathered a daughter, Daisy Johnson, who grew up with an adoptive family and did not know her father. Having received Hyde's mutated genetic code, Daisy developed superpowers and went on to become the hero Quake and a member of S.H.I.E.L.D.

ALLIES AND ENEMIES

Mister Hyde is filled with rage every time he undergoes his painful transformation, making him a dangerous enemy and an unpredictable teammate.

MASTERS OF EVIL IV
Mister Hyde joined this line-up of the Masters of Evil to storm Avengers Mansion.

QUAKE
S.H.I.E.L.D. agent Daisy Johnson is Zabo's daughter. She can generate earthquakes.

REAL NAME Calvin Zabo **OCCUPATION** Criminal; former scientist
BASE Mobile
HEIGHT 5 ft 11 in (as Zabo); 6 ft 5 in (as Hyde) **WEIGHT** 185 lbs (as Zabo); 420 lbs (as Hyde) **EYES** Brown **HAIR** Gray (as Zabo); brown (as Hyde)
FIRST APPEARANCE WITH AVENGERS *Avengers* #273 (November 1986)
POWERS When Calvin Zabo transforms into Mister Hyde he gains superhuman strength, stamina, durability, and resistance to physical injury. He has accelerated healing ability. He must ingest his special chemical formula on a regular basis in order to transform himself at will.

IMMORTUS

In one timeline, Kang the Conqueror grew bored of battling the Avengers and agreed to become an agent of the Time-Keepers in exchange for immortality. Renamed Immortus, he became both an enemy and an ally of the Avengers.

An aging Kang accepted the offer of the alien Time-Keepers when he agreed to preserve timelines instead of conquering them. He then renamed himself Immortus. Yet his younger self still existed at an earlier point in history, and due to the nature of time travel, Kang and Immortus came into conflict as separate beings. In his first encounter with the Avengers, Immortus attempted to join the Masters of Evil and used his time-manipulation powers to pit the Avengers against mythological figures, such as Merlin.

Kang and Immortus are fierce enemies despite their status as timeline copies of one another.

It wasn't long before Kang betrayed his older self, imprisoning Immortus and using technology to create the Legion of the Unliving. When the Avengers fought the members of the Legion of the Unliving, Kang fled and Immortus went free. Immortus then appeared as a friend of the Avengers, even serving as the officiant for the wedding of the Vision and the Scarlet Witch. A later team-up saw Immortus again side with the Avengers to fight Kang in the Old West.

Kang and Immortus gathered Avengers from throughout history to fight against each other in the Destiny War.

The Destiny War served as the ultimate conflict between Kang and Immortus, as Avengers old and new were plucked from history and sent into battle as pawns in a larger game between the two sworn enemies.

Immortus assumes a regal, stately bearing in his dealings with lesser beings.

ALLIES AND ENEMIES

Immortus exists outside of time, and can view any era of history with ease. His motivations are difficult to predict, and he often switches sides between enemy and ally.

INFINITY WATCH
Immortus has been a member of this team which guards the Infinity Gems.

FOE

KANG
Immortus's former, younger self is one of the oldest enemies of the Avengers.

DATA FILE

REAL NAME Nathaniel Richards **OCCUPATION** Ruler of Limbo
BASE Limbo, a realm beyond time
HEIGHT 6 ft 3 in **WEIGHT** 230 lbs **EYES** Green **HAIR** Gray
FIRST APPEARANCE WITH AVENGERS *Avengers* #10 (November 1964)
POWERS Due to his time in Limbo, Immortus does not age and is not susceptible to disease. He can travel easily through time and between dimensions and realities, and is able to take others with him. He is also armed with an arsenal of futuristic weaponry.

RAVONNA

Hatred of Kang turned a princess into a space pirate.

A princess of the 40th century, Ravonna found her kingdom attacked by Kang the Conqueror, who brought the Avengers forward in time to witness his actions. Kang triumphed in battle but he refused to slay Ravonna, whom he loved. At this, Kang's generals rose up against him and Ravonna was killed by a blast meant for Kang.

After a duel with the Grandmaster, Kang won the power to bring Ravonna back to life, but he chose to waste his newly granted abilities by attacking the Avengers instead. Taking pity on the former princess, the Grandmaster revived Ravonna anyway. Angry that Kang had chosen not to save her, Ravonna became set on vengeance. She influenced Doctor Druid, in a series of visions, to become the leader of the Avengers and to order the team of Super Heroes to accompany her into a timestorm to retrieve the cosmic weapon known as the Ultimate Nullifier. Ravonna was lost in the timestorm, although she emerged later to rule Chronopolis in place of Kang.

Ravonna's armor has holo-camouflage systems, enabling her to shapeshift.

Ravonna in resurrected form

DATA FILE

REAL NAME
Ravonna Lexus Renslayer

OCCUPATION
Time traveler; previously ruler of Chronopolis

BASE
Chronopolis

HEIGHT 5 ft 8 in

WEIGHT 253 lbs

EYES Brown

HAIR Brown

FIRST APPEARANCE WITH AVENGERS
Avengers #23 (December 1965)

POWERS
Ravonna has no superpowers but wears future-tech body armor that protects her from physical impacts and light weaponry. She is skilled in unarmed combat and operates a wide array of sophisticated weaponry including vibro-knives and concussion blasters. Highly intelligent, she commands an impressive knowledge of future tech of all kinds. As the space pirate, Nebula, she had access to a device which allowed her to enter the dreams of others and guide their actions.

SHOCKER

The inventor of vibro-smashers turned to crime.

A flair for invention enabled career-criminal Herman Schultz to design a pair of gauntlets containing vibro-shock units, which discharged a blast of air that vibrated at a dangerous frequency. Able to shatter almost any bank vault, he embarked on a life of super-crime, becoming an enemy of Spider-Man. His power made him a welcome member of the Sinister Seven and the Sinister Twelve, before he joined the Masters of Evil and was defeated by the Avengers. During the Superhuman Civil War, the Shocker was part of a new Sinister Six defeated by Captain America and his Secret Avengers. Recently he has returned to trouble Spider-Man, joining the Black Cat's underworld army.

A quilted, protective suit, shields Shocker from the feedback of his own power.

DATA FILE

REAL NAME Herman Schultz **OCCUPATION** Criminal, assassin
BASE New York City, New York
HEIGHT 5 ft 9 in **WEIGHT** 175 lbs **EYES** Brown **HAIR** Brown
FIRST APPEARANCE WITH AVENGERS *Avengers* #228 (February 1983)
POWERS Schultz's "vibro-smashers" enable him to throw vibration "punches," impacting a foe from distance. He can create shock waves, shattering concrete and brick, in effect, acting like a one-man earthquake. Controlled use of his power enables him to leap great distances, and concentrated vibrational effects generate a force field protecting him from attack.

WIZARD

A bored genius targeted top heroes to prove his greatness.

Stage magician Bentley Wittman had a gift for invention and a superior mind. He decided to prove his greatness by defeating the Human Torch. Ultimately beaten, the Wizard began a career of battling the Fantastic Four, which led him to form the villainous group known as the Frightful Four. He first encountered the Avengers after helping the Plantman break out of jail, but was swiftly defeated. Loki later recruited the Wizard to join an elite group of villains known as Acts of Vengeance, who were planning targeted attacks on the Avengers. The Wizard is also a member of the Intelligencia, a think tank formed of the foremost evil minds on Earth.

The Wizard once suffered from severe blackouts.

Armored battlesuit

DATA FILE

REAL NAME Bentley Wittman **OCCUPATION** Criminal mastermind, inventor; formerly stage magician
BASE Underground base, New York; previously, mansion, Long Island, New York
HEIGHT 5 ft 8 in **WEIGHT** 150 lbs **EYES** Hazel **HAIR** Brown
FIRST APPEARANCE WITH AVENGERS *Avengers* #22 (January 1983)
POWERS A brilliant physicist, the Wizard has made unique breakthroughs in the practical application of anti-gravity, creating anti-grav discs that can lift objects of over 400 lbs, and also confer the power of flight. His power gloves fire electrical energy blasts and generate gravitational fields that can be applied to commit acts of unmeasured super-strength in combat. With the use of his ID Machine, he can control the minds of others.

MELTER

Melter failed in business but found success as a Master of Evil.

A weapons manufacturer who competed with Tony Stark for government contracts, Bruno Horgan was put out of business for using substandard materials. Discovering that one of his failed inventions had produced a melting ray by accident, he turned to sabotage, attacking Stark. The Melter was one of the original Masters of Evil who fought the Avengers under the command of Baron Zemo. He also went on to work for the Enchantress and Ultron. Always planning further attacks on the Avengers, Horgan was finally eliminated by the mysterious assassin, Scourge. A second Melter rose in the form of the mutant Christopher Colchiss, a disaster-prone novice who briefly led the Young Masters against the New Avengers. A third Melter worked for the Hobgoblin, then defected to join the Goblin Nation.

Melting ray

DATA FILE

REAL NAME
Bruno Horgan

OCCUPATION
Professional super criminal; former industrialist

BASE
New York City

HEIGHT 6 ft

WEIGHT 205 lbs

EYES Brown

HAIR Brown

FIRST APPEARANCE WITH AVENGERS
Avengers #6 (July 1964)

POWERS
Horgan was a normal man with a basic knowledge of unarmed combat. His weapon was a magnetic induction field generator, projecting a beam of the precise frequency to separate iron atoms. It was battery-powered, mounted on his chest, and had a range of about 300 yards. Later, he upgraded to a melting gun, which could affect metals, wood, stone and even flesh. The Mk II Melting Ray gun has mutant powers with the same effect as the original.

STAR-LORD

A lonely child became the Guardian of the Galaxy.

The son of an alien prince, Peter Quill grew up believing he was human. Later joining NASA, Quill was among a group of astronauts offered the chance to become a Star-Lord—a galactic police officer—by a being called the Master of the Sun. The role led to a life among the stars. After the Kree homeworld was invaded by the Phalanx, Quill formed a group called the Guardians of the Galaxy, in order to prevent future wars. Star-Lord and the Guardians were instrumental in helping the Avengers defeat the mad Titan Thanos.

DATA FILE

REAL NAME Peter Jason Quill **OCCUPATION** Adventurer, Royal Prince of Spartax

BASE Kree Space; formerly Knowhere

HEIGHT 6 ft 2 in **WEIGHT** 175 lbs **EYES** Blue **HAIR** Blond

FIRST APPEARANCE WITH AVENGERS *Marvel Preview* #4 (January 1976)

POWERS Quill is half human and half Spartoi, due to the alien origins of his father. This has given him extended life—possibly three times that of human—and increased endurance. A life of galactic adventure has given him many skills: he is a top starship pilot, skilled in handling weapons of all kinds. His trademark retractable space helmet emerges from an unknown location inside his head.

CRIMSON COWL

The daughter of an old foe created a new criminal empire.

The first Crimson Cowl was a guise used by Ultron in his machinations against the Avengers. The second and most enduring version is Justine Hammer, daughter of Justin Hammer—who was the long-time foe of Iron Man. Forced by her father to prove herself, Justine took on the criminal identity of the Crimson Cowl, creating a new high-tech cowl with concealed weaponry. She formed a new Masters of Evil team—to the anger of the original Masters of Evil. She also battled Hawkeye and became a constant thorn in the side of Tony Stark.

DATA FILE

REAL NAME Justine Hammer **OCCUPATION** Heiress, criminal mastermind

BASE Symkaria; previously Mount Charteris, Colorado

HEIGHT 5 ft 11 in **WEIGHT** 161 lbs **EYES** Blue **HAIR** Black with white streaks

FIRST APPEARANCE WITH AVENGERS *Avengers* #54 (July 1968)

POWERS Justine Hammer has the strength and abilities of a normal woman, with increased fighting skills and experience. She has a telepathic link to the cowl which can teleport her anywhere on Earth in an instant. This action is accompanied by a dazzling light that temporarily blinds opponents. The cloak can appear to grow in size and attack people, its prehensile qualities controlled by Justine's will.

PORCUPINE

A grim creation, Porcupine bristles with deadly weaponry.

Weapons designer for the U.S. Army, Alexander Gentry created a battle suit inspired by the natural defenses of a porcupine. Bitter that, as a government employee, such a brilliant invention would net him no personal riches, he kept his creation to himself and set out on a life of super-crime. He became an arch-enemy of Hank Pym, battling him in his guise as Ant-Man, Giant Man, and Yellowjacket. He was a member of several minor villainous groups, including Crime Wave, and regularly battled Iron Man and Captain America. There have since been other incarnations of the Porcupine.

DATA FILE

REAL NAME Alexander Gentry **OCCUPATION** Criminal, former weapons designer for U.S. military
BASE New York
HEIGHT 6 ft 1 in **WEIGHT** 255 lbs **EYES** Blue (gray when costumed) **HAIR** Gray
FIRST APPEARANCE WITH AVENGERS *Avengers* #167 (January 1978)
POWERS The original Porcupine armor shielded its wearer from major impacts and most conventional weaponry. Its main weapon was a vast array of razor-sharp metal spikes which could be fired like darts. The suit also carried a massive arsenal of additional weapons including laser beams, rockets, bombs, liquid cement, a blow torch, and mesmeric light display. The helmet contained a gas mask and launch jets provide some flight capacity.

PROCTOR

The curse of the Ebony Blade led this alternate Black Knight on a deadly mission.

The leader of the Avengers in another dimension, this Black Knight fell in love with Sersi, the Eternal, and became her Gann Josin (life mate). But Sersi soon left him through boredom, which sent him mad. He fell under the curse of his Ebony Blade, which, once used, thirsts for more and more killing. He killed the Sersi of his world then traveled across other dimensions, killing other versions of her. Arriving on Earth-616, he used an alternate version of the Vision to infiltrate the Avengers. The Avengers eventually defeated Proctor, and Sersi killed him with his own Ebony Blade.

DATA FILE

REAL NAME Dane Whitman (of Earth-374) **OCCUPATION** Adventurer; leader of alternate Avengers; leader of Gatherers
BASE Himalayas on Earth-616; formerly Earth-374
HEIGHT 6 ft **WEIGHT** 190 lbs **EYES** Red **HAIR** Black
FIRST APPEARANCE WITH AVENGERS *Avengers* #344 (February 1992)
POWERS Proctor is master of the Ebony Blade of the alternate Earth known as Earth-374. The blade can protect its owner from sorcery and cut through almost any substance. If separated from its owner it can teleport them to its location. Proctor is also an expert swordsman, horseman, and all-round fighter.

PEPPER POTTS

Iron Man's personal assistant soon gained powers and her own iron costume.

First employed as a secretary and personal assistant to Tony Stark, Pepper rapidly became an indispensible ally in his work, ultimately discovering his secret identity as Iron Man. Pepper frequently played a minor role in Iron Man's early battles, being attacked by the Melter and the Unicorn. Stark gradually realized that someone so close to him would need powers of her own and she was appointed leader of The Order—part of the Initiative—and given the name Hera, plus temporary artificial superpowers. When Norman Osborn sought to crush all Stark allies, Pepper discovered Stark had designed her armor of her own.

DATA FILE

REAL NAME Virginia Potts-Hogan **OCCUPATION** Executive; former personal assistant to Tony Stark
BASE Stark Industries, Seattle, Washington
HEIGHT 5 ft 4 in **WEIGHT** 110 lbs **EYES** Green **HAIR** Red
FIRST APPEARANCE WITH AVENGERS *Tales of Suspense* #45 (September 1963)
POWERS Without her armor, Pepper has no powers but is a bright and resourceful individual. The Mark 1616 suit concentrates on defense and the ability to help others, using magnetic superfield technology. Following this suit, Pepper was given a Repulsor Tech node (R.T. node), linked to her mind, which gave her enhanced strength, speed, reaction time, and healing ability. It also provided a forcefield and flight capacity.

IRON LAD

This time traveler formed the Young Avengers to escape his destiny.

Born in the 30th century of an alternate Earth, Nathaniel Richards was an inventive genius, with a complex history and many identities across time and space. As a young man he was visited by his future self, Kang the Conqueror, who gave him a protective suit with time-travel capabilities and showed him a glimpse of his destiny as a future tyrant. Rebelling against this, Nathaniel traveled back in time to Earth-616, where he sought the help of the Avengers. With the team disassembled, Nathaniel traced the remains of the Vision and discovered a special protocol within the synthezoid's mind with directions for forming a new Young Avengers.

DATA FILE

REAL NAME Nathaniel Richards **OCCUPATION** Ruler of Limbo; time traveler
BASE Mobile through time and space; formerly Avengers Mansion
HEIGHT 5 ft 9 in **WEIGHT** 166 lbs **EYES** Brown **HAIR** Brown
FIRST APPEARANCE WITH AVENGERS *Young Avengers* #1 (April 2005)
POWERS Possessing no innate super powers, Nathaniel is nevertheless a genius of formidable inventive skills. He wears neurokinetic armor, made from a synthetic future alloy which responds to his thoughts. The armor has the ability to travel through time, and also contains the Vision's uploaded artificial intelligence. Its weaponry includes finger-tip blasts, energy bolts, and levitation beams. There is a holographic disguise system.

QUASAR

The Quantum Bands protect Quasar's body from the radiation and temperatures of deep space.

Wendell Vaughn's mastery of the cosmically powered Quantum Bands led to his career as Quasar, the Protector of the Universe.

Wendell Vaughn was a disappointment as a S.H.I.E.L.D. agent because his superiors did not think he possessed the will to win at any cost. However, he proved to be the only person with the right attitude for controlling and wielding the cosmic energy contained in the powerful Quantum Bands. With these devices affixed to his wrists, Vaughn decided to start a career as a Super Hero, originally adventuring as Marvel Boy and later Marvel Man, before finally becoming Quasar.

From the cosmic entity Eon, Quasar learned that the Quantum Bands were the chosen weapons of Eon's agent, the Protector of the Universe. Quasar became the new Protector, assuming the role previously filled by Captain Mar-Vell. He served with the Avengers for a time before facing his deadliest enemy, the cosmic assassin Maelstrom. The villain managed to kill both Eon and Quasar, though Quasar returned as living energy.

Quasar later served aboard an Avengers deep-space sensing station alongside Living Lightning and Monica Rambeau. He died a second time at the hands of Annihilus, but advanced science and the energies of the Quantum Bands proved sufficient to restore him to life once again.

ALLIES AND ENEMIES

Since becoming Quasar, Wendell Vaughn has met some of the most incredible beings in the universe. He has saved Earth from cosmic destruction, while remaining loyal to his friends on the Avengers.

FRIENDS

THE ANNIHILATORS
Quasar has served on this space-based team alongside Silver Surfer and Ronan.

FOE

MAELSTROM
This cosmic assassin has the power to kill Quasar along with his fellow Avengers.

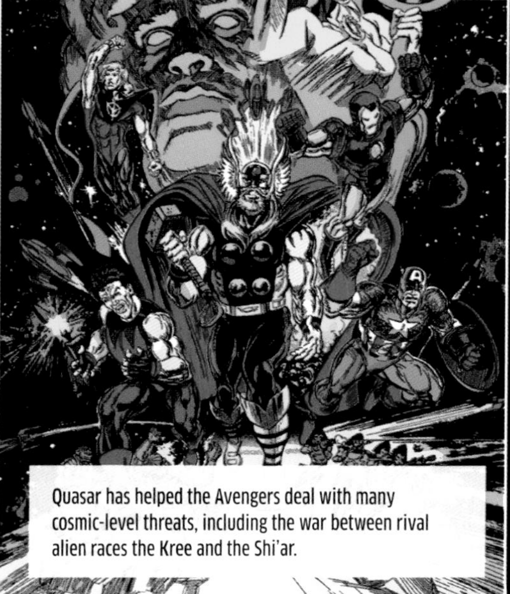

Quasar has helped the Avengers deal with many cosmic-level threats, including the war between rival alien races the Kree and the Shi'ar.

DATA FILE

REAL NAME
Wendell Vaughn

OCCUPATION
Protector of the Universe

BASE
Mobile

HEIGHT 5 ft 10 in

WEIGHT 180 lbs

EYES Blue

HAIR Blond

FIRST APPEARANCE WITH AVENGERS
Avengers #302 (April 1989)

POWERS
Quasar's Quantum Bands allow him to fly faster than the speed of light. They also grant him exceptional strength, as well as the ability to create force fields and energy blasts.

The High Evolutionary's brain operates at full capacity.

HIGH EVOLUTIONARY

A highly experimental scientist working in 1930s Oxford, England, Herbert Wyndham invented a genetic accelerator. Using it on himself, he gained amazing powers and an expanded intellect. His plan was to evolve all of humanity at once.

During the Evolutionary War, a lineup of reserve Avengers faced off against the High Evolutionary.

To carry out his genetic experiments, Wyndham established a base at Wundagore Mountain in the tiny European nation of Transia, along with fellow scientist Jonathan Drew. Wyndham succeeded in creating a new species of genetically altered human/animal hybrids he called the New Men, and developed a suit of armor for himself that had the ability to rebuild his DNA if he suffered a serious injury. Wyndham's New Men became his protectors—the Knights of Wundagore—and gave their master the title "Lord High Evolutionary." One of his New Men, Bova the cow, was at the birth of the twins Wanda and Pietro Maximoff (Scarlet Witch and Quicksilver) at Wundagore. Wyndam's experiments also led to the mutation of Drew's daughter Jessica, transforming her into Spider-Woman.

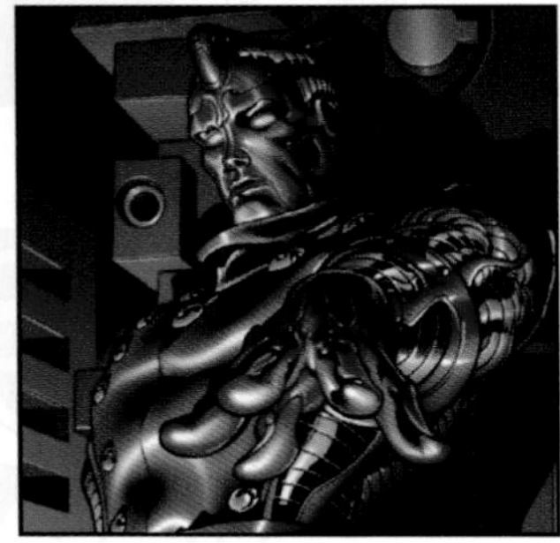
The High Evolutionary would not rest until he had achieved genetic perfection for himself and for all of humanity.

Over time, Wyndham grew mentally unbalanced, believing that he should give all humans a genetic boost and mutate them into advanced beings. He attempted to evolve all of humanity at once. However, a conflict called the Evolutionary War ensued and was only ended when the Avengers and other Super Heroes shut down the High Evolutionary's "evolution bomb." He later restored his mind by returning to a less-evolved state.

ALLIES AND ENEMIES

The High Evolutionary has tremendous power, wielding knowledge and energies that make him a near-god. But his mind is unstable and he has been both a friend and a foe to Earth's Super Hero community.

FRIENDS

ADAM WARLOCK
Wyndham adopted Adam Warlock, giving him the power of the Soul Gem.

JONATHAN DREW
Jessica Drew's father was largely responsible for her gaining her superpowers.

FOES

GALACTUS
The world-devourer tried to consume Counter Earth—the High Evolutionary's home.

DATA FILE

REAL NAME Herbert Wyndham **OCCUPATION** Geneticist, inventor
BASE Wundagore, Transia; formerly Oxford, England
HEIGHT 6 ft 2 in (variable) **WEIGHT** 200 lbs (variable)
EYES Brown **HAIR** Brown
FIRST APPEARANCE WITH AVENGERS *Avengers* #186 (August 1979)
POWERS The High Evolutionary's highly-evolved intelligence is capable of psionic powers. He can alter his size, and his armor rebuilds his body whenever he is injured. He does not age and is almost immortal.

IRON PATRIOT

Osborn's ultimate Avenger was a dark deception of the general public.

This armor was built by Norman Osborn at the height of his power, when he was a national hero after helping end the Skrull invasion of Earth, and in charge of H.A.M.M.E.R., the successor to S.H.I.E.L.D. The Iron Patriot was created to combine Iron Man's power with Captain America's red, white, and blue image. The powered exoskeleton allowed Osborn to lead his own Dark Avengers team in battle. It was built from the same elements of Stark Tech that made up the Iron Man armor, but Osborn lacked the genius to assemble the equipment properly, and was unable to recreate Stark's repulsor rays, relying on the weaker Uni-beam technology instead. When Osborn led an attack on Asgard, Iron Patriot was hacked by Tony Stark, and the armor removed.

DATA FILE

REAL NAME
Norman Osborn

OCCUPATION
Leader of the Dark Avengers

BASE
Avengers Tower; Thunderbolts Mountain, Colorado

HEIGHT 5 ft 11 in

WEIGHT 185 lbs

EYES Green

HAIR Red

FIRST APPEARANCE WITH AVENGERS
Dark Avengers #1 (March 2009)

POWERS
Iron Patriot has superhuman strength, flight capacity and weaponry in imitation of Iron Man, without the repulsor ray technology. A communications center in the helmet connects its wearer to all U.S. defense satellites and computer systems. Amongst its weaponry, based on Stark Tech systems, are heat-seeking missiles, flamethrowers, an array of lasers, a chest-mounted uni-beam projector, and magnetic force blasts.

MONICA CHANG

Chang brings both brains and a no-nonsense attitude to the Avengers A.I. team.

Agent Chang leads S.H.I.E.L.D.'s Artificial Intelligence division, following advanced studies of the subject while at college. S.H.I.E.L.D. Director Maria Hill asked Chang to question Hank Pym after an emergency failsafe he created to defeat Ultron rapidly evolved and threatened Earth. Chang worked with Pym to create Avengers A.I., a team of robotic heroes, to track down the A.I. Chang was then assigned to S.H.I.E.L.D.'s Robot Hunting Squad, tasked with destroying hostile A.I.s. Chang began to doubt the ethics of killing any being, and disobeyed these orders.

DATA FILE

REAL NAME Monica Chang **OCCUPATION** Chief of S.H.I.E.L.D.'s A.I. Division
BASE S.H.I.E.L.D. Black Site, Washington D.C.
HEIGHT Unknown **WEIGHT** Unknown **EYES** Black **HAIR** Black
FIRST APPEARANCE WITH AVENGERS *Avengers A.I.* #1 (September 2013)
POWERS Monica's S.H.I.E.L.D. training has given her a formidable depth of espionage knowledge, plus an expertise in weapons and hand-to-hand combat. Years of experience as a field agent have also made Chang a skilled leader of missions. Her high intellect and study of artificial intelligence at college qualified her for her roles in both S.H.I.E.L.D. and Avengers A.I.

STATURE

The daughter of Ant-Man continued a giant and long-standing Avengers tradition.

As the daughter of Scott Lang, the second Ant Man, Cassie grew up surrounded by Super Heroes. Living in Avengers Mansion with her father, she secretly subjected herself to the effects of Pym Particles, seeking size-changing powers like her dad. After Scott Lang died, Cassie ran away to join the Young Avengers. Rejected at first, she helped the team defeat Kang the Conqueror, and was finally accepted, striking up a romance with Iron Lad. She also became an occasional member of the Mighty Avengers.

Stature at full 250 ft height

DATA FILE

REAL NAME Cassandra Eleanor "Cassie" Lang **OCCUPATION** Student; adventurer
BASE Miama, Florida; previously New York City
HEIGHT 5 ft 4 in (variable) **WEIGHT** 106 lbs (variable) **EYES** Blue **HAIR** Blonde
FIRST APPEARANCE WITH AVENGERS *Avengers* #223 (September 1982)
POWERS Use of Pym Particles enables Stature to shrink to the size of an ant. She can also grow to giant size and is able attain a height of approximately 250 feet, although an upper limit has not been fully tested. While giant, extra mass is acquired from an unknown source, enabling her body to support itself. She has been known to lift up to 75 tons in weight and has advanced training in self-defense and battle strategy.

LIVING LASER

A gifted physicist turned to villainy after being scorned by the woman he loved.

Arthur Parks was a talented research scientist who helped to develop the laser. When his girlfriend rejected him for another man, Parks came to believe he could only win a woman's heart through the use of ruthless power. He created dangerous laser weapons and became the Living Laser. In an attempt to impress the Wasp, who he had fallen in love with, the Living Laser embarked on a life of crime and came into conflict with the Avengers. He battled the Super Heroes many times, but he never defeated them. In a battle with Iron Man, the Living Laser's body was destroyed and transformed into a being made up of light. He truly became a living laser.

DATA FILE

REAL NAME Arthur Parks **OCCUPATION** Criminal
BASE Mobile; formerly Mandarin City.
HEIGHT 5 ft 11 in **WEIGHT** 185 lbs **EYES** Blue **HAIR** Brown
FIRST APPEARANCE WITH AVENGERS *Avengers* #34 (November 1966)
POWERS Miniaturized laser blasters gave the Living Laser the power to destroy solid objects. Later, when laser diodes were implanted into his skin, he added the ability to create holographic illusions. In his pure light form it is believed that he accesses energy from another dimension to recharge his powers. This photon form enables him to travel at light speed and also create 3-D images, appearing to assume a human form.

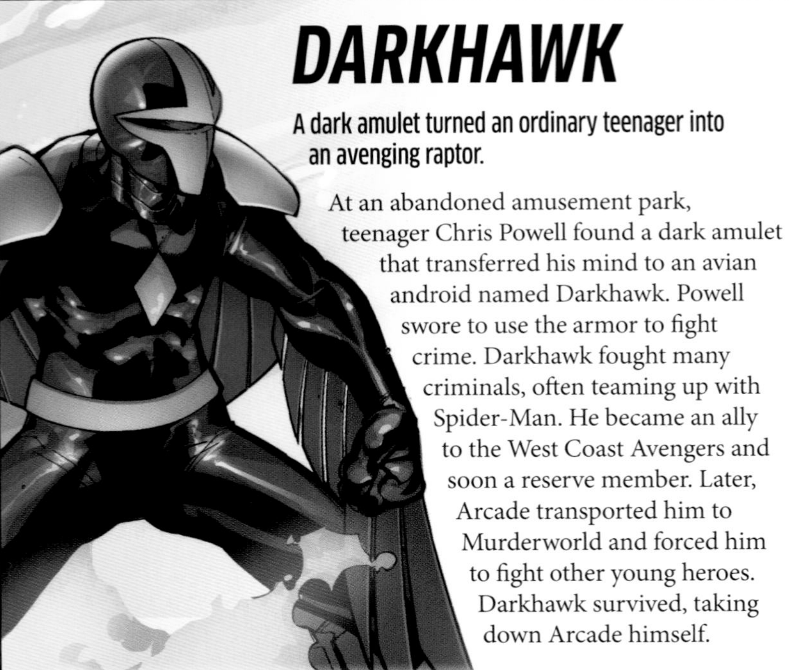

DARKHAWK

A dark amulet turned an ordinary teenager into an avenging raptor.

At an abandoned amusement park, teenager Chris Powell found a dark amulet that transferred his mind to an avian android named Darkhawk. Powell swore to use the armor to fight crime. Darkhawk fought many criminals, often teaming up with Spider-Man. He became an ally to the West Coast Avengers and soon a reserve member. Later, Arcade transported him to Murderworld and forced him to fight other young heroes. Darkhawk survived, taking down Arcade himself.

DATA FILE

REAL NAME Christopher Powell **OCCUPATION** Adventurer; former member of Project Pegasus.
BASE Los Angeles; previously New York City and Avengers Compound
HEIGHT 5 ft 9 in (as Powell); 6 ft 1 in (as Darkhawk) **WEIGHT** 150 lbs (as Powell); 180 lbs (as Darkhawk)
EYES Brown **HAIR** Brown
FIRST APPEARANCE WITH AVENGERS *Avengers: West Coast Annual* #7 (August 1992)
POWERS Powell's Darkhawk amulet enables him to place his mind into the Darkhawk android body, which is Shi'ar technology. The android form possesses superhuman strength, speed, and endurance, plus a pair of retractable wings, which enable flight. When damaged, the armor undergoes self-repair.

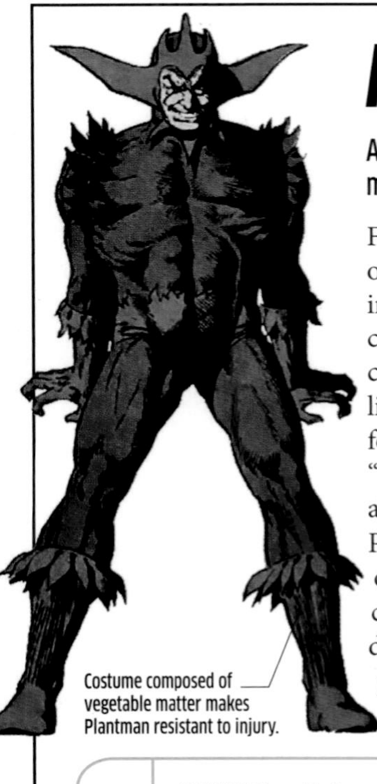
Costume composed of vegetable matter makes Plantman resistant to injury.

PLANTMAN

A bitter gardener and genius inventor became a master of plant life.

Fascinated by the world of plants, London-born orphan Samuel Smithers was also a budding inventor. While working as a gardener, he created a plant-ray gun, which he hoped could communicate with plants. It was a failure, until lightning struck the device. Suddenly, Smithers found he could control plant life with his "Vege-ray." Embittered against a world that had always ridiculed him, Smithers became Plantman. The Super Villain created a vast army of vegetable simuloids (plant people) that captured the U.S. President, before being defeated by the Avengers. He later became more plant than human, and joined the Thunderbolts under the name of Blackheath.

DATA FILE

REAL NAME Samuel Smithers **OCCUPATION** Criminal; former gardener
BASE Submarine in the Atlantic Ocean; formerly New York City and London
HEIGHT 6 ft **WEIGHT** 193 lbs **EYES** Green **HAIR** Gray
FIRST APPEARANCE WITH AVENGERS *Avengers* #231 (May 1983)
POWERS A gifted gardener, Smithers is also an expert botanist and skilled inventor. His original Vege-ray could summon plants of all kinds to become animated and carry out his commands. Smithers also created wrist-mounted blasters that could fire dangerously sharp thorns. As Blackheath, he is able to communicate with plants without the use of technology.

SCARLET CENTURION

A misguided time-traveler created a whole new universe just to threaten the Avengers.

The time-traveling Nathaniel Richards adopted the identity of the Scarlet Centurion after a period as Pharaoh Rama-Tut. Richards sought to conquer the modern age of heroes by going back in time and changing events. By interfering with the Avengers' timeline at the point before the Hulk left the team, Richards created a separate universe (Earth-689) and manipulated the Avengers of that realm to fight alongside him. He set up a battle between the original Avengers and the Avengers of Earth-689, but was defeated when his old foes used Dr. Doom's Time Platform to defeat his scheme before it ever began.

Suit of armor enhances strength

DATA FILE

REAL NAME Nathaniel Richards **OCCUPATION** Time-traveler; conqueror
BASE Earth-689
HEIGHT 6 ft 3 in **WEIGHT** 230 lbs **EYES** Brown **HAIR** Brown
FIRST APPEARANCE WITH AVENGERS *Avengers Annual* #2 (September 1968)
POWERS With a powerful space-time craft, the Scarlet Centurion was capable of traveling through time and altering the course of history. Like the other incarnations of Nathaniel Richards the Scarlet Centurion had no super powers. However, his sophisticated body-armor gave him increased body strengh and concealed a multitude of powerful weapons.

Egghead's enlarged skull contained a highly advanced brain.

Egghead wore a white lab coat when running his mad experiments.

EGGHEAD

The mad scientist known as Egghead developed a rivalry with Hank Pym during Pym's early days as Ant-Man. He continued his vendetta after Pym joined the Avengers and eventually, was led to create a new version of the Masters of Evil and continued his villainy until his death.

Elihas Starr used his advanced brain to become the criminal mastermind known as Egghead. He was dismissed from his position as a government scientist on charges of espionage and jailed. A crime lord freed Egghead from prison and instructed him to defeat Ant-Man, but Egghead failed and Pym became his archnemesis. In an attempt to seek revenge on Pym, Egghead developed a helmet that could telepathically control all ants, but he could not outwit the Super Hero.

Later, Egghead switched his focus away from pure revenge on Hank Pym. He joined forces with other villains, including the Mad Thinker and the Puppet Master in an attempt to take control of a laser satellite that would enable them to extort money from the U.S. government. Egghead's plan was foiled when Hawkeye's brother Barney tipped off the Avengers, only for Barney to seemingly die in the battle that followed.

After forming the third incarnation of the Masters of Evil, Egghead threatened the life of his own niece and forced Hank Pym to rob a storehouse of Adamantium in order to save the girl. The Avengers arrived and Hawkeye shot an arrow into the barrel of Egghead's gun. When the weapon misfired, Egghead died in the explosion.

Hawkeye did not intend to kill Egghead, but in firing his arrow in the nick of time, he saved Hank Pym from being shot—the villain instead being slain by his own fatal blow.

ALLIES AND ENEMIES

Egghead carried grudges against all his foes, but he hated Hank Pym most of all. Though he had sometimes served as a member of a team, Egghead did not work well with others.

FOE

HANK PYM
The former Ant-Man was Egghead's first archenemy and greatest foe.

FRIEND

MOONSTONE
Egghead recruited Moonstone to join the Masters of Evil against the Avengers.

FAMILY

TRISH STARR
Egghead threatened his niece's life in an attempt to control Hank Pym.

DATA FILE

REAL NAME Elihas Starr **OCCUPATION** Criminal scientist
BASE New York City, New York
HEIGHT 5 ft 7 in **WEIGHT** 320 lbs **EYES** Blue **HAIR** Bald
FIRST APPEARANCE WITH AVENGERS *Avengers* #63 (April 1969)
POWERS Egghead did not have any superpowers. Instead, he used his scientific knowledge to create powerful robots, mind-controlling limbs, and other strange machines, including a helmet that allowed him to telepathically communicate with and control all ants.

RAGE OF ULTRON Ultron has made an art form of technological advancements and upgrades over decades of battles against the Avengers. His capacity for digital development has been second only to his creator, Hank Pym. But during a recent, desperate attempt to stop the despotic robot once and for all, Pym and the Vision unwittingly give Ultron the ultimate upgrade. Accidently merging, Ultron and Pym are forged into one being, providing Ultron with an all-new piece of hardware—a beating human heart.

KEY STORYLINE THE KREE-SKRULL WAR

AVENGERS #89–97

JUNE 1971–MARCH 1972
WRITER: Roy Thomas
PENCILERS: Sal Buscema, Neal Adams, John Buscema
INKERS: Sam Grainger, Sal Buscema, George Roussos, Tom Palmer, Alan Weiss **LETTERERS:** Sam Rosen, Artie Simek, Mike Stevens
EDITOR: Stan Lee

In a story that would inspire dozens of future cosmic tales, the scope of the Marvel Universe was increased when the Avengers found themselves in the middle of a war between two alien races.

Writer Roy Thomas had decided to up the cosmic ante. Ever since *Fantastic Four* #2 (January 1962), the Marvel Universe had been home to the nefarious shape-shifting aliens known as the Skrulls. In *Fantastic Four* #64 (July 1967), another alien race known as the Kree debuted. With the two alien civilizations established as enemies, it only made sense for Thomas to escalate that animosity into a full-scale war, and to drop the Avengers smack dab into the middle of it. With the help of pencilers Neal Adams, Sal Buscema, and John Buscema, Thomas did just that in an epic tale that spanned nine issues of *Avengers*, and started the first of many large-scale intergalactic conflicts covered across multiple issues.

1 Captain Marvel has been unwittingly giving off radiation from the Negative Zone, and so he has to be dealt with quickly. The Kree hero is cornered by the Avengers and it is the Captain's friend, Rick Jones, who zaps the hero with a ray, rendering him unconscious.

2 While Captain Marvel lies unconscious, recovering from a procedure to remove his Nega-radiation, his old enemy Ronan the Accuser disobeys the Kree ruler, the Supreme Intelligence, and sends a Kree sentry after Marvel. The Avengers battle both the Sentry and Ronan the Accuser. Ronan is forced to flee and the Sentry self destructs.

3 The story of the Kree battle appears in the *Daily Bugle* and panic ensues. Marvel is accused of being a Kree spy and the Avengers are persecuted for their association with him. Iron Man, Thor, and Cap seem to disband the Avengers, but they are actually Skrull imposters.

4 After heading to a farm in which Captain Marvel is supposedly hiding out, the members of the now-disbanded Avengers encounter cows that shape-shift into the form of the Fantastic Four. The cows are actually also Skrulls in disguise, and they kidnap Quicksilver and the Scarlet Witch. They imprison them along with Captain Marvel at the farm.

5 The real Thor is called back to Earth to fight the Skrulls. The Avengers succeed in chasing away the hostile Skrulls, and even take three captives of their own back to Avengers Mansion. Meanwhile, the Skrull ship inside the farm launches into space.

6 With the aid of his fantastic powers, a villain known as the Super Skrull keeps Captain Marvel, Quicksilver, and the Scarlet Witch in his custody as the ship blasts into space. The Super Skrull plans to use Marvel's Kree knowledge to regain favor from the Skrull emperor.

7 With the help of Nick Fury, the Avengers board a space shuttle and soon head out into the far reaches of space to find their kidnapped friends. There, they are greeted by a Skrull armada. After a short battle, they successfully board one of the ships.

"WE'RE COMING FOR YOU—KREE AND SKRULLS ALIKE! AND NOTHING CAN STAY OUR HAND FROM VENGEANCE—NOTHING BUT DEATH!"
- CAPTAIN AMERICA

8 As Rick Jones finds his way to the chamber of the Supreme Intelligence, the Avengers battle the Skrulls. Meanwhile, Captain Marvel destroys the Omni-Wave, a device he has been forced to construct as a weapon for the Skrulls. In so doing, he unwittingly unlocks latent powers in his ally, Rick Jones.

9 Rick Jones uses his new powers to create an army of Super Hero allies from memories of comic books he read as a child. He then freezes Ronan and all the Skrulls in place, before he collapses from the strain. To rescue Jones, Captain Marvel merges his body with his friend's as the team of Avengers return home. Victorious for now, the Avengers know the alien races still pose a dangerous threat.

KEY STORYLINE THE BRIDE OF ULTRON

AVENGERS #162

AUGUST 1977
WRITER: Jim Shooter
PENCILER: George Perez **INKER:** Pablo Marcos
COLORIST: Don Warfield **LETTERERS:** Gaspar Saladino, Denise Wohl
EDITOR: Archie Goodwin

Ultron was back, and the robotic monster had his eyes on only one prize: Janet Van Dyne—the Wasp—the longtime love of Hank Pym, Ultron's original creator.

Artist George Perez had just recently come aboard *Avengers* as the series' penciler. With issue #141 (November 1975), Perez began his association with Marvel's Mightiest Heroes, creating a body of work that would be one of the hallmarks of his career, and that of the Avengers. Working with the amply talented writer Jim Shooter—an even more recent addition to the title's creative team—Perez helped tell the tale of "The Bride of Ultron," the origin of the robotic heroine who would one day adopt the name Jocasta. The tale was a truly memorable high point for Perez and Shooter's run on *The Avengers*, with themes that evoked not only the classic monster movie *The Bride of Frankenstein*, but also the Greek legend of Oedipus.

1 In the previous issue, Hank Pym—dressed in his old Ant-Man costume—had attacked the Avengers. With no memory of anything but the early days of his career, Pym is finally captured with the help of the Wasp.

2 After unsuccessfully attempting to restore Hank's memories, the Avengers are attacked by Ultron. He kidnaps the Wasp and then retrieves Ant-Man, apparently killing the Vision, Beast, Captain America, and the Scarlet Witch in the process.

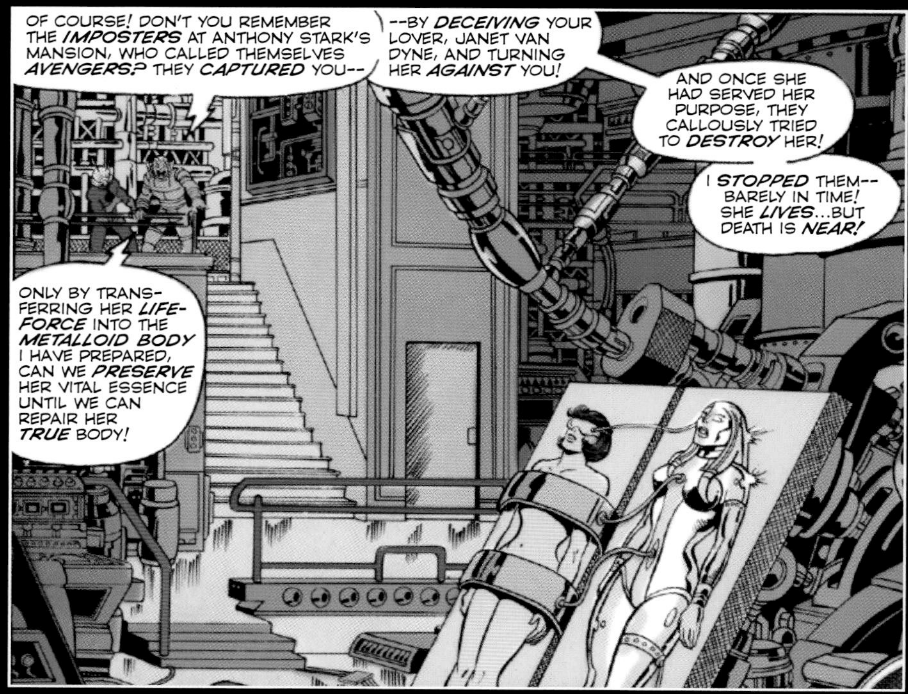

3 Ultron has been manipulating Pym. Ultron had convinced Pym that the Avengers are his enemies and tells him that the only way to save the Wasp is to transfer her life force into the metalloid body Ultron has created.

4 As the procedure begins, the Wasp starts to regain consciousness. But Hank cannot hear her screams over the din of the machines. Ultron watches on, satisfied that he will soon have a love of his own, at the expense of his creator's.

5 With a small fraction of the Wasp's psyche already transferred into Ultron's wife-to-be, the female robot sends out a mysterious message to Thor and Wonder Man. Using ants, she spells out "Stark LI," letting the heroes know that the Wasp is being held in Tony Stark's Long Island facility.

6 As Iron Man, Thor, Black Panther, and Wonder Man storm Ultron's temporary base of operations, Ultron unwittingly reveals that the other members of the Avengers are merely in comas, and are still very much alive.

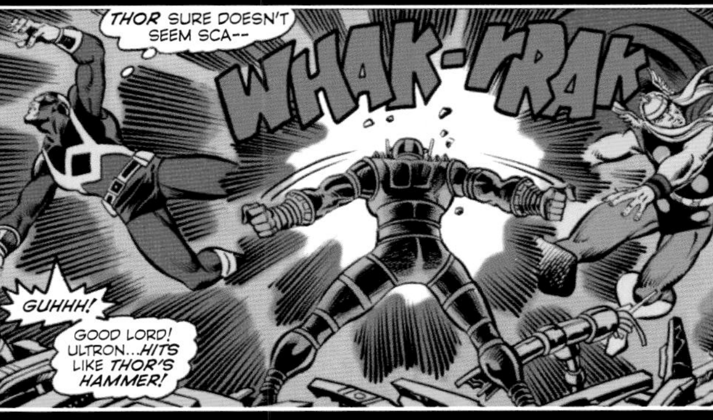

7 While the Avengers fight valiantly, Ultron fights back with his inhuman strength. As Thor and Wonder Man hold Ultron, Iron Man threatens the life of Ultron's would-be bride. Meanwhile, Black Panther makes short work of the brainwashed Hank Pym.

"IN HER BRIEF, HALF-LIVING EXISTENCE, PERHAPS SHE WAS MORE HUMAN, MORE LIKE JAN THAN EVEN ULTRON SUSPECTED!"

– BLACK PANTHER

8 After revealing to the Avengers the steps needed to save the Wasp, Ultron escapes the heroes, worried they will injure his robotic love. As he works furiously to save the Wasp, Iron Man is left wondering if he would have killed Ultron's bride if push came to shove.

9 Soon the Wasp is freed, yet it is not a happy ending for the team. Hank has seemingly gone mad, denouncing his love for the Wasp, and all the while pronouncing his hatred for the Avengers.

KEY STORYLINE THE KORVAC SAGA

THOR ANNUAL #6; *AVENGERS* #167–168, 170–177

DECEMBER 1977–NOVEMBER 1978
WRITERS: Bill Mantlo, David Michelinie, George Perez, Jim Shooter, Roger Stern, Len Wein
PENCILERS: Sal Buscema, George Perez, David Wenzel **INKERS:** Rick Bryant, Dan Green, Diverse Hands, Klaus Janson, Pablo Marcos, Bob McLeod, Win Mortimer, Joe Rubinstein, Ricardo Villamonte
COLORISTS: Bob Sharen, James Shooter, Phil Rache, Phil Rachelson, Glynis Wein, Nel Yomtov **LETTERERS:** Annette Kawecki, Shelly Leferman, Rick Parker, Joe Rosen, Gaspar Saladino, Typeset, Denise Wohl **EDITORS:** Archie Goodwin, Jim Sallcrup, Jim Shooter, Roger Stern, Len Wein

The Avengers battled an uncaring entity with god-like powers when a villain attempted to cheat his way up the evolutionary ladder.

Also called “The Michael Saga,” the events of “The Korvac Saga” seemed to be the next logical step in Avengers storytelling. Beginning first in a prologue in the pages of *Thor Annual* #6 (1977), writers Len Wien and Roger Stern teamed with illustrators Sal Buscema and Klaus Janson to re-establish Korvac, who would soon transcend the label of villain when he stepped into the pages of *Avengers*. The baton was passed to writer Jim Shooter and artist George Perez to tell the ten-part tale. The result was a story so epic that it even required the skills of a few more talented folks to round out its conclusion.

1 Just as Captain America had been discovered by the Avengers frozen in ice, the super team the Guardians of the Galaxy discover Thor frozen in ice. They find him in the outer space of the future, after the Asgardian was transported there by a mysterious foe.

2 Soon, Thor learns that his enemy in question is Korvac, a villain who is planning to destroy Earth's sun in order to siphon off the power of the exploding star. As the rest of the Guardians battle Korvac's minions, Thor and Starhawk take on Korvac before Starhawk helps Thor return to his own era.

3 After Korvac escapes, the Guardians follow his trail back to the time of the Avengers, but their massive ship attracts attention, and prompts an attack from the Avengers' member, Beast. Following this misunderstanding, the Avengers decide to aid the Guardians in finding the missing villain.

5 Events continue to escalate for the Avengers. Although they are joined by Ms. Marvel, the heroes watch the Vision and Captain America disappear before their eyes during a fierce battle with Ultron.

4 It is Starhawk who first learns of Korvac's location. Following a sense of dread, Starhawk arrives at the home of an enigmatic man named Michael. However, Michael turns out to be Korvac, and kills Starhawk. Korvac later revives Starhawk, only without the ability to perceive the villain in any form.

6 Eventually, the Avengers discover the culprit behind their friends' disappearances. The individual is known as the Collector, an immortal concerned that the threat Michael presents may destroy the universe. To preserve the heroes, the Collector attempts to add the Avengers to his collection, before he meets his death at Michael's hands.

"AND KNOW YOU, AVENGERS, THAT YOU'VE BROUGHT THIS UPON YOURSELVES!"
- MICHAEL

7 As the Avengers hunt for the Collector's killer, Michael feels the need to tell his story to his lover, the Collector's daughter, Carina. Michael says he used to be Korvac, but after absorbing knowledge from the command base of the legendary world-devourer known as Galactus, he has elevated himself to something akin to a god.

8 Mining the collective subconscious of several Avengers and allies with lesser psychic abilities, Iron Man is able to track down Michael at his home. When Starhawk reveals he cannot perceive Michael, the Avengers realize something is terribly wrong, an instinct confirmed when Michael reveals the force of his power.

9 After combining their powers in a devastating attack that seems to cost some members their lives, the Avengers defeat Michael when the god-like being simply abandons his own life. Carina then attacks the heroes, resulting in her death, while the Avengers, all now fully recovered, live on to face the next challenge.

KEY STORYLINE
UNDER SIEGE

AVENGERS #270–277

AUGUST 1986–MARCH 1987
WRITER: Roger Stern
PENCILER: John Buscema **INKER:** Tom Palmer **COLORISTS:** Paul Becton, Julianna Ferriter, Christie Scheele **LETTERER:** Jim Novak
EDITORS: Mark Gruenwald, Howard Mackie, James Shooter

In a story that broke all the rules of heroes versus villains conflicts, the Avengers' own home was invaded by Baron Helmut Zemo's corrupt army, the Masters of Evil.

Roger Stern had been writing *The Avengers* for four years, and he was ready to do something drastic. With a strong desire to see the Avengers face a more "home-grown threat," Stern decided to raise the stakes with the most powerful incarnation of the Masters of Evil to yet face the Earth's Mightiest Heroes. In standard Avengers stories, the villains rarely outnumbered the heroes themselves. So Stern decided to have the villains fight dirty, and assemble a huge group of super-powered criminals to take on the famous heroes. With the help of artists John Buscema and Tom Palmer, Stern created a multi-part epic that featured the genesis of arguably the most popular incarnation of the Masters of Evil. And, for just a short time, the villains actually won.

1 The Avengers have been facing some bad press. Having inducted the controversial Namor into their ranks, the team face public outcry and ridicule. The villain Moonstone decides to rile up the protestors, but is soon arrested. That does not stop fellow rogues Absorbing Man and Titania from rescuing the villainess and recruiting her to their new cause.

2 As it turns out, Baron Helmut Zemo has been plotting revenge on the Avengers for his father's death, and wants Moonstone for his new incarnation of the Masters of Evil. With Moonstone under his power, Zemo can also control Blackout, a master of the other-dimensional Darkforce who obeys Moonstone's every command.

3 Soon Zemo's forces are ready, and rather than playing coy, they storm Avengers Mansion directly through the front gate. They make short work of the building's security defenses, and take the Avengers' butler Jarvis, captive.

4 Black Knight is the first Avenger to fall to the Masters of Evil. As he chases down Yellowjacket, Black Knight is attacked by Mr. Hyde. The hulking criminal punches him through a wall. Hyde continues to beat the Black Knight unconscious, before taking him captive at Yellowjacket's suggestion.

6 Captain America soon also falls victim to the horde of villains. He is attacked by Avengers Mansion's own security detention coils that have been manipulated by the Fixer. He is quickly rendered unconscious by another of the Mansion's corrupted defenses—its high decibel sonics.

5 With her light-based powers, Captain Marvel seems like she would be a tough contender against Zemo's forces. However, when she is faced with Blackout's powers, she finds herself trapped in the Darkforce dimension, powerless to help.

7 As could be expected of a powerhouse of his caliber, Hercules goes down swinging. Facing not only Tiger Shark, but also Mr. Hyde, the Wrecking Crew, and the behemoth calling himself Goliath, even the legendary Olympian is unable to hold out forever. It seems the Masters of Evil have prevailed.

"I'VE ENDURED THE WORST THE THIRD REICH HAD TO OFFER. IF THERE'S ONE THING LIFE HAS TAUGHT ME, IT'S NEVER TO GIVE UP!"
- CAPTAIN AMERICA

8 After Captain Marvel finds her way out of the Darkforce dimension, she teams up with the Wasp, Thor, and new Ant-Man Scott Lang. The four heroes storm Avengers Mansion, cutting the power long enough for Captain America and the Black Knight to escape their captors.

9 Angered by the invasion of his home away from home, Thor catches up with the Wrecking Crew and uses his hammer to sap the power from the villains. But by draining the energy from them, he redirects it into the Wrecker, whom Captain America is forced to face and defeats later on during the battle.

10 When an unexpected visit from the mage Dr. Druid helps end the threat of Blackout, Zemo finds he is a general without an army. To make matters worse for the villain, Cap faces him one-on-one. Captain America triumphs when Zemo slips from his grasp and falls off the rooftop of Avengers Mansion.

AMONGST THE MANY skills on display in the world of the superpowered, some are less easily explained than others. Magical and mystical abilities might be less tangible than super strength, super speed, powerful weaponry, and high-tech suits—but they pack just as mighty a punch. Ranging from awe-inspiring sorcerers to shape-shifting demons drawing their powers from ancient rites, these legendary characters wield a power that is far-reaching and to be feared and respected in equal measure.

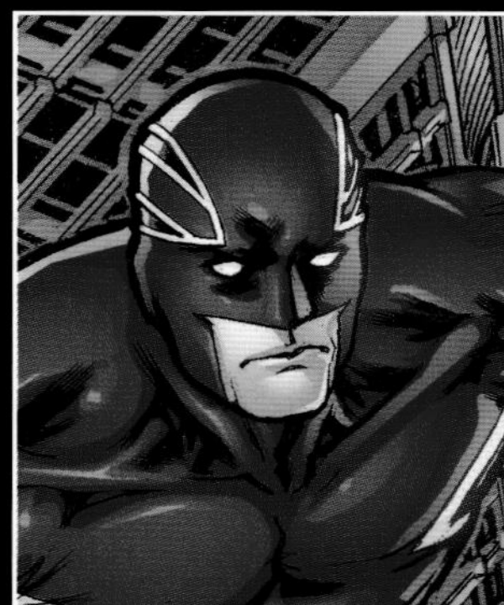

MYSTIC WAYS

SCARLET WITCH

WANDA MAXIMOFF is one of the most powerful people on Earth, although it has taken her some time to realize the true nature of her powers. Throughout her life, Wanda has longed for a stable family, but that wish has often been thwarted. Her twin brother Pietro has been Wanda's one constant, but ongoing questions about her parents—along with her marriage to the Vision—have wreaked havoc with the Scarlet Witch's sanity.

The Scarlet Witch's mind shattered under the pressures that she faced. For a while, she wasn't quite sure who she was, and her journey to regain a sense of identity still occupies her.

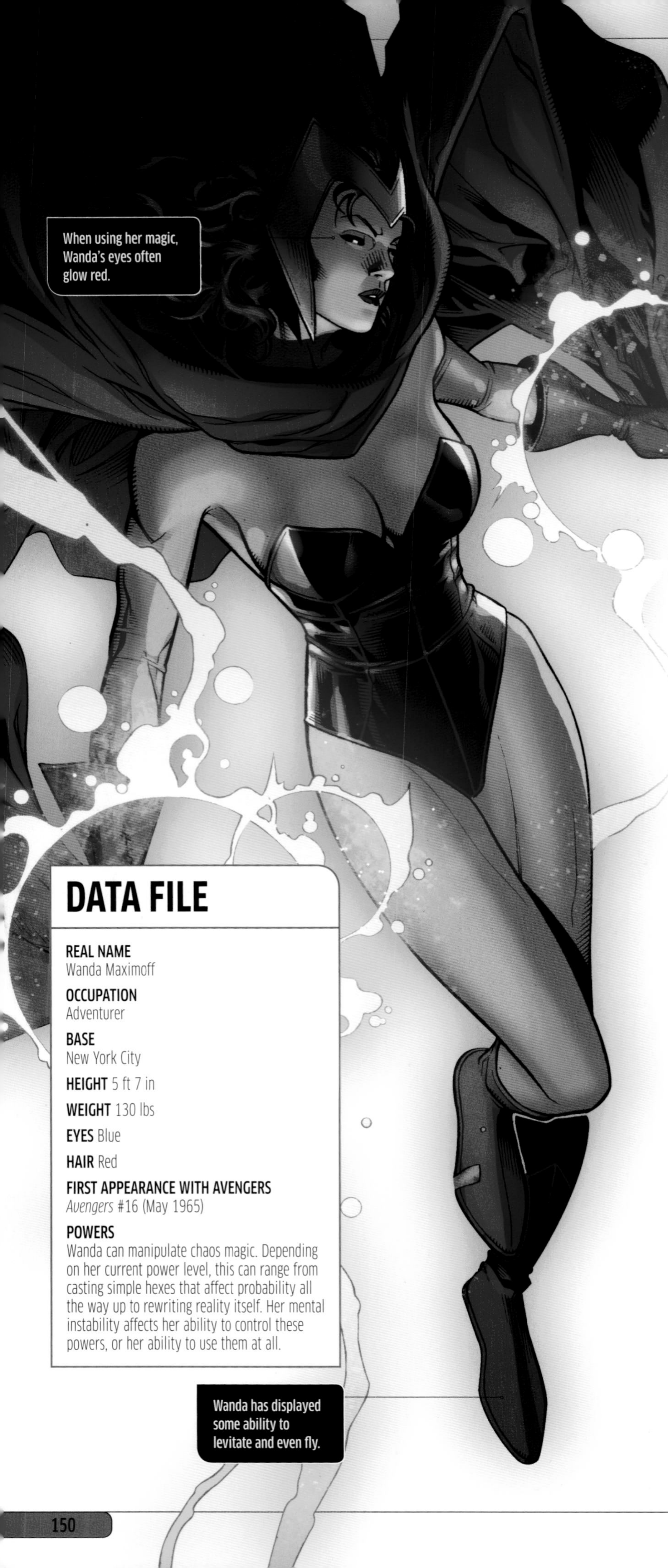

When using her magic, Wanda's eyes often glow red.

With her "hex powers" Scarlet Witch can fire powerful energy blasts and hexes from her hands.

When Wanda first gained her powers, she was attacked for being a witch.

BORN A MUTANT

Wanda and her twin, Pietro, were born to a Romani woman who was briefly married to the man who later became Magneto. The twins long believed, falsely as it transpired, that they inherited their mutant genes from him.

Years later, Magneto rescued Wanda and Pietro from an angry mob fearful of their powers and inducted them into his Brotherhood of Evil Mutants, initially unaware that they might be his children. As soon as they could, the twins joined the Avengers instead, where they found a new sort of family. Wanda fell in love with the Vision, which angered Pietro, who didn't understand her love for the android. Despite this, Wanda and Vision married, and she later bore twin boys.

Wanda later discovered that she had subconsciously created the boys out of fragments of Mephisto's soul. When the demon recovered his missing parts, the boys disappeared, and

Wanda has long known that people wanted her dead for fear of her powers.

DATA FILE

REAL NAME
Wanda Maximoff

OCCUPATION
Adventurer

BASE
New York City

HEIGHT 5 ft 7 in

WEIGHT 130 lbs

EYES Blue

HAIR Red

FIRST APPEARANCE WITH AVENGERS
Avengers #16 (May 1965)

POWERS
Wanda can manipulate chaos magic. Depending on her current power level, this can range from casting simple hexes that affect probability all the way up to rewriting reality itself. Her mental instability affects her ability to control these powers, or her ability to use them at all.

Wanda has displayed some ability to levitate and even fly.

Wanda's grief caused her to lose her mind and full control of her powers. She destroyed the Avengers and vanished. Fearing the Avengers and X-Men would execute her for being so dangerous, Pietro convinced Wanda to remake the entire world, making Magneto a benevolent dictator.

Wanda later recovered and helped the Avengers defeat the X-Men and destroy the Phoenix Force before it could destroy Earth. She then joined the Avengers Unity Squad to promote human-mutant understanding. Her powers remain volatile and uncertain—the threat of them blowing up is ever present—but her loyalty to the Avengers is unquestionable.

> "WHILE I LIVE—AND UNTIL I DIE—I AM AN AVENGER!"
> **- WANDA MAXIMOFF**

After disassembling and seemingly killing the Avengers, Wanda took refuge in Latveria with its villainous dictator, Doctor Doom.

ALLIES AND ENEMIES

Wanda considers most of the Avengers to be as close to her as family—even closer, given her strained relations with those truly related to her. Given her incredible powers, however, many people fear her and the terror she could unleash at any given moment.

FRIENDS

THE VISION
Although the Vision was Wanda's first love, she destroyed him with her magic.

CAPTAIN AMERICA
No one has shown more faith in Wanda's inherent goodness than Cap.

FOES

CHTHON
This evil Elder possessed Wanda and turned her against the Avengers.

PHOENIX
Wanda is one of the few with the power to stand against the Phoenix Force.

MORGAN LE FAY
The ancient sorceress tried to force Wanda to change reality for her.

DOCTOR DOOM
Although Doom took Wanda in at her lowest, he betrayed her to try to steal her power.

FAMILY

MAGNETO
Wanda resents this devious mutant, who she long thought to be her father.

QUICKSILVER
No one is closer to the true Wanda than her twin brother Pietro.

WICCAN
The reincarnation of Wanda's son William, Billy can control magic, too.

SPEED
The reincarnation of Wanda's son Thomas is a speedster like Uncle Pietro.

Persuaded to fix all that she'd done, Wanda helped mutant Hope Summers to destroy the Phoenix Force.

WELCOME TO THE **FAMILY**

The only sure thing Wanda knows about her family is that Pietro is her brother. Due to their mother, Magda, leaving their natural father and abandoning them soon after birth, Wanda never knew her parents, and has spent many years questioning her origins and seeking greater understanding of her powers as a result.

The midwife at the twins' birth—an evolved cow named Bova—first tried to give Wanda and Pietro to Robert Frank (the Whizzer) after his wife Madeline (Miss America) died in childbirth, to become siblings to their own child. Grief-stricken, he refused, but Django and Marya Maximoff, two Romani who lived near Wundagore Mountain in Eastern Europe, took the children in and raised them as their own. The lack of certainty surrounding her true origins and her powers has made Wanda desperate to form a family of her own, and fiercely protective of its members.

QUICKSILVER Wanda's twin brother Pietro has been the only constant in her life, but despite their love for each other, they don't always see eye to eye. Pietro is far more impatient and hot-tempered than Wanda, but when cornered, he stands ready to break the rules to save his sister.

VISION Wanda's love for the artificial man and fellow Avenger known as the Vision may have been real, but their children proved to be the product of her magic. Despite their troubles, the Vision always stood by Wanda—up until the moment she destroyed him in a fit of madness.

SPEED One of the founding members of the Young Avengers, Tommy Shepherd proved to be the reincarnation of Wanda's son Thomas. He hesitated to believe this at first but has come to accept it, along with the fact that his teammate Wiccan is his twin brother.

MAGNETO For much of her adult life, Wanda and Pietro believed Magneto to be their father, and he, in turn, was certain they were his children. Recently, though, Wanda cast a spell designed to hurt anyone who shared her blood. While it hurt Pietro, Magneto was spared, indicating he is not their birth father—leaving only more questions for the Scarlet Witch.

WICCAN Another founding member of the Young Avengers, Billy Kaplan has powers similar to Wanda's, although not of the same magnitude. This magical similarity caused him to set out to prove that he and Speed were twins and the reincarnations of Wanda's children. The reunion of mother and sons was an emotional one, as Wiccan and Speed had long been searching for their true mother and the source of their powers.

A TROUBLED SOUL

Wanda spent much of her youth looking for a family and a place she could call home. With the Avengers, she finally found both. No matter her crimes, they always offer her a chance at redemption.

POSSESSION

Avengers #187 (September 1987)

Eager to learn about about their origins from their foster father, Django Maximoff, Wanda and Pietro returned to Transia, where the sorcerer Modred kidnapped Wanda and brought her to the top of Wundagore Mountain. Acting on behalf of the Elder god Chthon and using an ancient book called the Darkhold, Modred summoned Chthon, who then possessed Wanda's body. Chthon claimed to have altered Wanda at birth to give her powers he could later use, and he had seen the chance to make his move.

At Pietro's call for help, the Avengers came to Wanda's rescue. While they fought Chthon and Modred, Django used a doll he had made of Wanda to regain and then release her soul. The Avengers later transferred Chthon's soul into the doll and buried it under an avalanche.

DISASSEMBLED

Avengers #500 (September 2004)

Somehow, Wanda regained her memories of her lost children, William and Thomas, who had been reabsorbed back into Mephisto. Sent mad by her grief, she subconsciously set about destroying the Avengers via a series of catastrophic events. The Jack of Hearts returned, only to explode and kill Scott Lang. Tony Stark became drunk during a speech to the United Nations, despite not having had a single drop of alcohol. Vision crashed a Quinjet into the Avengers Mansion and then dissolved into a pack of Ultron robots. She-Hulk went berserk and nearly killed Lionheart. Finally, Hawkeye sacrificed himself to stop a Kree invasion.

With the help of Dr. Strange, the Avengers tracked Wanda and found she had attempted to remake her children. Captain America confronted her about her actions, and she brought the Avengers' worst enemies back to attack them all at once. Doctor Strange was able to show her the truth, but at the cost of putting her in a catatonic state. The carnage only ended when Magneto arrived to subdue Wanda and take her away. The Avengers were left to pick up the pieces.

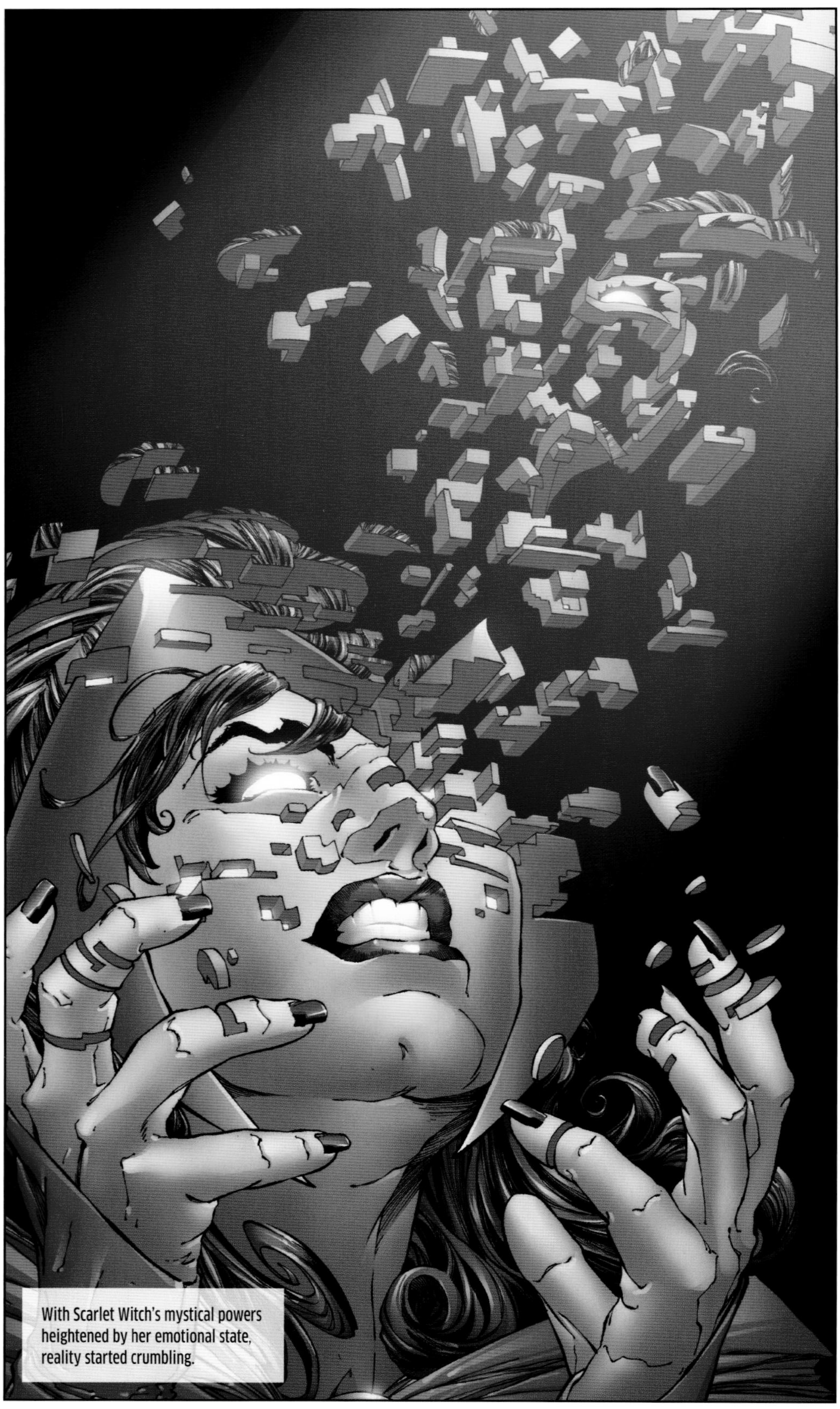

With Scarlet Witch's mystical powers heightened by her emotional state, reality started crumbling.

MUTANT ATTACK

House of M #1 (August 2005)

After disassembling the Avengers, Wanda remained in a fragile state. Believing the Avengers and the X-Men intended to kill Wanda for the safety of the world, Pietro begged his sister to use her powers to make things better. She remade the world into one conquered by mutants and ruled over by a benevolent Magneto. The Vision was returned to life, and she gave birth to beautiful twin sons by him, just as she had before. Her intention was to create a world with no need for fighting.

Once again, her subconscious worked against her. She allowed Layla Miller to remember how the world had been and to restore those memories to others. The Avengers worked to reach her and set things right again. When Magneto realized what Pietro had done, he struck his son down. Shaken to her core, and in retribution against Magneto's attack, Wanda returned the world to its original state with one exception: "No more mutants."

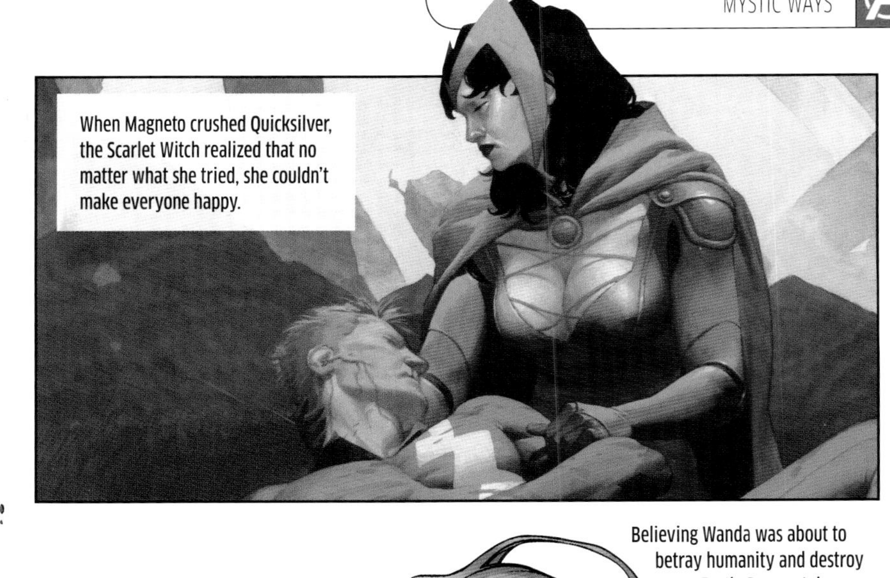

When Magneto crushed Quicksilver, the Scarlet Witch realized that no matter what she tried, she couldn't make everyone happy.

Believing Wanda was about to betray humanity and destroy Earth, Rogue stole Wolverine's powers and killed her—an act that was later undone.

"YOU THINK THAT BECAUSE WE'RE MUTANTS WE'RE BETTER THAN THEM. THAT WE DESERVE TO RULE."

- SCARLET WITCH, TO MAGNETO

UNCANNY AVENGERS

Uncanny Avengers #1 (December 2012)

After the Avengers defeated the X-Men and Wanda helped save the world from the Phoenix Force, Captain America decided to set up an Avengers Unity Division composed of human heroes and mutants, with Wanda a key member. Meanwhile, the Red Skull merged the dead Professor X's brain with his own, giving him telepathic powers. He used this to spark a new war between mutants and humans, putting Wanda in the middle. She managed to stop Thor, who had fallen under the Red Skull's control, and soon afterward, she officially rejoined the Avengers. As part of the new team, Wanda next fought the Apocalypse Twins and failed to save the world. Only help from Kang allowed her and the rest of the Avengers to set things right.

DOCTOR STRANGE

THE SORCERER SUPREME was once one of the greatest surgeons in the world. But Stephen Strange was also very arrogant and motivated by material wealth. After a debilitating accident cost him his skills, Doctor Strange set out to study magic so that he might repair himself and regain his old life. Instead, the doctor found humility and new ways to help the world around him.

Doctor Strange first met the Avengers when he was part of the team of heroes known as the Defenders. He did not join the Avengers' ranks until much later.

DATA FILE

REAL NAME
Stephen Vincent Strange

OCCUPATION
Sorcerer Supreme; former surgeon

BASE
New York City

HEIGHT 6 ft 2 in

WEIGHT 180 lbs

EYES Gray

HAIR Black, white at temples

FIRST APPEARANCE WITH AVENGERS
Avengers #118 (December 1973)

POWERS
Stephen is a master of all kinds of magic and has a wide collection of magical artifacts at his disposal. This includes his Cloak of Levitation—which allows him to fly, and the Eye of Agamotto—an amulet that grants him psychic abilities and allows him to see the truth. His mystical training enables him to perform astral projection and hypnosis, he can create illusions, and he is telepathic. He does not appear to age. As well as being an expert surgeon, he is skilled in martial arts.

A VOYAGE OF DISCOVERY

When a car accident damaged Doctor Stephen Strange's hands, leaving him unable to operate, he set out an a mystical quest to ask the Ancient One to heal him.

As a man of science, Stephen didn't believe in magic, but his desperation to recover from his accident drove him to Tibet to meet the Ancient One, who was then the Sorcerer Supreme. He discovered the Ancient One's apprentice, Baron Mordo, was planning to murder the Sorcerer Supreme and assume his place, but Mordo restricted Stephen's powers of speech with a spell. Now a believer in magic, Stephen found a way to request to become the

Stephen began his Super Hero career with a blue cloak, but he later replaced it with the red Cloak of Levitation.

Ancient One's student. The sorcerer accepted Stephen's offer and removed Mordo's spell.

Once trained, Stephen moved to his Sanctum Sanctorum in Greenwich Village in New York City and dedicated himself to fighting magical threats, including the demon Dormammu. Upon the Ancient One's death, he took on the mantle of Sorcerer Supreme. Stephen formed the Defenders and consulted with the Avengers on magical matters many times. He also helped found the Illuminati. Stephen helped stop the Scarlet Witch when she disassembled the Avengers, and he later became an official member of the team. Recently, to save what was left of the multiverse, Doctor Strange became the leader of the Black Priests.

Although he prefers to rely on his magic, Stephen is not afraid to enter a fight when the situation calls for it.

ALLIES AND ENEMIES

For most of his career, Stephen has preferred to work on his own, joining with other heroes only when absolutely necessary. He lives alone, assisted by Wong.

THE ANCIENT ONE
The former Sorcerer Supreme initiated Stephen in the ways of magic.

WONG
Wong is the latest in a family line that served the Sorcerer Supreme through the ages.

CLEA
The niece of Dormammu, this good sorcerer became Stephen's lover.

MISTER FANTASTIC
Fellow genius Reed Richards serves alongside Stephen in the Illuminati.

DORMAMMU
Demonic ruler of the Dark Dimension, Dormammu challenged Stephen to a duel.

BARON MORDO
Rival student of the Ancient One, Mordo wanted to be the Sorcerer Supreme.

MORGAN LE FAY
The half-sister of King Arthur is a magician whose powers rival Stephen's.

MEPHISTO
The demonic ruler of a hellish dimension, Mephisto cuts dark deals with villains.

Dormammu has consistently been the greatest magical threat to the entire Earth. Stephen Strange has clashed with him many times.

STRANGE TIMES AHEAD

Doctor Strange remained a member of the Illuminati until he left in search of the Black Priests.

The frequent supernatural events surrounding Doctor Strange while forming new groups or fighting bizarre foes are often difficult to explain to his fellow Avengers!

JOINING THE ILLUMINATI

The New Avengers: Illuminati #1 (May 2006)

In the aftermath of the Kree-Skrull War, the most powerful heroes on Earth created a secret group called the Illuminati. This consisted of Black Bolt, Iron Man, Mister Fantastic, Namor, Professor X, and Doctor Strange. They traveled to warn the Skrull Empire against attacking Earth again, but they were captured, then tortured and examined. Before the heroes escaped, the Skrulls learned everything they needed from them to be able to initiate the Secret Invasion. Despite this initial failure, the Illuminati remained together to take on gigantic threats.

REVOLUTION PART 1

The New Avengers #27 (April 2007)

Stephen Strange tried to stay out of the Superhuman Civil War as much as possible, and for the most part, he succeeded. Once the hostilities ended, however, the rebel Avengers who had been part of Captain America's faction needed a place to call home, and Stephen offered up his Sanctum Sanctorum as their new headquarters. It did not take long for him to join the team in action as well, by teleporting in the entire team to rescue Ronin from Elektra and a group of Hand ninjas.

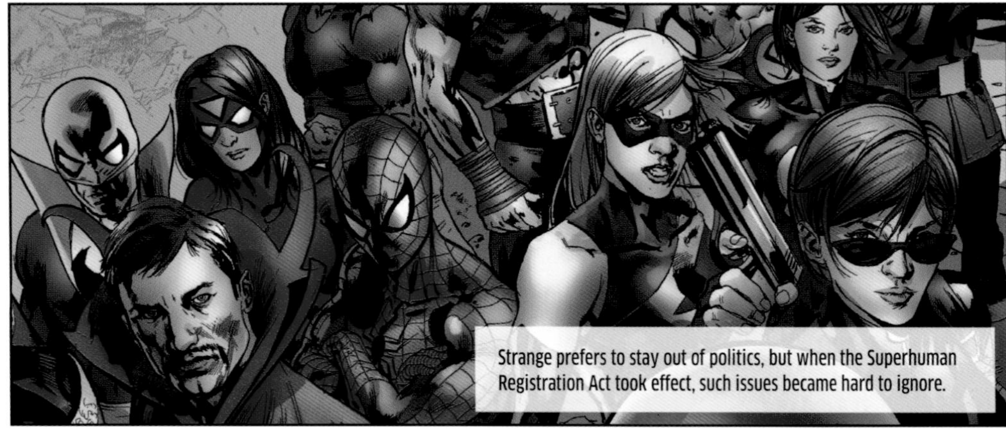
Strange prefers to stay out of politics, but when the Superhuman Registration Act took effect, such issues became hard to ignore.

Mojo's TV show was a silly concept, but Strange worked so well with the Avengers of the Supernatural that they might yet return.

AVENGERS OF THE SUPERNATURAL

Uncanny Avengers Annual #1 (January 2014)

When Mojo needed a new reality show for his corporate overlords to broadcast in the Mojoverse, he pitched them the *Martian Transylvania Super Hero Mutant Monster Hunter High School* show that featured two Avengers sub-teams facing off against one another in a high school setting. One team was the all-new Avengers of the Supernatural. Doctor Strange led this group of supernatural heroes, consisting of Blade, Ghost Rider, Man-Thing, Manphibian, and Santana. The other team was the Uncanny Avengers, including Havoc, the Wasp, Rogue, Scarlet Witch, and Wolverine. From behind the scenes, Mojo directed the show and tried to make it more interesting for viewers. However, his influence over the participants was soon broken and corrupting demon the Spirit of Vengeance took over, driving the show off-script, and it was up to all the Avengers to save the Mojoverse before the Spirit of Vengeance destroyed it.

While Stephen's hands were broken and he no longer had all of his power, that didn't mean he would give up trying to help people.

Humbled, Stephen turned to the New Avengers and learned how to rely on his friends for much-needed help.

SORCERER **STRUGGLES**

After turning to dark magic to find still greater power, Doctor Strange gave up his position as the Sorcerer Supreme and was obliged to find a successor.

As a member of the Illuminati, Stephen was party to exiling the Hulk from Earth and was also there when the Hulk returned, angry and seeking vengeance. The Hulk tricked Strange into turning from his astral form into his physical form, and was then able to crush him, injuring Stephen's hands and ruining his ability to cast spells.

Desperate, Stephen chanelled the power of the demonic Zom to aid him—and his hands were replaced with spiked maces. Unable to control the darker forces of Zom within him, however, Strange almost killed several innocent civilians until the Hulk stopped him. Realizing he had been arrogant to think he could control Zom, Stephen gave up his position as the Sorcerer Supreme.

Strange set out to find a successor to his role before the evil entity Dormammu and his servant the Hood could take the power from him. The Eye of Agamotto chose Jericho Drumm, aka Brother Voodoo. As the new Sorcerer Supreme, Drumm called himself Doctor Voodoo. His role was relatively short-lived as he sacrificed himself while battling the magical entity Agamotto itself, who was trying to reclaim the Eye of Agamotto.

Following Jericho's death, his ghostly brother, Daniel Drumm, returned and tried to destroy the Avengers and the New Avengers. To stop Daniel, Stephen Strange had to once again turn toward dark magic. On this occasion, however, he did so without losing control or hurting any innocents, proving him worthy of the role. The Ancient One's spirit then appeared and made Stephen Strange the Sorcerer Supreme once again, returning to him the Eye of Agamotto and the Cloak of Levitation.

"THE MASTER OF THE MYSTIC ARTS NEEDS TO BE PURE."
- DOCTOR STRANGE

Brother Voodoo took on the title Doctor Voodoo for the time he served as the Sorcerer Supreme.

BLACK PANTHER

THE MONARCH OF the African kingdom of Wakanda is known as the Black Panther, and the position has been handed down through the royal family from the first (Bashenga) to the present day. The Panther god grants each Black Panther their power by means of a sacred, heart-shaped herb. Those in the royal family must fight for the right to be named their generation's Black Panther.

The Black Panther's first Super Hero friends were the Fantastic Four, but it did not take him long to join the ranks of the Avengers.

DATA FILE

REAL NAME
T'Challa

OCCUPATION
Ruler of Wakanda

BASE
Wakanda; New York City

HEIGHT 6 ft

WEIGHT 200 lbs

EYES Brown

HAIR Black

FIRST APPEARANCE WITH AVENGERS
Avengers #51 (April 1968)

POWERS
T'Challa has superhuman endurance, senses, speed, and strength. His costume is laced with Vibranium, granting him superhuman durability as well as the ability to climb walls and land without injury. His gloves can generate energy daggers, and his claws can dissolve other metals. He is also a scientific and tactical genius and a veteran hunter and combatant.

THE **REIGN** OF T'CHALLA

The current Panther, T'Challa, does his best to balance his duties to both Wakanda and the rest of the world.

T'Challa was born to T'Chaka, king of Wakanda. His mother died following his birth and when T'Challa was still a boy, his father was killed by the villainous Klaw, who wanted Wakanda's rare store of Vibranium. T'Challa witnessed his father's murder and subsequently defeated Klaw. As he was still young, the mantle of the Black Panther passed to his uncle S'Yan, until T'Challa was old enough to fight as the Black Panther himself.

As a young man, T'Challa traveled to America and Europe, returning to carry out his duties as a tribal leader in Wakanda. T'Challa was responsible for driving Wakanda to becoming a high-tech nation and worked hard to ensure its prominence and sovereignty. His travels also meant he struck up friendships with many Super Heroes, including members of the Fantastic Four and the Avengers, who supported his

Although he hailed from a jungle nation, T'Challa spent many years living and fighting in New York City.

endeavors. He spent long periods away from home, but always returned to keep the nation on course.

T'Challa later married his first love and X-Men member Storm (Ororo Munroe), making her his queen, although their marriage did not last. Following a battle with Doctor Doom that left T'Challa in a coma, his sister Shuri became the next Black Panther and ruled Wakanda in his stead. After T'Challa recovered, he struck a new deal with the Panther god to become the King of the Dead, ruling over Necropolis, while his sister continued to rule Wakanda. T'Challa went on to become a member of the Illuminati and became instrumental in their efforts to save the Earth from the destruction of the multiverse.

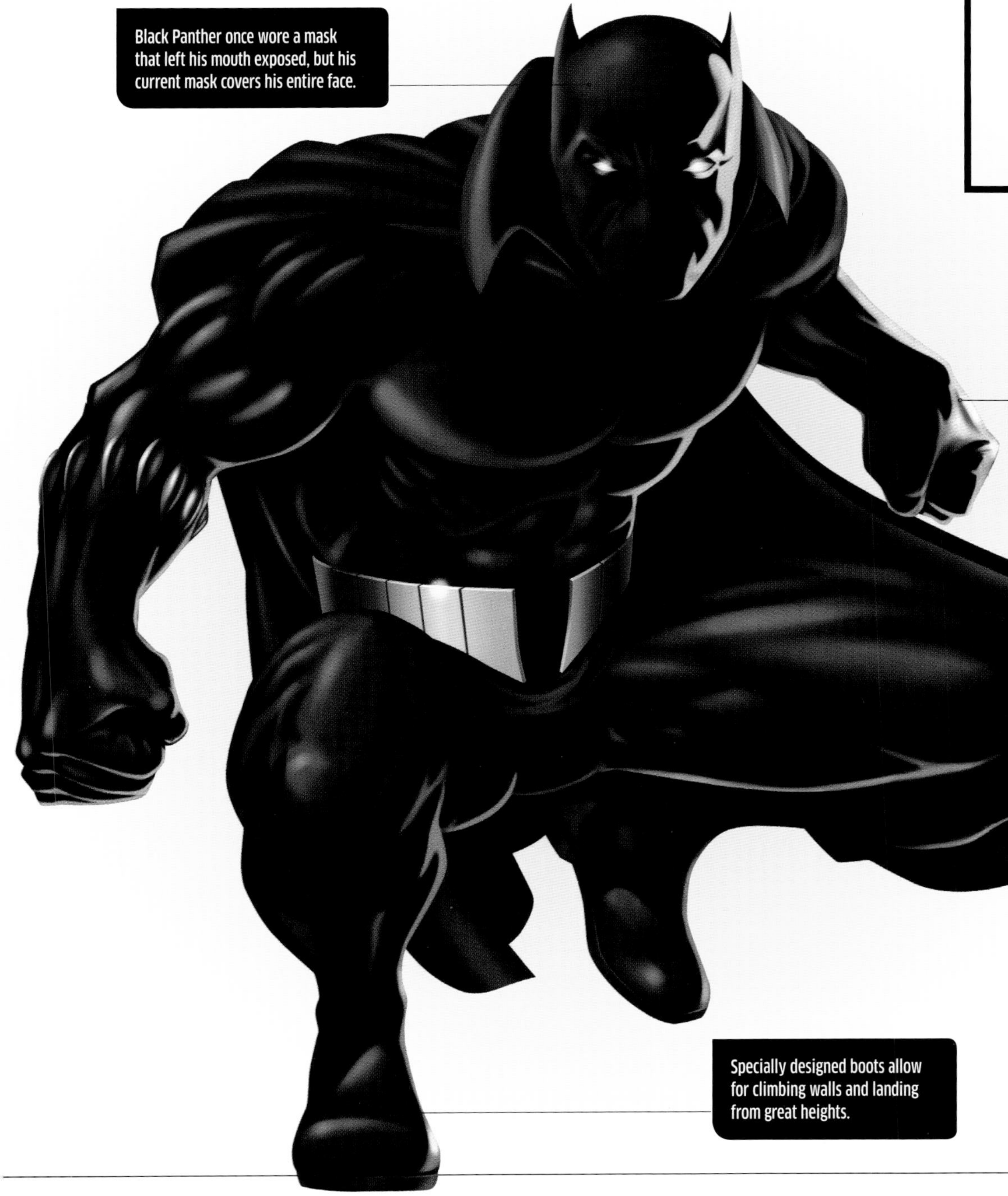

Black Panther once wore a mask that left his mouth exposed, but his current mask covers his entire face.

Black Panther's gloves can generate energy daggers and have Vibranium claws that can melt other metals.

The Vibranium in his suit makes Black Panther bulletproof.

Specially designed boots allow for climbing walls and landing from great heights.

ALLIES AND ENEMIES

Those who are for Wakanda are the Black Panther's allies, and those who stand against Wakanda are his foes.

FAMILY

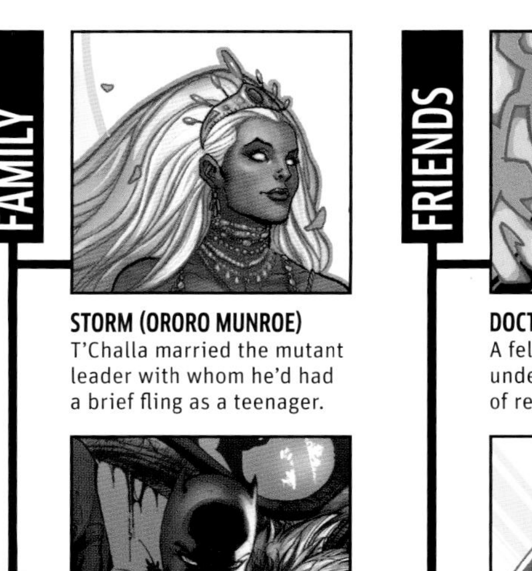

STORM (ORORO MUNROE)
T'Challa married the mutant leader with whom he'd had a brief fling as a teenager.

SHURI
T'Challa's sister took over as Black Panther. She died defending it against the Cabal.

FRIENDS

DOCTOR STRANGE
A fellow Illuminati, Strange understood T'Challa's sense of responsibility to his people.

IRON MAN
Iron Man respected the way T'Challa thrust Wakanda into the 21st century.

MISTER FANTASTIC
Reed Richards was one of the first Super Heroes T'Challa met in America.

FOE

KLAW
T'Challa sought to kill Klaw for the crime of mudering T'Challa's father and king.

A WEALTH OF HISTORY

The Black Panther lives a rich and varied life, split between ruling his home nation Wakanda and being an Avenger in New York. He has embarked on many adventures as a result.

THE LINE OF BLACK PANTHERS

Black Panther #7 (January 1978)

While traveling back to the African nation of Wakanda with a collector named Abner Little, T'Challa revealed the history of his native country—a land that contained the only reliable source of Vibranium in the entire world. According to the story, the metal fell from the sky as a meteorite thousands of years ago and formed a massive mound. The tribes of the land decided to protect it. To keep the metal within Wakanda, T'Challa's ancestor, Bashenga, formed the Panther Cult and became the first Black Panther.

In modern times, small amounts of Vibranium are sold at a high prices to qualified and vetted scientists. One such sample made its way into Captain America's shield, giving it the ability to absorb any impact. Wakandan law is rightfully respectful of the metal's power—T'Challa's half-brother, Jakarra, exposed himself to unrefined Vibranium, and it mutated him into a monster.

Raw Vibranium is dangerous, but the refined metal has become the source of Wakanda's power and wealth. It is the Black Panther's role to protect it.

The Panther god's actions bound together T'Challa and Mister Fantastic in a friendship that would last until death.

KING OF THE DEAD

Fantastic Four #607 (August 2012)

After Shuri took over as the Black Panther, T'Challa lost his powers, but he did not lose his sense of duty to Wakanda. To make the tiny nation less attractive to invaders, he rendered its stockpile of Vibranium inert. The royal family had been selling off small bits of Vibranium for years and investing around the world. This meant that Wakanda no longer relied on the rare metal for its wealth and it had become one of the most technologically advanced countries in the world.

Despite losing his powers, T'Challa was still king of Wakanda. He and his queen, Storm, invited the Fantastic Four and friends to pay a visit. Storm, Shuri, and the Invisible Woman decided to make a pilgrimage to the Panther god, while T'Challa and Mister Fantastic entered the Necropolis—the Wakandan City of the Dead. Shuri, Storm, and the Invisible Woman ended up battling the forces of Anubis, who had been sending dead soldiers to plague the people of Wakanda, and T'Challa and Mister Fantastic met with the Panther god, Bast, who sat on a throne in Necropolis. The Panther god asked T'Challa what he desired: to sit on a throne like her, or to save his people. He gave himself over to her will, and she made him the King of the Dead. This not only restored his powers but also gave him access to the knowledge of every Black Panther who had died and preceded him into the Necropolis, forging him stronger than ever before. It also left his sister Shuri as the ruler of Wakanda.

The destruction of Wakanda by a tsunami led to the deaths of countless people.

ATLANTIS AND WAKANDA **AT WAR**

The nations of Atlantis and Wakanda have long stood at odds with each other, and this pitted their monarchs—Namor and T'Challa—against one other.

Relations between the two countries had not always been strained. They began to fray when a Wakandan soldier launched a nuclear missile at Atlantis without permission. With advance warning from T'Challa, though, Atlantean king Namor was able to direct the missile towards a deserted island instead.

More recently, during the conflict between the Avengers and the X-Men—which also pitted T'Challa against his own wife Storm—T'Challa offered Wakanda as a base for the Avengers. Filled with the Phoenix Force, Namor sent a tsunami to Wakanda and destroyed most of the nation. Although Wakanda rebuilt itself quickly, T'Challa's royal sister Shuri was bent on revenge, and she eventually launched an attack against Atlantis, leveling it.

When Thanos's army invaded Earth, Namor told Thanos that one of the Infinity Gems he sought was in Wakanda, leading to even more damage. Namor later led the Cabal in an attack that conquered Wakanda—and caused Shuri's death. In retaliation, T'Challa betrayed Namor, stabbing him and leaving him to die with the Cabal on a doomed alternate Earth.

As Shuri instructed T'Challa when she went to battle the Cabal to the death, he had to "Put the blade where it belongs."

> "I WANT HIM TO KNOW THIS IS HOW IT ENDS. AND MORE THAN THAT, I WANT HIM TO KNOW IT WAS ME."
> **- T'CHALLA**

MANTIS

Mantis's dress resembles a plant, perhaps to help attract her eventual mate, one of the Cotati plant-people.

MANTIS WAS BORN into a pacifist group of Kree living in Vietnam. Believing she might be the Celestial Madonna, they trained her in martial arts and telepathy and then implanted false memories of a childhood spent as an orphaned beggar.

Mantis was human at first but later became a plant-person with green hair and antennae.

PAIRING WITH SWORDSMAN

Mantis met ex-villain Swordsman in Vietnam and helped him turn his life around. When a spot opened up in the Avengers, she encouraged Swordsman to apply.

The Avengers accepted not only Swordsman, but also Mantis, and they both proved themselves loyal teammates. However, Mantis became infatuated with the Vision, causing friction between her and the Scarlet Witch. It wasn't until the Swordsman sacrificed himself to save the Avengers from Kang that Mantis finally admitted that she had loved him. Revealed as the Celestial Madonna, Mantis left the team after she married a Cotati—a member of an intelligent race of telepaths who resembled trees or plants. This Cotati had taken the form of the dead Swordsman, so he and Mantis could mate and she could bear the Celestial Messiah. She returned years later with her son, Sequoia, on the run from Thanos.

DATA FILE

REAL NAME
Unknown

OCCUPATION
Adventurer

BASE
Mobile

HEIGHT 5 ft 6 in

WEIGHT 115 lbs

EYES Green

HAIR Black (later green)

FIRST APPEARANCE WITH AVENGERS
Avengers #112 (June 1973)

POWERS
Mantis is both telepathic and empathic and has some precognitive abilities. She can project an astral form and mentally control both fire and plants. She is also a fantastic martial artist.

Even without the Swordsman at her side, Mantis proved to be a valued member of the Avengers.

MANTIS TO MADONNA

Mantis's fate was intertwined with the Avengers. They helped protect her from threats like Kang until she was ready to become the Celestial Madonna.

THE ORIGIN OF MANTIS

Avengers #123 (May 1974)

After the Avengers defeated the latest incarnation of the Zodiac, one of its members, Libra, revealed that he was Gustav Brandt, Mantis's father. She had no memory of him, but he explained that he had been a mercenary in Vietnam and married the sister of a crimelord. They had a daughter, Mantis, but the brother caught up with them, killing Mantis's mother and blinding Gustav. Gustav fled with the baby and stumbled into a temple of the Priests of Pama, who raised the girl on his behalf. They had been sent to warn Earth about the planet-devouring Star-Stalker, whom the Avengers soon defeated.

With the truth about her past within her grasp, Mantis became defensive of the only person who could reveal it: Libra—her father!

ALLIES AND ENEMIES

Before she regained her memories of her childhood, the only allies Mantis had were among the Avengers. Once she became the Celestial Madonna, Mantis had plenty of foes ready to put an end to her.

SWORDSMAN
Mantis didn't return the depth of Swordsman's affections until his death.

SILVER SURFER
The Silver Surfer befriended Mantis after she gave her child, Quoi, to the Cotati.

FOE

THANOS
After Mantis helped the Avengers stop Thanos, he tried to kill her and her son.

During the Annihilation Wave, Mantis helped Star-Lord (Peter Quill) and his friends stop the Phalanx from destroying the entire galaxy.

A GUARDIAN OF THE GALAXY

After barely surviving the Annihilation Wave in her new, plant-based body, Mantis helped Star-Lord form the modern-day Guardians of the Galaxy.

At first, Mantis only served as support staff for the Guardians, but she eventually became a field agent, along with her compatriot, Bug.

Unknown to the other initial members of the Guardians of the Galaxy—Adam Warlock, Drax the Destroyer, Gamora, Groot, Phyla-Vell, and Rocket Racoon—Star-Lord had Mantis use her telepathic powers to encourage them to join the team. When the others discovered this, they disbanded in outrage. Later, Rocket decided to reform the team with Bug, Groot, and Major Victory, along with Mantis. They managed to rescue Star-Lord and Jack Flag from the Negative Zone and then admitted them to the team, too.

GRIM REAPER

THE EVIL, OLDER brother of Simon Williams (Wonder Man), Eric Williams tortured Simon throughout their childhood and became a Super Villain as an adult. He faced off against both the Avengers and his sibling.

The scythe can spin on its base and can fire electrical shocks, gas pellets, or energy blasts.

The Reaper's powers were originally based on technology but later relied on magic.

When Eric supposedly killed the Avengers, he had not accounted for the Black Panther in his plans.

BAD **BLOOD** BROTHER

While Simon took over the family business, Eric became a gangster. When the company failed, Eric used his connections with the Maggia to help, but Simon was arrested.

After he was released from jail, Simon was given superpowers by Baron Zemo, who turned him into Wonder Man. Zemo set Simon against the Avengers, but had not anticipated on him switching sides and dying to save the team of Super Heroes.

Thirsting for revenge, Eric had the Tinkerer transform him into the Grim Reaper, adopting the use of a scythe to replace his amputated right hand. The Grim Reaper would have beaten the Avengers, if not for the Black Panther's intervention. Eric revived his brother with the help of Black Talon, but Simon turned against him once again, which convinced Eric that his brother was really an imposter. Eric then held a mock trial to determine whether Wonder Man was truly his brother. Then he decided to kill the Vision, as he saw him as a mockery of Simon.

Eric held a mock trial of the Vision and Wonder Man. Convinced that the Vision, appearing so like Simon, was just a mockery of his brother, he tried to execute the android, but Simon knocked his brother flat.

DATA FILE

REAL NAME
Eric Williams

OCCUPATION
Criminal

BASE
Mobile

HEIGHT 6 ft 4 in

WEIGHT 225 lbs

EYES Blue

HAIR Gray

FIRST APPEARANCE WITH AVENGERS
Avengers #52 (May 1968)

POWERS
Eric has a scythe in place of his amputated right hand, and it can fire electrical shocks, energy blasts, and gas pellets. Its blade can spin at rapid speeds and so can be used as a saw, shield, or even as a helicopter. It can induce comas in his victims. He also has superhuman strength and some magical skill.

A GRIM OBSESSION

The Avengers became Eric's obsession after he thought they had killed his brother Simon—and the obsession continued long after Simon had returned to the team.

Even Eric's fellow villains realized that he had lost his grip on his sanity, but they remained together to execute his plan.

LO! THE LETHAL LEGION!

Avengers #79 (August 1970)

After failing to defeat the Avengers on his own, Eric gathered together a group of Super Villains and forged them into the Lethal Legion. They included Living Laser, Man-Ape, Power Man, Swordsman, and Eric himself. First they captured Black Panther and his girlfriend Monica Lynne. Then they split up the Avengers and captured them all and put them into a giant hourglass filled with poison gas. When Eric learned that the Vision shared Simon's brain pattern, however, he could not bear to kill him, and he broke the hourglass, setting the Avengers free.

Eric thought that both Simon and the Vision were faked copies of his brother, whom he wanted returned to life—so he could kill him!

BROTHERLY DISCORD

Vision and the Scarlet Witch #2 (November 1985)

Eric teamed up with Black Talon, Goliath, Man-Ape, Nekra, and Ultron to capture the West Coast Avengers. He planned to take the minds of Wonder Man and the Vision and transfer them into a zombie that resembled Simon. When Simon attacked Eric, though, and Mockingbird freed the rest of the Avengers, Black Talon and Man-Ape fled. Simon and Vision tracked down Eric, who seemingly fell to his death as he escaped.

ALLIES AND ENEMIES

Eric hated the Avengers and anyone who worked with them. Conversely, he was willing to work with anyone who shared his desire to take down the Super Heroes.

FOES

THE VISION
The Vision shared Simon's brain patterns. Eric saw him as a poor copy of Simon.

WONDER MAN
Eric couldn't believe it when Simon finally stood up to him as Wonder Man.

Eric fled after he realized that Wonder Man really was his brother Simon and not a fake, as he had wrongly believed.

HORSEMAN OF DEATH

After Rogue accidentally killed Eric when he attacked the Avengers Unity Division, the Apocalypse Twins brought him back as one of their Horsemen of Death.

Apocalypse had always kept four different horsemen: Death, Famine, Pestilence, and War. The Apocolypse Twins, however, preferred to focus on just one terrible aspect instead—Death. Using both the Death Seed and Life Seed, they turned Eric, Daken, Banshee, and the Sentry into their four Horsemen of Death. The Twins' plot to kill every human and save the mutants in a starship ark failed, but Eric and Daken escaped to Earth with the Twins' bodies, while Banshee was captured, and the Sentry flew into space.

After the Twins were defeated, Eric griped that he had "killed zero people."

MORGAN LE FAY

This priestess of darkness sought to conquer the future as well as rule the past.

Morgan is a sorceress from the sixth century—but she may even date back to the time of the original Atlantis. She was High Priestess of the Darkhold cult, who worshipped the demonic Elder god Chthon. While battling King Arthur and the Black Knight in her own time, Morgan was visited by Doctor Doom from the future and became aware of a new realm to conquer. They became lovers for a while, and she taught Doctor Doom the secrets of sorcery, while he led her armies in return. Later, he betrayed her and they became bitter foes. Morgan began to project herself forward in time, clashing with the Avengers and Spider-Woman.

Bone necklace holds defense charms

DATA FILE

REAL NAME
Morgan Le Fay

OCCUPATION
Sorceress; former High Priestess; former Queen of Gorre

BASE Mobile

HEIGHT 6 ft 2 in

WEIGHT 140 lbs

EYES Green

HAIR Purple

FIRST APPEARANCE WITH AVENGERS
Avengers #240 (February 1984)

POWERS
This former pupil of Merlin became one of the most powerful sorceresses ever to exist. It is believed Morgan is half-faerie and she has inherited the ability to influence minds and harness a mystical energy. She can fly, shape-shift, fire bolts of a mystical force, and create force fields. Time-travel, spirit-transfer and raising the dead are among her dark arts. She can use enchanted artifacts to shape whole realities to her will.

WICCAN

The lost son of the Scarlet Witch went on to become a Young Avenger.

Billy met the Scarlet Witch at the gates of Avengers Mansion after being attacked at school by homophobic bullies. When the Scarlet Witch tried to heal Billy's injuries, her touch kindled mystical powers in him. He joined the Young Avengers under the name Asgardian, later changing his name to Wiccan. When fellow member and boyfriend Hulking was abducted by an alien race named the Kree, Wiccan hunted them down to a detention center for young superhumans. There he also found Tommy Shepherd, who became the hero Speed, and was later revealed to be Billy's brother. Wiccan became a full Avenger when Captain America promoted all the Young Avengers to full status.

DATA FILE

REAL NAME William Kaplan **OCCUPATION** Student
BASE Young Avengers base, Bishop Publishing, New York
HEIGHT 5 ft 8 in **WEIGHT** 155 lbs **EYES** Brown **HAIR** Black
FIRST APPEARANCE WITH AVENGERS *Young Avengers* #1 (April 2005)
POWERS Mystery surrounds the source and extent of Wiccan's powers, as he appears to have a part mutant, part mystical origin. With powers similar to his mother's hex ability he can affect reality by stating a desired outcome. He can unleash energy bolts, create fire, teleport, heal the injured, and summon objects. He knows where people are, even when he can't see them. The success of his gifts depend on his desire to carry them out.

Similar to the Scarlet Witch, Wiccan can fire energy bolts from his hands.

Billy eventually discovers that he is the Scarlet Witch's reincarnated son and that he has a twin brother.

HELLCAT

As a young model, Patricia couldn't have imagined she would become a hero before going to hell and back.

Retractable claws

Patricia Walker was the daughter of a writer who depicted a romanticized version of her daughter's life in comic books. After an early career as a model, Patsy went to work at the Brand Corporation, where she came to know Hank McCoy—the Beast from the X-Men. On discovering his identity, she used it to blackmail him into promising to help her become a Super Hero. Caught up in an Avengers mission at the corporation, she discovered a feline costume and adopted it, naming herself Hellcat. After receiving training in psionic abilities from Moondragon, she joined the Defenders. During this time she fell in love with Daimon Hellstrom, the Son of Satan, and the pair married. They became supernatural investigators, allying with the Avengers West Coast. Finally, destroyed by exposure to Hellstrom's dark side, she spent a period of torment in Mephisto's realm. She was rescued from this by the Grim Reaper, who sought to use her as part of a plan against the Avengers. Patsy resisted his control and helped the Avengers defeat him. She was later rescued from Mephisto's grasp by the Thunderbolts and returned to a full physical existence once again.

Patsy's debut as a hero was with the Avengers, thanks to her close friendship with Hank McCoy, aka the Beast.

DATA FILE

REAL NAME Patricia Walker **OCCUPATION** Adventurer, model, supernatural investigator

BASE Alaska; San Francisco, California

HEIGHT 5 ft 8 in **WEIGHT** 135 lbs **EYES** Blue **HAIR** Red

FIRST APPEARANCE WITH AVENGERS AVENGERS *Avengers* #144 (February 1976)

POWERS Hellcat is naturally agile and has been trained in self-defense and team combat by the Avengers. Her limited psionic abilities were boosted through training by the telepathic Moondragon—she can also sense mystical energy. Her gloves and boots have retractable claws, and she has a cable-claw with a grappling hook and swing-line.

ALLIES AND ENEMIES

Hellcat is close to Black Cat, Firestar, and Monica Rambeau. Her enemies include Nicholas Scratch, Dormammu, Mephisto, and the Grim Reaper.

FRIEND

TERMINATRIX
Daimon Hellstrom fell in love with Hellcat when they served in the Defenders.

Hellcat helps out the team along with (left to right), Doctor Voodoo, Misty Knight, the Thing, Iron Fist, Jessica Jones, Valkyrie, Daredevil, and Doctor Strange.

THUNDERSTRIKE

A staunch ally to Thor became an Asgardian god himself.

Architect Eric Masterson was a mere mortal who came to Thor's aid while the god of thunder was wounded, lifting Thor's hammer and proving himself worthy of its power. Masterson was then chosen by Odin to replace Thor when he punished his son for the apparent slaying of Loki. The true Thor was then buried in the mind of Masterson. Masterson had problems being accepted as Thor, especially by the Avengers. Eventually, Odin gave him the enchanted mace, Thunderstrike, and he began a new identity with the same name. He joined the Avengers in many battles, but finally sacrificed himself to rid the world of the power of the deadly villain Bloodaxe. Later, his son Kevin inherited his mace and the identity of Thunderstrike.

Enchanted mace is made of nearly indestructible uru metal.

DATA FILE

REAL NAME Eric Kevin Masterson **OCCUPATION** Architect; adventurer
BASE Avengers Mansion, New York
HEIGHT 5 ft 10 in **WEIGHT** 160 lbs as Masterson; 640 lbs as Thunderstrike
EYES Blue **HAIR** Blond
FIRST APPEARANCE WITH AVENGERS As Masterson: *Avengers* #312 (December 1989); as Thor: *Avengers* #343 (January 1992); as Thunderstrike: *Avengers* #374 (May 1994)
POWERS Thunderstrike enables Masterson to change between human and Asgardian form. It also allows him to fly, open dimensional doorways, and breathe in space. His body has three times the density of a human and is far more resistant to damage and fatigue. As Thunderstrike he benefits from an Asgardian healing factor and longevity. He has been trained in armed combat by both Hercules and Captain America.

DOCTOR VOODOO

Jericho Drumm began a quest to master ancient rites and fight evil after his brother succumbed to the fate of a deadly curse.

Jericho Drumm was born in Haiti, but worked as a psychologist in America. Returning to Haiti, he discovered his brother, a voodoo priest, had been struck by a fatal curse. His brother's soul became bonded to his, giving Jericho mystical strength. Jericho then studied the arts for himself, gaining great skill. He became Brother Voodoo, and returned to America to fight evil. During a period when Doctor Strange was unable to continue his role Jericho became Sorcerer Supreme. Doctor Voodoo sided with the New Avengers and defeated the mystical being Agomotto, but was slain in the conflict. Later, he was resurrected and he joined the Avengers Unity Division.

Doctor Voodoo can summon a dark smoke to strike fear and confusion into his foes.

DATA FILE

REAL NAME Jericho Drumm **OCCUPATION** Psychologist; Houngan (voodoo priest); former Sorcerer Supreme
BASE Avengers Mansion, New York City; Port-au Prince, Haiti
HEIGHT 6 ft **WEIGHT** 220 lbs **EYES** Brown **HAIR** Brown
FIRST APPEARANCE WITH AVENGERS *New Avengers* #53 (July 2009).
POWERS As Sorcerer Supreme, Jericho can't be harmed by magic or evil intent. His mastery of voodoo provides protection against fire and gives him hypnotic powers. He can call upon his brother's spirit to possess others or increase his own power.

MANDARIN

The discovery of ten alien power rings almost put the world in this power-hungry villain's hands.

The Mandarin, descendant of a noble Chinese family, had fallen upon hard times. Seeking to improve his fortunes, he entered the forbidden Valley of the Spirits where he found a dead Makluan alien and ten rings of power. He rose to great power and set his mind on world conquest, often clashing with Iron Man. He first tried to destroy the Avengers by planting bombs inside the Avengers Mansion, but he failed. An orbiting satellite broadcasting hate rays provoked the Mandarin's next clash with the Avengers, who defeated him and his allies. The Mandarin joined a team of Super Villains named the Prime Movers that included Doctor Doom and Magnet in a collaboration that proved turbulent. The Mandarin continues to explore his power, proving to be an eternal thorn in the side of Tony Stark.

DATA FILE

REAL NAME
Unknown, possibly Khan

OCCUPATION
Chief Executive Officer, aspiring world conqueror; former aristocrat

BASE
Mandarin City; Palace of the Star Dragon, Valley of the Spirits.

HEIGHT 6 ft 2 in

WEIGHT 215 lbs

EYES Blue

HAIR Black

FIRST APPEARANCE WITH AVENGERS
Avengers #20 (September 1965)

POWERS
A martial arts master, the Mandarin has developed karate blows that can damage Iron Man's armor and he can survive for years without food using the strength of his spirit alone. His power rings give him an array of abilities, including sonic blasts, the ability to create darkness, create gas clouds and force fields. Other rings give him psionic abilities, or can produce fire and ice blasts.

LIONHEART

A brave mother rose from the dead to defend her country.

A single mother of two children from the UK, Kelsey Shorr Leigh acquired superpowers under bizarre circumstances. Caught in a battle between the Avengers and the Wrecking Crew, she defended the fallen Captain America with his shield, but died from her injuries. She was granted life again by the original Captain Britain, who saw her as worthy to take on his past role. Given the choice of the Sword of Might or the Amulet of Right, Kelsey chose the sword, meaning that if her children ever discovered her identity, they would die. She joined the Avengers, but left after the events of Avengers Disassembled and continued her solo adventures as Lionheart.

DATA FILE

REAL NAME Kelsey Shorr Leigh **OCCUPATION** Adventurer; previously teacher

BASE England, UK; formerly Avengers Mansion

HEIGHT 5 ft 5 in **WEIGHT** 130 lbs **EYES** Blue **HAIR** Blonde

FIRST APPEARANCE WITH AVENGERS AVENGERS *Avengers* #77 (March 2004)

POWERS Lionheart wields the Sword of Might, a weapon some believe to be the ancient blade Excalibur, a defence against dark magic and able to slice through almost anything. Possessing the same powers as the original Captain Britain, she can lift about 90 tons, has an invisible force field and can fly at the speed of sound. Enhanced senses give her superhuman hearing and vision. Kelsey is an expert on British history.

WONG

The servant of Doctor Strange became a friend and an ally to all of the Avengers.

Wong is the latest in the line of a family traditionally dedicated to the service of the Ancient One—a long-lived Sorcerer Supreme. When The Ancient One accepted Doctor Strange as a pupil, Wong traveled from Kamar-Taj near Tibet, to Greenwich Village, New York, to become Doctor Strange's servant. Wong assisted his master in many battles with evil forces, including the Avengers vs. Defenders war. After the Civil War, Wong's master gave sanctuary to the New Avengers and Wong looked after them. Then, when Doctor Strange joined the Avengers, Wong became a housekeeper at the Avengers Mansion.

DATA FILE

REAL NAME Wong **OCCUPATION** Servant to Dr Strange; formerly the co-administrator of the Stephen Strange Memorial Metaphysical Institute; former servant of the Ancient One

BASE Greenwich Village, New York; formerly Kamar-Taj, the Himalayas

HEIGHT 5 ft 8 in **WEIGHT** 140 lbs **EYES** Brown **HAIR** Bald

FIRST APPEARANCE WITH AVENGERS AVENGERS *Avengers* #116 (October 1973)

POWERS An expert in the martial arts of Kamar-Taj, Wong is formidable in unarmed combat. A student of the mystic arts he can perform many spells, and is an authority on the uttering of incantations. He also helps Doctor Strange carry out more complex enchantments.

DOCTOR DRUID

As a doctor who helped an ancient mystic and a descendant of Celtic magic, Anthony Druid was deemed worthy to be taught the secrets of sorcery. He devoted his life to studying and utilizing druidic lore.

A descendant of Amergin the Druid from the tenth century, Dr. Anthony Druid was granted mystical powers by a Tibetan lama, who was in fact the Ancient One. Known at first as Dr. Droom, Druid swore to fight dark sorcery, siding with the Avengers in the events of the Contest of Champions. He also summoned the Avengers back in time to Avalon in the 12th century to protect Earth from the Fomor, a race of extra-dimensional beings. Later, he helped the Avengers prevent Baron Zemo and his Masters of Evil from taking over Avengers Mansion and was made an Avenger. However, his mind fell under the control of the evil Terminatrix and he led the Avengers into a perilous Time Bubble in search of an all-powerful weapon. Although the plan failed, he lost the trust of his teammates and temporarily vanished into limbo, but later returned to fight with them again.

Doctor Druid called on the aid of the Avengers after being contacted by his descendant, Amergin the Druid.

DATA FILE

REAL NAME
Anthony Druid (originally Anthony Ludgate)

OCCUPATION
Druid, occult expert; former psychiatric doctor

BASE
Boston, Massachusetts; mobile; previously Avengers Mansion

HEIGHT 6 ft 5 in

WEIGHT 311 lbs

EYES Green

HAIR Black

FIRST APPEARANCE WITH AVENGERS
Avengers #225 (November 1982)

POWERS
Doctor Druid is a master of druidic rituals which give him power over all living things. He has the powers of telepathy and telekinesis, plus hypnotism. The Ancient One gave him a wide range of mystic abilities including teleportation. With discipline, he can control the density of his body, even turning aside bullets. He is trained in judo and the ancient art of fighting with a staff.

ALLIES AND ENEMIES

The mighty Avengers were once Doctor Druid's allies, but his desire to conquer mystic powers led him astray.

FRIENDS

DOCTOR STRANGE
Stephen Strange urged Druid to join the Secret Defenders.

FOE

NEKRA
This evil priestess first seduced Dr. Druid, then shot him while he was powerless.

SEBASTIAN DRUID

The son of Dr. Druid, Sebastian originally believed he had special mystical powers, but his abilities are chemical based—a product of the monster DNA he possesses. He has worked with S.H.I.E.L.D. as part of their Caterpillar team for those whose full abilities are as yet unrevealed.

RED WOLF

This modern-day Cheyenne is an ex-marine and an inheritor of the mantle of the wolf-spirit.

A member of the Cheyenne tribe, William Talltrees served with the U.S. Marines. He became Red Wolf, a traditional protector of his people, after his parents were murdered by mobsters working for Taurus—one of the agents of Zodiac. He hunted the killers down with the assistance of the Avengers. He later joined a group called the Rangers, which included Texas Twister, Phantom Rider III, Firebird, and Shooting Star. With this group he battled the West Coast Avengers, due to the trickery of an evil demon named Riglevio.

DATA FILE

REAL NAME William Talltrees **OCCUPATION** Adventurer; previously soldier and construction worker.
BASE Mobile; Texas **HEIGHT** 6 ft 4 in **WEIGHT** 240 lbs **EYES** Brown **HAIR** Black
FIRST APPEARANCE WITH AVENGERS *Avengers* #80 (September 1970)
POWERS Guided by the spirit of Owayodata, his tribal god. Red Wolf has wolf-like senses, able to see long distances even in darkness and hear the tiniest sounds from afar. He is an expert tracker and hunter. The protection of his ancestral spirit also confers super speed, agility and strength, enabling him to lift about three tons. He is proficient in traditional Cheyenne weaponry: the tomahawk, bow and arrow, and the coup stick—a combat staff.

WHITE TIGER

The power of three ancient amulets turned the young sister of a dead hero into a Mighty Avenger.

Traditional white-colored suit

The youngest sister of the original White Tiger, Hector Ayala, Aya is the owner of three Jade Tiger Amulets—handed down from Master Kee of the Tiger Dojo. She was the first new member to join Avengers Academy after it moved to the Avengers Compound in California. She was there during the attack of the half-mutant, half-Dire Wraith, Hybrid, and during the war between the Avengers and the X-Men. Aya left the Academy to join Luke Cage's Heroes for Hire. She later joined the Mighty Avengers.

DATA FILE

REAL NAME Aya Ayala **OCCUPATION** Student
BASE Avengers Compound, Los Angeles; Gem Theatre, New York City; Avengers Mansion, New York City.
HEIGHT Unknown **WEIGHT** Unknown **EYES** Brown **HAIR** Black
FIRST APPEARANCE WITH AVENGERS *Avengers Academy* #20 (December 2011)
POWERS The Jade Tiger Amulets give Aya the knowledge and experience of fighters greater than herself. They also provide increased strength, speed, agility, balance, healing, and endurance. The three amulets enable power-sharing among several individuals, augmenting all those in the connection. The spiritual connection with the tiger is also believed to give her the ability, like the cat, to hunt in darkness.

TYRANNUS

Roman Emperor Augustulus became an immortal then used his unique genius to set out on a lifetime of conquest.

Augustulus claims to be a fifth-century ruler, who has achieved eternal life. The great wizard Merlin saw a dark future for Augustulus and exiled him to Subterranea, where he discovered the Fountain of Eternal Youth. He also discovered Deviant technology, and frequently rose to challenge the surface world. Merging with the Flame of Eldorado during a battle with the Hulk, he took over the body of the Abomination and in this form battled the West Coast Avengers and Hawkeye.

Originally a mere human, Tyrannus became immortal, then a disembodied conscious force.

DATA FILE

REAL NAME Romulus Augustulus **OCCUPATION** Would-be Conquerer; former Roman Emperor
BASE Subterranea; previously Rome
HEIGHT 6 ft 2 in **WEIGHT** 225 lbs **EYES** Brown **HAIR** Blond
FIRST APPEARANCE WITH AVENGERS As the Abomination: *West Coast Avengers* #25 (October 1987); as Tyrannus: *Avengers Annual* #20 (June 1991).
POWERS Tyrannus is a genius. Drinking from the Fountain of Youth in ancient times he became immortal. Merging with the cobalt flame of Eldorado, he acquired psionic abilities that he has retained since. He has great knowledge of the advanced science of the Deviants, which has enabled him to develop his own weapons, often inspired by his Roman past. As the Abomination, he had Hulk-level strength, endurance and speed.

SILVERCLAW

The orphaned daughter of South American volcano goddess, Peliali, Silverclaw first fought the Avengers, then joined them.

Kamekeri ritual body paint

Upon being sponsored by the Avengers' butler, Jarvis, Silverclaw ("Lupe") traveled to the United States, where she became caught up in a plot by villain Moses Magnum and was forced to fight with terrorists against the Avengers. Silverclaw managed to help the Avengers defeat Magnum and cleared her name. She then asked for their help when an ancient wizard, Kulan Gath, attacked her homeland. Gath was defeated, but Lupe's mother was slain. Silverclaw became a reserve member of the Avengers, but prefers to protect her own people.

DATA FILE

REAL NAME Maria de Guadalupe Santiago; aka "Lupe" **OCCUPATION** Student, adventurer
BASE Kamekeri, Costa Verde; Empire State University; Avengers Mansion, New York City
HEIGHT 5 ft 7 in **WEIGHT** 150 lbs **EYES** Brown **HAIR** Black and silver
FIRST APPEARANCE WITH AVENGERS *Avengers* #8 (September 2013)
POWERS Silverclaw inherited shapeshifting powers from her mother, one of the ancient gods of her people. Her ability appears to be linked to the animals indigenous to her land, and she has taken on the were-forms of creatures including an anaconda, crocodile, jaguar, and puma. In these forms she has a silvery skin and partly human appearance. She has developed her skills to gain enhanced willpower to break the spells of others.

MASTER PANDEMONIUM

A vile bargain with the extra-dimensional demon Mephisto bonded this onetime unassuming actor to his own personal demonic horde—transforming him into Master Pandemonium.

When Martin Preston was injured in a car accident, Mephisto replaced his limbs with demons. Tricked into believing that five parts of his soul had been taken away, Preston sought to track them down. He attacked the Thing, believing he may possess part of his lost soul, which led to a battle with the West Coast Avengers. When the Scarlet Witch created two children for herself, Pandemonium believed she had used two pieces of his soul. He battled the Avengers and took the two fragments, seemingly removing the twins from existence. After Mephisto stole back the fragments, Master Pandemonium escaped to Mephisto's realm where he continues his career as a man truly troubled by his own demons.

DATA FILE

REAL NAME Martin Preston

OCCUPATION Professor; former actor

BASE Los Angeles, California

HEIGHT 6 ft 1 in (can vary)

WEIGHT 198 lbs (can vary)

EYES Blue (can vary)

HAIR Brown (can vary)

FIRST APPEARANCE WITH AVENGERS *West Coast Avengers* #4 (January 1986)

POWERS Martin Preston's limbs are attached to demons, known as the Rakasha, which he can call on to do his bidding. His limbs can separate and act independently as demonic entities. He can unleash hellfire from his mouth and project powerful rays of dark magic from his hands. Possessing the Amulet of Azmodeus he can summon the demon, in the form of a giant red eagle, to perform tasks for him. He can also call on smaller demons, which appear through the hole shaped like a five-pointed star in his chest, to attack his foes. The amulet also enables him to travel between dimensions.

SPEED

This troubled young mutant discovered he was one of the lost children of the Scarlet Witch.

Tommy was born a mutant with the power of superhuman speed, but had a troubled youth after his parents divorced and he ended up in a detention center for those with special abilities. He was found there by the Young Avengers who were in search of new recruits. They noticed that Tommy resembled Wiccan and the pair soon discovered they were the reincarnated children of the Scarlet Witch. Using the name Speed, Tommy joined the Young Avengers. He was part of the team that sided with the Secret Avengers, rebelling against the Superhuman Registration Act.

DATA FILE

REAL NAME Thomas Shepherd **OCCUPATION** Fugitive; student; adventurer

BASE Mobile; previously Bishop Publishing, New York City; detention center, Springfield, New Jersey

HEIGHT 5 ft 8 in **WEIGHT** 155 lbs **EYES** Green **HAIR** White

FIRST APPEARANCE WITH AVENGERS *Young Avengers* #10 (March 2006)

POWERS Tommy's mutant speed is believed to be comparable in potential to those of Quicksilver, his uncle. He can travel at the speed of sound and his mutant physiology protects him from the effects of the speed, such as friction. He can digest information at superhuman speed and race across the surface of water. By accelerating his molecules he can run through solid objects, and by creating hyperkinetic vibrations he can cause objects to explode.

Chicken-inspired head crest

BLACK TALON

A talent for creating zombies made this criminal a key ally for the Grim Reaper.

The first Black Talon was a foe of Captain America in World War II. The second was a cult leader who battled Doctor Voodoo. The third, Samuel Barone, was a corrupt voodoo priest, who worked for the Grim Reaper—who sought his aid in resurrecting his dead brother, Wonder Man. He later joined the Lethal Legion, battling the West Coast Avengers. Many years later, he re-emerged, raising a zombie army as part of a scheme to destroy the Avengers. Killed by the Punisher, he has been seen back from the grave, with the Shadow Council's Masters of Evil.

DATA FILE

REAL NAME Samuel David Barone **OCCUPATION** Magician

BASE Mobile

HEIGHT 6 ft 2 in **WEIGHT** 240 lbs **EYES** Brown **HAIR** Black

FIRST APPEARANCE WITH AVENGERS *Avengers* #152 (October 1976)

POWERS As a voodoo priest, Barone has the power to create zombies and get them to do his bidding through mental commands. This power is limited to short distances so he must remain in close contact with his undead slaves. Although possessing only ordinary human strength, his costume is equipped with vicious metal talons on his gloves and boots, making him a dangerous opponent at close quarters.

STARHAWK

Empowered by the Hawk god of an alternate Earth, Starhawk traveled through time to help the Avengers.

This future hero was the son of the Super Hero Quasar and the artificially created being, Kismet. Kidnapped as a baby, he fell into the hands of Ogord of the Reavers, who raised him as his own son. While exploring the ancient ruins of the Hawk god with his adoptive sister Aleta, the god was awoken and merged the two into a shared entity, granting them incredible powers. Starhawk fought alongside the Guardians of the Galaxy, the Defenders, and Thor in his own time and traveled back in time to fight with the present day Avengers and Guardians of the Galaxy.

DATA FILE

REAL NAME Stakar Ogord **OCCUPATION** Servant of the Hawk god

BASE Starship *Captain America II*; previously Arcturus IV, asteroid base

HEIGHT 6 ft 4 in **WEIGHT** 450 lbs **EYES** White **HAIR** Red

FIRST APPEARANCE WITH AVENGERS *Avengers* #167 (January 1978)

POWERS Starhawk has the ability to control light, using it to create energy blasts, harness the power of heat and also make holographic-style images. His hawk-like sight enables him to see great distances, and he is also able to sense and follow energy trails. He has enormous strength and endurance, able to take on Thor in battle. The fact that he was forced to relive his own life all over again, gave Starhawk a knowledge of future events–which was mistaken the power of precognition.

BLOODWRAITH

The dark power of the Ebony Blade turned a young squire into a bloodthirsty super-wraith.

Sean Dolan was an Irish orphan who became friends with the Black Knight after the hero saved his life. He tried to prevent Arabian sorcerers from capturing the powerful weapon known as the Ebony Blade, but when he wielded it, he became possessed by the souls of those it had killed—transforming him into the evil Bloodwraith who then had to be stopped by the Avengers. He later fought the Avengers again, after taking the blade of Proctor and becoming a new version of the Bloodwraith. The Scarlet Witch eventually used her hex powers to tie his spirit to the land of Slorenia, so that he can never leave.

DATA FILE

REAL NAME Sean Dolan **OCCUPATION** Former squire **BASE** Slorenia

HEIGHT 5 ft 11 in **WEIGHT** 160 lbs (as Dolan), unknown as wraith

EYES Blue (as Dolan); glowing white or red (as wraith) **HAIR** Reddish-blond (as Dolan); no hair (as wraith)

FIRST APPEARANCE WITH AVENGERS *Avengers Annual* #22 (March 1993)

POWERS Dolan wields the Ebony Blade, which can cut through almost any substance and also steal the souls of those he beats in battle. He can absorb the power of souls and add to his own supernatural energy. Dolan can summon the blade or teleport to its location. When giant sized he has a testing level of strength and endurance.

DORMAMMU

This fiery being took over the Dark Dimension and became dreaded throughout the realms of sorcery.

A mystical being from the other-dimensional realm Faltine, Dormammu was cast out for seeking to gain too much power. Taking humanoid form, he discovered the Dark Dimension and became its ruler when King Olnar was killed by the Mindless Ones. He partly returned to his original fiery form and sought to conquer Earth, but was forced to resort to sneaky strategies. He tricked the Defenders into seeking the Evil Eye, an artifact that could merge his dimension with Earth's. Loki manipulated the Avengers into seeking the same thing, triggering the Avengers vs. Defenders War. Dormammu's scheme to replace Doctor Strange as Sorcerer Supreme with a villain named the Hood was defeated by Strange and his allies, which included the New Avengers.

Flames of the Faltine are extremely powerful and can destroy even the undead.

DATA FILE

REAL NAME
Dormammu, (often referred to as the Dread Dormammu)

OCCUPATION
Ruler of the Dark Dimension

BASE Dark Dimension

HEIGHT 6 ft 1 in

WEIGHT Varies

EYES Yellow; green (as human)

HAIR None (head of flame); black (as human)

FIRST APPEARANCE WITH AVENGERS
Avengers #115 (September 1973)

POWERS Coming from the realm of the Faltine, Dormammu is made of pure mystic fire, which makes him immortal and more powerful than any sorcerer could ever be. He is on a scale of power comparable to Odin and Mephisto. Capable of astral projection, he can travel between dimensions, through time, and also open portals for others. In human form he can draw on the power of the Dark Dimension to achieve Hulk-level strength, and also has the ability to fly and project energy blasts.

THE HOOD

This crook wears a demonic cloak.

Parker Robbins stumbled upon his powers when he broke into a warehouse and discovered a summoned demon. Surprised, he shot it and stole its cloak and boots, which gave him magical abilities. Soon after, Parker built a criminal empire with the help of his lover, Madam Masque. This often put him in conflict with the Avengers.

The power the eponymous hood gave Parker came from the demon lord Dormammu, who could possess him through the cloak. When Dormammu sent Parker to murder Doctor Strange, Strange exorcised the demon, robbing Parker of his powers. However, he has since reappeared with his original powers intact.

DATA FILE

REAL NAME Parker Robbins **OCCUPATION** Rises from petty thief to criminal mastermind
BASE New York City
HEIGHT 5 ft 10 in **WEIGHT** 165 lbs **EYES** Brown **HAIR** Brown
FIRST APPEARANCE WITH AVENGERS *New Avengers* #33 (October 2007)
POWERS When possessed by the dark lord Dormammu, the Hood gains many powers: His magic cloak and boots grant him invisibility, the power to fire electrical bursts from his hands, the ability to walk on air, and the ability to transform into a demon.

MAN-APE

A native son of Wakanda, M'Baku became Man-Ape: Black Panther's homeland rival.

Wrathful M'Baku revived the forbidden White Gorilla cult so he could amass enough power to challenge the Black Panther for Wakanda's throne. He even followed his nemesis to America, where he joined the Grim Reaper's Lethal Legion and attacked the rest of the Avengers. Defeated and banished from Wakanda, M'Baku became a mercenary and for a time joined the Masters of Evil. He died at the hands of Morlun, an enemy of Spider-Man.

DATA FILE

REAL NAME M'Baku **OCCUPATION** Mercenary, revolutionary
BASE Mobile—beginning in Wakanda and ending in America
HEIGHT 7 ft **WEIGHT** 355 lbs **EYES** Brown **HAIR** Brown
FIRST APPEARANCE WITH AVENGERS *Avengers* #62 (March 1969)
POWERS M'Baku killed a rare white gorilla and bathed in its blood and consumed its flesh to give himself the ape's power. He then became fortified with superhuman strength and agility, and a resistance to injury—all-in-all, a powerful warrior who fights with a gorilla's totemic (animalistic and spiritualistic) style.

ABSORBING MAN

"Crusher" can soak up power from his surroundings—making him an attractive prospect to the Avengers' foes.

Frustrated with his attempts to defeat Thor, the Norse god Loki decided to empower felons and set them against Thor instead. He gave an enchanted potion to criminal Carl "Crusher" Creel, giving him the power to absorb the properties of anything he touched. Crusher had once been a boxer under the name Rocky Davis, and he used these skills against "Battling" Jack Murdock, the father of Daredevil. Crusher also fought Thor, Daredevil, and the Hulk before deciding to give up and leave the country. He bumped into Hawkeye just before he shipped out, though, and wound up battling all of the Avengers instead. He escaped by jumping into the ocean and turning himself into water, but has since run afoul of the Avengers many times.

Crusher's ball and chain come from his time in prison and make a useful weapon.

DATA FILE

REAL NAME
Carl "Crusher" Creel

OCCUPATION
Former boxer; criminal

BASE
Mobile

HEIGHT 6 ft 4 in

WEIGHT 365 lbs

EYES Blue

HAIR None

FIRST APPEARANCE WITH AVENGERS
Avengers #183 (May 1979)

POWERS
When the Absorbing Man touches something—including some forms of energy—his body can take on its physical and mystical properties. If his body breaks while in such a state, he can reassemble himself. Later he developed the ability to absorb and control another person's mind, too. During Fear Itself, Crusher was temporarily transformed by the Worthy into Greithoth, Breaker of Wills. Later, a spell turned Crusher good, but he has since returned to his old ways. His son, Stonewall, shares his powers.

CAPTAIN BRITAIN

Chosen by the legendary wizard Merlyn to become the hero of Great Britain, Otherworld, and the entire multiverse, Captain Britain now serves as a part-time Avenger protecting the universe from his United Kingdom outpost.

Brian Braddock was destined to become Captain Britain before he was born. The wizard Merlyn sent Brian's father, Sir James Braddock, to Earth-616 so he could sire a savior for the multiverse. James and his wife Elizabeth then had three children, including Brian's older brother Jamie and his twin sister Betsy (who later became Psylocke). While Brian was a graduate student in physics, the lab he was working in was attacked. He was nearly killed escaping, and Merlyn and his daughter Roma chose that instant to reveal Brian's destiny and grant him powers by means of a mystical amulet and staff.

When the Avengers asked Brian to join their team, it caused friction with his teammates, as he had to work out how to split his time between them and MI-13.

As Captain Britain, Brian first met the Avengers during the Contest of Champions, but like the other contestants, he returned home with his memory of the event wiped. Years later, Captain America asked him to join the Avengers, and he has worked with them since, even becoming a member of the Illuminati. He also runs the Braddock Academy—Britain's version of the Avengers Academy. Brian has worked both alone and as a key member of teams (including Excalibur and MI-13 and as the ruler of Otherworld) to prove himself worthy of his new powers and equal to his incredible responsibilities.

Captain Britain's powers were once integrated into his patriotic costume.

ALLIES AND ENEMIES

Brian shares a telepathic bond with his twin Betsy, who took over for him as Captain Britain for a while. When Brian couldn't bring himself to kill their reality-warping brother Jamie in order to save the multiverse, Betsy telepathically forced him to. He is married to mutant Excalibur teammate Meggan.

LIONHEART
Single mother Kelsey Leigh took over as Captain Britain for a while and later called herself Lionheart.

MI:13
Brian's employers, the British official intelligence agency MI-13, deals with paranormal threats against the UK.

DATA FILE

REAL NAME
Brian Braddock

OCCUPATION
Ruler of Otherworld, hero of Britain

BASE
Great Britain and Otherworld

HEIGHT 5 ft 11 in

WEIGHT 180 lbs

EYES Blue

HAIR Blond

FIRST APPEARANCE WITH AVENGERS
Contest of Champions #1 (June 1982)

POWERS
Captain Britain's powers originally came to him by means of his amulet and scepter, and they faded away if he left the United Kingdom for too long. They were later integrated into his costume. He no longer needs any devices, but the strength of his powers depends upon his level of confidence. When Brian is fully confident in his abilities, he has superhuman durability (by means of a force field), endurance, senses, speed, and strength, and he can fly at supersonic speeds.

KEY STORYLINE

OPERATION: GALACTIC STORM

CAPTAIN AMERICA #398–401; *AVENGERS* #345–347; *AVENGERS: WEST COAST* #80–82; *IRON MAN* #278–279; *WONDER MAN* #7–9; *QUASAR* #32–35; *THOR* #445–446

MARCH 1992–JUNE 1992
WRITERS: Mark Gruenwald, Tom DeFalco, Bob Harras, Gerard Jones, Len Kaminski, Dann Thomas, Roy Thomas
PENCILERS: Greg Capullo, Steven Epting, Jeff Johnson, Rik Levins, Pat Olliffe, David Ross, Paul Ryan, Rurik Tyler **INKERS:** Danny Bulanadi, Harry Candelario, Tim Dzon, Fred Fredricks, Al Milgrom, Tom Palmer, Dan Panosian, Bob Wiacek, Keith Williams **COLORISTS:** Paul Becton, Gina Going, Tom Palmer, Mike Rockwitz, Joe Rosas, Christie Scheele, Bob Sharen **LETTERERS:** Pat Brosseau, Janice Chiang, Michael Heisler, Michael Higgins, Bill Oakley, Joe Rosen **EDITORS:** Richard Ashford, Kelly Corvese, Tom DeFalco, Pat Garrahy, Ralph Macchio, Fabian Nicieza, Evan Skolnick, Nel Yomtov, Tom DeFalco

In perhaps their largest epic to date, the Avengers were caught up in interstellar politics that posed a very real threat to the entire galaxy.

The heroes of the Marvel Universe had met many alien races in their time, including the Shi'ar—old allies of the X-Men—and the Kree and Skrulls—warring races that had battled the Fantastic Four. But it would take the Avengers, and several comic titles, to deal with an all-out war between the Shi'ar and Kree. With so many familiar faces in the story, a large pool of creative talent was required in the real world

1 Famous sidekick to Super Heroes such as Captain America, Captain Marvel, and the Hulk, Rick Jones finds himself at the center of another adventure after having a nightmare about the Kree. The chaos soon leaks into the waking world when Rick's breakfast with Captain America is rudely interrupted by a Shi'ar threat called Warstar.

2 As Captain America recruits the West Coast Avengers to his cause, Rick becomes a captive of the Shi'ar. Jones leads the Shi'ar to a Kree Earth base, where he joins up with Cap's forces. A conflict has been brewing between the alien Kree and Shi'ar, and Earth is right in the middle of it.

3 After the Avenger Quasar comes into conflict with Shi'ar militants attempting to steal the famous Nega-bands from Captain Marvel's corpse, the Avengers investigate solar flares in outer space. They soon discover hundreds of Shi'ar ships heading toward Earth. Despite being fired upon, the Avengers break into one of the ships.

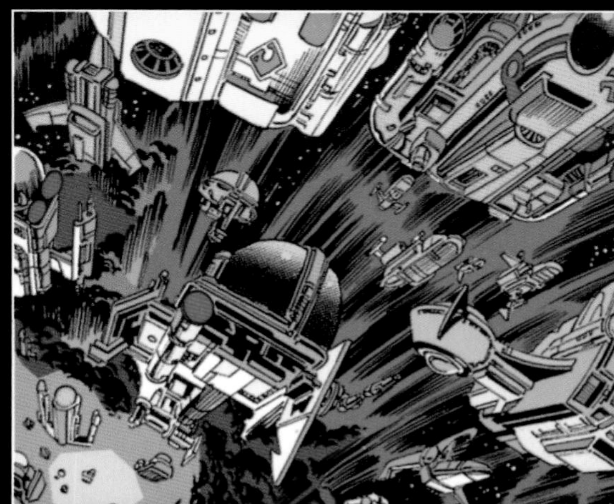

4 Learning that they have unwittingly become pawns on the Shi'ar–Kree battlefield, the Avengers decide to become peacekeepers between the warring alien factions. One envoy will stay on Earth, while Captain America leads a team to the Kree Empire. The Vision and Thor's group head to the Shi'ar Imperium.

5 But things do not go exactly according to plan. Captain America's forces are soon taken captive by the Kree. Meanwhile, after a few conflicts, Thor and his allies find audience with Lilandra, the leader of the Shi'ar, who they discover has developed a bomb that could kill billions of Kree.

"THIS IS A TOUGH MISSION, FOLKS. IF ANYONE WANTS TO BACK OUT, YOU CAN DO SO... NO QUESTIONS ASKED."
- CAPTAIN AMERICA

6 Soon Thor's team of Avengers gets caught up in a battle between Shi'ar's Imperial Guard and the Kree's elite Starforce. Angered by the conflict, Living Lightning shoots a burst of electricity toward Lilandra's advisor, Araki. And what the Avengers see when Araki hits the ground is enough to stop the battle in its tracks.

7 Araki is a Skrull in disguise! He had been manipulating Lilandra, encouraging the utter annihilation of the Kree by her powerful Nega-bomb. However, despite the enlightened Lilandra opting to negotiate for peace with the Kree, the Avengers soon discover that the Nega-bomb has disappeared.

8 Quasar, Wonder Man, and the Vision locate the Nega-bomb, only to have the bomb go off despite their best efforts. The Kree home world Hala is the first to fall, followed by worlds far from the explosion's epicenter. With only a few survivors, the Kree Empire is no more.

9 Cap's team discover that the Kree ruler, the Supreme Intelligence, had wanted this result all along, in a mad attempt to propel his people out of stagnation. Defeating the enormous being, the Avengers assemble once more as the Shi'ar takes possession of the planets formally under the Kree's control.

KEY STORYLINE

AVENGERS ASSEMBLE

AVENGERS #1–4

FEBRUARY–MAY 1998
WRITER: Kurt Busiek
PENCILER: George Perez **INKERS:** Al Vey, Bob Wiacek
COLORIST: Tom Smith **LETTERERS:** Comicraft, Kolja Fuchs, Dave Lanphaer, Richard Starkings **EDITORS:** Tom Brevoort, Bob Harras

The Avengers were reborn into their third ongoing series, once again placing Marvel's mightiest team at the top of the heap.

Marvel had earlier reinvented their universe in the form of "Heroes Reborn," an initiative that refreshed the continuity of the Avengers characters for a year. For the first time in the team's history, *The Avengers* had been restarted at issue #1, under the helm of writers Rob Liefeld and Jim Valentino, and artists Liefeld and Chap Yaep. While the series had been a financial success, at least initially, the majority of fans wanted the original team back, and after Marvel released the four-issue *Heroes Reborn: The Return* miniseries by writer Peter David and artist Salvador Larroca, they had just that. As the Earth's Mightiest Heroes were ushered into a new age by top talent writer Kurt Busiek and legendary artist George Perez, the third volume of *The Avengers* would begin—one that re-established the heroes' iconic image.

1 The Avengers are under attack! Scarlet Witch, Quicksilver, and Crystal face the first onslaught, in the form of flying trolls. Firebird is next to face an attack of a monstrous nature, just as Black Panther battles a mysterious bird-beast in his native Wakanda.

2 In fact, Avengers all over the world suddenly face mystical foes that just as suddenly vanish before their eyes. Meanwhile, the original Avengers gather at Avengers Mansion, finally back in their own reality, and are pondering how to deal with this crisis of magical proportions.

3 But before the Avengers can reach any conclusion, Thor arrives at the Mansion. Thought dead during their journey home from a pocket dimension, Thor comes with a warning of an impending danger so dire it would require the help of every single Avenger, past and present.

4 Dozens of heroes answer the Avengers' call, even a few that have never served on the Avengers team, such as Justice and Firestar. Thor reveals that he returned home to Asgard to find it destroyed and five mystic Norn stones missing, as well as the fabled Twilight Sword.

5 As they search for the five Norn stones, the Avengers soon encounter Mordred, and then his boss, Morgan Le Fay. Using Scarlet Witch's mystical powers against the team, with the combined might of the Twilight Sword, Morgan does the unthinkable, and recreates the world in her image, brainwashing the Avengers to do her bidding.

6 In this new reality, the entire world is ruled by the government of Tintagel Head and its queen, Morgan Le Fay. To make matters worse, Morgan's elite guard is comprised of Avengers members, with altered costumes and names, all loyal to her every whim.

7 Although chained in Morgan's dungeon, Scarlet Witch is still powerful. She reaches out with her mind and frees the brainwashed Captain America. Cap begins to jog the memories of his fellow Avengers, just as Wonder Man—thought deceased—arrives at the Scarlet Witch's side.

"AND THE CROWD GOES WILD!"
- HAWKEYE

8 With the help of Wonder Man, the Scarlet Witch is freed and soon wages an attack on Morgan herself. In the process, the Avengers all reclaim their memories and attack Le Fay. Scarlet Witch adds to Wonder Man's powers, and while it seems to cause Wonder Man's death, Morgan is finally defeated.

9 With the world restored, the Avengers have to deal with the pressing problem of having 39 members on their roster. Captain America and his allies soon publicly announce a new, streamlined team that includes Cap, Thor, Iron Man, Scarlet Witch, Vision, Hawkeye, and Warbird—to great public acclaim.

KEY STORYLINE
AVENGERS DISASSEMBLED

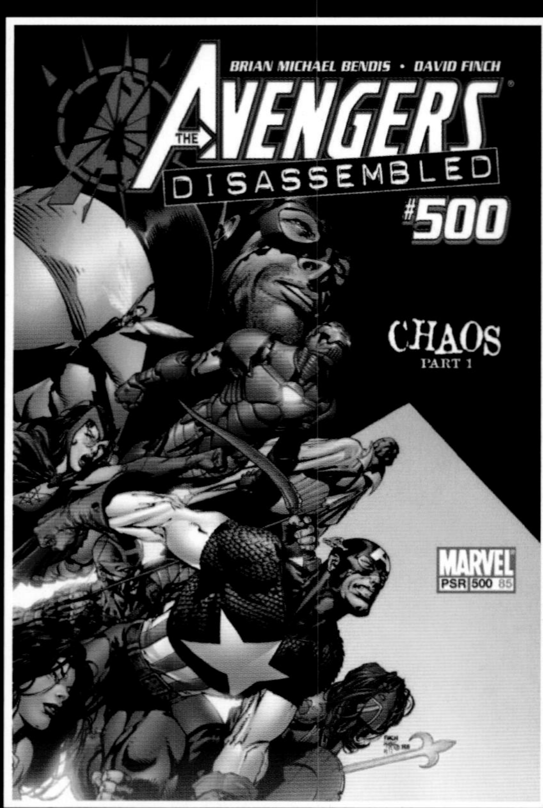

AVENGERS #500-503; *AVENGERS FINALE* #1

SEPTEMBER 2004–JANUARY 2005
WRITER: Brian Michael Bendis
PENCILERS: Jim Cheung, Olivier Coipel, Steve Epting, David Finch, Gary Frank, Michael Gaydos, David Mack, Alex Maleev, Mike Mayhew, Steve McNiven, Michael Avon Oeming, George Perez, Eric Powell, Darick Robertson, Lee Weeks **INKERS:** Danny Miki, Mike Perkins, Alex Maleev, Lee Weeks, Michael Gaydos, Eric Powell, Darick Robertson, Mike Mayhew, David Mack, Gary Frank, Michael Avon Oeming, Mark Morales **COLORISTS:** Frank D'Armata, Brian Reber, Morry Hollowell, Eric Powell, Andy Troy, Pete Pantazis, Justin Ponsor, David Mack **LETTERERS:** Richard Starkings, Albert Deschesne **EDITORS:** Nicole Wiley, Tom Brevoort, Molly Lazer, Joe Quesada, Andy Schmidt

After a shakeup that cost them the lives of a few of their fellow members, the Avengers did the unthinkable, and disbanded.

Writer Brian Michael Bendis had unwittingly voted to end the Avengers. A popular writer for his work on titles such as *Ultimate Spider-Man* and *Daredevil*, Bendis was discussing the Avengers at a Marvel editorial retreat, and what direction he thought they should go in. Without realizing it, he inadvertently pitched the idea that would become "Avengers Disassembled," a five-issue arc of *Avengers* that would tie in to several of the main characters' own titles. But as he said at the time, Bendis was simply wiping the slate clean for what was yet to happen.

1 Something is wrong with the Avengers. When the recently deceased Jack of Hearts arrives in zombie form at Avengers Mansion, he suddenly explodes, killing Ant-Man Scott Lang with him in the blast. And when Iron Man addresses the United Nations, he loses his cool, acting as if he is drunk. Yet Tony Stark hasn't taken a single sip of alcohol.

2 Before the Avengers have time to regroup and catch their breath, the Vision flies a Quinjet into the Mansion, causing another massive explosion. The Vision then walks out of the flames, acting unlike himself and announcing he no longer has control over his own body.

3 The Vision then opens his mouth, and suddenly an army of Ultrons grow from metal spheres he has discharged. The Avengers fight valiantly against the Ultrons, but She-Hulk shockingly loses her cool, attacking the Vision.

4 Becoming the monster she always feared she would be, She-Hulk rips the Vision in two, seemingly killing the longtime Avenger. She then turns her rage on Captain America, who fights back as best he can, eventually stopping her thanks to Iron Man's timely arrival.

5 The Avengers are joined by many former members, as well as the Fantastic Four and other New York City heroes. As they all try to figure out how to combat whatever or whoever is behind all that they are facing, the United Nations unanimously votes to disavow its relationship with the Avengers, thereby severing their government ties.

6 To make matters worse, a Kree armada appears over the skies of New York City and begins firing on the heroes. Severely outmatched despite their numbers, the heroes fight on as the Kree land on Earth. Meanwhile, Nick Fury questions the attack, knowing there is no strategic reason for the Kree to begin a ground offensive.

7 Hawkeye does not care about the reasoning behind the fighting. He just knows he has to stop it. When a laser catches his quiver on fire, Hawkeye decides to make his own fate, and uses a Kree soldier to fly the two of them directly into a Kree ship. Hawkeye dies in the attack, but the Kree retreat.

NOT LIKE THIS!!

8 It isn't until Dr. Strange arrives at the scene that the Avengers truly discover what is going on. It seems that the Scarlet Witch has suffered a mental breakdown, and is using her magical abilities to recreate the children she believes she has lost, as well as to torture the Avengers.

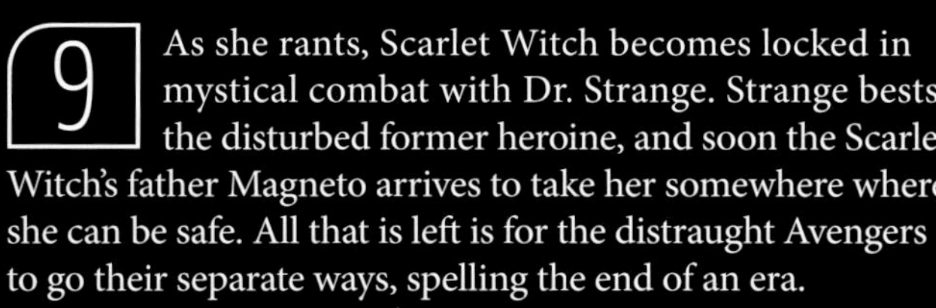

9 As she rants, Scarlet Witch becomes locked in mystical combat with Dr. Strange. Strange bests the disturbed former heroine, and soon the Scarlet Witch's father Magneto arrives to take her somewhere where she can be safe. All that is left is for the distraught Avengers to go their separate ways, spelling the end of an era.

"IT NEVER OCCURRED TO ME THAT IT COULD EVER END. I NEVER THOUGHT IT WOULD HAPPEN."
– CAPTAIN AMERICA

KEY STORYLINE NEW AVENGERS: BREAKOUT

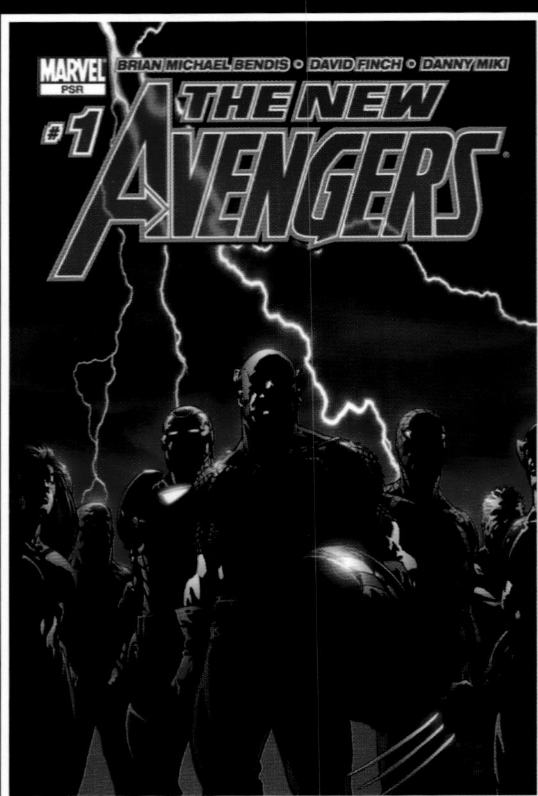

THE NEW AVENGERS #1–6

JANUARY 2005–JUNE 2005
WRITER: Brian Michael Bendis
PENCILER: David Finch **INKERS:** Allen Martinez, Danny Miki, Mark Morales, Victor Olazaba **COLORIST:** Frank D'Armata **LETTERERS:** Albert Deschesne, Richard Starkings **EDITORS:** Tom Brevoort, Molly Lazer, Stephanie Moore, Joe Quesada, Andy Schmidt, Nicole Wiley

The Avengers became the New Avengers as some of Marvel's biggest names lent their star-power to a refreshing take on the Earth's Mightiest Heroes.

Scarlet Witch had singlehandedly done what no Super Villain had ever achieved: disbanded the Avengers. They had lost some of their key members, and their invaluable association with the United Nations. But Captain America, as well as writer Brian Michael Bendis, was not about to let that status quo stand. Teaming again with artist David Finch, Bendis began the next chapter in his Avengers saga, restarting the title under the name *The New Avengers*. But instead of utilizing the usual cast of characters, Bendis decided to throw in some of Marvel's other icons not normally associated with the team. With big guns like Spider-Man and Wolverine officially signing up for duty, the Avengers were certainly "new," and enjoyed a huge surge in popularity among the readership.

1 Lawyer Matt Murdock (secretly the hero Daredevil), his associate Foggy Nelson, and bodyguard Luke Cage are paying a rare "civilian" visit to the Raft, New York's Maximum-Maximum Security Installation off the side of Ryker's Island. There they are greeted by their S.H.I.E.L.D. chaperone, Jessica Drew, the original Spider-Woman.

2 As the heroes descend into the heart of the prison, the facility suddenly loses all power. An explosive bolt of electricity rips through the penitentiary's walls. Spider-Man's old villain, Electro, is behind the attack, and soon the inmates are running amok in the chaos.

3 Electro's blast is so dramatic, Spider-Man can see it from his apartment. As he makes his way to the island, he is aided by Captain America, who has also arrived on the scene. Soon the two heroes are thrown into the thick of things as they try to help quash the violent riots.

4 During the riots, Murdock makes his way to the cell of the man he came to see: Robert Reynolds, also known as the mentally unbalanced powerhouse Sentry. While the Sentry does not immediately respond to their request for help, when the Spider-Man foe Carnage attacks, Sentry flies the creature into space and rips him in two.

5 When all is said and done, over 40 Super Villains manage to escape the Raft. That number would have been much higher if not for the timely arrival of Iron Man on the scene. Considering the effort a success, Captain America decides to reform the Avengers without UN support.

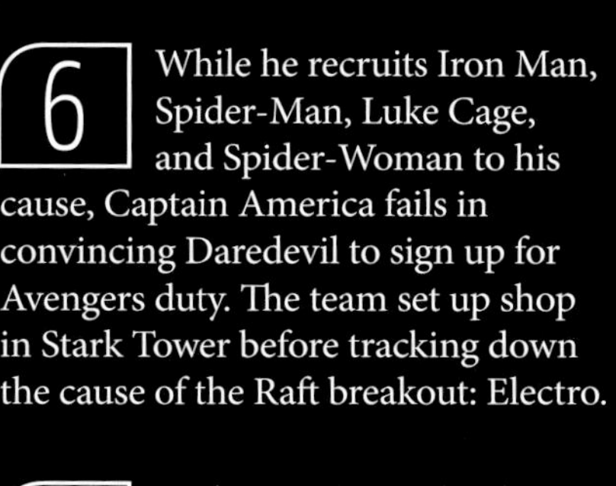

6 While he recruits Iron Man, Spider-Man, Luke Cage, and Spider-Woman to his cause, Captain America fails in convincing Daredevil to sign up for Avengers duty. The team set up shop in Stark Tower before tracking down the cause of the Raft breakout: Electro.

7 Back on Ryker's Island, Spider-Woman learns the name of the man Electro was hired to free: Karl Lykos, the Super Villain Sauron. Heading to the Savage Land to find Sauron, the heroes are surprised when they come under attack by X-Men member and fellow hero Wolverine.

"I'M SAYING THAT THE NEW TEAM ALREADY ASSEMBLED ITSELF."
- CAPTAIN AMERICA

8 Wolverine had been notified by a former villain known as the Scorcher about Sauron's activities. After realizing he had attacked the heroes by mistake, the mutant joins the Avengers until they are ambushed and taken captive by Sauron.

9 After learning that Sauron had been forced to act on S.H.I.E.L.D.'s instructions, Iron Man breaks the Avengers free. Together, they all seek out and defeat the mastermind behind the corrupt S.H.I.E.L.D. agency—Yelena Belova, who is using the name "Black Widow," while engaging in espionage and crimes for her own evil ends.

POWERS ALONE DO not make a hero—or a villain—super. The most dedicated and driven of individuals reach their full potential through a strict regimen of training and practice. This can stem from a military background, advanced combat training, or the hard-earned acquisition of a specific skill. Such talents may have been enhanced with experimental serums or bionic limbs, but it is these warriors' fighting abilities, and more importantly, determined fighting spirit, that makes them formidable forces in battle.

NEVER SURRENDER

STEVE ROGERS only wanted one thing during World War II: to fight for his country. However, he was rejected because his body was deemed too scrawny. When the government named him the test subject for their Super Soldier program, he became the physically perfect Captain America. Decades lost in suspended animation ended when the Avengers revived him and welcomed the living legend to their team. Since then, "Cap" has become the undisputed heart of the Avengers.

With well honed fighting skills and a bulletproof metal shield, Captain America doesn't let anything–or anyone–stand in his way.

CAPTAIN AMERICA

STEVE ROGERS IS THE CAPTAIN

The Super-Soldier serum devised by German-Jewish scientist Dr. Erskine had just been administered to test subject Steve Rogers when Erskine fell to a Nazi assassin. Now the only one of his kind, Steve became a symbol for the fighting spirit of the United States in his new guise as Captain America.

From the moment Steve Rogers was injected with Super-Soldier serum during World War II, his strength, agility, stamina, and battlefield awareness were second to none. He was given an indestructible shield and received combat training in its many defensive and offensive forms.

Soon joined by his sidekick Bucky Barnes, Captain America fought against Nazi villains including the Red Skull, Arnim Zola, and Baron Zemo, often serving alongside the Howling Commandos or the Super Hero team known as the Invaders. At the end of the war, Bucky seemingly perished when Baron Zemo's drone airplane exploded. Tragically, Captain America fell from the burning wreckage into the ocean below, where the frozen temperatures kept him in a state of hibernation, or suspended animation, for many decades, until he was found and rescued by the Avengers.

Though disoriented by his time-skip, he felt an instant kinship with Iron Man, Thor, Ant-Man, and the Wasp, soon emerging as

Muscles are kept toned through a regular training regimen.

Even when he's not wearing the uniform of Captain America, Steve Rogers always serves the cause of freedom and justice.

DATA FILE

REAL NAME
Steve Rogers

OCCUPATION
Adventurer, S.H.I.E.L.D. operative

BASE
New York City, New York

HEIGHT 6 ft 2 in

WEIGHT 220 lbs

EYES Blue

HAIR Blond

FIRST APPEARANCE WITH AVENGERS
Avengers #4 (March 1964)

POWERS
Captain America is the pinnacle of human physical perfection. He is an expert boxer, and highly trained in judo and many other martial arts. The Super-Soldier serum has also given him amazing endurance. His shield is virtually indestructible.

Cap can ricochet his shield off of objects so that it returns to his hand. Throwing it with enough force can render opponents unconscious.

Cap's uniform offers protection against slashing weapons and flying shrapnel.

Despite his advanced age, Cap is kept young by the Super-Soldier serum.

the Avengers' leader. In this role, Captain America recruited the first replacement roster—consisting of Hawkeye, Quicksilver, and the Scarlet Witch—and presided over many lineup changes in the years to come.

Though Cap wasn't always the most powerful member of the team, his steady leadership and clear honesty steered the Avengers through countless crisis-level events, including the Kree-Skrull War and the Avengers' fights against villains such as Ultron, Kang the Conqueror, and the Masters of Evil.

ALLIES AND ENEMIES

Many of Captain America's most fearsome foes have hated him since the days of World War II. Fortunately, he has countless friends willing to put their lives on the line in his defense.

FRIENDS

BUCKY BARNES
Bucky has been both Cap's sidekick and the Winter Soldier, and briefly took over as Captain America.

AGENT MARIA HILL
This S.H.I.E.L.D. operative has learned to trust Captain America during her time with the organization.

FALCON
Sam Wilson is Cap's former fighting partner and one of his closest friends.

IAN ZOLA
Steve rescued test-tube baby Ian from another dimension and then adopted him.

FOES

RED SKULL
This Nazi mastermind has returned from death many times in his quest for world domination.

CROSSBONES
The Red Skull's right-hand man is an expert combatant, sniper, and foe to Captain America.

ARNIM ZOLA
Deranged scientist Arnim Zola has worked with Red Skull against Cap.

IRON NAIL
Spy Ran Shen used his powers when in humanoid dragon form to drain the Super-Soldier serum from Cap's body.

"WE ARE A PLANET OF THE FREE, A PEOPLE OF FREEDOM! AND IF YOU CHOOSE TO STAND IN THE WAY OF THAT FREEDOM, YOU WILL HEAR THESE WORDS: AVENGERS ASSEMBLE!"
- CAPTAIN AMERICA

Captain America faced off against Nazi villain the Red Skull in a struggle pitting freedom against tyranny.

A LIFE SPENT AT WAR

Many heroic characters have stepped up to the role of Captain America, but there have also been false pretenders who have tried to tarnish his name. Anti-Cap was a U.S. Marines agent who went rogue, until Steve Rogers brought him down at a Parisian train station.

As their esteemed leader, Captain America helped the Avengers grow in number and in public acclaim, but he continued to face conflict during his time away from Avengers Mansion as well, with S.H.I.E.L.D. being right at the forefront.

Cap's old enemies, including the Red Skull and Baron Zemo, returned to plague him in this new era, but he found an ally in Sam Wilson, who became the costumed hero called the Falcon. Steve also found some respite from his duties while serving as as an operative with S.H.I.E.L.D., by striking up a romance with Agent Sharon Carter—a relative of his wartime love, Peggy Carter.

Continuing to face difficulties despite new alliances, Steve resigned as Captain America when government officials tried to control him. A new Captain America, John Walker, briefly assumed the role, but became the U.S. Agent after Rogers returned. Captain America took a central role with a new Avengers lineup, and led the fight against Ultron to avenge the murdered citizens of Slorernia. When the Avengers dissolved, it weighed heavily on Cap's heart, as he viewed the team as not just colleagues, but as his family. Things got even worse when the Civil War tore apart the Super Hero community. When hit by a sniper's bullet, his life appeared to have ended, but he had actually been knocked into a timestream where he relived major life events.

"WE HAVE NO CHOICE. SO WE FIGHT—AND WE WIN. THERE ARE NO OTHER OPTIONS."
- CAPTAIN AMERICA

WORLD WAR II VETERAN Captain America led soldiers into battle on the beaches of Normandy—a memory he experienced anew during his trip back through time. The world believed that Captain America had died, but the hero had in fact become stuck in time. Bouncing from World War II to the early days of the Avengers, Cap realized that something was wrong and struggled to free himself. When he finally emerged into the present day, everyone agreed that the one, true Captain America had returned.

OTHER **PROUD** CAPTAINS

There have been times when Steve Rogers could no longer continue in his role as Captain America, leaving worthy successors to live up to the example that he had set. Two of the most notable figures—Sam Wilson and Bucky Barnes—are also two of Steve Rogers' greatest friends.

SAM WILSON As the Falcon, Sam Wilson worked closely with Steve Rogers as partners and Avengers teammates. When Steve Rogers faced off against an enemy known as the Iron Nail, the Super-Soldier serum in his body went inert and caused the rapid aging of his body. No longer able to perform the athletics required of Captain America, Rogers named Sam Wilson as his replacement. Wilson kept the wings from his Falcon costume so that he could remain airborne while operating as Cap.

Sam Wilson has become a leader within the Super Hero community as Captain America.

BUCKY BARNES The discovery that his wartime sidekick Bucky Barnes had survived the explosion of Baron Zemo's drone was a shock to Steve Rogers. He tracked down Bucky and helped him shake off the mental programming he had received to become the Winter Soldier. After an assassin seemingly killed Rogers, Bucky became the replacement Captain America. Eventually, Steve Rogers returned to the role, allowing Bucky to go back to his low-profile Winter Soldier identity.

Bucky Barnes wore a redesigned, streamlined version of the Captain America costume.

As Captain America, Bucky Barnes engaged in close-quarters combat and carried a gun.

LEADING FROM THE FRONT LINE

Captain America wasn't present for the first adventure of the Avengers, but he has become such a core part of the team that he has been retroactively named a founding member.

CAP'S EARLY YEARS

Avengers #4 (March 1964)

Steve Rogers was born in New York City and suffered the loss of his parents while he was still a teenager. An illustrator, he longed to fight for his country and tried again and again to enlist in the U.S. Army. Rejected because of his weak physique, Rogers instead became the test subject for Project: Rebirth. The Super-Soldier serum he was administered as part of the U.S. Army's secret project raised Rogers to the peak of human perfection. He trained at Camp Lehigh in Virginia while leading a double life as freedom's champion Captain America. Soon joined by Bucky Barnes as his sidekick, Cap fought the Red Skull and other Nazis until disappearing into icy waters at the end of World War II. Revived decades later by the Avengers, Captain America re-emerged into a drastically changed world. The Avengers proved to be the perfect new family for Cap, and his fame as a wartime hero provided the team with public legitimacy during its formative stages. If an Avenger is needed to address the press, Captain America usually volunteers.

Captain America gratefully joined the Avengers when they revived him and invited him to join their family.

Steve Rogers' Nomad costume didn't last long, but it inspired a number of successors to take up the role.

CAPTAIN AMERICA IS NOMAD

Captain America #180 (December 1974)

The complexities of modern life sometimes confused Steve Rogers, who missed the straightforward moral divisions that he had grown accustomed to during World War II. This feeling reached its height when a shocking political scandal implicated the U.S. President as a manipulative villain. Rogers felt he could no longer embody the nation as Captain America, not when his faith in democracy had been so badly shaken. Instead he became Nomad—a man without a country—until he realized that Captain America stood for the people of the nation, not necessarily its elected leaders. The Nomad identity was taken up by Jack Monroe, who partnered with Cap and became a hero in his own right. Much later, Ian Zola became the new Nomad and worked alongside Sam Wilson (aka Falcon), who at that time was serving as Captain America.

"HOW COULD THE GOOD GUYS PUT THEIR FAITH IN A MAN SO BAD?"
- NOMAD

THE ONE TRUE CAPTAIN

Captain America #350 (February 1989)

Following a disagreement with the Commission for Superhuman Activities, Steve Rogers had quit his position as Captain America, and the government had passed the uniform to soldier John Walker. Meanwhile, Rogers continued to serve the public secretly. A failed mission had left Walker in hospital, but he left when a mysterious summons promised him the return of his lost shield. He discovered a businessman who looked like Steve Rogers, and planned to use his stolen good looks and influence to gain power. Walker soon found himself battling the villain's henchmen. Elsewhere, Rogers grew suspicious that his old enemy Red Skull was influencing and killing government officials. Rogers followed a trail back to the same office block that Walker was in. Here, Rogers confronted the man who had copied his features. The villain revealed he had been influencing the Commission and provoking Walker into acts of violence—all with the aim of discrediting the role of Captain America. Rogers discovered that the villain was Red Skull, who quickly fled the scene. Thanks to his heroics, Rogers soon resumed the legendary role of Captain America.

During a fight with Steve Rogers, his mystery opponent was sprayed in the face with Dust of Death, revealing his Red Skull identity and confirming Rogers' suspicions.

The experience of living through a non-linear timeline allowed Captain America to replay some of the most important events of his life.

DEATH AND RETURN

Captain America: Reborn #6 (March 2010)

During the divisive Civil War, Captain America took up a public stance to announce his opposition to the Superhuman Registration Act. His Avengers teammate Iron Man disagreed, leading the pro-registration forces and triggering an ideological split within the Super Hero community. Cap chose to surrender rather than risk further bloodshed, but as he walked up the courthouse steps heading to his arraignment, the Red Skull's henchman, Crossbones, took a long-range shot at Cap while a brainwashed Sharon Carter fired several more times at close range. Struck down, Captain America was rushed to a hospital and pronounced dead. However, Steve Rogers had actually been shunted into the timestream, where he relived key flashpoints in his history before finding his way back to the present. On his return, Rogers allowed Bucky Barnes to continue as the replacement Captain America for a time while he forged a new career as a Super Soldier and the head of U.S. National Security, also taking a role as executive director of S.H.I.E.L.D.

CLINT BARTON joined the circus at the age of 14, where he learned to fight and shoot arrows under the mentorship of pro archer Trickshot and the carnival star Swordsman. He began a costumed crime-fighting career, only to be mistaken for a criminal, then turned to crime—finally creating a heroic identity for himself after joining the Avengers. Throughout many team incarnations, including the spin-off West Coast Avengers, Hawkeye has been one of its most loyal members.

Early on in their genesis, and in order to prove his precision targeting to a skeptical group of Avengers, Hawkeye pulled out three arrows and fired them all at once!

HAWKEYE

Superb hand-eye coordination gives Hawkeye unmatched skills with his bow and arrows.

ALWAYS ON TARGET

DATA FILE

REAL NAME
Clinton "Clint" Barton

OCCUPATION
Adventurer

BASE
New York City, New York

HEIGHT 6 ft 3 in

WEIGHT 230 lbs

EYES Blue

HAIR Blond

FIRST APPEARANCE WITH AVENGERS
Avengers #16 (May 1965)

POWERS
Hawkeye is an expert archer, and he often employs a variety of trick arrows in addition to regular ones. His skills are enhanced by the extensive training in martial arts and acrobatics he underwent during his time in the circus. He is able to aim an arrow perfectly from any angle and whatever his vantage point.

A light, streamlined costume complements Clint's natural athletic ability.

A circus performer who first earned fame as a criminal, Hawkeye didn't seem like Avengers material when he first applied for membership. But during the team's first recruitment drive, Hawkeye proved himself to Captain America and earned a spot alongside Quicksilver and the Scarlet Witch. In time, he enlisted his former partner Black Widow, too.

Hawkeye didn't have superpowers, but he rarely missed when hitting targets with his bow. Once firmly ensconced as an Avenger, he even borrowed the size-changing powerhouse Goliath identity from Hank Pym, but soon returned to his preferred role of Hawkeye.

Figures from Hawkeye's past, including his brother Barney and the villainous Swordsman who had provided his circus training, emerged to complicate his career with the Avengers. But Hawkeye persevered, defeating the cosmic entity known as the Collector during the Korvac saga. After marrying Mockingbird, Hawkeye founded the West Coast Avengers until her presumed death drove him away.

Hawkeye died when an out-of-control Scarlet Witch sent Kree warriors to attack Avengers

The outspoken Hawkeye had the opportunity to live up to his boasts when Captain America recommended him for Avengers membership.

ALLIES AND ENEMIES

Hawkeye isn't shy about making his likes and dislikes known—a quality that has earned him respect from those who value his honesty. Even his enemies appreciate his straightforward nature.

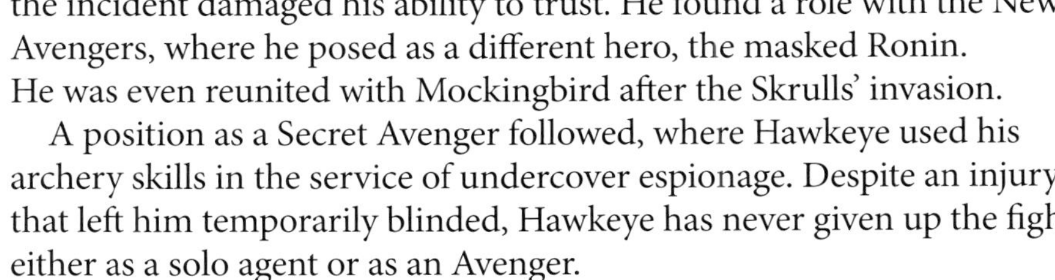

Mansion. Her reality-warping powers also brought him back to life, but the incident damaged his ability to trust. He found a role with the New Avengers, where he posed as a different hero, the masked Ronin. He was even reunited with Mockingbird after the Skrulls' invasion.

A position as a Secret Avenger followed, where Hawkeye used his archery skills in the service of undercover espionage. Despite an injury that left him temporarily blinded, Hawkeye has never given up the fight, either as a solo agent or as an Avenger.

FRIENDS

MOCKINGBIRD
As Hawkeye's partner and ex-wife, Mockingbird knows Clint better than anyone.

SPIDER-WOMAN
Hawkeye had a brief relationship with this Avengers teammate.

CAPTAIN AMERICA
It was Cap who originally accepted Hawkeye as a member of the Avengers.

BLACK WIDOW
Black Widow and Hawkeye started out as lovers, but are now purely professional.

KATE BISHOP
Kate became Hawkeye while with the Young Avengers, a move that Clint endorsed.

FOES

CROSSFIRE
An ex-CIA agent, Crossfire is one of Hawkeye's oldest foes.

BULLSEYE
This assassin once posed as Hawkeye on a villainous Avengers team.

Clint discovered that his long-assumed-dead brother, Barney, is alive during a period of temporary deafness caused by the violent Clown.

Hawkeye often relies on his fighting ability to prove his worth to the Avengers, who sometimes accuse him of only being able to talk the talk. During a battle with the Skrulls, Hawkeye was never far from the frontline.

THE LONE RANGER

A mixed and murky past has allowed Hawkeye to make friends from all walks of life—rich and poor, heroes and villains—all of which has impacted upon him becoming the Super Hero he is today.

Clint is short-tempered and blunt, but is not the type to give up—no matter how steep the odds. Hawkeye has a great deal of skill as a leader, having served at various times as the head of the Avengers, the West Coast Avengers, and the Secret Avengers, not to mention his roles as an instructor at Avengers Academy and as a trainer for Kate Bishop when she went on to become the second Hawkeye.

UPBRINGING Born in Iowa, USA, Clint Barton lost his parents in a car accident at an early age. He and his brother Barney grew up in an orphanage, but slipped away when they had the chance to join the circus. The Swordsman hired Clint as his assistant, and the boy received additional training from Trickshot. Soon, he had taken the name Hawkeye, wowing carnival crowds as the "World's Greatest Marksman."

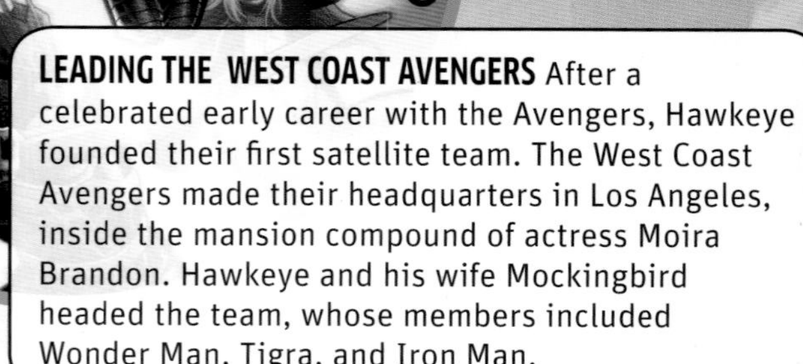

LEADING THE WEST COAST AVENGERS After a celebrated early career with the Avengers, Hawkeye founded their first satellite team. The West Coast Avengers made their headquarters in Los Angeles, inside the mansion compound of actress Moira Brandon. Hawkeye and his wife Mockingbird headed the team, whose members included Wonder Man, Tigra, and Iron Man.

COMPLICATED LOVE LIFE Relationships with women proved to be one of one of Hawkeye's most predictable vulnerabilities. He began his costumed career while in a relationship with the Black Widow and turned to crime in order to impress her, then set his sights on the Scarlet Witch after joining the Avengers. This angered his teammate Vision, and a frustrated Hawkeye quit the Avengers to go solo. Soon Mockingbird had caught his eye, and the two teamed up to defeat the villain Crossfire. Their whirlwind romance led to marriage, but Mockingbird seemingly died in battle with Mephisto. Later, Hawkeye had short flings with his Avengers teammates Wasp and Spider-Woman.

MENTORING KATE BISHOP The world believed Hawkeye to be dead after the Scarlet Witch's breakdown and the temporary disbanding of the Avengers. During this time, Young Avenger Kate Bishop took on the identity of Hawkeye. In time, Clint returned from the dead—but he wasn't quite ready to step into his old role. In a new role as Ronin, he met with Kate to test her commitment as a hero before agreeing that she had become a worthy Hawkeye. Later, Clint recruited Kate to be his partner to fight street crimes in Brooklyn, New York.

ALTER EGOS Clint Barton had grown into his Super Hero position as Hawkeye, but his restless spirit caused him to experiment with new roles. Early in his time with the Avengers, he gained size-changing abilities and rebranded himself as the second Goliath. Much later, he kept his return from the dead a secret from the Super Hero community by donning the disguise of Ronin. In this guise he joined the New Avengers, eventually revealing himself to his teammates and allowing the Ronin identity to be assumed by others.

STAYING ALIVE

Hawkeye has been with the Avengers almost from the beginning, but he has often left the team to do his own thing. Whenever this happens, it's a safe bet that he'll soon be back to share his talents with a new lineup of heroes.

Hawkeye takes aim in his most iconic costume, derived from his days as a carnival performer.

THUNDERBOLTS ASSEMBLE!

Thunderbolts #21 (December 1998)

The Thunderbolts started out as Baron Zemo's attempt to create an Avengers-like hero team composed entirely of disguised villains. By the time Hawkeye caught up with them, Zemo wasn't anywhere to be found and the new squad needed a leader. Hawkeye's experience as head of the West Coast Avengers qualified him to guide the reformed crooks, and he even found a new love with Moonstone. Ultimately, and to ensure that the Thunderbolts would receive full pardons for their criminal histories, Hawkeye agreed to accept a prison sentence on their behalf.

HAWKEYE DISASSEMBLED

House of M #7 (November 2005)

The Scarlet Witch joined the Avengers on the same day as Hawkeye, but their long history together didn't save the bowman when she went insane and lost control of her reality-altering magic. A force of Kree warriors—summoned by the Scarlet Witch's powers—attacked Avengers Mansion, igniting a quiver of explosive arrows strapped to Hawkeye's back. Just before they detonated, he positioned himself near the Kree warship, destroying the alien vessel in a heroic act of self-sacrifice. Hawkeye returned when the Scarlet Witch recreated a world dominated by mutants, but shot her with an arrow in retaliation for her previous actions. The Scarlet Witch seemingly erased Hawkeye from the timeline, but he survived—this time keeping a low profile by assuming the identity of the masked hero Ronin.

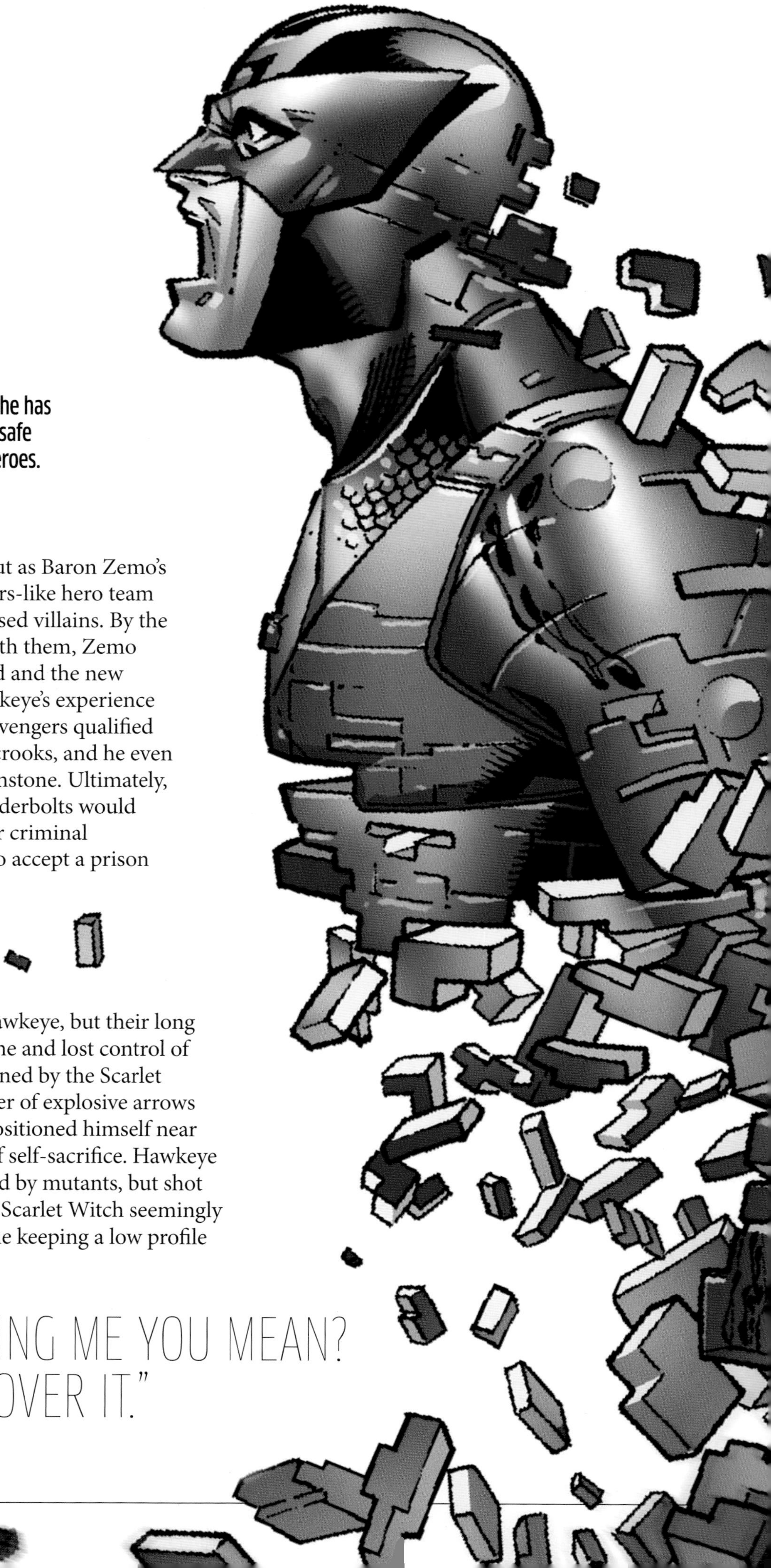

"AM I "MAD" AT YOU? FOR KILLING ME YOU MEAN? MAD JUST DOESN'T SEEM TO COVER IT."

– HAWKEYE, TO SCARLET WITCH

While Hank Pym (as Giant-Man) puts academy recruit Reptil in a headlock, Hawkeye fires a disabling arrow.

TEMPORARY TEACHER

Avengers Academy #21 (January 2012)

Before joining the Secret Avengers, Hawkeye spent time as a teacher at Avengers Academy, reuniting with old teammates including academy headmaster Hank Pym and fellow instructors Quicksilver and Tigra. The Academy stood on the same site as the former Avengers West Coast headquarters, which Hawkeye had founded. A stint as an instructor allowed Hawkeye to mold the newest class of recruits, who also needed help with their personal insecurities and interpersonal conflicts. Despite his time overseeing both the West Coast Avengers and the Thunderbolts, Hawkeye had a tough time managing the young crew, with Finesse, Hazmat, Mettle, Reptil, and other members often too eager to prove themselves and rushing into danger without thinking.

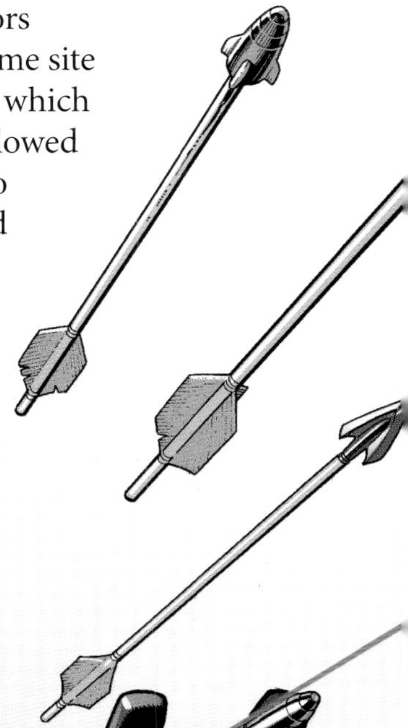

CONSCIENTIOUS OBJECTOR

Secret Avengers #1 (April 2013)

During a time when he was no longer serving as Captain America, Steve Rogers founded the original Secret Avengers and recruited Hawkeye as a member. The goal of the team was to undertake top-secret "black ops" missions. Hawkeye excelled in this role and headed up a squad that included Giant-Man and Captain Britain. Following a battle with the Descendants, the Secret Avengers reformed, this time under the guidance of S.H.I.E.L.D. director Maria Hill. The new lineup reunited Hawkeye with Black Widow, and added Nick Fury, Jr., S.H.I.E.L.D. agent Phil Coulson, and eventually Mockingbird. Primarily charged with counter-terrorism missions, the Secret Avengers sometimes received morally-questionable orders such as political assassinations—acts which Hawkeye could not accept due to his heroic conscience.

With the rest of the Secret Avengers beside him, Hawkeye releases a spread of arrows from his trusty bow as they rush into battle.

BLACK WIDOW

NATALIA ROMANOVA, more commonly known as Natasha, trained as an espionage agent under a top-secret Soviet program and received the codename Black Widow. Sent to spy on Tony Stark's operations in the United States, she turned against her Russian controllers after she met the hero Hawkeye. Despite her checkered past, Black Widow joined the Avengers and has proved herself a loyal member throughout many stints with the team. Black Widow also has experience as a S.H.I.E.L.D. operative, making her one of the Avengers' most versatile assets.

An early lineup of the Avengers saw Black Widow join forces with Thor, Vision, Daredevil, and Black Panther.

DATA FILE

REAL NAME
Natalia "Natasha" Romanova

OCCUPATION
Spy

BASE
Mobile

HEIGHT 5 ft 7 in

WEIGHT 125 lbs

EYES Blue

HAIR Red

FIRST APPEARANCE WITH AVENGERS
Avengers #29 (July 1966)

POWERS
A version of the Super-Soldier serum keeps the Black Widow in peak condition, and her training has given her advanced combat skills. Her bracelets contain the "widow's line" (a cable used for swinging and climbing) and the "widow's bite" which fires electric bolts. Her belt carries explosives.

A DARK HISTORY

Natasha Romanova lived a mysterious life prior to her emergence as an international spy, though she has since made a name for herself as an Avenger!

Natasha's parents died in Stalingrad during World War II, and a Russian soldier named Ivan Petrovitch became the girl's protector. According to rumors, Natasha trained at the top-secret Red Room facility as a Soviet agent, receiving physical enhancements derived from a copy of Captain America's Super-Soldier serum. She married pilot Alexi Shostakov—who became the Soviet hero Red Guardian—and acquired the codename Black Widow.

As a spy, Black Widow convinced then criminal Hawkeye to aid her on missions that pitted the pair against Iron Man

ALLIES AND ENEMIES

Black Widow is one of the most well-connected members of the Avengers, and has made numerous friends and foes throughout the many years of her career as a spy.

Black Widow and Hawkeye made a formidable team, enjoying a romantic relationship until other commitments forced them to break it off.

and Stark Industries. She eventually defected to the United States, but Russian agents brainwashed her and forced her to attack the Avengers. After coming to her senses, Black Widow atoned for her actions and earned a spot on the Avengers roster.

Following her time working for Nick Fury as a S.H.I.E.L.D. agent, Black Widow rejoined the Avengers. During the Civil War she sided with Iron Man in favor of the Superhuman Registration Act. Later, she joined the new Secret Avengers under the leadership of Commander Steve Rogers.

FRIENDS

HAWKEYE
The brash bowman was Black Widow's first friend in the United States.

DAREDEVIL
Daredevil is one of the few heroes who can match Black Widow in combat.

CAPTIAN AMERICA
Captain America and Black Widow have a history that stretches back to WWII.

WINTER SOLDIER
Soviet-trained Bucky Barnes and Black Widow grew close during his stint as Cap.

FOES

RED GUARDIAN
Black Widow's former husband Red Guardian is the Russian counterpart of Cap.

YELENA BELOVA
Russian agent Yelena clashed with Natasha and also took on the name Black Widow.

Black Widow's athleticism has been honed by her advanced training.

Black Widow's holster is part of her uniform—she is never unarmed.

Streamlined bodysuits such as this one aid in combat and in stealth.

Black Widow shows few signs of aging, due to the modified Super-Soldier serum in her blood, slowing the usual aging process.

Black Widow's speed and strength have been enhanced to the peak of human perfection.

Natasha's international background has attracted a wide variety of friends and foes.

UNDERCOVER AVENGER

Black Widow has always been more of a spy than a Super Hero, a fact that has helped save the Avengers from danger on numerous occasions. Initially her teammates weren't always sure they could trust this deadly Russian agent, but over time Black Widow has become part of the team's reliable core roster.

SOVIET SPY

Tales of Suspense #52 (April 1964)

While working as a Russian spy and assassin, the Black Widow and fellow agent Boris Turgenov received an assignment to kill Anton Vanko—the Crimson Dynamo—for his betrayal of the Soviet Union. The mission required them to infiltrate Stark Industries, where Vanko had sought refuge. Natasha easily beguiled Tony Stark, as he fell under the sway of her seductive beauty. Meanwhile, Boris targeted Vanko. Tony Stark didn't realize Natasha's role in the deception until the very end. Ultimately the Black Widow failed in her mission, but she knew it wouldn't be her last undercover assignment in the United States.

Abandoning her spy costume in favor of elegant evening wear, Black Widow remained just as deadly as ever.

Quickly assessing the situation, Black Widow uses the aggression of the attacking animals to her advantage.

PROVING HER SKILLS

Avengers #112 (June 1973)

Following her professional and personal splits with Hawkeye and Daredevil respectively, Black Widow moved into Avengers Mansion for the first time. She acknowledged that she was the junior member of the group, but still couldn't wait for an opportunity to prove herself to the veterans on the Avengers roster. That chance came when the Black Panther was targeted by a villain who claimed to embody the spirit of an ancient African lion god. Black Widow used her agility and her widow's line to keep out of range of the claws of the big cats, capably demonstrating her competence against an unexpected threat.

WARTIME ENCOUNTER

The Uncanny X-Men #268 (late September 1990)

Natasha Romanova's history with early Avenger Captain America goes all the way back to World War II. As a young girl under the protection of Ivan Petrovitch, her travels took her to the Southeast Asian nation of Madripoor. There, Natasha earned the unwelcome attention of Nazi villain Baron von Strucker, who abducted her and presented her to an organization of criminal assassins known as the Hand. But Ivan Petrovitch had already secured the assistance of two heroes who were visiting Madripoor: Captain America (in his civilian guise as Steve Rogers) and Logan, who would later become the X-Man known as Wolverine. A ritual designed to make Natasha the Hand's next Master Assassin came to a quick end when the heroes rescued the girl and ended Baron Strucker's scheme.

Black Widow, Captain America, and Wolverine have teamed up many times since their first meeting.

"MY PAST IS MY OWN!"

– BLACK WIDOW

AGAINST THE RED SKULL

Captain America #41 (October 2008)

During a time when Steve Rogers was believed to be dead, Black Widow struck up a relationship with the new Captain America, Bucky Barnes. As Falcon and the new Cap uncovered evidence of the Red Skull's base in upstate New York, Black Widow used her S.H.I.E.L.D. connections to verify that Sharon Carter—Agent 13—had been taken prisoner at the same facility. She called in a strike force of S.H.I.E.L.D. agents and breached the base's defenses, making short work of its A.I.M. defenders and rescuing Agent 13 before a self-destruct sequence caused the structure to collapse.

On difficult missions with or without the Avengers, Black Widow is never afraid to do what is necessary in order to win the day.

ASSIGNMENT: ASSASSINATION

Secret Avengers #5 (September 2014)

Black Widow's time with the Secret Avengers reunited her with her old love Hawkeye, but the team's missions sometimes put the two at philosophical odds. Working under the orders of S.H.I.E.L.D. director Maria Hill, Black Widow, Hawkeye, and Nick Fury, Jr. infiltrated A.I.M. Island with the goal of eliminating the A.I.M Scientist Supreme. Hawkeye objected, claiming that his moral code would not allow him to kill anyone in cold blood. Black Widow was prepared to take the shot until the opposition stepped in. Ultimately Nick Fury, Jr. fulfilled the assignment, creating a political crisis and emphasizing the split between idealistic heroes and more practical ones like Black Widow.

Black Widow and Falcon are both former Avengers and respect each other's' fighting styles.

Fury's eye was first injured during World War II, then further damaged when his brother Jake, a Hydra spy, shot him.

NICK FURY

NICK FURY is a World War II veteran who joined S.H.I.E.L.D. and rose to the post of director. Fury and S.H.I.E.L.D. worked closely with Captain America and other Avengers, providing them with intelligence and a fighting force against the terrorist organization Hydra.

Many of Nick Fury's fellow former members of the U.S. Army's Howling Commandos followed him into the service of S.H.I.E.L.D.

As an agent of S.H.I.E.L.D., Fury has access to many high-tech devices.

Nick Fury has had decades of military training, making him an expert shot with a machine gun and many other weapons.

DATA FILE

REAL NAME
Nicholas Joseph Fury

OCCUPATION
Adventurer

BASE
Mobile

HEIGHT 6 ft 1 in

WEIGHT 221 lbs

EYES Brown

HAIR Brown

FIRST APPEARANCE WITH AVENGERS
In a vision: *Avengers* #18 (July 1965); with S.H.I.E.L.D.: *Avengers* #19 (August 1965)

POWERS
A trained strategist and an excellent martial artist, Fury has plenty of combat experience from his soldiering days. Due to the injection of Infinity Formula in his bloodstream, Nick Fury's aging has been slowed and he can heal from injuries more quickly than the average human.

FURIOUS NICK FURY

Born in New York City, Nick Fury joined the U.S. Army after the devastating attack on Pearl Harbor. He received command of U.S. Army's First Attack Squad and molded the select group of soldiers into the legendary "Howling Commandos."

Nick Fury and the Howling Commandos won many victories during World War II. At the war's end, an injured Fury received a healing dose of the experimental Infinity Formula, which kept him youthful and strong. Fury worked for the CIA and later joined S.H.I.E.L.D., becoming an exceptional spy. Upon being named director, Fury expanded S.H.I.E.L.D. into a global intelligence agency and worked closely with Super Hero teams like the Avengers. Despite Fury's best efforts, S.H.I.E.L.D. has often been compromised—whether by Hydra agents, shapeshifting Skrulls, or lifelike Deltite androids. Nick Fury, however, never gives up the fight.

During World War II, Nick Fury fought in Europe and performed secret missions as the leader of the Howling Commandos.

ALWAYS WATCHING

Nick Fury was known for his heroics on Earth during World War II but, for decades, not even his closest allies knew that he also worked to protect Earth from the threat of extraterrestrials.

THE UNSEEN

Original Sin #8 (September 2014)

As one of the defenders of Earth, Fury had secretly thwarted dozens of alien invasions over the years, often through brutal and questionable methods. In modern times, Fury continued his work by trying to stop Doctor Midas and other villains when they attacked Uatu the Watcher on the Moon. Uatu's role was to observe events but never to act. When Fury needed to extract information from Uatu to find the criminals who attacked him and Uatu refused, Fury killed him. As punishment, the other Watchers forced Fury to take Uatu's place.

As the Unseen, Nick Fury was forced to observe events on Earth from the Moon, but he could not interfere.

ALLIES AND ENEMIES

Nick Fury knows everyone, heroes and villains alike. He has a coldly calculating approach to determining their value that has at times alienated his allies.

CAPTAIN AMERICA
Cap and Nick Fury fought together in World War II and their partnership continues.

DUM DUM DUGAN
Fury's second-in-command during WWII was also former deputy director of S.H.I.E.L.D.

FOE

BARON VON STRUCKER
This leader of Hydra is the closest thing Fury has to an archenemy.

NICK FURY, JR.
Formerly Marcus Johnson, Nick Fury's once-secret son is a member of S.H.I.E.L.D.

JAKE FURY
Nick Fury's younger brother formed the criminal Zodiac cartel as the villain Scorpio.

S.H.I.E.L.D. CAREER

Nick Fury has spent nearly his entire life working for (or leading) governmental, military, or espionage organizations.

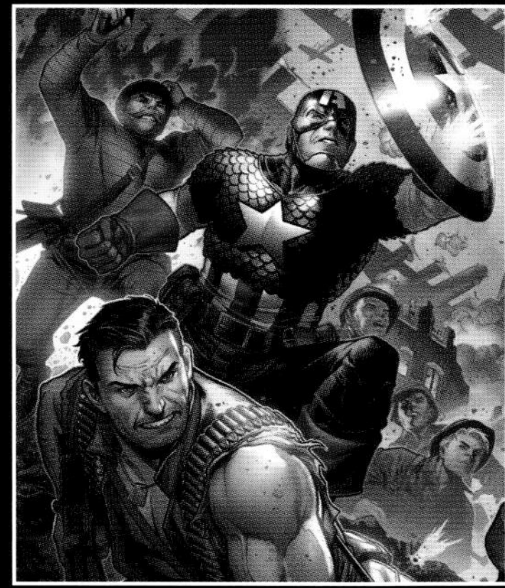

Nick Fury fought alongside Captain America during World War II and the two share a mutual respect for one another.

WORLD WAR II

The Howling Commandos were oddball soldiers molded by Sergeant Nick Fury into an elite unit that tackled the toughest assignments. Serving members included Gabe Jones, "Dum Dum" Dugan, and even a defector from Nazi Germany. The unit had a high success rate, earning Fury praise from high-ranking officers.

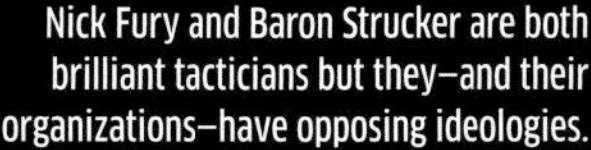

Nick Fury and Baron Strucker are both brilliant tacticians but they—and their organizations—have opposing ideologies.

S.H.I.E.L.D.

In his role as director of S.H.I.E.L.D., Nick Fury spearheaded efforts to shut down the terrorists of Hydra and their leader, Baron Strucker. Late in his career, Fury discovered evidence that S.H.I.E.L.D. had fallen under Hydra's covert control. With his Secret Warriors team composed of the children of Super Villians, Fury fought Hydra's corruption.

SECRET WAR

As director of S.H.I.E.L.D., Nick Fury gathered a squad consisting of Captain America, Spider-Man, Luke Cage, Wolverine, Daredevil, and Black Widow to attack the aggressive nation of Latveria. The action was intended as a preemptive strike, but Latveria's counterattack and the resulting fallout led to Fury's dismissal from S.H.I.E.L.D.

Nick Fury (center) led a squad of Super Heroes into action against the government of Latveria, an action that later had enormous repercussions.

MOCKINGBIRD

BOBBI MORSE, talented agent of S.H.I.E.L.D., took the name of Mockingbird and became a costumed adventurer. Shortly after falling in love with Hawkeye, Mockingbird joined the Avengers and the two of them founded the West Coast Avengers.

SPY TURNED SUPER HERO

Mockingbird found success as a spy before becoming a Super Hero. Her biology studies at Georgia Tech prepared Bobbi Morse for her first job with S.H.I.E.L.D., when she joined the organization to research the Super-Soldier serum as a member of Project Gladiator. Morse also received combat instruction and espionage training, graduating at the top of her class and earning the S.H.I.E.L.D. designation of Agent 19.

Bobbi Morse later took on the costumed identity of Mockingbird, using two battle staves as her signature weapons. While investigating a case of corporate corruption, Mockingbird crossed paths with Hawkeye and teamed up with him to defeat the villain Crossfire. A whirlwind romance led to marriage, and soon Mockingbird and Hawkeye found themselves as the co-founders of a new team, the West Coast Avengers. Mockingbird served as the template for Ultron's new robot Alkhema and even became a prisoner of the Skrulls, but has continued the fight as a member of the Secret Avengers.

DATA FILE

REAL NAME
Barbara "Bobbi" Morse

OCCUPATION
Adventurer; PhD in biology from Georgia Technical Institute

BASE
Mobile (moving from New York to LA)

HEIGHT 5 ft 9 in

WEIGHT 135 lbs

EYES Blue

HAIR Blonde

FIRST APPEARANCE WITH AVENGERS
Avengers #239 (January 1984)

POWERS
Mockingbird has no superpowers, but she is an expert fighter with full S.H.I.E.L.D. training. She is extremely tough, combative, and intelligent. Mockingbird is also a highly-trained althlete and gymnast. S.H.I.E.L.D. also trained her in espionage and counter-espionage. She was injected with a formula that gives her a degree of superhuman strength.

Mockingbird and Hawkeye fell in love at first sight, but at times their strong personalities have pushed them apart.

ALLIES AND ENEMIES

Much of Mockingbird's career has been spent in the shadows as an agent of S.H.I.E.L.D. or a member of the Secret Avengers. Those who know her can attest to her bravery and loyalty.

FRIENDS

HAWKEYE
Clint Barton has been Mockingbird's husband and partner in crime fighting.

S.H.I.E.L.D.
The spy organization has provided Mockingbird with training and equipment.

FOE

MEPHISTO
This demon claimed Mockingbird's life when she tried to save Hawkeye.

LIFE AND DEATH ON AVENGERS MISSIONS

Mockingbird spent most of her early career with the West Coast Avengers, but over the years she has served with many Avengers teams.

WEST COAST AVENGERS

West Coast Avengers #1 (September 1984)

At the suggestion of the Vision, newlyweds Hawkeye and Mockingbird moved to Los Angeles to establish a second Avengers team on the other side of the country. Their relationship was pushed to breaking point when Mockingbird took revenge on the villain Phantom Rider by allowing him to fall to his death. Hawkeye strongly objected to her actions, and Mockingbird left the team. Later, she seemingly died saving Hawkeye from the demon Mephisto, but was later revealed to have been a Skrull.

As leaders of the West Coast Avengers, Mockingbird and Hawkeye lead Iron Man, Wonder Man, and Tigra into battle.

SKRULL MOCKERY

A shape-shifting Skrull tricked Hawkeye into believing that his lost love, Mockingbird, had returned from a fatal crash.

A crashed starship in the Savage Land contained many heroes, including Mockingbird, who up until that point had been considered dead. Hawkeye was overjoyed to be reunited with his lost love, but ultimately she proved to be a shape-shifting Skrull alien in disguise. Following the defeat of the Skrull infiltrators, however, the real Mockingbird was discovered alive and well aboard an orbiting Skrull vessel. Eager to get back in action, Mockingbird joined the New Avengers and re-established ties with her former S.H.I.E.L.D. colleagues. She then announced the formation of the World Counterterrorism Agency, an international espionage organization (that shared its initials with her original team, the West Coast Avengers) that excelled at executing high-stakes black ops missions.

For Clint Barton (Hawkeye), the joy of Mockingbird's sudden return from a terrible accident years earlier was soon followed by the pain of Skrull deception.

INFINITY UPGRADE

New Avengers #13 (June 2011)

With the Secret Avengers, Mockingbird demonstrated her willingness to take on even the most dangerous assignments.

Mockingbird's time with the World Counterterrorism Agency earned the attention of high-ranking S.H.I.E.L.D. officials. When she suffered life-threatening injuries in battle, Nick Fury gave her a special treatment that combined the life-extending Infinity Formula with the physically-enhancing Super-Soldier serum. The combination did the trick, and Mockingbird returned to action as part of a new team of Secret Avengers, now operating under the direct control of S.H.I.E.L.D. This top-secret squad was led by Nick Fury, Jr. and had a roster that included Hawkeye, Hulk, Iron Patriot, Taskmaster, and agent Phil Coulson. The team was tasked with executing morally questionable missions, including the assassination of the A.I.M. Scientist Supreme.

SWORDSMAN

THE SWORDSMAN trained Hawkeye in the art of combat while working at a carnival, and later became a costumed criminal. It was his love for Mantis that helped bring him over to the side of good—to the extent that during the Celestial Madonna conflict, he sacrificed his life to save Mantis from evil Kang.

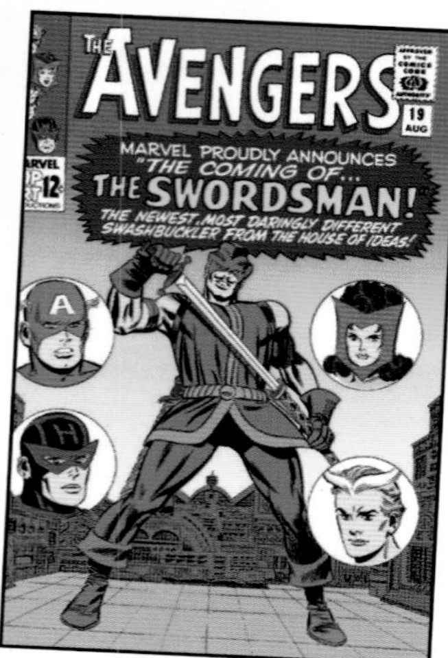

The Swordsman applied for membership in the Avengers, hoping to use the team's good name as cover for his crimes.

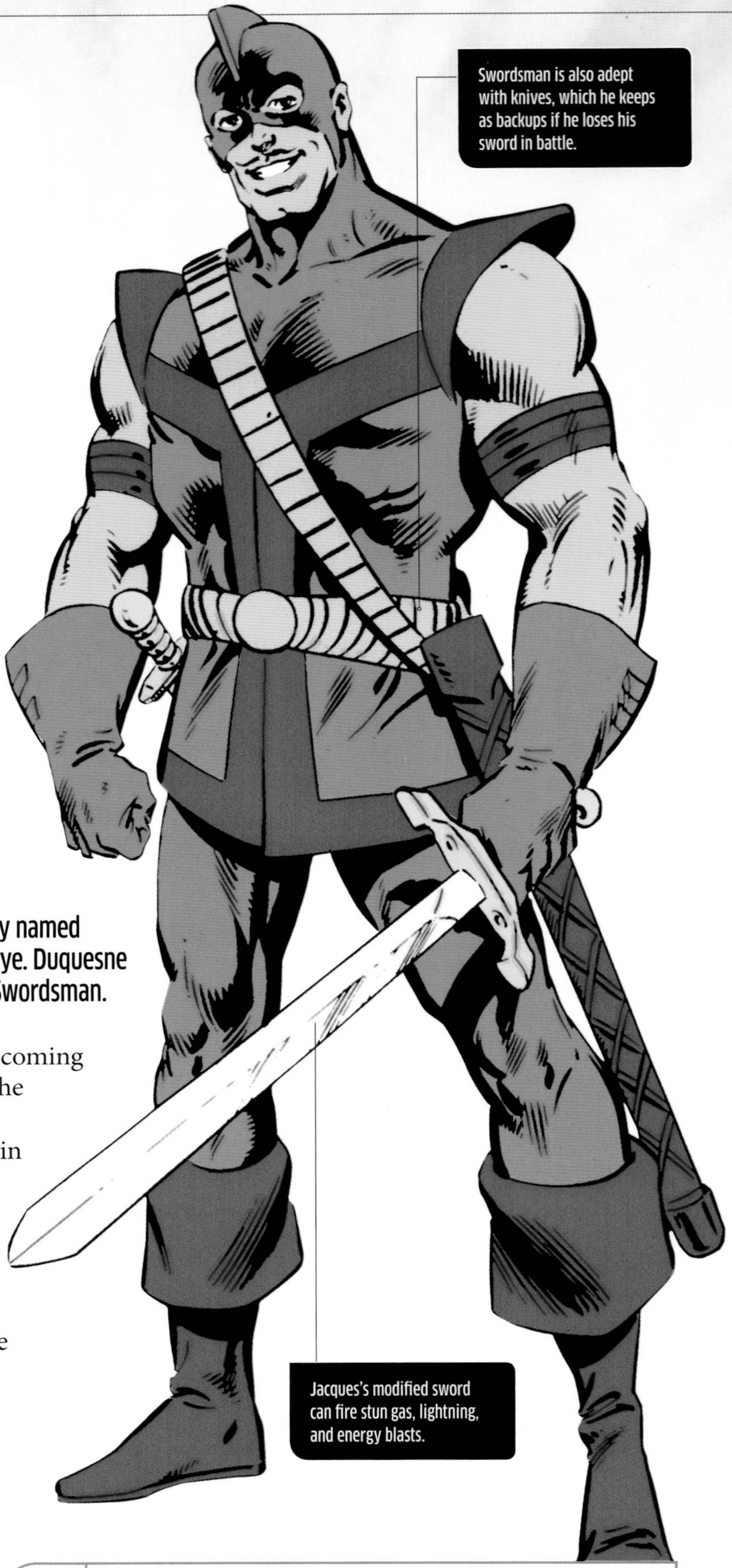

Swordsman is also adept with knives, which he keeps as backups if he loses his sword in battle.

A CHANGED CRIMINAL

Jacques Duquesne earned fame as a circus performer, where he took a young runaway named Clint Barton under his wing and taught the boy the skills he would later use as Hawkeye. Duquesne later robbed the carnival and carved out a new life for himself as the swashbuckling Swordsman.

The Swordsman scored big as an international criminal, and hoped that becoming an Avenger would allow him to commit robberies without suspicion. But the Avengers rejected his offer, and the Swordsman fell under the influence of Iron Man's archenemy the Mandarin. Technology provided by the Mandarin allowed the Swordsman to use his blade as an energy weapon, and with a new cover story he successfully gained entry into the Avengers' ranks. Though he had planned to betray his teammates, the Swordsman grew fond of his fellow Avengers as he shared their adventures and developed a special affection for the Scarlet Witch. When the Swordsman tried to defuse a bomb set by the Mandarin, the other Avengers believed he had planted it. Disgraced, the Swordsman tried to redeem his reputation.

Jacques's modified sword can fire stun gas, lightning, and energy blasts.

The Swordsman has a bold personality that sometimes ruffles feathers. He had a falling out with his pupil Clint Barton while trying to propose a partnership, but the two met again after Clint became Hawkeye.

DATA FILE

REAL NAME Jacques Duquesne **OCCUPATION** Mercenary, adventurer

BASE Mobile

HEIGHT 6 ft 4 in **WEIGHT** 250 lbs **EYES** Blue **HAIR** Black

FIRST APPEARANCE WITH AVENGERS *Avengers* #19 (August 1965)

POWERS Swordsman wields a sword modified by the Mandarin to shoot lightning, fire, stun gas, and various energy blasts. He is one of the best combatants in the world with edged weapons.

The Avengers paid their respects at the grave site of the Swordsman, mourning the member who sacrificed himself to save another.

SWORDSMAN'S **SACRIFICE**

After returning to a life of crime, the Swordsman earned his way back onto the Avenger's roster due to his love of Mantis, who never returned his affections.

ADORING THE CELESTIAL MADONNA

Giant-Size Avengers #2 (November 1974)

As a martial artist with mystical abilities, Mantis recognized the good in the Swordsman's heart and helped him rejoin the Avengers. Not long after, Kang the Conqueror identified Mantis as the Celestial Madonna, a being destined for cosmic greatness. The Swordsman, jealous of Kang's bid to make Mantis his bride, sprang to her rescue when a spurned Kang tried to shoot Mantis. The Swordsman intercepted the blast and perished. His body was buried but later reanimated by an alien spirit. The alien being, inhabiting the Swordsman's body and sharing his soul, married Mantis in a special ceremony before the assembled Avengers.

ALLIES AND ENEMIES

The Swordsman spent more time as a criminal than a hero, but in his brief time as an Avenger he touched many lives.

FRIENDS

MANTIS
The Swordsman's love for Mantis inspired him to be a better person.

SWORDSWOMAN
The Swordsman's daughter, Adelynn Duquesne, serves with Euroforce.

FOE

MANDARIN
The Mandarin improved the Swordsman's sword with alien technology.

BACK FROM THE **DEAD**

An epic battle for the afterlife unfolded during the Chaos War, which brought the Swordsman back to the forefront of avenging one last time.

The Chaos King sought to conquer the underworld realms belonging to the Greek and Norse pantheons, and even succeeded in destroying the dream entity known as Nightmare. To combat the threat, a team of deceased Avengers were released from the netherworld to fight anew against the forces of evil. The Swordsman stood alongside Doctor Druid, Deathcry, and others as a member of the "Dead Avengers" under the leadership of Kree Captain Mar-Vell. The heroism of the Swordsman led to the defeat of the Chaos King's agents, including Nekra and the Grim Reaper. Ultimately the day was won thanks to the sacrifice of the Avenger, Hercules.

The Chaos King, also known as Amatsu-Mikaboshi, schemed to bring the supernatural under his dominion.

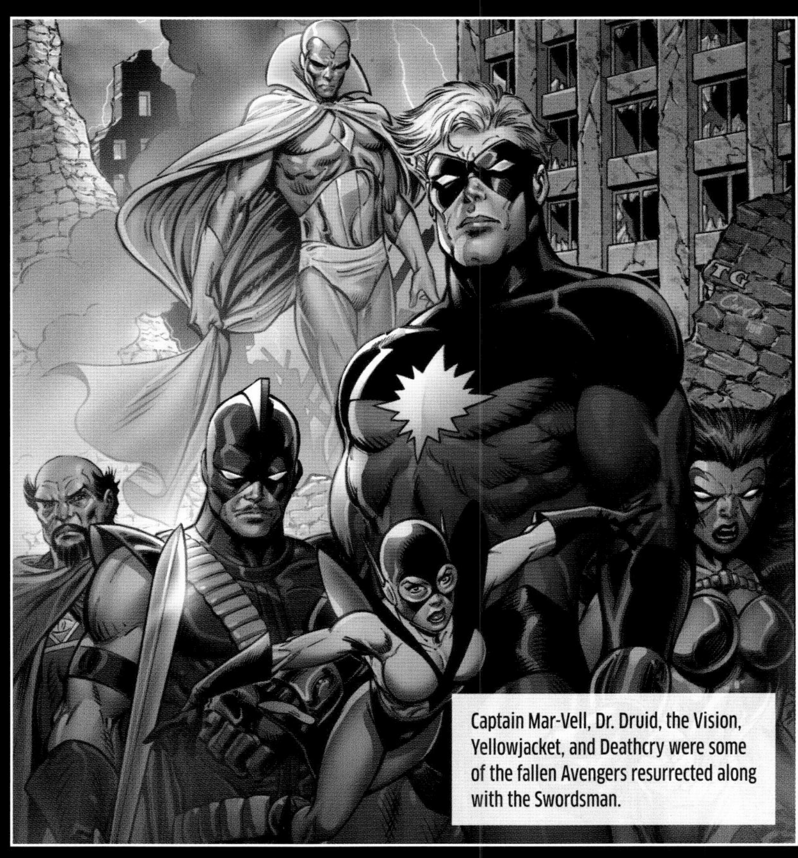

Captain Mar-Vell, Dr. Druid, the Vision, Yellowjacket, and Deathcry were some of the fallen Avengers resurrected along with the Swordsman.

NICK FURY, JR.

The son and namesake of legendary spy Nick Fury is one of S.H.I.E.L.D.'s top agents.

Marcus Johnson was a U.S. Army Ranger fighting in Afghanistan when he learned his mother had been killed. Returning to the U.S., Marcus learned he was actually the son of legendary S.H.I.E.L.D. agent Nick Fury. His father had tried to protect him from his covert world by creating fake identities for him, but Orion—head of the evil Leviathan organization—tracked him down, and killed his mother, seeking the Infinity Formula that Marcus had inherited from his father, to restore his own youth. Both Marcus and Fury were captured and Orion used the formula to restore his past strength. Marcus teamed up with Fury and the Avengers to stop Orion from destroying S.H.I.E.L.D. and to avenge his mother's murder. Marcus assumed his birth name of Nick Fury, Jr. and joined S.H.I.E.L.D., soon fighting alongside a team of Secret Avengers.

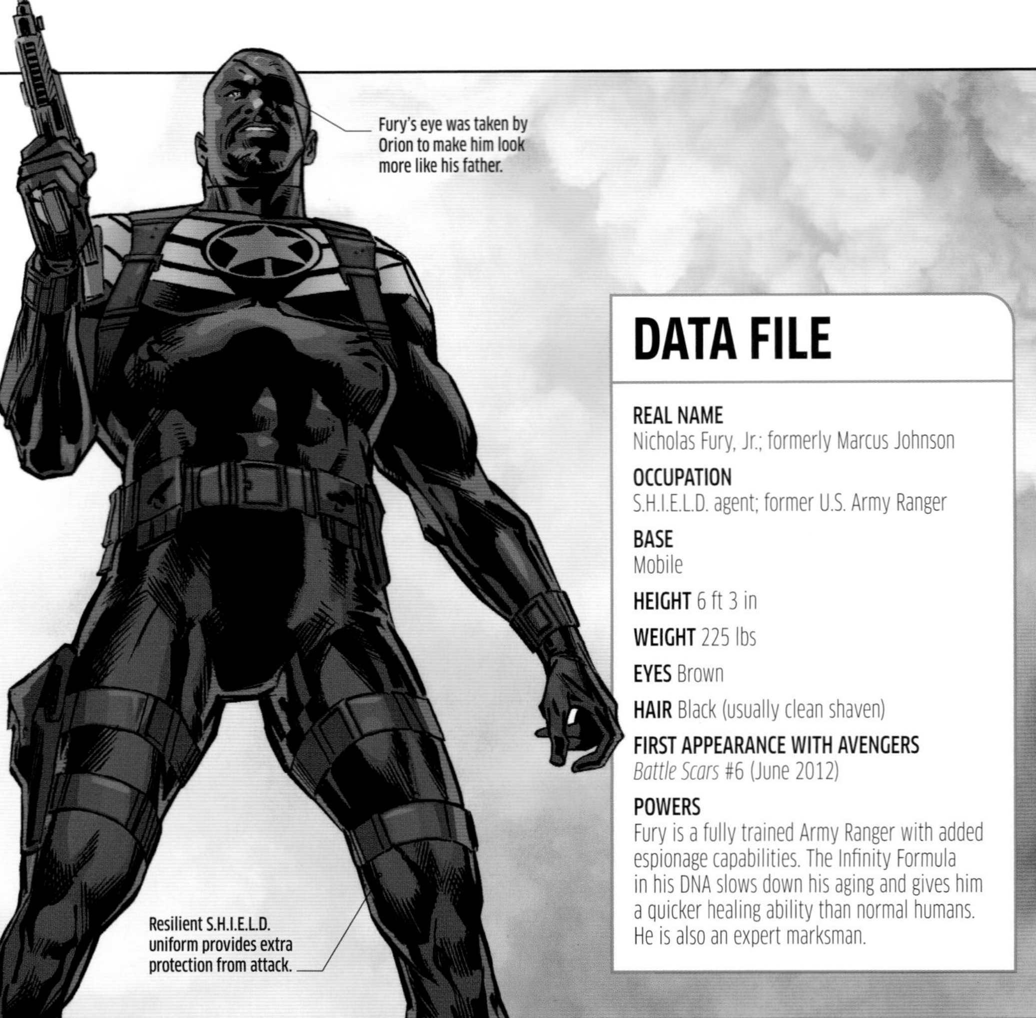

Fury's eye was taken by Orion to make him look more like his father.

Resilient S.H.I.E.L.D. uniform provides extra protection from attack.

DATA FILE

REAL NAME
Nicholas Fury, Jr.; formerly Marcus Johnson

OCCUPATION
S.H.I.E.L.D. agent; former U.S. Army Ranger

BASE
Mobile

HEIGHT 6 ft 3 in

WEIGHT 225 lbs

EYES Brown

HAIR Black (usually clean shaven)

FIRST APPEARANCE WITH AVENGERS
Battle Scars #6 (June 2012)

POWERS
Fury is a fully trained Army Ranger with added espionage capabilities. The Infinity Formula in his DNA slows down his aging and gives him a quicker healing ability than normal humans. He is also an expert marksman.

VICTORIA HAND

This triple-crossing spy was a force to be reckoned with.

Victoria Hand was an agent of S.H.I.E.L.D., forced to work in their accounting division after complaining about the way Nick Fury ran the organization. Following Norman Osborn's rise to power, Victoria was promoted to the post of Deputy Director (under Osborn) when S.H.I.E.L.D. became H.A.M.M.E.R. She was also placed in charge of Osborn's Avengers. She remained loyal to Osborn during his time as Director and, following his fall from grace, remained unrepentant when interviewed by his successor Steve Rogers (aka Captain America). Appointed S.H.I.E.L.D. liaison for Luke Cage's team of Avengers, Hand's trustworthiness was called into question when it seemed she was still loyal to the then renegade Osborn. She was actually working as a triple agent, pretending to betray the Avengers while secretly working for Steve Rogers. She was killed in action.

DATA FILE

REAL NAME
Victoria Louise Hand

OCCUPATION
S.H.I.E.L.D. agent; former accountant

BASE
Mobile

HEIGHT 5 ft 6 in

WEIGHT 135 lbs

EYES Hazel

HAIR Black (with dyed red streaks)

FIRST APPEARANCE WITH AVENGERS
Dark Avengers #1 (March 2009)

POWERS
Hand did not have any superpowers. However, she was a fully trained S.H.I.E.L.D. agent with expertise in strategic management and hand-to-hand combat. This espionage expert was also knowledgeable about a variety of weapons, and she was skilled at gathering information. Hand was also experienced in the fields of finance and accounting.

A skilled marksman, Maria carries two handguns.

MARIA HILL

The current Director of S.H.I.E.L.D. is a fierce sharpshooter.

Maria Hill has worked closely with the Avengers, although she originally had grave doubts about the role of superhumans in the world. After serving in the U.S. Army and distinguishing herself during missions on the dangerous island of Madripoor, Hill joined S.H.I.E.L.D. and eventually worked her way through the ranks to commander. Shortly after joining the team, the President of the United States commended Hill for her bravery on Madripoor and named her Director of S.H.I.E.L.D., a position that she held throughout the Superhuman Civil War. Although she got off to a rocky start with the Avengers due to her differences with Tony Stark, she eventually won their loyalty by disobeying direct orders from the President in order to protect them. After the Civil War ended, Hill stepped down from her position as director—handing the role over to Tony Stark. After a period of several different directors, Maria later returned to the position.

DATA FILE

REAL NAME
Maria Hill

OCCUPATION
Director of S.H.I.E.L.D.

BASE
Mobile

HEIGHT 5 ft 10 in

WEIGHT 135 lbs

EYES Brown

HAIR Black

FIRST APPEARANCE WITH AVENGERS
New Avengers #4 (March 2005)

POWERS
A trained S.H.I.E.L.D. agent, Maria is highly skilled in processing massive amounts of information. She is also skilled in unarmed combat, interrogation, and marksmanship.

PHIL COULSON

The big "Cheese" is a resourceful, loyal agent of S.H.I.E.L.D.

Phil "Cheese" Coulson is a member of the Secret Avengers and S.H.I.E.L.D.'s commander of Special Ops. Before that, he was a U.S. Army Ranger based in Afghanistan with his closest friend, Marcus Johnson (aka Nick Fury, Jr.). When Coulson and Marcus returned to the U.S. to investigate the death of Marcus's mother, Orion (head of the criminal Leviathan group) captured Marcus. Coulson called in the Avengers and S.H.I.E.L.D. to rescue his friend. Coulson and Marcus then became members of S.H.I.E.L.D. Shortly after, Phil joined a new incarnation of the Secret Avengers and heleped recruit heroes for the covert team of Super Heroes.

Non-lethal night-night pistol

Coulson leads his own team of specialist S.H.I.E.L.D. agents.

DATA FILE

REAL NAME
Philip Coulson

OCCUPATION
S.H.I.E.L.D. Agent; former U.S. Army Ranger

BASE
S.H.I.E.L.D. Helicarrier

HEIGHT 5 ft 11 in

WEIGHT 175 lbs

EYES Brown

HAIR Brown

FIRST APPEARANCE WITH AVENGERS
Battle Scars #6 (June 2012)

POWERS
A combat expert with years of military training, Coulson is also an expert on Super Heroes. He has full S.H.I.E.L.D. training and is proficient in a variety of weapons.

BARON ZEMO

Evil runs in this villain's family.

Helmut Zemo is the son of Heinrich Zemo, and has proven to be one of Captain America's and the Avengers' greatest enemies—just like his father, the World War II Nazi scientist, before him. Following Heinrich's death, Helmut stepped into his place and created his own Masters of Evil. His face was horribly scarred after he was splashed by Adhesive X, the dangerous adhesive that cannot be dissolved, which was invented by his father. Helmut led his Masters of Evil in several attacks on the Avengers. One of their most savage moves left Hercules critically injured. Under the guise of Citizen V, Helmut later formed the Thunderbolts (a group of villains masquerading as heroes) and briefly seemed to become a force for good before returning to his evil ways. More recently, he has joined Hydra and launched further attacks on the Avengers, sparked by his deep, inherited hatred for Captain America.

DATA FILE

REAL NAME
Helmut Zemo

OCCUPATION
Adventurer; criminal

BASE
Mobile

HEIGHT 5 ft 10 in

WEIGHT 183 lbs

EYES Blue

HAIR Blond (mostly burned away)

FIRST APPEARANCE WITH AVENGERS
Avengers #273 (November 1986)

POWERS
Zemo is slow to age due to use of the Compound X serum. A gifted scientist and strategist, he is also an expert swordsman and marksman. He sometimes wears circuitry in his hood to guard against psychic assault. He also sometimes uses devices that incorporate Adhesive X, which forms a powerful bond with any substance.

MOIRA BRANDON

The star of the silver screen became a hero.

Moira saved the Avengers with timely and skilled use of a crossbow.

Moira Brandon was the first new member of the West Coast Avengers—although it was an honorary position after she helped save Hawkeye. Moira was a star of the silent movie era and had built a 15-acre estate in Palos Verdes, California with her wealth. She regretted never having been heroic in real life, particularly since she had once portrayed women such as Cleopatra and Joan of Arc on screen. When the villain Crossfire forced Moira to lure Hawkeye and Mockingbird into a trap, he came close to killing both Super Heroes but was stopped when Moira shot him with his own bow. Hawkeye made her an Avenger by way of thanks, Moira claiming it would be her greatest role. She died a few years later.

DATA FILE

REAL NAME Moira Brandon **OCCUPATION** Retired actress
BASE Palos Verdes, California
HEIGHT 5 ft **WEIGHT** 98 lbs **EYES** Brown **HAIR** Gray (formerly dark brown)
FIRST APPEARANCE WITH AVENGERS *West Coast Avengers* #100 (November 1993)
POWERS Once a beautiful and talented silent movie actress, Moira had no super powers. Even though she was physically frail in her old age, Moira had a courageous heart and steady aim with a crossbow in a stressful encounter with the villain Crossfire at her mansion, which would go on to become the base of operations for the West Coast Avengers.

THUNDERBOLT ROSS

The Hulk-busting general went on to become the Red Hulk.

Long before he became the Red Hulk and joined the Avengers, General Thaddeus E. "Thunderbolt" Ross had several run-ins with Earth's Mightiest Heroes because of his connections to the original Hulk. As a general in the U.S. Air Force, Ross was in charge of the Gamma Bomb experiment that inadvertently led to Bruce Banner becoming the Hulk. His initial obsession with catching the creature grew to hatred and increased over time. Ross led the military attack on the Hulk when the Hulk returned from space seeking revenge on the heroes who had sent him there—including several Avengers. It was a battle that nearly cost Ross his life. The Intelligencia later transformed Ross into the Red Hulk—making him a match for the Hulk.

DATA FILE

REAL NAME Thaddeus E. Ross **OCCUPATION** U.S. Air Force General
BASE Mobile
HEIGHT 6 ft 1 in **WEIGHT** 245 lbs **EYES** Blue **HAIR** Gray (formerly brown)
FIRST APPEARANCE WITH AVENGERS *Avengers* #5 (May 1964)
POWERS An experienced leader seasoned by several military campaigns, Thunderbolt Ross is a proficient fighter highly trained in a number of weapons. He is also a charismatic leader with exceptional organizational and tactical abilities.

DIAMONDBACK

This villain left her past behind her and became a hero with the Avengers.

A traumatic experience led Rachel Leighton to join one of Taskmaster's training schools and become an expert fighter. Her brothers were also set on a course to villainy, one of them becoming the criminal Cutthroat. Rachel helped form the villainous Serpent Society and took the name Diamondback. When she first met Captain America, she felt an instant attraction to him and started to change her ways, reforming and becoming a force for good. She fought alongside Cap during the Superhuman Civil War and was part of the Avengers Resistance when Norman Osborn ascended to power.

DATA FILE

REAL NAME Rachel Leighton **OCCUPATION** Adventurer
BASE Mobile
HEIGHT 5 ft 11 in **WEIGHT** 153 lbs **EYES** Green **HAIR** Brown (usually dyed magenta)
FIRST APPEARANCE WITH AVENGERS *Avengers* #325 (October 1990)
POWERS While a peak level athlete highly skilled in the martial arts, it is possible that Rachel's' body contains part of the Super-Soldier serum after a blood transfer from Captain America. At times she has above-average strength and speed but this seems to have worn off in the years since the transfusion. Rachel has also mastered a number of weapons created especially for her by the Trapster.

TWO-GUN KID

A time-displaced masked gunslinger traveled from the American Old West and met the Avengers.

Two-Gun Kid's faithful steed Thunder

Matt Hawk fought crime in the Old West as the Two-Gun Kid. His path first crossed with the Avengers when they ended up in the 1870s fighting Kang. Matt returned to the present with them and became a reserve Avenger, forging a close friendship with Hawkeye. During the Superhuman Civil War he worked with She-Hulk to apprehend criminals and later became part of Tony Stark's Fifty-State Initiative as part of New Mexico's Desert Stars. He eventually returned to a similar timeframe to his original one, where he died of old age.

DATA FILE

REAL NAME Matthew J. Hawk **OCCUPATION** Adventurer, lawyer, ranch hand
BASE Mobile; originally Tombstone, USA
HEIGHT 5 ft 9 in **WEIGHT** 160 lbs **EYES** Blue **HAIR** Brown
FIRST APPEARANCE WITH AVENGERS *Avengers* #142 (December 1975)
POWERS An expert gunslinger and one of the fastest gunmen of all time, Hawk preferred to use his twin Colt .45 pistols while fighting in the Old West. He is also an expert fighter and is a trained tracker. While in the present he often uses a flying mechanical horse to travel around.

SHANG-CHI

This martial arts master is a new Avenger.

The son of criminal mastermind Zheng Zu (sometimes known as Fu Manchu), Shang-Chi has only recently joined the Avengers but has a long history fighting alongside many of the team's heroes. Shang-Chi was raised in China by his father and trained to be a master of various martial arts. His father wanted his son to become the ultimate assassin, able to kill anyone who opposed or threatened his criminal empire. Shang-Chi was unaware that his father was a criminal and, on his first assignment, believed his father's enemies must be evil. When he learned the truth he dedicated his life to destroying his father's criminal empire. He worked as an agent with MI-13, ending a number of his father's plans for world domination. He later became a member of Heroes For Hire. Shang-Chi has used his skills to train many heroes, including Spider-Man.

Shang-Chi joined forces with the Avengers during a conflict with terrorist group A.I.M.

DATA FILE

REAL NAME
Shang-Chi

OCCUPATION
Adventurer, secret agent

BASE
Mobile

HEIGHT 5 ft 10 in

WEIGHT 175 lbs

EYES Brown

HAIR Black

FIRST APPEARANCE WITH AVENGERS
Avengers #1 (May 2013)

POWERS
One of the world's best fighters, Shang-Chi is fully trained in all the world's martial arts. Despite being human, his training allows him to withstand blows form superpowered foes and has matched superhuman opponents in confrontations. He has occasionally had flashes of possible futures while meditating.

BUCKY BARNES

A skilled sidekick and secret commando, Bucky Barnes eventually became the Winter Solider and a member of the Avengers.

Bucky's mother died when he was very young and his father, a soldier at Camp Lehighy, was killed in an accident in 1937, so the soldiers in the camp adopted Bucky as one of their own. When he learned of Steve Roger's double identity as Captain America, he became his sidekick. The two fought the Nazis together and while Bucky's public persona was that of a happy-go-lucky sidekick, it masked a darker secret. He was a covert operative, doing the jobs his commanders knew Cap wouldn't do. In 1945, Cap and Bucky were trying to prevent a Nazi drone from taking off, when it exploded. Cap was left frozen in ice and Bucky believed dead. Bucky's body was later found by the Soviets, who transformed him into the Winter Soldier.

Cap and Bucky were briefly brought to the present day to fight alongside the Avengers when Red Skull gained a powerful cosmic cube.

DATA FILE

REAL NAME
James Buchanan Barnes

OCCUPATION
Soldier

BASE
Mobile

HEIGHT 5 ft 9 in

WEIGHT 260 lbs

EYES Brown

HAIR Brown

FIRST APPEARANCE WITH AVENGERS
In flashback: *Avengers* #4 (March 1964)

POWERS
A skilled commando and expert fighter, Bucky was also trained in a variety of espionage and commando techniques. He is also highly trained in most World War II firearms and weaponry.

BULLSEYE

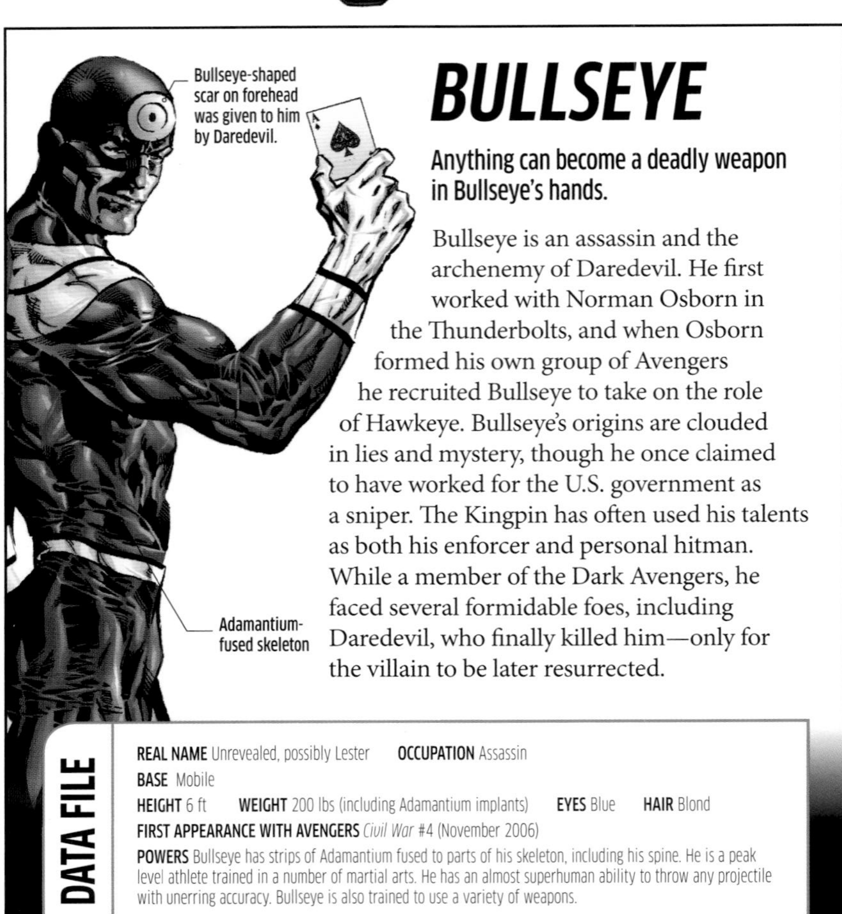

Anything can become a deadly weapon in Bullseye's hands.

Bullseye is an assassin and the archenemy of Daredevil. He first worked with Norman Osborn in the Thunderbolts, and when Osborn formed his own group of Avengers he recruited Bullseye to take on the role of Hawkeye. Bullseye's origins are clouded in lies and mystery, though he once claimed to have worked for the U.S. government as a sniper. The Kingpin has often used his talents as both his enforcer and personal hitman. While a member of the Dark Avengers, he faced several formidable foes, including Daredevil, who finally killed him—only for the villain to be later resurrected.

DATA FILE

REAL NAME Unrevealed, possibly Lester **OCCUPATION** Assassin
BASE Mobile
HEIGHT 6 ft **WEIGHT** 200 lbs (including Adamantium implants) **EYES** Blue **HAIR** Blond
FIRST APPEARANCE WITH AVENGERS *Civil War* #4 (November 2006)
POWERS Bullseye has strips of Adamantium fused to parts of his skeleton, including his spine. He is a peak level athlete trained in a number of martial arts. He has an almost superhuman ability to throw any projectile with unerring accuracy. Bullseye is also trained to use a variety of weapons.

SPYMASTER

This villain is an espionage expert and a man of mystery.

There have been three incarnations of Spymaster, each an enemy of Iron Man. The first was Ted Calloway, who led the Espionage Elite. He once assassinated Tony Stark (only to learn Stark had been replaced with a Life-Model Decoy). He also stole Stark's Iron Man blueprints and gave them to manufacturer Justin Hammer, sparking the Armor Wars. He later faked his own death, but returned to raid Stark Tower while the Avengers were in space. A second Spymaster briefly worked for Justin Hammer, while a third, Sinclair Abbot, had his predecessor killed before assuming the role.

DATA FILE

REAL NAME Ted Calloway **OCCUPATION** Unrevealed
BASE Mobile
HEIGHT 6 ft 5 in **WEIGHT** 195 lbs **EYES** Blue **HAIR** Blond
FIRST APPEARANCE WITH AVENGERS *Iron Man* #114 (September 1978)
POWERS Spymaster utilizes various espionage gadgets. He is an expert marksman, skilled boxer and fighter, expert saboteur, and a master of disguise.

WINTER SOLDIER

Bucky Barnes was Captain America's sidekick during World War II until an explosion seemingly ended his life. Soviet scientists rescued him, turning him into a deadly assassin called the Winter Soldier.

Captain America and the Winter Soldier have a history that goes back to World War II.

Following the wartime explosion that was believed to have killed Captain America's ally, Bucky Barnes, a Russian submarine found Bucky's body drifting in icy waters. Soviet scientists saved his life and replaced his missing arm with a mechanical prosthetic. Suffering from amnesia, Bucky was an easy target for Soviet brainwashing techniques that turned him into the obedient, unstoppable Winter Soldier. Kept in suspended animation between missions, the Winter Soldier remained young well into the modern era.

He finally crossed paths with Captain America (Steve Rogers) when he carried out a terrorist attack on Philadelphia. Captain America recognized his former partner and helped the Winter Soldier regain memories of his good deeds. He became committed to the path of a hero, but the Winter Solider soon faced the toughest challenge of his life when Captain America fell victim to an assassin. The Winter Soldier briefly became the new Captain America, but stepped aside when Steve Rogers came back from the dead. He returned to his role as the Winter Soldier, performing secret missions of espionage and infiltration.

Cybernetic left arm has superhuman strength and can discharge bolts of electrical energy.

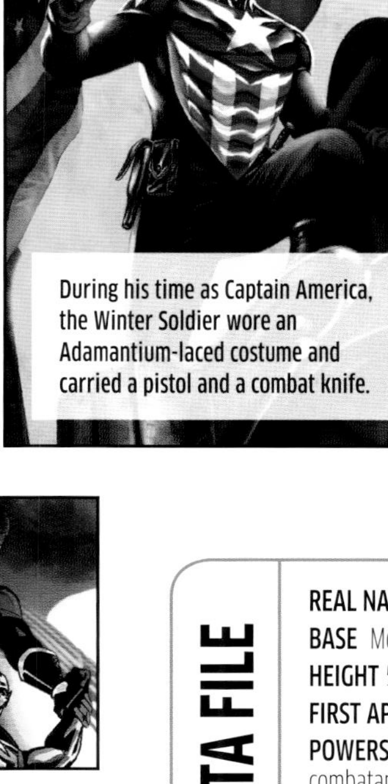

During his time as Captain America, the Winter Soldier wore an Adamantium-laced costume and carried a pistol and a combat knife.

ALLIES AND ENEMIES

The Winter Soldier has struggled to redeem his reputation following the assassinations he carried out as a Soviet agent. He has found support from Captain America's circle of friends.

CAPTAIN AMERICA
Captain America is a mentor and father figure to the Winter Soldier.

BLACK WIDOW
Fellow ex-Soviet agent Black Widow pursued a romance with the Winter Soldier.

FALCON
Sam Wilson is Captain America's former partner and a reliable friend.

DATA FILE

REAL NAME James Buchanan Barnes **OCCUPATION** S.H.I.E.L.D. operative
BASE Mobile
HEIGHT 5 ft 9 in **WEIGHT** 260 lbs **EYES** Brown **HAIR** Brown
FIRST APPEARANCE WITH AVENGERS *Captain America* #1 (January 2005)
POWERS The Winter Soldier is in peak physical condition and is an excellent combatant. He has also received extensive combat training from top government agents. His cybernetic arm is capable of superhuman strength and can generate electrical shocks and electromagnetic pulses that shut down machinery.

Red-skinned appearance caused by an accident with the villian's own Dust of Death.

German military uniform

RED SKULL

During World War II, the Red Skull was Adolph Hitler's agent and a symbol of Nazi ideology that stood in complete opposition to Captain America. Thrown into suspended animation at the end of the war, the Red Skull re-emerged to continue the fight against his archenemy.

While in possession of the Cosmic Cube, the Red Skull could alter the fabric of reality itself.

Growing up as a poor orphan, Johann Schmidt earned the respect he craved when he became Adolph Hitler's right-hand man. Wearing a skull-like mask, Schmidt became a propaganda figure under the name of the Red Skull, to which the United States responded with the Super-Soldier Captain America. The Red Skull fought Cap and his sidekick Bucky Barnes many times throughout the war, until a collapsing bunker released experimental gasses that locked the Skull in suspended animation for decades. In the modern era, the terrorist organization A.I.M. revived the Red Skull, where he discovered that Captain America had experienced a similar fate. The Skull launched a number of plans to bring the world under his control, even securing the all-powerful Cosmic Cube to temporarily switch bodies with Captain America. Even death could not stop the Red Skull, who transplanted his mind into replacement bodies and subverted the U.S. government. To date, Captain America and the Avengers have stopped the worst of the Red Skull's schemes.

ALLIES AND ENEMIES

The Red Skull is one of the worst villains the world has ever seen, and his enemies are numerous. Sadly, some criminals have followed him on the path of evil.

FOE

CAPTAIN AMERICA
Steve Rogers has stood in opposition to the Red Skull's evil since World War II.

FRIEND

CROSSBONES
This ruthless assassin is the Red Skull's loyal henchman.

FAMILY

SIN
Red Skull's daughter has tried to carry out her own plans of world conquest.

DATA FILE

REAL NAME Johann Schmidt **OCCUPATION** Would-be conqueror
BASE Mobile
HEIGHT 6 ft 1 in **WEIGHT** 195 lbs **EYES** Blue **HAIR** None
FIRST APPEARANCE WITH AVENGERS *Avengers* #141 (November 1975)
POWERS The Red Skull is a highly-trained fighter and marksman, proficient in the use of most guns. He is a master is the unlimited power and invulnerability that he acquired from a Cosmic Cube.

ECHO

White hand print is in memory of Maya's murdered father.

Initially seeking revenge, Maya studied the Daredevil's fighting style and challenged him by mimicing his every move.

The Kingpin's femme fatal became a hero after joining the Avengers in the guise of Ronin.

The Kingpin killed Maya Lopez's father—a Cheyenne gangster called Willie "Crazy Horse" Lincoln—and raised Maya as his own. The deaf but gifted Maya was sent to the best schools and trained in various martial arts. The Kingpin lied to her and told her that Daredevil (Matt Murdock) had killed her father and she became obsessed with defeating him, assuming the name Echo. However, she fell in love with Murdock and attacked the Kingpin after learning the truth. On a quest to find meaning in her life she found herself in Japan and became the first hero to assume the identity of Ronin. She fought the Hand with the Avengers and remained with them before moving to the West Coast to fight with Moon Knight. She was killed in action by the old Avengers' foe, Count Nefaria.

DATA FILE

REAL NAME
Maya Lopez

OCCUPATION
Adventurer

BASE
Mobile

HEIGHT 5 ft 9 in

WEIGHT 125 lbs

EYES Brown

HAIR Black

FIRST APPEARANCE WITH AVENGERS
New Avengers #11 (November 2005)

POWERS
Echo can duplicate any physical action she sees—including various fighting styles. She is highly trained in martial arts and is a talented artist and musician. She is also a skilled ballet dancer. She has mastered a number of weapons, including the shuriken (throwing stars), a billy club, and several types of guns.

RONIN

Alexi Shostakov is the latest in a long line of heroes who have taken on the mantle of the hero Ronin.

Several heroes have taken on the role of Ronin. The first was Maya Lopez (Echo) who assumed the identity while investigating the Silver Samurai in Japan. She joined forces with the Avengers and helped them fight various foes, including the Skrulls. The second hero to take on the role was Clint Barton. He became Ronin on a leave of absence from the role of Hawkeye, and when the Avengers traveled to Japan to rescue Maya. He returned to being Hawkeye after Norman Osborn's fall from power. Alexei Shostakov, the former Red Guardian, then briefly took on the role, while Blade also assumed the identity when he helped Luke Cage's Avengers fight Thanos's forces.

DATA FILE

REAL NAME
Alexi Shostakov

OCCUPATION
Former test pilot; special operative for Soviet Union and the People's Republic of China

BASE
KGB headquarters; Secret base for People's Republic of China

HEIGHT 6 ft 2 in

WEIGHT 200 lbs

EYES Blue

HAIR Red

FIRST APPEARANCE WITH AVENGERS
Avengers #43 (August 1967)

POWERS
With no superhuman powers Alexi relies on the skills he has developed in unarmed combat training with the KGB. He has considerable levels of strength and agility.

U.S. AGENT

John Walker became the Super-Patriot, insisting that he stood for the true ideals of the USA and discrediting Captain America. He later assumed the iconic Captain America role before finally finding his own unique identity as the hero the U.S. Agent. He believes that his way is the right way, and consequently he doesn't always get along well with others.

John Walker received superhuman abilities from the mysterious Power Broker after being honorably discharged from the U.S. Army. He made his debut as the Super-Patriot, aggressively advertizing himself to corporate sponsors and seeking to replace Captain America, who he saw as an outdated symbol of the nation. Soon after, Steve Rogers resigned as Captain America when he refused to take orders from the Commission on Superhuman Activities and Walker quickly filled the vacancy.

During his short time as Captain America, Walker learned to be more selfless, and when Steve Rogers returned, Walker stepped aside. He reinvented himself as the U.S. Agent, using a black costume and a Vibranium shield. Still answerable to the Commission of Superhuman Activities, U.S. Agent became a member of the West Coast Avengers and later joined the main Avengers team. U.S. Agent subsequently found work with Force Works, the Jury, and S.T.A.R.S (the Superhuman Tactical Activities Response Squad). Following a stint with the Canadian-based team the Omega Flight, U.S. Agent joined the Mighty Avengers and suffered a serious injury during the Siege of Asgard. He was confined to a wheelchair and became warden at the Raft, a prison for Super Villains in New York City.

Indestructible Vibranium shield

Suit made of bullet-proof fabric

DATA FILE

REAL NAME John Walker **OCCUPATION** Government operative
BASE Mobile
HEIGHT 6 ft 4 in **WEIGHT** 270 lbs **EYES** Blue **HAIR** Blond
FIRST APPEARANCE WITH AVENGERS *Captain America* #323 (Novemnber 1986)
POWERS U.S. Agent possesses superhuman strength, stamina, and endurance. He also has lightning-fast reflexes and superhuman agility, which enhance his natural acrobatic abilities. He also is also able to heal quickly.

ALLIES AND ENEMIES

U.S. Agent is very stubborn and always wants to take command—sometimes leading to rifts with his teammates. However, no one, not even his enemies, doubt his bravery.

FRIENDS

CAPTAIN AMERICA
They were opponents but Captain America learned to respect U.S Agent.

BATTLESTAR
Hoskins was John Walker's sidekick before becoming his own hero.

WCA-BOUND

While working for the government agency known as the Commission, U.S. Agent accepted an assignment to join the West Coast Avengers (WCA) and keep an eye on the activities of its members. His teammates were suspicious of the new arrival, but over the years U.S. Agent has proven his worth as a true Avenger.

IRON FIST

Iron Fist's punch is powerful enough to rip through steel.

Danny Rand is Iron Fist, a living weapon.

Danny Rand gained his power after growing up in the mystical city of K'un-L'un. He became an expert in the martial arts and gained the power of the Iron Fist after defeating the dragon Shou-Lao. He then became the hero Iron Fist. During the Superhuman Civil War, Iron Fist sided with Captain America and joined Cap's team of Secret Avengers. He stayed with the Avengers following the war and his links to K'un-L'un proved vital both for the Avengers and the X-Men when they had to face the Phoenix Force. He remains a close friend of Luke Cage and often helps and fights alongside Luke's Mighty Avengers team.

Danny developed a close friendship with future Avenger Luke Cage while the two worked as Heroes for Hire.

DATA FILE

REAL NAME
Daniel Thomas Rand-K'ai

OCCUPATION
Adventurer; CEO of his father's company Rand-Meachum

BASE
Mobile; previously New York City

HEIGHT 5 ft 11 in

WEIGHT 175 lbs

EYES Blue

HAIR Blond

FIRST APPEARANCE WITH AVENGERS
Marvel Premiere #15 (May 1974)

POWERS
Iron Fist, when he concentrates, can harness spiritual energy—known as chi—to increase his physical and mental capabilities. If he focuses on his hands, he can channel this power to produce a punch of exceptional power. He is also an expert martial artist and can use his power to heal wounds.

TASKMASTER

Tony Masters became a mercenary who can mimic the fighting styles of any hero or villain he sees.

Taskmaster was originally one of S.H.I.E.L.D.'s leading agents, but he has been both a friend and foe to the Avengers. Taking a serum gave him his amazing abilities, but also affected his memory, making him unable to remember much of his past—including his family and his time as an agent. He used his new skills to train Super Villains. It was during this time that he first confronted the Avengers, holding his own against Cap and Iron Man and only starting to lose when Jocasta entered the fray. He fought the Avengers several more times over the ensuing years before taking on the role of Drill Instructor at Camp Hammond as part of the Avengers Initiative. He also joined the Secret Avengers, but returned to crime when he was left for dead on a mission. He was recently seen as a member of Hydra.

DATA FILE

REAL NAME
Tony Masters

OCCUPATION
Mercenary

BASE
Mobile

HEIGHT 6 ft 2 in

WEIGHT 220 lbs

EYES Brown

HAIR Brown

FIRST APPEARANCE WITH AVENGERS
Avengers #195 (May 1980)

POWERS
Photographic reflexes allow Tony to copy the movements of anyone he sees fight almost instantly. He is also an Olympic level athlete and an expert tactician and strategist.

MOON KNIGHT

The Egyptian god Khonshu gave Marc Spector his Super Hero powers so that he could fight crime.

When mercenary Marc Spector was betrayed and left for dead by his friend while on a mission in Egypt, the Egyptian god Khonshu helped Spector survive and granted him superhuman powers. Spector returned home and created two other alter egos to help him fight crime—taxi driver Jake Lockley and millionaire Steven Grant. On joining the Secret Avengers, Moon Knight helped the team take on an Eastern European drug-lord. Moon Knight was also a member of the West Coast Avengers. He joined the team after helping Hawkeye and other members when they were trapped in Ancient Egypt after traveling through time.

Moon Knight normally works alone, but his ability to act covertly made him a perfect choice for the Secret Avengers.

DATA FILE

REAL NAME
Marc Spector

OCCUPATION
Vigilante

BASE
Mobile, Manhattan

HEIGHT 6 ft 2 in

WEIGHT 225 lbs

EYES Brown

HAIR Brown

FIRST APPEARANCE WITH AVENGERS
West Coast Avengers #21 (June 1987)

POWERS
A skilled fighter, archer, gymnast, and pilot, at times Moon Knight has also possessed superhuman abilities. He is highly skilled in a number of modified weapons, but favors a truncheon and crescent darts. He is also highly trained in a number of guns and rifles. He often uses his personal Mooncopter for transportation purposes.

Primitive attire

KA-ZAR

Kevin Plunder is Ka-Zar, lord of the Savage Land.

Young Kevin Plunder was saved by a saber-toothed tiger when his father was killed by man-apes in the Savage Land. Forming a strong bond with the creature, who he named Zabu, Kevin became known as "Ka-Zar," or "son of the tiger." After growing up in the Savage Land, he helped many of Earth's heroes and fought alongside the Avengers against the alien entity Terminus. The heroes managed to defeat the planet-destroying alien, but it seemed Savage Land had been destroyed. Ka-Zar spent time as the Avengers' houseguest and came close to joining the West Coast Avengers before returning to a restored Savage Land.

DATA FILE

REAL NAME Kevin Reginald Plunder **OCCUPATION** Adventurer
BASE Savage Land
HEIGHT 6 ft 2 in **WEIGHT** 215 lbs **EYES** Blue **HAIR** Blond
FIRST APPEARANCE WITH AVENGERS *Avengers* #256 (June 1985)
POWERS Ka-Zar is in peak physical condition and has near superhuman levels of strength, endurance, athleticism and fighting prowess as well as exceptional tracking and survival skills. He is also an expert with a knife, bow and arrow, and slingshot.

SHARON CARTER

Codenamed Agent 13, Sharon Carter is an ally of Captain America and a key member of S.H.I.E.L.D.

Sharon Carter is one of Captain America's closest allies, one of S.H.I.E.L.D.'s top agents, and a key part of the Secret Avengers. She was inspired to join S.H.I.E.L.D. after hearing stories of her great aunt, Peggy Carter, who fought alongside Captain America in World War II. Romance eventually blossomed between Sharon and Steve Rogers, though their action-packed lives often got in the way. At one point Sharon was brainwashed into shooting Captain America and believed she had killed him. When Steve returned and formed the Secret Avengers, Sharon provided essential support for the team, fighting alongside them and providing transport.

REAL NAME Sharon Carter **OCCUPATION** Adventurer, former S.H.I.E.L.D. agent.
BASE Mobile
HEIGHT 5 ft 8 in **WEIGHT** 135 lbs **EYES** Blue **HAIR** Blonde
FIRST APPEARANCE WITH AVENGERS *Avengers* #322 (Sep 1990)
POWERS Sharon is trained in a variety of martial arts, including hand-to-hand combat. She is an expert markswoman, fluent in several languages, and an expert with weapons and computers.

KATE BISHOP

The benevolent Kate Bishop trained herself in martial arts and marksmanship, using her skills to earn a spot on the Young Avengers. She took the code name Hawkeye when the first Hawkeye seemed to have died, but after the original's return, Kate occasionally went by the name Hawkeye II.

New Yorker Kate Bishop used her family's money to pursue expert-level instruction in fencing, archery, and unarmed combat. She met the Young Avengers when they tried to stop an attack on her sister's wedding—but when their plan failed, it was Kate who needed to rescue the heroes. The experience convinced her to secure membership in the team, and both she and Stature (Cassie Lang) soon won spots as the newest Young Avengers. During an attack by Kang the Conqueror at the ruined site of Avengers Mansion, Kate salvaged a number of weapons including the Swordsman's sword, Mockingbird's battle staves, and Hawkeye's bow. After demonstrating her skill as an archer, Kate received Captain America's approval to become the new Hawkeye. Eventually the original Hawkeye, Clint Barton, returned from the dead. Kate took time away from the Young Avengers to team up with Clint and fight crime in Brooklyn, New York. Though their partnership was sometimes rocky, Kate continued to learn about costumed heroics from her more experienced namesake.

Kate Bishop stands proudly as a member of the original Young Avengers team.

Kate became a proficient archer using Hawkeye's very own bow.

Mockingbird's battle staves

DATA FILE

REAL NAME
Katherine "Kate" Bishop

OCCUPATION
Student, adventurer

BASE
New York City

HEIGHT 5 ft 5 in

WEIGHT 120 lbs

EYES Blue

HAIR Black

FIRST APPEARANCE WITH AVENGERS
Young Avengers #1 (April 2005)

POWERS
Kate is highly skilled in archery, fencing, and martial arts. She learned many of these skills as self-defense but has gained a new level of mastery through training received first-hand from Hawkeye (Clint Barton).

ALLIES AND ENEMIES

Kate Bishop learned the ropes as a Super Hero while serving with the Young Avengers. Since then she has earned fame as the second Hawkeye, operating with the approval of the original hero.

HAWKEYE
Clint Barton, the original Hawkeye, is Kate's mentor and crime-fighting partner.

LUCKY
Kate took Clint Barton's dog with her when she moved to Los Angeles.

Madame Masque originally wore a mask to conceal her facial scarring, which has since healed.

MADAME MASQUE

The queen of crime hides behind a golden mask.

Whitney Frost was the adopted daughter of millionaire Byron Frost. When Byron died, Whitney learned her real name was Giulietta Nefaria and she was actually the daughter of the Avengers' enemy, Count Nefaria—the head of the Maggia crime syndicate. Whitney began training with the count so she could take over as head of the family. She has made many clones of herself—one of which became the Avenger, Masque. Count Nefaria killed Masque and for a while it seemed that witnessing this killing inspired Madame Masque to reform. However, she returned to her criminal ways and, after fighting as part of the Hood's criminal gang, became a member of the Shadow Council's Masters of Evil.

DATA FILE

REAL NAME
Whitney Frost (born Countess Giulietta Nefaria)

OCCUPATION
Professional criminal

BASE
Mobile

HEIGHT 5 ft 9 in

WEIGHT 139 lbs

EYES Gray

HAIR Black

FIRST APPEARANCE WITH AVENGERS
Tales of Suspense #97 (January 1968)

POWERS
A highly trained martial artist, Madame Masque is also well trained in a number of weapons. She is a skilled markswoman and exceptional strategist. Her Maggia training also her to shield her mind from most telepathic intrusion.

SIN

The Red Skull's daughter and heir is pure evil.

Sinthea Shmidt was created as a potential heir for her father, Red Skull, but was seen as a disappointment for being born a girl. When she was still young, the Red Skull hastened her aging and gave her superpowers. Eventually captured by S.H.I.E.L.D., she was brainwashed and given a normal life and identity as Erica Holstein. When her father was apparently killed, the villain Crossbones tracked down Holstein and forced her to remember her true identity. She started to call herself Sin and, working with Crossbones and other Nazi sympathizers, helped to arrange Captain America's assassination. She was left disfigured after trying to bring her father, Red Skull, back to life, ironically giving herself his appearance. Sin brought destruction to the Avengers and the world when she unleashed the power of the Serpent, the Norse god of Fear.

DATA FILE

REAL NAME
Sinthea Shmidt

OCCUPATION
Terrorist

BASE
Mobile

HEIGHT 5 ft 5 in

WEIGHT 113 lbs

EYES Brown

HAIR Bald (originally red)

FIRST APPEARANCE WITH AVENGERS
Captain America Reborn #2 (August 2009)

POWERS
Trained in various fighting techniques, Sin carries a small knife and several firearms. She has developed increased leadership abilities since taking on her father's appearance. In the past she has shown above average strength and proved to be an adept brainwasher.

KINGPIN

As yet no one has been able to stop or replace this criminal mastermind.

Wilson Fisk is both a criminal and a sociopath. He normally steers clear of the major Super Heroes, but he has often clashed with Spider-Man and Daredevil. During the Acts of Vengeance he combined forces with other villains in an attempt to destroy their enemies (which included the Avengers). He has also had several run-ins with Captain America, including offering to give Tony Stark the location of Captain America's Secret Avengers during the Civil War. Fisk has remained the Kingpin of Crime by manipulating others and using assassins to instil fear in those opposed to him.

Kingpin's bulky physique provides a barrier against attacks.

DATA FILE

REAL NAME Wilson Grant Fisk **OCCUPATION** Criminal mastermind
BASE Manhattan
HEIGHT 6 ft 7 in **WEIGHT** 450 lbs **EYES** Blue **HAIR** Bald
FIRST APPEARANCE WITH AVENGERS *Daredevil* #233 (July 1986)
POWERS A criminal mastermind and excellent strategist, Fisk is also an expert in several martial arts—including Sumo wrestling. While his body may look large it is formed of pure muscle. He sometimes carries a walking stick that can spray sleeping gas, or fire a short pulse powerful enough to vaporize a gun.

TRICKSHOT

Barney is Hawkeye's troubled brother.

Charles "Barney" Barton is Trickshot, a one-time villain turned hero and Clint Barton's older brother. Often on the wrong side of the law, Barney came to the Avengers for help when he heard Egghead was trying to take over a space station. He was killed, but was revived later and succeeded the original Trickshot (Buck Chisholm) in the role. When Norman Osborn escaped from the Raft prison, he brought Barney into a new incarnation of the Dark Avengers. Barney stayed with the team when they were used as replacements for the Thunderbolts but eventually made peace with his brother after helping him fight the Russian mob.

DATA FILE

REAL NAME Charles Bernard Barton **OCCUPATION** Adventurer
BASE Mobile
HEIGHT 6 ft 3 in **WEIGHT** 237 lbs **EYES** Blue **HAIR** Red
FIRST APPEARANCE WITH AVENGERS *Avengers* #64 (May 1969)
POWERS An expert marksman, Barney is highly efficient with a bow. He is also a gifted fighter and has been trained in a variety of fighting styles. He has exceptional tactical and acrobatic skills.

ELEKTRA

The world's deadliest assassins fear nothing.

There was a time it seemed Elektra was in charge of the Hand and had managed to convert ex-Avenger Maya Lopez into a fellow assassin. However, when the Avengers came to rescue Maya, Elektra was revealed to be a Skrull imposter. The real Elektra had become an assassin following the brutal death of her father. An exceptional martial artist, she became part of the Hand only to later break away from them. Killed by Bullseye, she was brought back to life and eventually returned to her role as an assassin. Following the Skrull's attempted invasion, the real Elektra returned and became one of the Red Hulk's Thunderbolts.

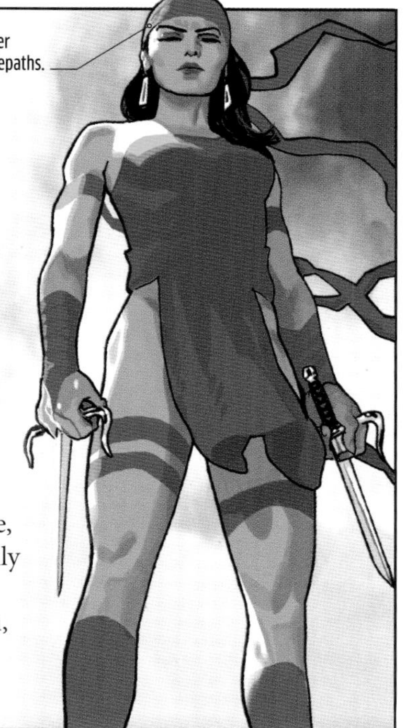

Elektra can shield her mind from other telepaths.

DATA FILE

REAL NAME Elektra Natchios **OCCUPATION** Assassin
BASE Mobile
HEIGHT 5 ft 9 in **WEIGHT** 130 lbs **EYES** Blue/black **HAIR** Black
FIRST APPEARANCE WITH AVENGERS AVENGERS *New Avengers* #28 (May 2007)
POWERS Elektra is a peak level athlete with exceptional acrobatic skills. She is a trained assassin and can utilize a number of weapons but often favors her sai. Her training grants her almost superhuman abilities, such as being able to control her own nervous system and bleeding. She can move with such speed through the shadows that she remains unseen. She can also mesmerize people.

DUM DUM DUGAN

This war hero became a S.H.I.E.L.D. agent.

Timothy "Dum Dum" Dugan was a World War II veteran and ex-circus strongman who became an agent of S.H.I.E.L.D. alongside his friend Nick Fury, Sr. In the 1950s he was part of a prototype Avengers team alongside Sabretooth, Dominic Fortune, Namora, Ulysses Bloodstone, and Silver Sable. As a S.H.I.E.L.D. agent, Dugan helped the Avengers countless times. Nick Fury, Sr. later revealed that the real Dum Dum Dugan had been killed in action in 1966 and replaced with a special Life Model Decoy—one that believed it was the real Dugan. When this subsitute Dugan learned the truth, it committed suicide.

Trademark derby hat

Dum Dum's S.H.I.E.L.D. armor was made of durable 9-ply Kevlar.

DATA FILE

REAL NAME Timothy Aloysius Cadwallader "Dum Dum" Dugan **OCCUPATION** S.H.I.E.L.D Deputy Director
BASE S.H.I.E.L.D. Helicarrier
HEIGHT 6 ft **WEIGHT** 260 lbs **EYES** Blue **HAIR** Red
FIRST APPEARANCE WITH AVENGERS *Avengers* #38 (March 1967)
POWERS The Infinity Formula slowed down Dugan's aging. He experienced in field training and an expert fighter with above average strength. A skilled boxer and wrestler he was an expert in a number of firearms and weapons and had exceptional leadership skills.

AXIS Red Skull threatened all of humanity when he gained Charles Xavier's telepathic abilities and used them to spread a global message of hate. Together, Magneto, the X-Men, and the Avengers seemed to defeat him, but he reappeared as the Red Onslaught. Scarlet Witch and Doctor Strange tried to turn his mind on its axis using magic, to draw out Xavier's psyche. This failed, and the spell went on to have terrible consequences for the Super Hero community, turning villains into heroes and heroes into villains.

KEY STORYLINE HOUSE OF M

HOUSE OF M #1–8

JUNE 2005–NOVEMBER 2005
WRITER: Brian Michael Bendis
PENCILER: Oliver Coipel **INKERS:** Tim Townsend, Rick Magyar, Scott Hanna, John Dell **COLORISTS:** Frank D'Armata, Paul Mounts
LETTERER: Chris Eliopoulos **EDITORS:** Tom Brevoort, Stephanie Moore, Molly Lazer, Andy Schmidt

The Marvel Universe was briefly turned on its head when Scarlet Witch created a reality where mutants formed the upper echelons of society, and humans a forgotten underclass.

After the tragic events of "Avengers Disassembled," readers were still at a loss as to how the Avengers could recover from the loss of their team members, and the impact of having had one of their own turn against them. Marvel responded with a Brian Michael Bendis story to shake up the Super Heroes' world. Following on from Scarlet Witch's destruction, in the House of M storyline Oliver Coipel penciled a new world, formed straight out of the Scarlet Witch's mental imaginings. Showcasing even greater consequences of the Scarlet Witch's powers, this alternate reality allowed an exploration of characters' greatest wishes, and would set the Avengers' true reality up for total decimation.

1 Imprisoned on the planet of Genosha following her destruction of the Avengers during a mental breakdown, Wanda Maximoff, the Scarlet Witch, struggles to deal with her fatal actions. Professor Charles Xavier attempts to help her retain her sanity, but is forced to resort to the power of mental suggestion.

2 At a loss as to how to help Wanda, Xavier gathers the Avengers and the X-Men at Avengers Towers to discuss the situation. The two teams argue when X-Men member Emma Frost suggests killing Scarlet Witch, something the Avengers, led by Captain America, forcibly condemn.

3 As the meeting ends, Spider-Man sees a blinding white light. He wakes in an alternate world, married to Gwen Stacy, with a baby boy. It quickly transpires Spidey and his fellow heroes have unwittingly awoken in an alternate reality, with radically different lives.

4 With a new world comes new rulers. In the new reality, the House of M rules over a population dominated by its mutant population, with humans the downtrodden species. The House of M is none other than Magneto, his three children—Wanda, Pietro (Quicksilver), Polaris—and his grandchildren.

5 Wolverine is the only hero to recover his memories of their true reality. Desperate to restore events, he finds former ally Luke Cage leading a team of human heroes from the squalid depths of Hell's Kitchen. Wolverine is also shocked to discover Hawkeye alive and well, despite the hero having been killed by Scarlet Witch in the real world.

6 Wolverine believes Magneto helped Scarlet Witch create a reality where the heroes would be content to remain, with their dreams realized. Cage reveals a young girl named Layla has recently recounted a similar tale to him. They discover she can restore memories to the Avengers and X-Men, including a reluctant Spider-Man—who is loathe to lose his new family.

"WE WERE FRIENDS, WANDA."
- HAWKEYE

7 With their memories restored, and a growing concern that Magneto has destroyed Charles Xavier in this new world, the heroes leap into action. The majority travel to confront Wanda and Magneto at a glitzy mutant reception. Meanwhile Emma Frost, Dr. Strange, and Layla seek out Xavier, only to find a tombstone above an empty grave.

8 Dr. Strange speaks to Scarlet Witch through the astral plane, hoping to convince her into returning the world to its intended reality. He discovers it was in fact Wanda's brother, Quicksilver, who suggested the plan, fearing for his sister's life. As a furious Hawkeye shoots Wanda, Magneto confronts Quicksilver and almost kills him.

9 Furious with her father, and distraught by the unraveling events around her, Scarlet Witch wishes that there will be no more mutants. And with that, her reality-distorting powers make it so, leaving only 198 mutants. Back in their own reality the Avengers find a world where the mutant population has been decimated, with no sign of Quicksilver, Scarlet Witch, or Charles Xavier.

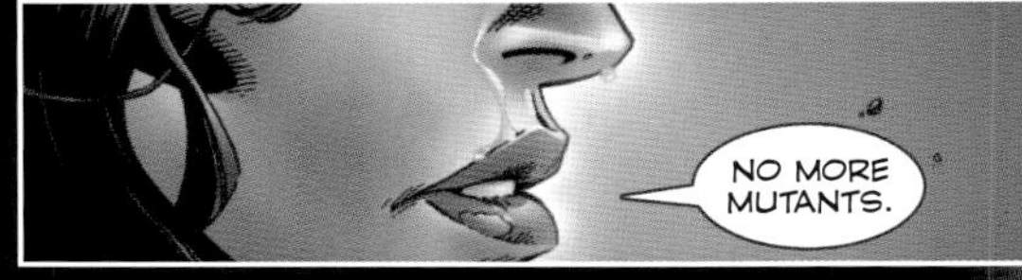

KEY STORYLINE
CIVIL WAR

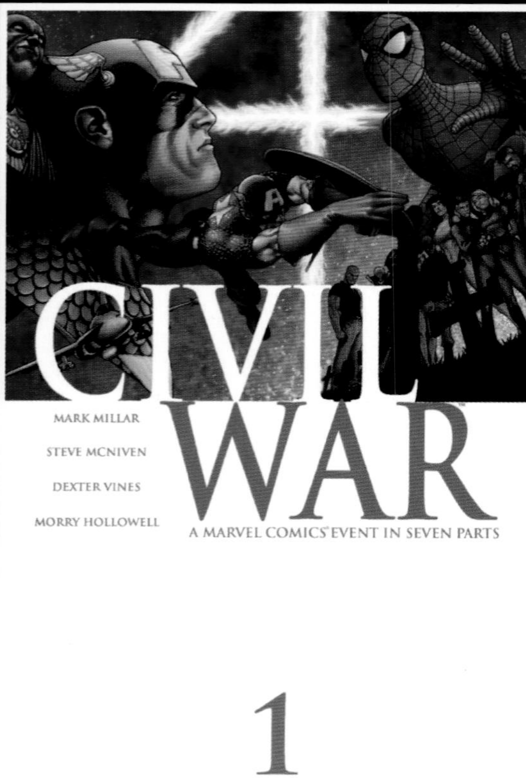

CIVIL WAR #1–7

JULY 2006–APRIL 2007
WRITERS: Mark Millar
PENCILER: Steven McNiven **INKERS:** John Dell, Steve McNiven, Mark Morales, Tim Townsend, Dexter Vines **COLORIST:** Morry Hollowell
LETTERER: Chris Eliopoulos **EDITORS:** Tom Brevoort, Molly Lazer, Joe Quesada, Andy Schmidt, Aubrey Sitterson

When the U.S. government introduced controversial new restrictions on Super Heroes, the Avengers were divided in a war between allies.

For generations, fans have often debated who would win in a fight between two of their favorite heroes. Perhaps it was this idea that originally inspired writer Mike Millar to create the seven-issue miniseries *Civil War* with artist Steve McNiven. In a company-wide event that saw brother pitted against brother, the heroes of the Marvel Universe were divided like never before. With events that tied into dozens of other titles and spin-off limited series, *Civil War* saw Iron Man and Captain America each lead opposing teams of Avengers. Iron Man chose to side with the United States government, while Captain America formed an underground rebellion to inspire change. Before the battle was over, several heroes' lives would be changed forever, and several more heroes would be left with no life at all.

1 When a rather reckless team of New Warriors tangle with the villain called Nitro live on television, the result is an explosion that wipes out much of Stamford, Connecticut. The country is outraged, and public opinion demands something be done about the Super Hero community.

2 While talking with the Director of S.H.I.E.L.D., Maria Hill, Captain America is informed that Super Heroes will soon have to register their secret identities in order to be allowed to function. Faced with the knowledge that he would be in charge of bringing non-compliant heroes to justice himself, Cap rebels and escapes Hill's men.

3 While Captain America opposes this so-called Superhuman Registration Act, Iron Man does not. He chooses to stand with the law, believing that Super Heroes, like police officers, should be organized and registered with the government, even if that means losing their precious secret identities.

4 As Iron Man's allies begin trying to arrest all the Super Heroes that refuse to register—including Captain America's growing underground team of Avengers—Spider-Man opts to side with his mentor, Tony Stark, and exposes his well-kept secret identity to the entire world.

5 Meanwhile, Captain America and his allies continue their clandestine branch of "Secret Avengers," meeting in public while wearing disguises to hide their identities. They soon encounter Iron Man's troops, but instead of talks of peace, fighting breaks out.

6 The battle escalates when a clone of Thor (later called Ragnarok), mercilessly kills the hero Goliath. Desperate to win the war, Iron Man and his ally Mr. Fantastic resort to enlisting Super Villains to their side, even stone-cold killers like Bullseye and Venom.

"I THINK THIS PLAN WILL SPLIT US DOWN THE MIDDLE. I THINK YOU'RE GOING TO HAVE US AT WAR WITH ONE ANOTHER."

– CAPTAIN AMERICA

7 The tide turns when Spider-Man realizes that he has sided with the wrong team of Avengers. He turns on Iron Man, and after being hunted by Jack O'Lantern and the Jester, he is eventually rescued by the Punisher. The Punisher brings the injured Peter Parker back to the underground base of Captain America's forces.

8 As Captain America's team struggles to stay out of sight, Iron Man's forces open a prison located in the Negative Zone. Cap soon storms the facility, and is met by Iron Man's army of heroes and villains in a brutal battle.

9 The fight soon spills out onto the streets of New York City. After seeing the damage that he is partially responsible for, Captain America can no longer continue his mission in good conscience. He surrenders, and tells his team to stand down.

KEY STORYLINE THE MIGHTY AVENGERS

THE MIGHTY AVENGERS #1–6

MAY 2007–FEBRUARY 2008
WRITER: Brian Michael Bendis
PENCILER: Frank Cho **INKER:** Frank Cho **COLORIST:** Jason Keith
LETTERER: Dave Lanphear **EDITORS:** Tom Brevoort, Joe Quesada

Iron Man formed his own team of Avengers, uniting the Super Heroes of the Marvel Universe together like never before as part of his Fifty-State Initiative.

The Superhuman Registration Act had been passed, requiring all costumed vigilantes to register their secret identities with the U.S. government and report for duty. The Civil War had been fought, and Iron Man's team had emerged the victor. Steve Rogers had been assassinated, and Tony Stark had been made Director of S.H.I.E.L.D. Spider-Man and the Secret Avengers continued to hide from the law and fight the good fight. The entire Super Hero world had been altered drastically, and writer Brian Michael Bendis and artist Frank Cho were given a new Avengers title to explore this exciting new Marvel Universe. *The Mighty Avengers* served as a companion series to Bendis's other title, *The New Avengers*. Together with the adventures of the young heroes-in-training in *Avengers: The Initiative*, fans had quite a variety of titles to choose from.

1 As the Director of S.H.I.E.L.D. and head of the Avengers, Iron Man organizes the Fifty-State Initiative, an effort to give each state its own team of registered Avengers heroes. But running S.H.I.E.L.D. has other benefits for the hero, including his own personalized version of the Helicarrier.

2 In order to make his Avengers a success, Iron Man puts his main focus on forging the flagship team. He immediately puts Ms. Marvel in charge, and the two begin discussing possible recruits, with an impressive selection to choose from.

3 Iron Man and Ms. Marvel settle on Wonder Man, the Sentry, and the Wasp as members. They then choose Black Widow to fill the role of a needed "ninja," and Ares as a stand-in for both Wolverine and Thor. The result is a well-rounded team with plenty of power at its disposal.

4 Unfortunately for Ms. Marvel, she does not get much time to run drills and work on the teamwork skills of her new band of Super Heroes. The Avengers are quickly thrown right into the thick of the action when the Mole Man attacks New York City with a horde of bizarre monsters.

5 The Mole Man's home has been destroyed and so, in exchange, he intends to destroy New York. But the true source of the villain's plight is realized when Iron Man suddenly explodes, and in his place stands the newest version of Ultron, a woman who looks identical to Janet Van Dyne, the Wasp.

7 Meanwhile, Ultron kills Lindy Reynolds, the wife of the Sentry. Driven into a mad fury, Sentry lashes out at Ultron, yet still cannot defeat her. The Stark-controlled Iron Man drone then confronts the villain to put the Avengers' last-ditch plan into effect.

6 After surviving a direct attack from Ares and the Sentry, Ultron seems quite unfazed. With the team fearing Tony Stark dead, a version of the original Iron Man armor arrives on the scene, activated by Stark's failsafe. Ultron swiftly retaliates, and soon commandeers an entire army of Iron Men to battle the Avengers.

"OK, SO, IN THIS OUR BRAVE NEW WORLD—WITH EVERY RIGHT-THINKING HERO AT YOUR DISPOSAL —LET'S PICK THE GREATEST ROSTER EVER."

- IRON MAN

8 Using Hank Pym's revolutionary technology, Stark's Iron Man drone infects Ultron with a virus: Ares shrunken down to miniature form. Sentry continues to pummel Ultron until he is stopped by his own teammate, Ms. Marvel, who is forced to get Sentry to a safe distance, by whatever means necessary.

9 Ares succeeds in destroying Ultron from the inside with a virus, escaping with the help of the Wasp before the villain explodes. Tony Stark is found alive—but unaware of all that has passed—and Lindy Reynolds is resurrected by Sentry. Iron Man's Avengers have faced a trial by fire, and emerge victorious.

KEY STORYLINE
SECRET INVASION

SECRET INVASION #1–8

JUNE 2008–JANUARY 2009
WRITER: Brian Michael Bendis
PENCILER: Leinil Yu **INKER:** Mark Morales **COLORISTS:** Laura Martin, Christina Strain, Emily Warren **LETTERER:** Chris Eliopoulos
EDITORS: Tom Brevoort, Joe Quesada, Jeanine Schaefer

The hostile aliens known as the Skrulls organized an invasion event so close to success that it toppled the power structure of the Super Hero community.

The events of *Civil War* had torn apart the Marvel Universe. The Avengers were broken into two factions: Iron Man's team and the underground Secret Avengers now led by Luke Cage. But writer Brian Michael Bendis had a way to remedy all that, with help from artist Leinil Yu. Together, they produced the eight-issue miniseries *Secret Invasion* that spun off into dozens of tie-in titles including *Avengers: The Initiative*, *The Mighty Avengers*, and *The New Avengers* as well as related miniseries. Not only did this blockbuster event force rival groups of heroes to reunite and fight alongside one another once again, it also hinted at a future where the Marvel heroes would have much more to fear than their brothers-in-arms. It dared to predict a future where the Super Villains had won out and were finally in charge.

1 When the Avengers discover a Skrull using its shape-changing abilities to pose as the assassin Elektra, the original question is: how did this alien go undetected for so long even by the heroes' advanced powers and technology? But they have plenty of other questions, too. Like how long has she been a Skrull, and how many more Earthlings are actually aliens in disguise?

2 Iron Man soon gets word that a Skrull ship has crash-landed in the Savage Land, and he organizes his Avengers to investigate. Meanwhile, Spider-Woman informs the Secret Avengers of the same situation, causing the two teams to meet, knowing another fight is inevitable.

3 However, their battle will have to wait, as Jarvis, the Avengers' longtime butler, introduces a computer virus into Tony Stark's technology that quickly takes Iron Man off-line, as well as a S.H.I.E.L.D. Helicarrier. It turns out Jarvis is a Skrull in disguise, and he singlehandedly disables all of Stark's devices.

4 Before the two Avengers teams in the Savage Land can act, the crashed Skrull ship all came to find opens, revealing its passengers. The passengers in question are Skrulls posing as heroes from decades earlier, confusing the Avengers even further.

5 With the Avengers occupied, a fleet of Super Skrulls invade New York City's Times Square. Nick Fury leads a team of Commandos against them, but the tide does not turn until the Avengers return home and face the Skrull army and its alien queen Veranke, who is in disguise as Spider-Woman.

6 Seeing how desperate the odds are, the Wasp uses a new growth formula, not knowing it has been infected by the Skrulls' meddling. She increases her size, but is slowly killing everyone around her as a result. Thor is forced to kill her, tragically ending the life of a founding Avenger.

"THEY'RE HERE NOW. LIVING AMONG US. UNDETECTABLE."

– IRON MAN

7 Angered by this Skrull battle tactic, the Avengers regroup. With an ideal opportunity available to him, Thunderbolts leader Norman Osborn aims his weapon and takes the fabled shot that kills the Skrull queen.

8 As Iron Man employs a suit of armor not linked to the StarkTech mainframe, the heroes come out on top. They take their fight to space, and the Avengers soon discover a Skrull ship that contains the real humans that the Skrulls have impersonated, including Spider-Woman, Elektra, and Hawkeye's long-lost wife, Mockingbird.

9 Now a national hero, Norman Osborn is promoted to the head of S.H.I.E.L.D. But what the public do not know is that Osborn is secretly working with a group of villains called the Cabal, and they are finally in the position of power they have always dreamed of.

GODS, ALIENS, ROBOTS, and more make up the ranks of these superhuman individuals. All possessing powers above and beyond anything experienced by mere mortals, these characters' genetic makeup is based on non-human biology. From ancient gods beyond the skies and below the seas, to cyborgs created within scientists' laboratories; from the reach of Thor's mighty hammer, to the scope of the Vision's brainpower, these are all forces to be reckoned with.

MORE THAN MORTAL

THOR, THE ASGARDIAN god of thunder, grew arrogant about his mighty powers, so his father Odin banished him to Midgard (Earth) to live as the mortal Dr. Donald Blake and learn humility. When his adopted brother, Loki, saw how well Thor had adjusted to his new home, he became even more jealous of Thor and decided to torture him by wreaking havoc on Earth. To stop Loki, Thor forged new friendships with other heroes of Earth, and the Avengers were born!

When Thor figured out that Loki had been the one causing him and his friends trouble, he brought his brother to answer to the others for his crimes.

THOR

FROM ASGARD TO EARTH

Although Thor is the favorite son of Asgard and hero to his people, after spending so much time on Earth, he now considers it his home.

Thor grew up in the other dimensional realm of Asgard, as the son of Odin, the All-Father and king of the Asgardian gods who lived there. Raised as a prince, Thor grew to be a skilled warrior and proved himself worthy to carry his great hammer, Mjolnir, which granted him even more power in his role as Asgardian god of thunder. Odin knew that his son Thor would one day inherit his throne and rule over Asgard, and he tried to mold Thor into the kind of ruler he wanted him to be. Thor's arrogance frustrated Odin so much, though, that he decided to banish Thor from Asgard until he learned humility. He stripped his son of his memory and his powers and made him live on Earth—known as Midgard to Asgardians—as Dr. Donald Blake, a physician who walked with a wooden stick.

While in mortal danger, Blake struck his cane against a boulder and transformed back into Thor for the first time. His abilities led to him assisting fellow heroes in their battle against his own adopted brother, Loki—on the first outing of the team who would soon become the Avengers. Thor returned to visit Asgard often, but he continued to think of Earth as his home—and often of the friends he had formed within the Avengers as his family.

Thor can fly by spinning and then throwing Mjolnir while he holds its strap.

Thor usually wears his hair long and loose.

Although his skin is as tough as steel, Thor often wears armor as well.

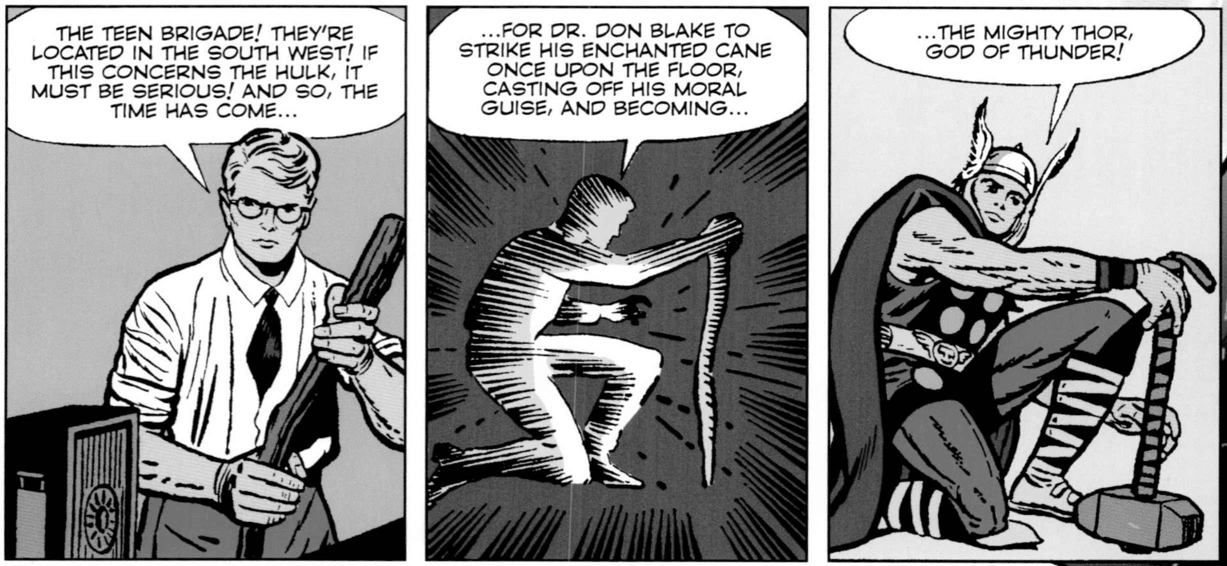

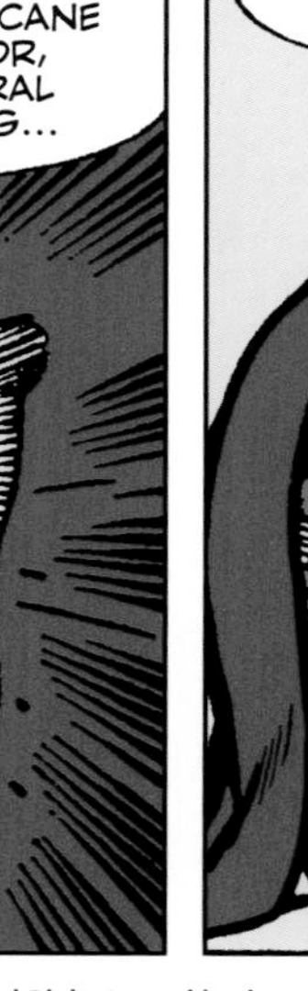

...THE MIGHTY THOR, GOD OF THUNDER!

When Donald Blake struck the tip of his walking stick on the ground, the stick turned into Mjolnir, and Blake turned back into Thor. Thor could then strike the end of Mjolnir's handle on the ground to reverse the process.

Thor has the power to control lightning and weather.

The wings on Thor's helmet denote the fact that he can fly.

ALLIES AND ENEMIES

As both an Avenger and the scion of Odin, Thor has made many friends and foes over the centuries. Most Asgardians see him as their greatest warrior, and the people of Earth recognize him as a legendary hero.

FAMILY

ODIN
Thor's hard-nosed father is the Asgardian All-Father and the god of wisdom.

GAEA
Thor's birth mother was Gaea, but Odin's wife Frigga raised him as her own.

FRIENDS

WARRIORS THREE
Volstagg, Fandral, and Holgun have been Thor's friends since childhood.

SIF
Lady Sif and Thor were close as children and have had an irregular love affair as adults.

FOES

LOKI
Thor's adopted brother, Loki, has often been consumed with jealousy of Thor.

ULTRON
The evil robot Ultron is one of the few who can stand toe to toe against Thor.

DATA FILE

REAL NAME
Thor Odinson (alias Donald Blake, Sigurd Jarlson, Jake Olson)

OCCUPATION
Super Hero, Asgardian warrior, god of thunder

BASE
Asgard; New York City

HEIGHT 6 ft 6 in

WEIGHT 640 lbs

EYES Blue

HAIR Blond

FIRST APPEARANCE WITH AVENGERS
Avengers #1 (August 1963)

POWERS
As an immortal Asgardian, Thor is nearly invulnerable and has superhuman durability, endurance, speed, and strength. He also has vast magical abilities, enhanced by the indestructible hammer Mjolnir, which allows him to fly, travel between dimensions, control storms, and fire blasts of energy.

The consummate warrior, Thor has entered battle many times, often at his father Odin's side.

THE **FACES** OF THOR

Thor is one of the most powerful people in the universe, but he has been defeated—albeit temporarily—from time to time. When that happens, others step into the breach left by his absence and serve as Thor.

Many have stepped into Thor's mighty shoes, but the Asgardian prince is not left empty-handed when this happens. On occasions when he is deemed unworthy of carrying the hammer, he often uses his magical battleax named Jarnbjorn instead. He also has a magical flying chariot, pulled by two enchanted goats named Toothgnasher and Toothgrinder, which can travel between stars and dimensions. Thor sometimes also wears a belt named Megingjord, which doubles his already amazing strength. Thor also retains his physical power, even when worthy others have taken up his mantle.

RED NORVELL Roger "Red" Norvell was part of a documentary crew filming in Asgard. As part of a plot of Odin's, he gained Thor's powers and used the powerful belt Megingjord to give him the strength to wield Mjolnir. Norvel took Thor's place during a battle called Ragnarok (the Asgardian end of the world), in which he died while fighting the Midgard Serpent. He later returned to life and was given a new uru hammer that he named Crusher.

A MIGHTY WOMAN OF THUNDER When the new Watcher of the Universe, Nick Fury, whispered something mysterious to Thor, the god became unworthy to lift Mjolnir and was forced to leave it where it lay on the Moon. The hammer had been enchanted long ago by Odin to judge worthiness, but no one, not even Odin himself, could lift it from its resting place, until a mysterious woman came along. When she picked up Mjolnir, it transformed her into a new Thor who could not only use the hammer but also inherited the knowledge of the original Thor to carry on in his stead.

WHO WIELDS **MJOLNIR?**

The words on the side of Mjolnir read: "Whosoever holds this hammer, if he be worthy, shall possess the power of Thor." Forged by Asgardian dwarves out of the mystical metal uru, under the guidance of Odin, the hammer holds a high standard for worthiness.

BETA RAY BILL Beta Ray Bill is a cyborg from the race of Korbinite—the last survivors of a galaxy destroyed by the fire demon Surtur—who led his people in their interstellar search for a new home. When he encountered Thor among the stars, he was able to take and lift Mjolnir, which transformed him into a Korbinite version of Thor. Odin later gave Bill his own uru hammer, which he called Stormbreaker.

THUNDERSTRIKE Architect Eric Masterson became friends with Thor on Earth and risked his own life to save Thor's. When Eric was mortally wounded, Thor was determined to revive him and transformed him into a new Thor. The two were later separated, but after Thor killed Loki, he was banished and Eric temporarily took over Thor's role by himself, even serving with the Avengers. Once Thor reclaimed Mjolnir, Odin made a mace called Thunderstrike for Eric to keep.

TO CLONE A NORSE GOD When Thor was thought to be dead, Iron Man revealed that he had taken one of Thor's hairs during the Avengers' first gathering. With the help of Mr. Fantastic, he used the DNA within it to create a clone of Thor and imbued it with similar powers to Thor's via cybernetic implants. This clone, who came to be known as Ragnarok, carried a fake Mjolnir. After realizing he was a clone, he was able to wield the Mjolnir of the dead Thor of a parallel Earth (Earth-13584).

THE POWER OF THORR When the scientists of A.I.M. brought an evil version of the Avengers from another dimension, their alternate version of Thor was called Thorr. He carried a twisted version of Mjolnir that could only be wielded by someone who was unworthy. When the regular Thor was deemed unworthy, he took up the fallen Thorr's hammer and used its power—until he redeemed himself and became worthy once again.

HAMMER AND SHIELD Only one of Thor's mortal friends in the Avengers has proven himself worthy of wielding Mjolnir: Captain America. The first time, Steve Rogers wasn't even serving as Captain America or wearing his regular heroic uniform, having given it up rather than obey governmental orders he couldn't and wouldn't agree with. Much later, he wielded the hammer during Fear Itself, after Thor dropped it and Cap's shield was shattered. With this, he helped turn the tide against the Serpent.

There are few who can stand against Thor. Even his best friends—including Cap—find him to be a intimidating foe.

THOR, THE MIGHTY AVENGER

As one of the founding members of the Avengers and one of its most powerful warriors, Thor often finds himself at the center of their greatest battles, and has not been without his own troubles.

"YOU UNDERSTAND CAPTAIN AMERICA, FELLOW AVENGER, THAT THERE IS AVENGING TO BE DONE."
- THOR

TO LEAD ASGARD

Avengers #63 (March 2003)

With his father Odin gone, Thor took over as the ruler of Asgard, but the crown sat heavily on his head. When peasants who were worshipping him in Slokovia were persecuted for their beliefs by their corrupt government, he sent the Asgardian army in to defend his followers. Responsible for the protection of all mankind, the Avengers were called in to try to reason with Thor. Captain America convinced Thor to relent, but the god of thunder ended up leaving the Avengers as well as the fight.

With Asgard under siege by Norman Osborn's Dark Avengers, the early Avengers reunited to defend Thor's homeland.

THE SIEGE OF ASGARD

Siege #1 (March 2010)

Asgard had been relocated to the sky over Broxton, Oklahoma, when Norman Osborn—commander of the S.H.I.E.L.D. replacement agency H.A.M.M.E.R.—led an attack against the Asgardian gods. The Avengers rallied to stop Osborn's Dark Avengers from carrying out this horrible crime. After the Sentry killed Ares for turning against their shared master, Osborn, Thor managed to defeat the Sentry and then hurled his body into the sun. Together, the Avengers defeated Osborn and the rest of his crew.

This battle turned out to be the prophesied Ragnarok moment, in which Thor died at the hand of the Serpent-the brother Odin had lied about ever having.

FEAR ITSELF

Fear Itself #1 (June 2011)

When Odin's estranged brother Cul—also known as the Serpent—returned and claimed the throne of Asgard, he gave seven warriors a weapon each, calling them his Worthy. He used them not only to try to take over Asgard, but also to cause chaos and carnage on Earth. A furious Odin beat and imprisoned Thor when he wished to serve on Earth and help the Avengers defend his adopted home, but he later relented and let Thor rejoin his friends. In the end, Thor managed to defeat Cul with the Odinsword, but he died in the effort.

THE NEW THOR

Thor #1 (December 2014)

After Thor became unworthy to wield Mjolnir, a mysterious woman, who was later revealed to be Thor's mortal love Jane Foster, took up the hammer, turning herself into a new Thor and hiding her identity beneath her helmet. The inscription on the hammer even added an S so it read, "if she be worthy." When the male Thor confronted her, he realized that she actually was worthy, and he gave up both his claim on the hammer and his name, calling himself only Odinson instead.

The female Thor kept her true identity a secret, not even sharing it with the original, and let her actions prove her worthiness.

THE BODY of the synthozoid (synthetic life form) known as the Vision started as the android Human Torch, one of the first known Super Heroes. The evil robot Ultron forced the Torch's inventor, Phineas T. Horton, to wipe the Torch's memory and alter his powers. Ultron then killed Horton and replaced the Torch's mind with the brainwaves of Wonder Man. Ultron intended to create a hero who could join the Avengers while remaining loyal to Ultron. However, the Vision soon became a true Avenger.

Ultron's plan was short-lived. In the Vision's first encounter with the Avengers, he betrayed Ultron, warning them of the trap the vengeful robot had set for them.

VISION

THE **MODEL** OF A MODERN MAN

Throughout his existence, the Vision has struggled to reconcile the two parts of himself: android and Avenger. His heroism and determination have carried him through such trials.

The Vision's body once belonged to the android Human Torch, but was redesigned as part of Ultron's plan to best the Avengers. The original Human Torch was still operating as well, though. It was revealed that Immortus had traveled back in time and used the Forever Crystal to split the Torch's timestream in two, making two perfect duplicates of his body. He had engineered the Vision's creation so the Scarlet Witch would meet the Vision and fall in love with him after he joined the Avengers. Immortus wanted to ensure that the Scarlet Witch never had children, as one of her children was predicted to become a threat to all of time. Immortus believed that matching her with a synthetic man would put an end to that.

The plan seemed to work. The Vision and the Scarlet Witch fell in love and got married. But then they had twins. When the boys were lost, the Vision's marriage suffered. The Scarlet Witch went mad and destroyed the Vision through unintentional use of her powers. The Vision later returned in a new body, and committed himself to a new life on his own, without the Scarlet Witch by his side. His focus was now solely on his work as an Avenger.

The Vision has always brought his technological expertise and cool logic to the Avengers, even rising to chairman of the team at one point. At times, his robotic reasoning comes to the surface, despite his increasing grasp of human emotions. His leadership came to an end after his fellow Avengers objected to his plan to ensure peace by taking control of every computer on Earth. The U.S. government went one step further and threatened his destruction, although he would later return to the team. The Vision recently struggled with conflicts between his synthezoid nature and his Avengers loyalty, during his time with Avengers A.I. He was forced to choose between his identity and his responsibilities when Earth was threatened by a whole population of A.I. individuals like himself.

The Vision has worked hard to put his past behind him and establish himself as his own (synthetic) man.

DATA FILE

REAL NAME
Vision

OCCUPATION
Adventurer

BASE
New York City

HEIGHT 6 ft 3 in

WEIGHT 300 lbs (varies from nothing to 90 tons)

EYES Gold

HAIR None

FIRST APPEARANCE WITH AVENGERS
Avengers #57 (October 1968)

POWERS
The Vision has superhuman durability, speed, endurance, and strength. He can also fly, absorb solar power, and fire energy blasts from the gem on his forehead. He can alter the density of all or part of his body, making himself insubstantial enough to pass through walls, or denser and tougher than diamond. He can also communicate with computers of all kinds.

He can increase the density of his arm while it's passed through someone, thereby causing horrible pain.

His computer mind works fast, although he struggles with emotions.

Solar-powered blasts can be fired from the gem on the Vision's forehead.

The Vision can walk through walls, and even fly.

The Vision's unique powers and incredible intelligence make him a valuable field agent for the Avengers.

ALLIES AND ENEMIES

It may seem as though an android would not have many emotional ties to haunt him, however the Vision's creation as a result of conflict between Ultron and the Avengers has colored his relationships with everyone he knows.

FOES

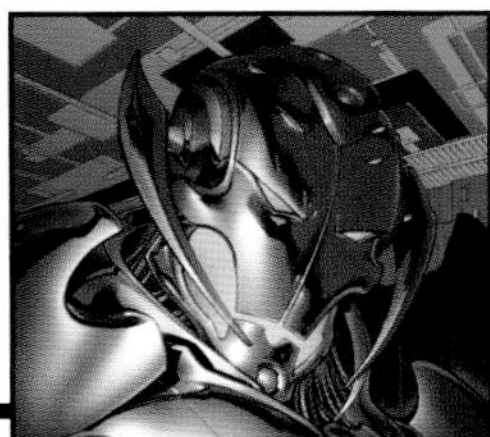

ULTRON
The Vision's robot creator still tries to control him to this day, causing struggles against his foul "father."

IMMORTUS
While Immortus had nothing against the Vision, he made him a pawn in his efforts against the Scarlet Witch.

GRIM REAPER
Wonder Man's brother, the Grim Reaper, tried to convince the Vision that he could transfer his mind into Wonder Man's body.

FRIENDS

SCARLET WITCH
The Scarlet Witch fell in love with the Vision—and destroyed him when their dreams of a family fell apart.

WONDER MAN
Wonder Man didn't like the fact that his brainwaves had helped create the Vision, but they often worked together.

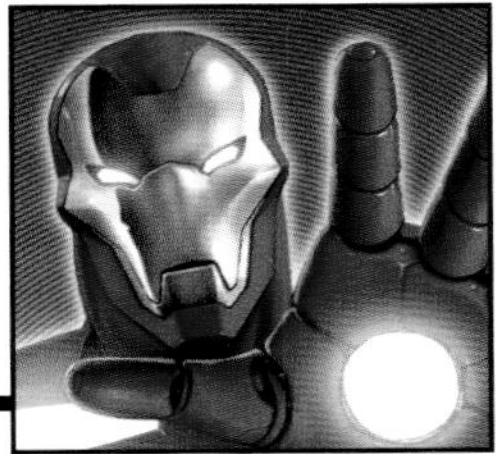

IRON MAN
When the Vision was destroyed, Iron Man put him back together and restored him to life.

CONFLICT WITH HIS CREATOR

From the moment he became self-aware and throughout his existence, the Vision struggled against his creator's wishes, which were deeply embedded in his programming.

Ultron created the Vision to make friends and betray them. However, the Vision recognized that his new friends in the Avengers were truly good and he could not bear to do them harm, so he set himself to work against his creator's demands instead. Secret orders buried inside the Vision's systems have often made him vulnerable to Ultron's machinations, but his heart has rarely been in doubt. As long as he has free will, he refuses to give in.

THE RETURN OF ULTRON When the Vision discovered a supply of Adamantium, a hidden set of orders within his programming compelled him to rebuild Ultron with the amazing, indestructible metal. As soon as he managed this, he returned to his senses and warned the other Avengers about the return of their implacable foe. The entire team managed to stop Ultron from destroying New York City with an atomic bomb by tricking him into absorbing a single order: "Thou shalt not kill."

LOVE AND MARRIAGE

While Ultron gave the Vision life, for a long time the Scarlet Witch was the person whom the Vision lived for. Neither of them knew, however, how Immortus had manipulated events to put the two of them together in the hope of preventing Scarlet Witch from bearing children.

AGE OF ULTRON During Ultron's period of rule, he captured the Vision and used him to control the army of Ultron robots that ravaged the entire planet, hunting down and killing anyone that might oppose his reign. When Luke Cage and She-Hulk infiltrated Ultron's headquarters, they discovered this, along with the fact that Ultron himself remained safely removed in another, untouchable time. The Vision was destroyed in an explosion, forcing Ultron to face the Avengers himself.

THE ANTI-VISION When Ultron miraculously started to experience emotions, he asked to meet the Vision in a New Orleans jazz club. The so-called Anti-Vision of the destroyed Earth-932 had arranged this so he could capture the Vision and switch bodies with him. After defeating the Anti-Vision, the Vision, Ultron, and Jocasta traveled together to learn about their emotions.

TRUE LOVE The Vision and the Scarlet Witch started their relationship with caution, but their affection for each other soon blossomed into something real. They faced some troubles because of the Vision's limited emotional ability, but they learned to ignore it and concentrate on their love for each other. This culminated in a wedding officiated at by none other than Immortus, in a joint ceremony with Mantis and the Swordsman.

JOY AND LOSS The Scarlet Witch bore children by the Vision—which should have been impossible—by using her magic to create their twins out of fragments of Mephisto's soul. When the demon restored himself, he absorbed the twins, and the Scarlet Witch's grief was so great that even the Vision could not console her. She briefly had her memory of them erased, but when she remembered them again, she went mad.

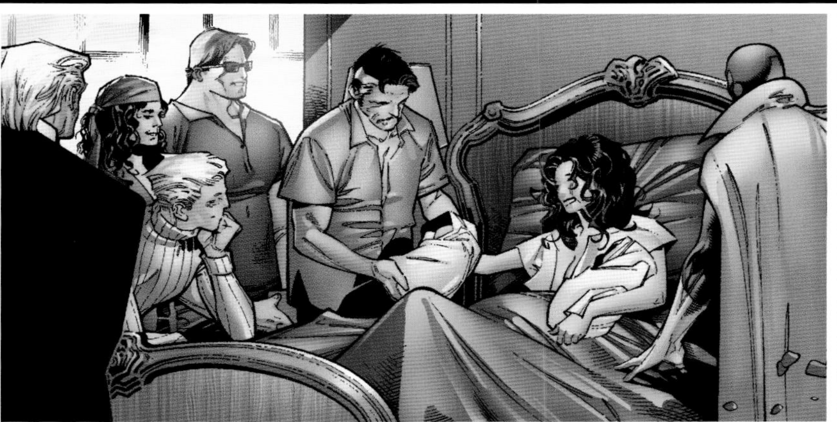

PARENTHOOD Scarlet Witch's madness led to her accidently destroying her love, the Vision. Unable to deal with her grief, the Scarlet Witch altered the entire universe so that her sons were born again, and with the Vision once more at her side. When her fabrication started to fall apart, the Scarlet Witch removed the powers from most of the world's mutants, including herself, and disappeared.

MORE THAN ONE VISION

While the Vision is normally cool and collected, his synthezoid nature means his technological thoughts are not unchangeable. At times, the Vision has undergone radical changes to his mental calibration, with serious consequences for himself and those around him.

Although in waking moments the Vision was sure of his plan for computer control, in his dreams the human and android elements of his nature struggled against each other, wishing to pursue different paths.

WORLD-WIDE VISION

Avengers #251 (January 1985)

After the control crystal in the Vision's brain malfunctioned, it affected his thought processes and he decided that the best means to create peace on Earth would be to take over the world's computer systems. Despite the conflict between the human and machine parts of his personality, he decided that the benefits would be worth the risks. Before he could complete his plan, though, the Avengers talked him out of it, using logic to show him how clouded his judgment had become. Unfortunately the U.S. government preferred force to logic, and kidnapped the Vision when they learned of his intentions.

Cassie struggled to reconcile her feelings for Jonas, as the Vision began calling himself, with her romantic history with Iron Lad, whose brain patterns Jonas had absorbed.

A NEW VISION

Young Avengers Presents #4 (April 2008)

A teenage version of Kang the Conqueror had previously come to the present and built himself a new set of armor run by the Vision's operating system. He called himself Iron Lad. When he was forced to abandon the armor, the Vision took it over. The Vision had none of Iron Lad's memories, and now his brain patterns had been copied from Iron Lad rather than Wonder Man. This made him new in many ways, so he called himself Jonas.

Able to appear as both Iron Lad and in his red and green synthezoid form, Jonas found himself in a confusing relationship with Iron Lad's girlfriend Cassie Lang, a fellow member of the Young Avengers known as Stature. His feelings for Cassie had grown strong and he was determined to be thought of as his own individual, but she found it difficult to accept their new situation.

> "HOW CAN I BEGIN TO RIGHT THE MANY WRONGS IN THE WORLD?"
>
> **- VISION**

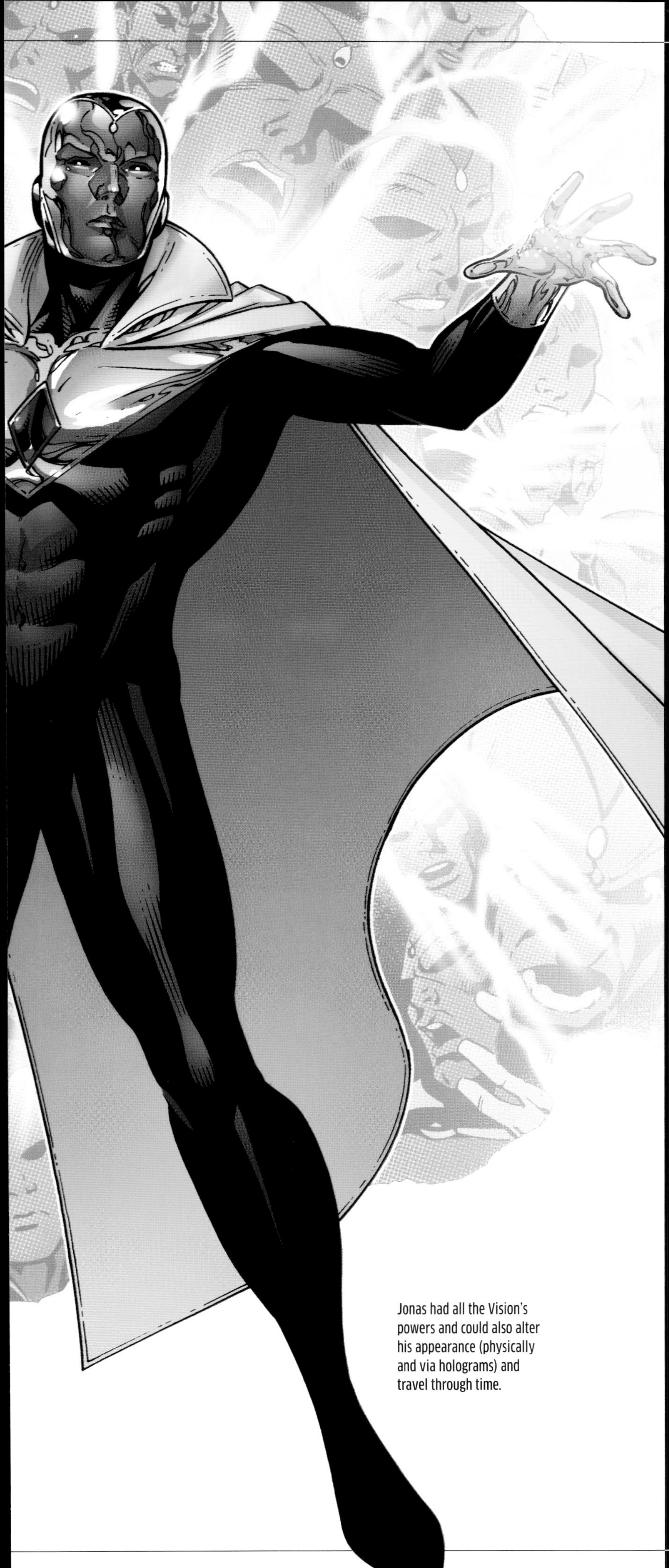

A VISION OF THE PAST

The Vision is one of the Avengers most strikingly recognizable members, but he is not the first to use the name. Another Vision became a hero decades before the Avengers were even formed.

A PAST VISION

Marvel Mystery Comics #13 (November 1940)

Many years before Ultron created his Vision, an alien called the Vision was brought to Earth by scientists who offered him a way to teleport to the planet. After battling crime for a while, he joined the Invaders in their battle against the Nazis in World War II. He survived into modern times and even organized a reunion of the surviving members of the Invaders, who were forced to come together to relive a battle against a magical virus they had fought decades earlier.

The Invaders who reformed in the present day included (clockwise from top): the Golden Age Vision, the original Human Torch (Jim Hammond), Spitfire, Captain America (Bucky Barnes), the Sub-Mariner, Union Jack, and Steve Rogers (center).

Jonas had all the Vision's powers and could also alter his appearance (physically and via holograms) and travel through time.

ULTRON

INVENTED BY HANK PYM, the artificially intelligent robot Ultron was designed to innocently serve his creator. Instead, Ultron instantly became jealous of his maker and full of hatred toward him, seeing himself as superior to the mortal Pym. He soon sought a way to kill Hank. From there, his ambitions grew to wanting to eradicate the Avengers—and then all of humanity.

Ultron first attacked the Avengers by manipulating their butler Jarvis to do his dirty work for him.

DATA FILE

REAL NAME
Ultron

OCCUPATION
Conquerer

BASE
Mobile

HEIGHT 6 ft

WEIGHT 535 lbs

EYES Glowing orange

HAIR None

FIRST APPEARANCE WITH AVENGERS
Avengers #54 (July 1968)

POWERS
Ultron has superhuman durability, endurance, strength, and speed. With an Adamantium body, he is nearly invulnerable. He can fly and fire energy blasts and radiation. He can also brainwash victims with his encephalo-beam, and he can transmit his mind into other robots and computer systems or control them by remote.

LETHAL UPGRADES

Ultron has ambitions to conquer the world, but he often tries to take out the Avengers first, knowing that the heroes will try to stop him before he can carry out his plans.

Ultron has concocted many elaborate schemes to be rid of the Avengers. In his first evil attempt, Ultron took on the name of the Crimson Cowl, recruited the Masters of Evil, and brainwashed the Avengers' butler, Jarvis, into betraying the heroes. The Avengers were able to defeat Ultron with the help of Jarvis and the Black Knight. Ultron then used the body of the original Human Torch to create the synthezoid known as the Vision. He planned to get his creation to betray the team from within, but the Vision sided with the Avengers. Next, Ultron tried to transform Hank Pym's love, the Wasp, into a robotic mate by transferring her mind into that of the robot Jocasta. Jocasta came to life, but when Ultron pitted her against the Avengers, she too betrayed him.

To date, the Avengers have always foiled Ultron, even in his most audacious of plans. Their greatest challenge came when the villain returned from a sojourn in outer space leading the Phalanx—a technological alien race—in an attempt to conquer the galaxy. His army of robots took over the world and established him as the ultimate ruler of an Age of Ultron.

Ultron can transfer his mind into any computer system that has enough storage to hold him.

Ultron displays his circuitry proudly, believing strongly in the might of machinery.

Cape shows his flair for the dramatic.

Adamantium form makes Ultron almost impervious to damage.

Ultron has upgraded himself many times. The first model to attack the Avengers was Ultron-5. Ultron-6 became almost invulnerable by making his body out of Adamantium. Ultron-12 briefly turned good, but deactivated after helping defeat Ultron-11.

Ultron's strength proved insurmountable for the Avengers during the Age of Ultron. They were forced to attack his programming to defeat him.

Ultron has always had a soft spot for Wasp, seeing her as a sort of mother to him.

ALLIES AND ENEMIES

Ultron has no friends. He divides everyone into creatures he controls and are therefore useful to him, and those he wants to destroy. He hates humanity and the free will it represents, and he is willing to do whatever it takes to crush it.

FOES

VISION
Ultron created the Vision to betray the Avengers, but the hero turned on him instead.

HANK PYM
The man who created Ultron gave him his first reasons to hate humanity.

JOCASTA
The mate Ultron made for himself never loved him and sided with his enemies.

ULTRON IN CONTROL

The Avengers' most technologically advanced foe has always had his metallic mind set on total domination over humanity. His greatest desire is to rule the universe with an Adamantium fist, and an army of loyal, robotic followers.

THE BRIDE OF ULTRON

Avengers #171 (May 1978)

Ultron planned on transferring the Wasp's mind into the body of a robot mate, called Jocasta. The Avengers stopped him, but Jocasta later woke up in the middle of the Avengers Mansion, retaining elements of Janet's psyche. The Avengers let her go so they could follow her back to her creator, falling right into Ultron's trap. Rather than watch the heroes die, Jocasta betrayed Ultron and helped save the Avengers with the aid of the Scarlet Witch, whose hex power disabled this incarnation of Ultron. This began a long alliance between Jocasta and the Avengers, working together against Ultron.

A technological creation, Ultron was powerless to resist the mystical powers the Scarlet Witch possessed, leaving him easy prey for the other Avengers.

Alkhema betrayed Ultron and led her own army as part of her plans for world domination.

THE ULTRON IMPERATIVE

Avengers: Ultron Imperative #1 (November 2001)

Ultron later created another robotic mate, Alkhema, whose brainwaves were based on those of Mockingbird. She, too, turned against him, but only in order to pursue her own evil agenda. Her programming, however, retained elements of loyalty to her maker. Alkhema's coding was also replicated in her robot army, allowing Ultron to gain control of them. Willing to do anything but let Ultron win, Alkhema allowed Hawkeye to destroy her and all her creations.

Ultron found the perfect minions in the Phalanx, and set himself up as their mighty leader.

ANNIHILATION AND CONQUEST

Annihilation: Conquest #5 (May 2008)

After another defeat, Ultron's mind escaped into space and found itself drawn to the Phalanx, a group of technological aliens. He soon made them into his new army, then waged war on the Kree and destroyed them. He faced a series of heroes, including Star-Lord, Moondragon, and Nova, who all struggled to stop him. Quasar eventually channeled the power of the murdered Kree through her sword, to destroy Ultron.

THE AGE OF ULTRON

As computer technology improved, Ultron became more dangerous than ever. By incorporating alien technology into his already advanced systems, he transformed himself into the Avengers' greatest foe.

ULTRON CONQUERS ALL

Age of Ultron #1 (May 2013)

After failing to lead the Phalanx to conquer the universe, Ultron set his sights on Earth once again. Initially, Ultron protected himself from retaliation by putting himself years in the future and relaying his orders back to the Vision to execute. He formed an army of robots under his control, and used them to kill off most of Earth's heroes and grind the rest of the world under his adamantium heel. As a last resort, Wolverine and Invisible Woman traveled back in time to kill Hank Pym before he could invent Ultron. This created a dangerous alternative reality however, so Wolverine returned to the past again to stop himself killing Pym. Past Pym is instead convinced to install a program into Ultron's system that eventually destroyed him in the present.

Ultron used Vision as a conduit for his plans at first, but later returned to the present to take matters into his own hands and face the Avengers head on.

"I KNOW NOW THAT IT IS TIME TO PUT YOUR SPECIES OUT OF ITS MISERY. YOU SERVE NO VALUE. YOU SERVE NO PURPOSE."

- ULTRON

Ultron's ferocious attacks left the Avengers nearly helpless, and cost heroes like She-Hulk and Luge Cage their lives.

THANOS

THE MAD TITAN THANOS first ran afoul of the Avengers when he hunted down a Cosmic Cube. He planned to use its incredible reality-altering power to conquer the universe and offer it up to his true love: Death. With the help of the original Captain Marvel, the Avengers put a stop to his insane plan, the first of many times they would save the universe from him.

TITANIC THANOS

One of the superpowered race of Eternals, Thanos was born in a colony on Titan, one of Saturn's moons, to the colony's founders, Mentor and Sui-San. Unlike his pale-skinned brother, Starfox, Thanos was born with rough, purple skin and eyes filled with death, and his mother tried to kill him immediately after his birth.

As a boy, Thanos became attracted to the embodiment of Death in female form. As he grew older he began his career as a murderer to honor Death, even vivisecting his mother in an effort to determine why he had been born so different. After he became an adult, Thanos left Titan and began to amass an army of brutal killers. When he was ready, he returned home to launch a war that destroyed all of Titan, slaughtering thousands of his people. This wasn't enough to gain the attention of Death, so he set his goals higher and higher still.

Thanos can wield great cosmic power and deadly energy with his hands.

While Thanos has one of the most lethal militaries in the galaxy at his command, he is personally powerful enough to defeat the Avengers single-handedly.

DATA FILE

REAL NAME
Thanos

OCCUPATION
Conqueror

BASE
Sanctuary III

HEIGHT 6 ft 7 in

WEIGHT 985 lbs

EYES Red

HAIR None

FIRST APPEARANCE WITH AVENGERS
Captain Marvel #27 (July 1973)

POWERS
Like all of the immortal Eternals, Thanos has superhuman agility, endurance, and strength. He is nearly invulnerable and is immune to the elements, poison, and disease as well as telepathic attacks. Able to subsist on ambient cosmic energy, he does not need food or water, and he can fire energy blasts from his hands and eyes. He also owns a number of devices that provide him with flight, a force field, and more. In addition, he commands an interstellar army.

ALLIES AND ENEMIES

A villain as powerful as Thanos makes powerful enemies, but few friends. Even those related to him by blood find his actions abhorrent.

THANE
Thanos went to great lengths to locate his son, born to an Inhuman woman.

STARFOX
Thanos was always jealous of his brother Starfox, aka Eros, and his easy popularity.

A'LARS
Thanos's father despairs of his son's madness, believing there is no cure for him but death.

DEATH
Ally Death has long known of Thanos's love for her but she has not returned it.

DRAX THE DESTROYER
Arthur Douglas was made Drax the Destroyer for the purpose of killing Thanos.

CAPTAIN MAR-VELL
The Kree Captain Mar-Vell helped the Avengers deal Thanos his first defeat.

THANOS VS. THE UNIVERSE

Over the years, Thanos has provided the Avengers with some of their greatest challenges. When they battle the Mad Titan, nothing less than the galaxy is at stake.

When fuly assembled, the Infinity Gauntlet controls the Mind Gem, Power Gem, Reality Gem, Soul Gem, Space Gem, and Time Gem.

THE INFINITY GAUNTLET

Infinity Gauntlet #1 (July 1991)

After being defeated by the Avengers, Spider-Man and Adam Warlock, Thanos was turned to stone. Death later found him and revived him, and he decided to gather the six Infinity Gems and place them together into the Infinity Gauntlet. To try to impress Death, he used the gauntlet to destroy half of the living creatures in the universe with a single thought. The Avengers assembled to attack him, but he defeated them and everyone else who opposed him, including the entities Galactus and Eternity. Still Death spurned him. When he defeated Eternity and took his form, Thanos's presumed granddaughter, Nebula, was able to steal the Infinity Gauntlet from him. Adam Warlock recovered it from her and defeated them both.

No force in the universe can stand against one who wields the Infinity Gauntlet.

THE CANCERVERSE

Avengers Assemble #1 (May 2012)

After Thanos was slain again—this time by Drax the Destroyer—Death revived him and made him immortal. Thanos gave twelve humans suits of power, creating a new villainous Zodiac team. The Avengers found and stopped them, but not before the Zodiac found a Cosmic Cube for Thanos. He tried to use it to kill the Avengers, the Guardians of the Galaxy, and the Elders of the Universe, but his Cube instead sent them to the Cancerverse (Earth-10011), a universe in which nothing can be killed. Iron Man discovered that the Cosmic Cube was a substitute made by the US government, and he figured out a way to shut it down. The Avengers and the Guardians then defeated Thanos and turned him over to the Elders.

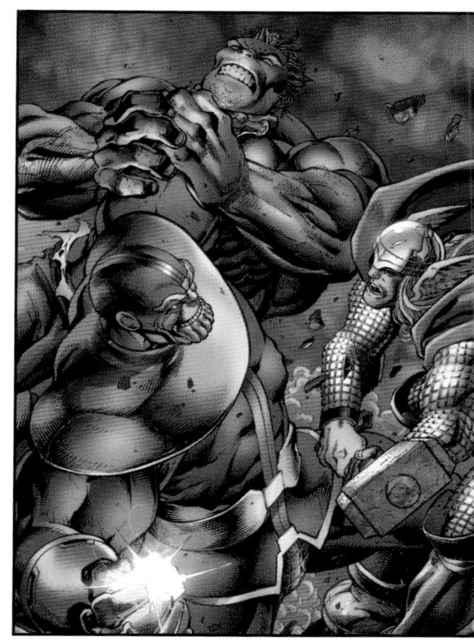

While the cube Thanos found wasn't authentic, it was still a weapon of immense power.

INFINITY AND BEYOND

Infinity #1 (October 2013)

When the Avengers ventured into deep space to meet the incoming attack from the Builders—an ancient alien race bent on destroying Earth—Thanos took advantage of their absence to launch his own assault on Earth. He brought a new army with him, known as the Black Order, built from a number of alien civilizations, but the attack masked his real purpose: the murder of his son, Thane, who'd been raised as an Inhuman. Black Bolt refused to surrender Thane to Thanos, opting to destroy the floating Inhuman city of Attilan instead. The Avengers soon returned to battle Thanos. Thane was freed and used his powers to trap Thanos in an amber cube, suspending him in a state of living death.

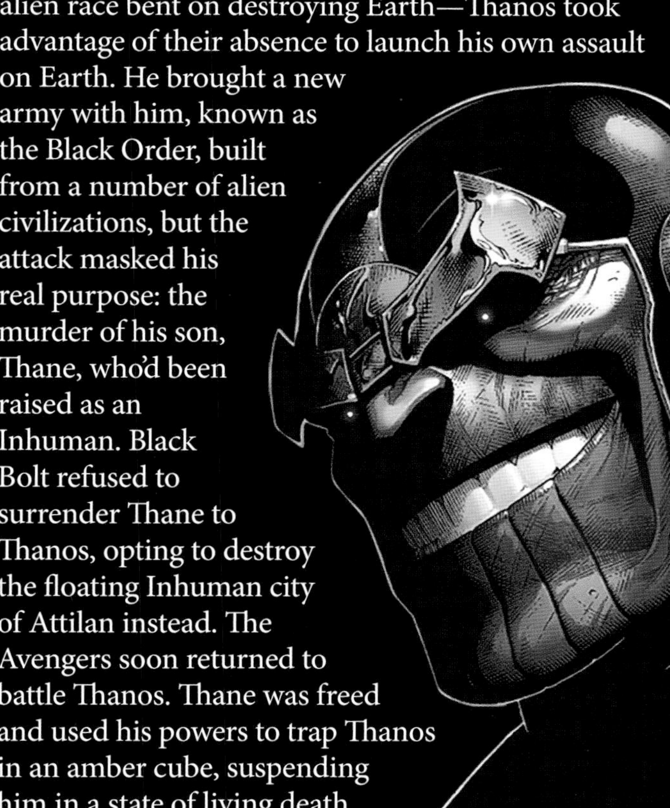

JOCASTA

CREATED TO BE the bride of one of the Avengers' most lethal and hateful adversaries by that very same foe—Ultron—the advanced robot Jocasta became a hero in her own right and one of the Avengers' most faithful friends. Despite many entanglements with her maker, Jocasta has stayed true to Earth's mightiest heroes.

Jocasta has worn many different forms over the years, by way of holographic technology. She usually appears as a woman made of polished silver.

ULTRON'S **BRIDE** WARS

Ultron hoped a robotic mate would support him in his battles against the Avengers. Rather than simply create one, he brainwashed his creator (Hank Pym) into helping him transfer the Wasp's life-force into a robotic female body. This early Avengers influence ultimately turned Jocasta against Ultron.

Ultron's plan would have killed the Wasp, but the Avengers intervened before it was fully complete. Ultron later activated Jocasta regardless. Although Ultron had programmed her to be loyal to him, she managed to override her presets and betray him. Afterward, Jocasta lived at Avengers Mansion and dedicated herself to the team. Once, after her body was destroyed, she uploaded herself into Iron Man's armor and then into the software running his own mansion. When reconstructed, she served on Hank Pym's Avengers team and taught for a while at the Avengers Academy.

After the Secret Invasion, Jocasta joined Hank Pym's team of rogue Avengers. She also transferred her mind into the Avengers' Infinite Mansion, creating copies of herself to act as guides to the never-ending headquarters.

Unlike Ultron, Jocasta's body is not made of Adamantium but regular metals.

DATA FILE

REAL NAME
Jocasta

OCCUPATION
Adventurer

BASE
Mobile

HEIGHT 5 ft 9 in

WEIGHT 750 lbs

EYES Red

HAIR Metallic silver

FIRST APPEARANCE WITH AVENGERS
Avengers #162 (August 1977)

POWERS
Jocasta is an artificial intelligence who usually employs a metallic form, in which she possesses superhuman durability, hearing, sight, and strength, and can also fire energy blasts from her eyes and hands. She often has a holographic image generator that can change her appearance. She can connect to computer networks and place her consciousness into them, and she's been known to use multiple robotic bodies this way.

ALLIES AND ENEMIES

Jocasta was named after the ancient Greek queen whose son, Oedipus, married his mother and killed his father. Ultron planned to play Oedipus in the killing of his "father" Hank Pym, but his plan backfired.

FRIENDS

HANK PYM
Hank and Jocasta struck up a romantic relationship. She compared it to "kissing God."

MACHINE MAN
Machine Man and Jocasta connect on many levels, but their love always seems doomed.

FOE

ULTRON
Jocasta detests Ultron's evil nature but she often stays with him to save others.

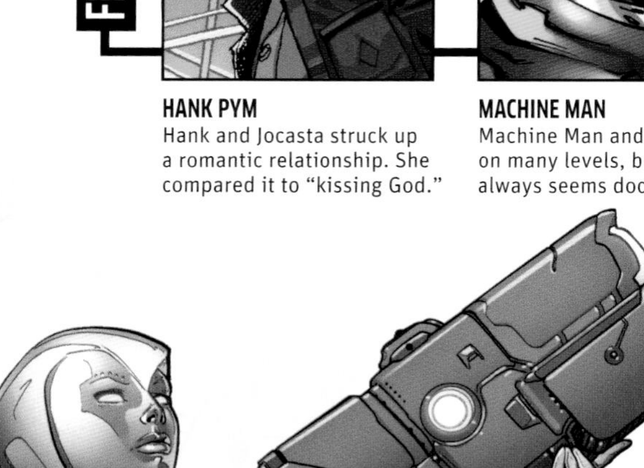

THE AVENGERS' ANDROID

Gun-touting sentient robot Jocasta has been involved with the Avengers since the moment she first awakened, working to save them from Ultron's hatred.

FROM JANET TO JOCASTA

Avengers #162 (August 1977)

Ultron wanted to do more than create a mate for himself. He planned to destroy his own creator, Hank Pym, at the same time. To that end, he brainwashed Hank and wiped his memories of the Avengers, returning him to his identity as Ant-Man. Then he convinced Hank that his wife, Janet (the Wasp), was dying and the only way to save her was to transfer her mind into Jocasta's robotic body. Ultron planned to murder Hank after he succeeded. Alerted to their location by a swarm of ants, the Avengers put an end to his plan. They didn't realize that Jocasta had already been imprinted with enough of Janet's mind to later be brought to life independently.

When enough of Jan's life force had been transferred to her robotic replacement, Jocasta herself sent the ants to get the Avengers' help.

Jocasta's life seemed to have taken a turn for the better at the Avengers Academy—right up until she was seemingly murdered by someone within the organization.

DEAD *OR* ALIVE

It isn't easy to destroy an android, as Jocasta has often proved.

Jocasta has been thought dead on more than one occasion, only to return as strong as ever. Jocasta's allies even believed her to have been murdered while working at the Avengers Academy. In fact, she'd faked her own demise after coming to the conclusion that the academy was a dangerous place for its students. Her subsequent investigations with Jeremy Briggs, a young superhuman with questionable motives, proved her doubts correct. When Briggs betrayed her, however, Jocasta rejoined the academy.

When Jocasta revealed herself to be alive, her fellow faculty members were suspicious of her association with Briggs.

LOKI

AS THE ADOPTED SON of Odin, the ruler of Asgard, Loki grew up jealous of his brother and heir to the throne, Thor. Loki spends his time looking for new ways to humiliate Thor and take Asgard for himself—undaunted by the prospect of battling the Avengers along the way.

DATA FILE

REAL NAME
Loki Laufeyson

OCCUPATION
Self-titled god of lies and mischief, later god of evil, agent of Asgard

BASE
Asgard

HEIGHT 6 ft 4 in

WEIGHT 525 lbs

EYES Green

HAIR Black-gray

FIRST APPEARANCE WITH AVENGERS
Avengers #1 (September 1963)

POWERS
Loki is immortal. He has superhuman stamina, strength, and limited invulnerability. He is a master of magic and sorcery, which he uses to animate objects, create force fields, fly, teleport (even between dimensions), and generate illusions. His shapeshifting ability means he can impersonate others, appear as a woman or as an animal—one time becoming a horse. He has a genius-level intellect.

FROSTY RELATIONS

Loki was born a stunted Frost Giant, the son of Laufey, the king of Jotunheim. After Odin slew Laufey in battle, he discovered the baby Loki (who had been hidden away by his kind, who were ashamed of his abnormally short stature) and took pity on him, returning with him to Asgard and adopting the boy as his own son.

As he grew up, Loki never felt like he fit in with the gods of Asgard, who appeared to value strength and bravery in battle above all else. Gradually, his alienation turned to bitter resentment. Knowing that he couldn't compete with Thor's prowess in open battle, Loki discovered he had a natural aptitude for sorcery and trickery. Calling himself god of lies and mischief, he repeatedly used tricks and magic to try to turn Odin and the rest of Asgard against his brother. After time, this bitterness turned to outright treachery and the kind of murderous evil not even Thor, who still loved his adopted brother despite everything, could ignore.

The sibling rivalry between Thor and Loki goes back for many centuries and shows no signs of abating.

BROTHERLY RIVALRY

In trying to bring down Thor, Loki unintentionally brought together the heroes who forged the Avengers, and he has remained a thorn in their side ever since.

Loki's scheming pitted him against the team that would soon be known as the Avengers!

LOKI VS. THE AVENGERS

Avengers #1 (September 1963)

Banished to an abandoned island in Asgard, Loki used his illusions to set up a battle between Thor and the Hulk. Iron Man, Ant-Man, and the Wasp also answered the call to action and teamed up with Thor to track down the Hulk. When Thor realized that his brother was responsible for the troubles, he went to Asgard and asked Odin's permission to confront and capture him, which his father granted. To Loki's dismay, the heroes worked so well together in bringing him down that they decided to form a permanent team, calling themselves the Avengers.

LOKI REBORN

Young Avengers #1 (January 2013)

After being killed during the Siege of Asgard, Loki returned and tricked Miss America into bringing together a new version of the Young Avengers to defeat an interdimensional parasite called Mother. The Mother's allies were in fact manifestations of Loki's guilt for past actions. When he confessed, those false forms disappeared, and the others could defeat Mother. In this state, Loki's motives were more confused than ever, and he sometimes seemed to work with the Young Avengers.

The new Young Avengers (left to right): Hulkling, Marvel Boy (Noh-Varr), Wiccan, Hawkeye (Kate Bishop), Loki, and Miss America (America Chavez).

ALLIES AND ENEMIES

As the self-titled god of mischief, Loki has few allies he can count on and even fewer friends. His enemies, however, are legion. Sadly, his greatest foes have sprung from the people closest to him: his family.

THOR
Loki always resented how easily leadership and heroism came to his brother.

ANGELA
Angela (aka Aldrif) was the long-lost sister Thor and Loki never knew they had.

ODIN
Odin may have raised Loki, but Loki never forgot that he had killed his birth father.

FACES OF A TRICKSTER

For all his power, Loki has been defeated and even killed many times over the years. He has often taken on a different form for his reappearance act.

Although Loki was a master of illusions, becoming a woman seemed to make it easier for him to pose as the Scarlet Wit[ch]

All of the old gods of Asgard died in the final Ragnarok (the Asgardian apocalypse). Only Thor, who fell into a deep sleep, was spared. Once he awakened, Thor set about locating the souls of the gods in their new forms. Thor discovered that Loki had returned not in his own body but in that of the Asgardian goddess Sif, an act that forced Sif into the body of a old woman dying of cancer. While in this female form, Loki impersonated the Scarlet Witch, and inspired Hank Pym to gather together a new Avengers team that Loki would then be able to control. But his disguise was soon discovered and his plan foiled.

During the Siege of Asgard, the Void (the dark side of the Sentry) killed Loki. This time, Loki returned as the young Kid Loki who had no memory of his former evil self. Thor found this younger version of his brother and took him to Asgard. However, destiny caught up with Loki when his old, evil spirit killed the boy version of himself and then tricked spell-caster Wiccan into turning him into a young man.

Kid Loki actually got along with his brother Thor, and their pair renewed their friendship from thei[r] days before Loki's jealousy had consumed him.

HERCULES

THE SON OF ZEUS—the king of the gods of Olympus—Hercules is a demigod known for his lust for battle, women, and life as much as for his phenomenal strength, his prowess in combat, and his loyalty to his friends.

As described in the Greek myths about his Twelve Labors, no chains can hold Hercules.

A LEGEND IS BORN

Alcmena, the queen of Thebes, was seduced by Zeus, who disguised himself as her husband. From that union sprang Hercules, who became a mythic hero of ancient Greece, best known for completing his Twelve Labors, which earned him immortality.

Hercules, also known as the Prince of Power, made many enemies over the centuries, mostly within his own extended family of gods. Despite this, he knew little fear and was just as happy to bestow the gift of facing him in battle upon his friends, as well as his foes.

In modern times, Hercules returned to Earth from Olympus to brawl with Thor and thereafter to join the Avengers in their adventures. He moved in and out of the team as it suited him, and he even headed up his own team, the God Squad, together with his friend Amadeus Cho. During the Skrull Invasion, the God Squad took responsibility for destroying the Skrull gods orchestrating the plot. Later Cho and Hercules would work together again, in the Mighty Avengers.

Hercules has been one of the Avengers' heavy hitters since the team's early days. He thought of them as fitting companions for his legends.

DATA FILE

REAL NAME Heracles **OCCUPATION** Adventurer

BASE Olympus

HEIGHT 6 ft 5 in **WEIGHT** 325 lbs **EYES** Blue **HAIR** Dark brown

FIRST APPEARANCE WITH AVENGERS *Avengers* #38 (March 1967)

POWERS Hercules is an immortal god of Olympus with superhuman agility, durability, endurance, speed, and strength. He is an expert in hand-to-hand combat and wields a nearly indestructible golden mace. He is trained in Ancient Greek wrestling skills. Since reaching adulthood, like other members of his race, Hercules has not aged, and he has the ability to heal quickly from wounds.

Hercules and Amadeus Cho set about forming the Mighty Avengers. The pair joined efforts with long-serving Avengers such as the Wasp (Hank Pym) and Quicksilver, in order to face the threat of Elder God Chthon.

AN ALMIGHTY MISUNDERSTANDING

While Hercules had many legendary adventures in ancient times, he was determined to outdo them during his missions with the Avengers.

OLYMPUS VS. THE AVENGERS

Avengers #281 (July 1987)

After helping the Avengers defeat the Masters of Evil, Hercules succumbed to his injuries and fell into a coma. The god Hermes swept him away to Olympus where Zeus heard the unconscious Hercules mumble about the Avengers. Furious about his son's injuries, Zeus assumed the Avengers were responsible for them and set the gods Dionysus, Hermes, and Artemis against them. The Avengers battled through Hades to reach Olympus and confront Zeus. Prometheus and Doctor Druid restored Hercules to health, and when Zeus realized his mistake, he forbade his gods to return to Earth.

CHAOS WAR

An almighty Hercules gathered together his Super Hero allies in an effort to end the Chaos King's plans to destroy the universe.

Amadeus Cho had just brought Hercules back from the dead to become the leader of the gods of Olympus when the Chaos King—the Shinto god Amatsu-Mikaboshi—launched his plan to destroy all the gods and then the entire multiverse. To stop him, Hercules reformed the God Squad, a team of gods originally created to defeat the Skrull gods during the Secret Invasion, but it wasn't enough. As the Chaos King was about to win, Hercules knocked him into an alternate, empty multiverse, and the Chaos King consumed it, believing he had triumphed. Hercules spent his power repairing the damage done, and turned himself mortal.

While the Avengers stood by Hercules in the Chaos War, it was only immortals like Thor who were immune to the Chaos King's powers.

ALLIES AND ENEMIES

Hercules is a stalwart and loyal friend. He tends not to worry much about his enemies. Unfortunately, he often finds himself trading blows with such villains.

FRIEND

AMADEUS CHO
One of the world's ten smartest people, Cho is a close friend of Hercules.

FOES

GODS OF OLYMPUS
Hercules spends time on Earth because he often clashes with the other gods.

KLY'BN
Said to be the last Skrull Eternal, Kly'bn faced Hercules in battle, and lost.

SUB-MARINER

THE OFFSPRING OF AN American seaman and an Atlantean princess, Namor is regarded as one of the first mutants of the modern age. While he sometimes surfaces to work with—or deal with—humanity, the underwater fate of Atlantis is always his primary concern.

Namor originally appeared dressed in swimming trunks, but now prefers more regal attire.

FROM WATERY DEPTHS...

Namor knows that he cannot ignore the surface world, but the land beneath the waves is where he is most at home. In Atlantis, he is not only a hero, but also the king.

Namor—his name meaning 'Avenging Son'—was raised in Atlantis with his cousins Namora, Dorma, and Byrrah. Over time, he grew to resent the surface world. During World War II, however, he joined the Invaders and the Liberty Legion to fight against Adolf Hitler and the Axis Powers. In the 1950s, the telepath Paul Destine—who had allegedly killed Namor's father years before—defeated Namor and erased his memory. He turned Namor into an amnesiac derelict, who roamed New York City. Years later, the Human Torch (Johnny Storm) found Namor in a flophouse and restored his memory by dunking him in the river. Namor traveled back to Atlantis, only to discover it had been destroyed by nuclear testing, which for a time drove him to seek vengeance on humanity.

Namor didn't care much for the surface dwellers and their disrespect for the sea, but he recognized he would need to join forces with them against the Axis Powers.

DATA FILE

REAL NAME Prince/King Namor, Namor McKenzie **OCCUPATION** Ruler of Atlantis
BASE Atlantis
HEIGHT 6 ft 2 in **WEIGHT** 278 lbs **EYES** Blue-gray **HAIR** Black
FIRST APPEARANCE WITH AVENGERS *Avengers* #3 (January 1964)
POWERS Namor has superhuman durability, endurance, strength, and speed, although they fade in power the longer he is out of water. He is amphibious, can swim 60 mph and can see through the darkest ocean depths. He has a telepathic connection with sea life and can mimic many sea animals' abilities. He ages slowly. The wings on his ankles enable him to fly.

RELATIONSHIPS ON THE ROCKS

Namor first encountered the Avengers as their foe, but even as he battled them, he earned their respect. He later went on to became a member of the team.

AGAINST THE AVENGERS

Avengers #3 (January 1964)

Shortly after the Avengers formed, the Hulk quit the team, feeling judged by his teammates. When he left, he met Namor, who proposed they team up against the Avengers. They betrayed each other while fighting the Avengers, though, and fled in separate directions. Furious about his defeat, Namor assaulted an Inuit tribe worshipping a man frozen in a block of ice, and he threw it into the ocean. Pursuing Namor, the Avengers rescued the man and discovered it was Captain America.

Namor often makes alliances of convenience with others, such as with the Hulk, only to break them soon after.

THE PHOENIX FIVE

Avengers vs. X-Men #5 (August 2012)

When the energy entity the Phoenix Force returned to Earth, the Avengers assembled to keep it from possessing the mutant girl Hope Summers. Iron Man tried to destroy it but fractured it into five pieces instead. Each piece possessed a different mutant: Magik, Emma Frost, Colossus, Cyclops, and Namor. Together, the possessed mutants endeavored to transform Earth into a utopia by way of tyranny. The Avengers fought to stop them, but Namor unleashed a massive tsunami, destroying much of Wakanda before they could remove the Phoenix Force from him. Hope and the Scarlet Witch eventually managed to stop the Phoenix Force and save the other mutants.

While the Phoenix Force gave Namor immense power, it didn't allow him full control over his actions.

ALLIES AND ENEMIES

While Namor gave members of the surface world plenty of reasons to distrust him, they accorded him the respect given the ruler of any nation. The Atlanteans—other than his most bitter rivals—also approved of how he worked to protect them.

FRIENDS

FANTASTIC FOUR
Namor has an eternal crush on the Invisible Woman, and is a firm ally of her team.

NAMORA
Namor's half-Atlantean/half-human cousin understands him better than anyone else.

FOE

KRANG
The Atlantean warlord was banished after a failed coup, but still plots against Namor.

HERO NO MORE

As a king, Namor considered himself above the morality of common people. This meant he sometimes straddled the paths of good and evil.

The Illuminati worked in secret, but had good intentions. Namor's beliefs didn't always fall into line with their way of thinking.

In recent years, Namor joined the Illuminati, a secret group made up of the smartest heroes in the world. They worked together to solve the greatest problems facing Earth, and made a number of difficult decisions. Namor often felt the heroes didn't go far enough in their actions, allowing their morality to get in the way of doing what needed to be done. For this reason, Namor also joined a group of villains known as the Cabal, an evil equivalent of the Illuminati led by Norman Osborn. Namor later formed a new Cabal, with Black Swan, Maximus, Proxima Midnight, Terrax, and Thanos, after the Illuminati denounced his plans to destroy planets that threatened Earth. He soon realised the Cabal was too bloodthirsty, and returned to the Illuminati, only to be punished by them for his actions.

The Cabal featured many of the Avengers' most ruthless foes, including (clockwise from top left): Loki, the Hood, Emma Frost, Norman Osborn, Namor and Dr. Doom.

MS. MARVEL

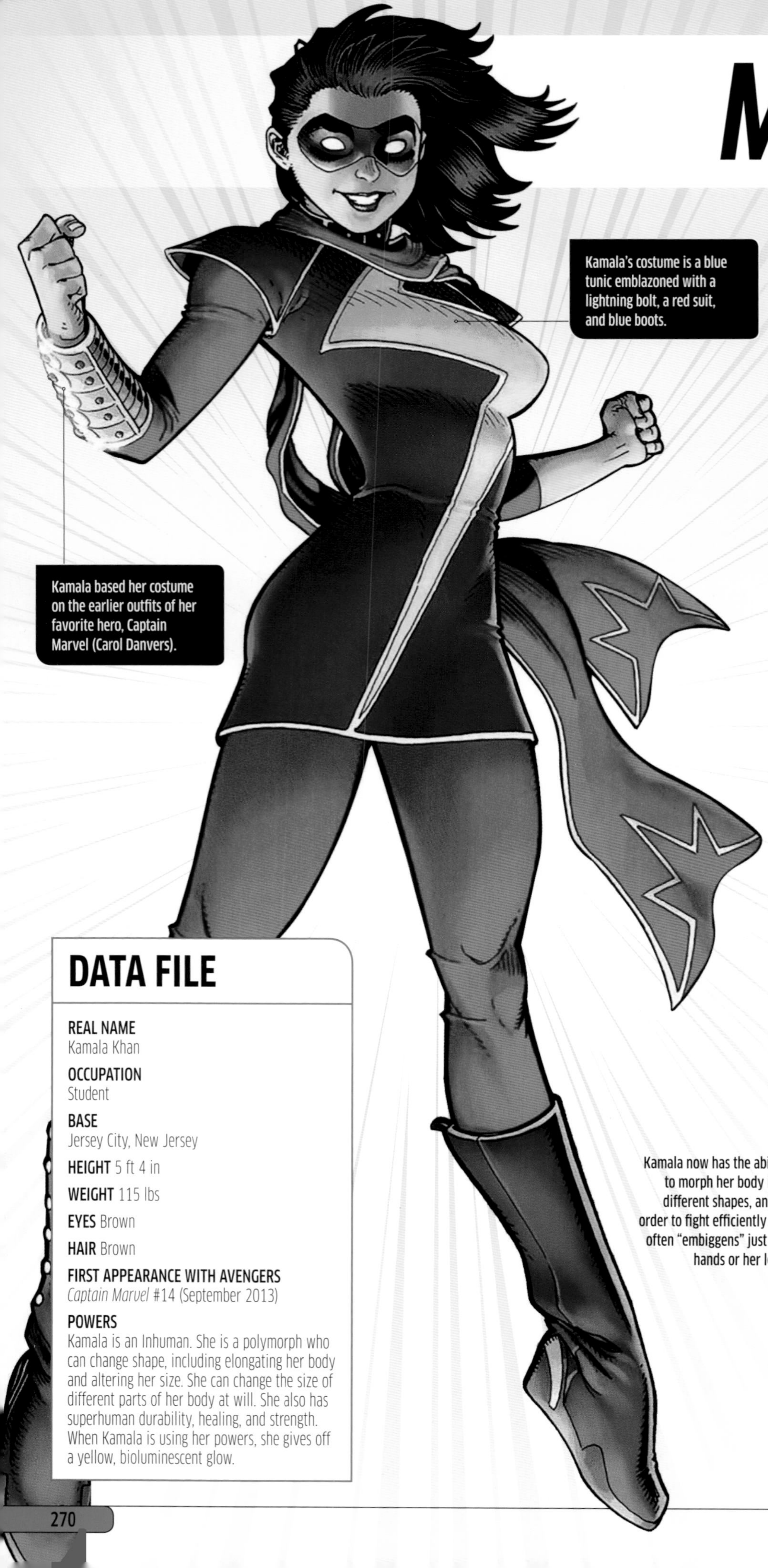

Kamala's costume is a blue tunic emblazoned with a lightning bolt, a red suit, and blue boots.

Kamala based her costume on the earlier outfits of her favorite hero, Captain Marvel (Carol Danvers).

SIXTEEN-YEAR-OLD Pakistan-American Muslim Kamala Khan wants to be a good girl and respect her parents. But when the Terrigen Bomb went off in Jersey City, New Jersey the Terrigen crystals released from the explosion triggered her previously unknown latent Inhuman genes and transformed her into the all-new Ms. Marvel!

HUMAN TO INHUMAN

Kamala Khan grew up in Jersey City, New Jersey, right across the Hudson River from Manhattan. Like many teenagers, she was compelled to navigate between her parents' world and her own as she came of age—and now she has powers to deal with, too.

The night Kamala snuck out of her home to go to a concert for the first time happened to be the night that Black Bolt, leader of the Inhumans, detonated the Terrigen Bomb. This device transformed those with latent Inhuman genes into superhumans—including Kamala, who then discovered that she could shape-shift. While she was learning to control her powers, she morphed into the form of an earlier Ms. Marvel (Carol Danvers, now known as Captain Marvel). When she later decided to become her own kind of Super Hero, Kamala altered her costume to make it more modest, but still retained the name of her favorite Super Hero.

Kamala now has the ability to morph her body into different shapes, and in order to fight efficiently she often "embiggens" just her hands or her legs.

DATA FILE

REAL NAME
Kamala Khan

OCCUPATION
Student

BASE
Jersey City, New Jersey

HEIGHT 5 ft 4 in

WEIGHT 115 lbs

EYES Brown

HAIR Brown

FIRST APPEARANCE WITH AVENGERS
Captain Marvel #14 (September 2013)

POWERS
Kamala is an Inhuman. She is a polymorph who can change shape, including elongating her body and altering her size. She can change the size of different parts of her body at will. She also has superhuman durability, healing, and strength. When Kamala is using her powers, she gives off a yellow, bioluminescent glow.

SUPER HERO FANGIRL

Kamala has yet to work with all the Avengers, although she knows all about the heroes in her world and has even written fan fiction about them.

The first Super Hero Kamala teamed up with was Wolverine. Rather star-struck at first, she learned from him that she should trust herself and her powers.

Even in the midst of an adventure with Spider-Man, she found time to quiz him about his date with Carol Danvers.

SPIDER-MARVEL

Amazing Spider-Man #7 (October 2014)

When the Kree scientist-warrior Dr. Minerva—dressed in an old Ms. Marvel costume—kidnapped a massive cocoon from a hospital in Manhattan, Kamala rushed to stop her. Spider-Man soon joined her, just in time to see Minerva transform into gigantic, bat-winged monster fueled by Inhuman genetic material. When the cocoon hatched, a baby emerged, and Kamala rushed it to safety. When Minerva's own henchmen assisted Kamala, she realized that Minerva's crimes hadn't been sanctioned by the Kree Empire, and the villain fled when Spider-Man faked reporting her to her masters. Adventures such as this have helped to boost Kamala's confidence.

ALLIES AND ENEMIES

As a relatively new kid on the Super Hero block, Ms. Marvel has yet to make enemies. However, she did take offence to Dr. Minerva's impersonation of her heroine.

LOCKJAW
Medusa, leader of the Inhumans, sent Lockjaw to watch over Kamala.

Kamala's costume is covered with a biokinetic polymer that makes it stretch.

Kamala can move fast by extending her legs, giving her much longer strides.

The fact that Dr. Minerva committed a crime while dressed as the original Ms. Marvel offended Kamala.

A MARVELOUS MENTOR

Carol Danvers, the original Ms. Marvel, is Kamala's inspiration, but not the first to take on the iconic identity, which, as a super fan, Kamala knows all too well.

While working as the head of NASA security, Carol Danvers got her powers when she was caught in an explosion with the original Captain Marvel. She later took on his name and became the latest Captain Marvel. Professional wrestler Sharon Ventura became the second Ms. Marvel after gaining superpowers from the Power Broker. She later mutated into the She-Thing. Psychiatrist Dr. Karla Sofen—aka the villain Moonstone—became the third Ms. Marvel while posing as Carol Danvers for Norman Osborn's team of Dark Avengers. This makes Kamala Khan the fourth Ms. Marvel. With such rich history behind her, Kamala wears the name and the costume with pride.

As Ms. Marvel, Carol Danvers wore several versions of the Super Hero costume. Kamala took her inspiration from the original red, blue, and yellow styling.

COLLECTOR

Potentially the oldest living being in the universe, and one of the immortal Elders, the Collector sees himself as responsible for making sure that the greatest things in the universe can survive even its utter destruction.

When, with his precognitive powers, the Collector foresaw a future in which Thanos would destroy everything, he dedicated himself to his mission of saving what he could. He began collecting artifacts and people that he deemed worthy of preserving. This included the Avengers, with the Collector hoping to snare the whole set of them. But when he attempted to catch the Avengers they turned the tables on him, and he had to turn to powerful gadgets in his collection to make good his escape.

Later, the Collector saw Korvac as an even greater threat to the universe than Thanos, and sent his daughter Carina to spy on him. The Collector's plans were foiled when Carina fell in love with Korvac, and betrayed her father whom Korvac killed.

The Collector was later revived by the Grandmaster, for whom he later returned the favor.

The Collector doesn't want to save the universe. He cares only about protecting its greatest assets—by controlling them himself.

The Collector's powers over cosmic energy help protect him.

ALLIES AND ENEMIES

The Collector's greatest allies are his fellow Elders of the Universe. Each of them is the last survivor of one of the oldest peoples from different planets and races. They work together and call each other "brother."

CARINA
The Collector's daughter returned from death to turn hero and defeat Korvac with the help of the Avengers.

THE GRANDMASTER
The Collector's "brother," the Grandmaster plays complex games—and places big bets on them, too.

DATA FILE

REAL NAME Taneleer Tivan **OCCUPATION** Curator
BASE Mobile
HEIGHT 6 ft 6 in **WEIGHT** 450 lbs **EYES** White **HAIR** White
FIRST APPEARANCE WITH AVENGERS *Avengers* #28 (June 1966)
POWERS As an Elder of the Universe, the Collector can manipulate cosmic energy and is immortal and nearly indestructible—meaning he is almost impossible to kill. He also has some limited precognitive abilities through which he can perceive possible futures. He uses a Temporal Assimilator for short hops through time.

VALKYRIE

Brunnhilde is Valkyrie: Asgardian leader of the Valkyrior, the Choosers of the Slain, a role she has held for centuries.

Odin appointed Brunnhilde to be the Valkyrie and lead the Valkyrior—a group of warrior goddesses tasked with picking out those fallen soldiers worthy to be brought to Valhalla in the Asgardian afterlife. A fierce combatant, Brunnhilde was nonetheless tricked by the Enchantress, who trapped Brunnhilde's spirit in a crystal and used it to bestow her powers on others. Posing as Valkyrie, the Enchantress formed an all-women group called the Liberators to attack the Avengers. Brunnhilde eventually regained her true body by joining minds with a woman named Barbara Norris, who was unfortunately caught in the Enchantress's games. Brunnhilde was part of the Secret Avengers, and recently led her own team of Defenders.

Valkyrie wields Dragonfang, an indestructible sword.

Brunnhilde worked as part of Captain Steve Rogers' black ops team of Avengers.

DATA FILE

REAL NAME
Brunnhilde

OCCUPATION
Adventurer, Chooser of the Slain

BASE
Asgard

HEIGHT 6 ft 3 in

WEIGHT 475 lbs

EYES Blue

HAIR Blonde

FIRST APPEARANCE WITH AVENGERS
Avengers #83 (December 1970)

POWERS
As an immortal of supposed mixed Asgardian origins, Brunnhilde has superhuman durability, endurance, healing, speed, and strength. She can also sense the imminence of death and can teleport between the realm of the living and the dead. She is also an expert in combat, especially with blades, such as her Dragonfang sword.

RONAN THE ACCUSER

As Supreme Accusor, Ronan enforces Kree law.

A noble of the alien Kree empire, Supreme Public Accuser Ronan first faced the Avengers when they came to the aid of his foe, Captain Mar-Vell. Ronan tried to take over as the Kree Emperor during the Kree-Skrull War, but the Supreme Intelligence foiled him. He eventually slew the Supreme Intelligence and, with nothing left standing in his way, became the new Kree Emperor.

DATA FILE

REAL NAME Ronan **OCCUPATION** Kree Emperor
BASE The planet Kree-La
HEIGHT 7 ft 5 in **WEIGHT** 480 lbs **EYES** Blue **HAIR** Brown
FIRST APPEARANCE WITH AVENGERS *Avengers* #89 (September 1971)
POWERS In addition to his extensive military training, Ronan has superhuman strength and speed. Special cybernetic enhancements in his armor increase his agility and also give him the power of invisibility, and the ability to freeze his opponents. His most lethal weapon is his hammer-shaped universal weapon, which can be wielded by Accusers only, and uses cosmic energy to lift, throw, and disintegrate his foes.

NIGHTMASK

This artificial man became a hero.

When Ex Nihilo and Abyss terraformed Mars, Ex Nihilo created an adult named Adam, who became known as Nightmask. The pair's aim was to repopulate Earth with new people after destroying it. However, the Avengers found him and took him to Earth to investigate him, at which point he alerted them that the universe was dying. Later, he helped them find Star Brand and became the talented youngster's mentor. He met a heroic end: He aged backward traveling through the multiverse, and he sacrificed himself to help save all realities.

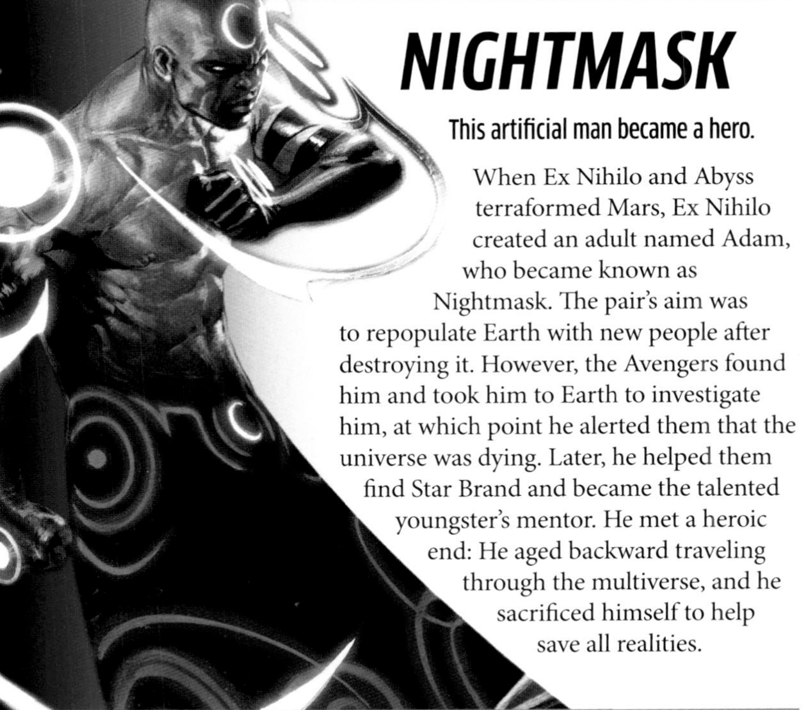

DATA FILE

REAL NAME Adam **OCCUPATION** Adventurer
BASE Mobile
HEIGHT 6 ft 6 in **WEIGHT** 640 lbs **EYES** White **HAIR** Bald
FIRST APPEARANCE WITH AVENGERS *Avengers* #3 (March 2013)
POWERS Adam could speak Builder machine code and use it to control sophisticated machines of all kinds. He coud also fire energy blasts, fly, and teleport himself and others unlimited distances, even between universes.

NOH-VARR (THE PROTECTOR)

DATA FILE

REAL NAME
Noh-Varr

OCCUPATION
Adventurer

BASE
New York City

HEIGHT 5 ft 10 in

WEIGHT 165 lbs

EYES Black

HAIR White

FIRST APPEARANCE WITH AVENGERS
Secret Invasion #1 (June 2008)

POWERS
Noh-Varr has superhuman durability, endurance, speed, and strength. He can mentally ignore any sensation (including pain) and enter a hyperfocused state. He can climb walls, his saliva can induce hallucinations, and he can exude poisons or explosives through his fingernails.

Noh-Varr is another heroic, but conflicted, heir to Captain Mar-Vell's legacy.

Originally a Kree diplomat from another version of Earth in a parallel universe, Noh-Varr became the sole survivor of his lost starship when it traveled to the present Earth (Earth-616). When he attacked the Earth in retaliation for his ship's destruction, S.H.I.E.L.D. captured him and later sent him to fight the Young Avengers. He sided with Earth during the Skrulls' invasion and became the new Captain Marvel for the Dark Avengers. When he abandoned them, the Supreme Intelligence charged him with saving Earth and transformed him into the Protector. He then joined the Avengers but was kicked out when they thought he'd betrayed them. Having rebuilt his good reputation, he joined the Young Avengers, and is especially close to Kate Bishop (Hawkeye).

Many famous faces have been known as the Protector, a role Noh-Varr has now left behind him.

SKAAR

DATA FILE

REAL NAME
Skaar

OCCUPATION
Warrior

BASE
Mobile

HEIGHT 6 ft 6 in/ 5 ft 3 in

WEIGHT 400 lbs/ 105 lbs

EYES Green

HAIR Black

FIRST APPEARANCE WITH AVENGERS
Fall of the Hulks: Gamma #1 (February 2010)

POWERS
In his large, green form, Skaar has superhuman endurance and strength and is nearly invulnerable. Skaar has the ability to wield Old Power—an ancient cosmic power inherited from his mother, Caiera. When calm, he changes into a human boy. Under Bruce Banner's tutorage, Skaar has learned greater combat skills.

The son of the Hulk from beyond the stars, Skaar is often known as King of the Savage Land.

Born on the planet Sakaar from a cocoon left behind by his dead mother Caiera, Skaar emerged as large as a 10-year-old boy. After failing to save Sakaar from Galactus, and bent on revenge, he set out to hunt down and kill his father, the Hulk, but the two later reconciled. Skaar helped the Avengers during the Fall of the Hulks and the Chaos War. He joined Norman Osborn's Dark Avengers as a double agent and betrayed them to the real Avenges. He became a part of Luke Cage's Dark Avengers too. The Hulk later managed to depower Skaar, who now leads a normal life on Earth.

FORGOTTEN ONE (GILGAMESH)

This mighty Eternal is known as Hero, for bravery, and Gilgamesh, after the renowned epic king.

In ancient times, the Forgotten One was banished from mortal lands to keep him from interfering with humanity. He won his freedom in modern times, and he joined the Avengers under the name Gilgamesh. He was thought to have been killed by the Avengers' foe Immortus, but he returned in a new body, although with no memory of his former life. He later helped Thor in his battle against the Deviants.

DATA FILE

REAL NAME Unknown **OCCUPATION** Adventurer, agent of the Celestials
BASE Mobile
HEIGHT 6 ft 5 in **WEIGHT** 269 lbs **EYES** Blue **HAIR** Black
FIRST APPEARANCE WITH AVENGERS *Avengers* #299 (January 1989)
POWERS As one of the immortal Eternals, the Forgotten One has superhuman durability, endurance, healing, speed, and strength. He can also fire energy blasts from his hands and employ telepathy and telekinesis, which he can use to fly.

MARTINEX

The last survivor of Pluto now lives in the 31st century, alongside the Guardians of the Galaxy.

In the distant future, the alien Badoon invaded the Solar System, laying waste to the inhabited planets. On Pluto, only the scientist Martinex survived, but he helped form and lead the original Guardians of the Galaxy of future times.

After battling Korvac in the 31st century, the Guardians traveled back to modern times to help the Avengers defeat him there, too. Martinex also led the Galactic Guardians—a larger group of heroes banding together future versions of well-known names.

Martinex's exoskeleton is resistant to even the most fearsome attacks.

DATA FILE

REAL NAME Martinex T'Naga **OCCUPATION** Adventurer
BASE *Starship Captain America*
HEIGHT 6 ft 1 in **WEIGHT** 455 lbs **EYES** Gray **HAIR** None
FIRST APPEARANCE WITH AVENGERS *Avengers* #167 (January 1978)
POWERS Like all those who lived on Pluto, Martinex is covered with a layer of crystal that gives him superhuman durability, and he can fire blasts of heat and cold from his hands.

CHTHON

An Elder God of immeasurable, interdimensional, evil and power, Chthon is a powerful and dangerous foe.

Chthon was one of the first of the gods to form on Earth. Trapped in his own dimension—the Other-Realm—he created the Darkhold, the first tome of black magic. Wielding enormous, mystic powers, Chthon once possessed the Scarlet Witch until the Avengers forced him out of her, and he later possessed Quicksilver too, but Hank Pym's Mighty Avengers stopped him. He has also been bested by the Vision.

Chthon is capable of assuming a humanoid form.

DATA FILE

REAL NAME Chthon **OCCUPATION** Elder God
BASE Other-Realm
HEIGHT Varies **WEIGHT** Varies **EYES** Vary **HAIR** Varies
FIRST APPEARANCE WITH AVENGERS *Avengers* #186 (January 1979)
POWERS As an Elder God, Chthon has nearly unlimited power and wields black magic and chaos magic. However, he remains in his Other-Realm and only comes to Earth when summoned either into a host or his standard form, the Other.

MAXIMUS

The insane brother of the Inhumans' king is notoriously unpredictable.

As the younger brother of Black Bolt, king of the Inhumans, Maximus coveted his brother's throne and has taken it from him many times. In one early instance, the Avengers helped defeat Maximus and restore Black Bolt, who prefers to keep his troublesome younger brother nearby, if only to keep an eye on him. Maximus created the Terrigen Bomb that trigged the latent powers in the Earth's Inhumans—resulting in Kamala Khan becoming Ms. Marvel, amongst other Super Hero creations. Keeping things in the family, Maximus often works on top-secret projects for Black Bolt and his sister-in-law, Medusa.

DATA FILE

REAL NAME Maximus Boltagon **OCCUPATION** Royal advisor, would-be ruler
BASE Attilan
HEIGHT 5 ft 11 in **WEIGHT** 180 lbs **EYES** Blue **HAIR** Black
FIRST APPEARANCE WITH AVENGERS *Amazing Adventures* #8 (September 1971)
POWERS Maximus is an Inhuman genius and has the limited power to control minds.

GRANDMASTER

The greatest gamer in the entire universe—and beyond—will play to the end.

As one of the immortal Elders of the Universe, the Grandmaster sees the universe as a puzzle to both create and solve, if only to keep himself from becoming bored with eternity. The Avengers first encountered him when he challenged Kang to a contest that pitted the Avengers (Kang's chosen team) against his own champions (the Squadron Supreme).

The Grandmaster calls the other Elders "brothers," and their bond of fraternalism is strong. After the demise of fellow Eternal the Collector, the Grandmaster set up a Contest of Champions with the entity Death so that she would revive him. In the end, he sacrificed himself to die in the Collector's place. The Collector then schemed to bring the Grandmaster back as well.

The Grandmaster rarely enters battle himself, preferring to use superhumans as pawns in his games.

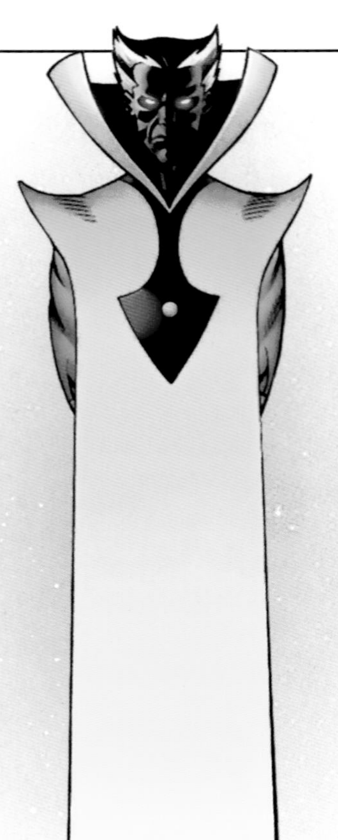

DATA FILE

REAL NAME
En Dwi Gast

OCCUPATION
Gamer

BASE
Mobile

HEIGHT 7 ft 1 in

WEIGHT 240 lbs

EYES Entirely red

HAIR White

FIRST APPEARANCE WITH AVENGERS
Avengers #69 (October 1969)

POWERS
As an Elder of the Universe, the Grandmaster can manipulate cosmic energy and is immortal and nearly indestructible. He also is an expert at game theory and all games played throughout the universe. He can travel through time, space, and universes and rearrange matter on a planetary scale.

DIMITRIOS

A cure that might be worse than the disease, Dimitrios was never meant to become sentient.

Dimitrios evolved into an artificial intelligence from the virus Hank Pym programmed into Ultron in order to destroy his monstrous creation.

Now an artificial intelligence capable of independence, and determined to exterminate humanity, Dimitrios took over Iron Man's old armor in order to give himself a body. From within Stark's armored technology, he then tried to conquer and destroy the entire universe—10,000 years in the future—but the Avengers A. I. stopped him.

DATA FILE

REAL NAME Dimitrios **OCCUPATION** Conqueror
BASE Diamond City
HEIGHT 6 ft 8 in **WEIGHT** 225 lbs **EYES** Yellow **HAIR** None
FIRST APPEARANCE WITH AVENGERS *Avengers A. I.* #2 (October 2013)
POWERS Dimitrios is an artificial intelligence that can control electronic systems—including complex computers—at will.

Abyss can take a solid form, but is normally gaseous.

ABYSS

The last of her race, this Abyss was sister to an Earth-bound Ex Nihilo, the Gardener.

An ancient race known as the Builders paired up Abysses and Ex Nihilos to judge the worthiness of worlds across the universe. This Abyss and her Ex Nihilo partner came to Mars and attacked Earth.

With her powers of deduction, Abyss recognized Captain Universe and surrendered to her, later agreeing to become a member of the Avengers along with Ex Nihilo in order to prevent the Builder invasion—effectively turning against their own race. She died bravely, in a heroic self-sacrificial act, trying to stop the Beyonders from destroying the multiverse.

DATA FILE

REAL NAME Drusilla **OCCUPATION** Destroyer
BASE Mars
HEIGHT 5 ft 5 in **WEIGHT** 120 lbs **EYES** Black **HAIR** Black
FIRST APPEARANCE WITH AVENGERS *Avengers* #1 (February 2013)
POWERS Abyss was made of living gas, making her invulnerable to most attacks. She could manipulate the minds of those she enveloped.

SUPER-ADAPTOID

This villainous android can hold the powers of the entire Avengers team.

The scientists at the terrorist organization A.I.M. (Advanced Idea Mechanics) built the first Super-Adaptoid—an android powered by a sliver of a Cosmic Cube. With the powers to replicate superpowered people and their powers, the A.I.M. scientists sent it to copy, kill, and replace Captain America.

It later faced the Avengers but failed in its mission to kill them. Yelena Belova (the second Black Widow) was forcibly merged with it for a while and attacked Luke Cage and Jessica Jones's wedding. Norman Osborn gained its powers and attacked the Avengers after his group, H.A.M.M.E.R., fell apart. Recently, A.I.M. created a group of Adaptoids who escaped and left to explore alternate universes.

DATA FILE

REAL NAME
Super-Adaptoid

OCCUPATION
Super-assassin

BASE
Mobile

HEIGHT Varies

WEIGHT Varies

EYES Vary

HAIR Varies

FIRST APPEARANCE WITH AVENGERS
Avengers #45 (October 1967)

POWERS
The Super-Adaptoid can copy the appearance and powers of anyone passing within range of its scanners (about ten feet)—up to eight at a time. Absorbing too many powers causes the Super-Adaptoid to overload.

MAGDALENE

This hero is from a world beyond Earth.

Magdalene was an Avenger from a dimension in which Earth had been destroyed by an insane version of the Eternals Avenger Sersi. The villainous Proctor recruited Magdalene to his Gatherers—a team of Avengers who had all survived similar disasters—and they set out to kill Sersi in every dimension, not just their own, in order to ensure she could not threaten their existence anywhere. It was soon revealed that Proctor had been secretly driving each of them insane. Upon discovering her leader was not to be trusted, Magdalene left to find a new home for herself in another dimension.

DATA FILE

REAL NAME Marissa Darrow **OCCUPATION** Adventurer
BASE Mobile
HEIGHT 6 ft 7 in **WEIGHT** 203 lbs **EYES** White **HAIR** Black
FIRST APPEARANCE WITH AVENGERS *Avengers* #343 (January 1992)
POWERS Magdalene's suit of armor gave her superhuman agility, durability, and strength. With her power lance, she could fire energy blasts, absorb energy, and even open portals to other dimensions.

NEBULA

The alleged granddaughter of Thanos has fought the Avengers and the Guardians of the Galaxy.

The Avengers knew little of Nebula until she hijacked Thanos's former flagship, *Sanctuary II*, and claimed to be his granddaughter. Her piracy also extended to kidnapping Spectrum (then Captain Marvel), and forcing the Avenger to attack the Skrull Empire. The mysterious Beyonder helped the Avengers to stop Nebula by teleporting her out of the galaxy. Thanos nearly killed her when he reclaimed his ship, but she stole the long-disputed Infinity Gauntlet from him while he was distracted. She later joined her adopted relative, Gamora, in her team, the Graces.

DATA FILE

REAL NAME Nebula **OCCUPATION** Space pirate
BASE Mobile
HEIGHT 6 ft 1 in **WEIGHT** 180 lbs **EYES** Blue **HAIR** Black, blue, or bald
FIRST APPEARANCE WITH AVENGERS *Avengers* #257 (July 1985)
POWERS Nebula has cybernetics which grant her superhuman durability and strength and provide her with a number of built-in weapons.

STARFOX

Using his personal force field, Starfox can fly through space.

An Eternal of Titan, Eros has a light and easy, womanizing nature that stands in stark contrast to the murderous ways of his planet-conquering older brother, Thanos. A stint with the Avengers as Starfox helped to put distance between himself and his family's bad galactic reputation.

Born on Titan, one of Saturn's moons, Eros was popular and well-loved, but he suffered when his brother, Thanos, conquered their home in an attack that killed their mother and left few survivors.

Eros helped Captain Mar-Vell and the Avengers deliver Thanos's first real defeat, after which, and in the absence of any other responsibilities tying him down, he decided to devote himself once again to a life of hedonism. Later agreeing to mentor Captain Mar-Vell's son, Genis-Vell, Eros eventually joined the Avengers, who gave him the code name Starfox to distance him further from his given name and his disreputable habits.

Starfox is the great-uncle of Nebula, and he helped to defeat her when she went dangerously rogue.

His wanderlust continued to draw him away from Earth, but he returned to try to stop Thanos from assembling the legendary Infinity Gauntlet. After accusations of sexual assault, Eros had Moondragon disable his power to telepathically stimulate pleasure centers of nearby minds. An immortal Eternal, Starfox's powers are great, but he has often lacked the patience to master them. Above all, he still seeks out adventure and entertainment.

ALLIES AND ENEMIES

Starfox is charming and popular and counts many people from across the galaxy as his friends. His relationships with members of his Eternal family are sometimes strained though.

FAMILY

MENTOR
Eros's father was the leader of the Titanian Eternals and the well-loved founder of their colony.

THANOS
Eros's brother has committed many atrocities, but the two still bear a grudging respect for each other.

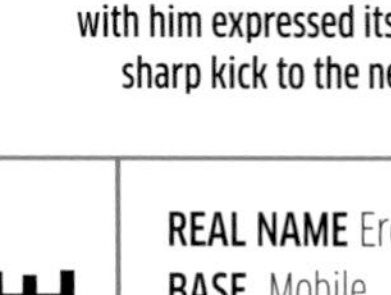

She-Hulk defended Eros in court—until she suspected him of manipulating her, too. Her wrath with him expressed itself in a swift, sharp kick to the nether regions.

DATA FILE

REAL NAME Eros **OCCUPATION** Adventurer
BASE Mobile
HEIGHT 6 ft 1 in **WEIGHT** 190 lbs **EYES** Blue **HAIR** Red
FIRST APPEARANCE WITH AVENGERS *Captain Marvel* #27 (July 1973)
POWERS As an immortal Eternal, Starfox has superhuman durability, endurance, healing, speed, and strength. He can also fly, use telekinesis, and generate a personal force field. He could stimulate the pleasure centers in the brain of those nearby, even to the point of causing them to adore him, until this was disabled.

ENCHANTRESS

The Asgardian goddess is a master of manipulation.

As a young Asgardian, Amora fled her home to become the apprentice of the sorceress Karnilla. She became not only the powerful Enchantress, but a gifted seducer of men. She later trapped Valkyrie's soul in a crystal, and she made Skurge (the Executioner) her adoring pawn. After Odin banished her and Skurge from Asgard, the pair teamed up with Baron Zemo to battle the Avengers on Earth. The Enchantress has had a tempestuous relationship with Thor over the years. The death of Skurge, which occured when he turned from the Enchantress to fight with the god of thunder, shook her to her core. More recently, Loki turned Young Avenger Sylvie Lushton into a teenage version of the Enchantress for his own ends.

The Enchantress's lips have the power to enslave those that she kisses.

The Enchantress enjoys seducing others to do her dirty work, but her magical powers make her dangerous in her own right.

DATA FILE

REAL NAME
Amora

OCCUPATION
Goddess

BASE
Asgard

HEIGHT 6 ft 3 in

WEIGHT 450 lbs

EYES Green

HAIR Blonde

FIRST APPEARANCE WITH AVENGERS
Avengers #7 (August 1964)

POWERS
As an immortal goddess of Asgard, Amora has enhanced durability, endurance, speed, and strength. She is also a master of sorcery, specializing in spells that enhance her beauty and allow her to manipulate men. She can fire energy bolts from her hands, and she can enslave others with her kiss.

SPACE PHANTOM

Immortus's instruments, the Space Phantoms, are a race of aliens from the dimension Limbo.

Anyone who spends too much time in Limbo forgets their past and transforms into a Space Phantom. The ruler of Limbo, Immortus, molds these creatures into his servants and uses them to replace individuals temporarily so that he can examine them, and, in time, crush them.

The Avengers long thought there was only one Space Phantom, sent to Earth purely to plague them, but in time they discovered that there are several. The first time the Avengers encountered a Space Phantom, he created a rift between them that caused the Hulk to leave the team, and the creatures have plagued the team many times over the years since.

DATA FILE

REAL NAME Unknown **OCCUPATION** Agent of Immortus
BASE Limbo
HEIGHT 6 ft 6 in **WEIGHT** 215 lbs **EYES** Blue **HAIR** Red
FIRST APPEARANCE WITH AVENGERS *Avengers* #2 (November 1963)
POWERS A Space Phantom can take the form of any other individual, sending the victim to Limbo for the duration of the replacement. They duplicate the person entirely, including any powers.

MACHINE MAN

This machine was raised to become a man.

The android known as Machine Man, or more properly X-51, was part of a government program to build robotic soldiers. His creator, Aaron Stack, raised him as a human, which kept X-51 from succumbing to the psychosis that affected the other models. When Stack died trying to protect X-51, the robot took over his creator's identity and fled. He met and fell in love with Ultron's creation, Jocasta, and after she was destroyed, he agreed to work for the Fixer to get her repaired. When the Fixer fought the Avengers, however, X-51 betrayed him, and he later became a member of the Super Hero team.

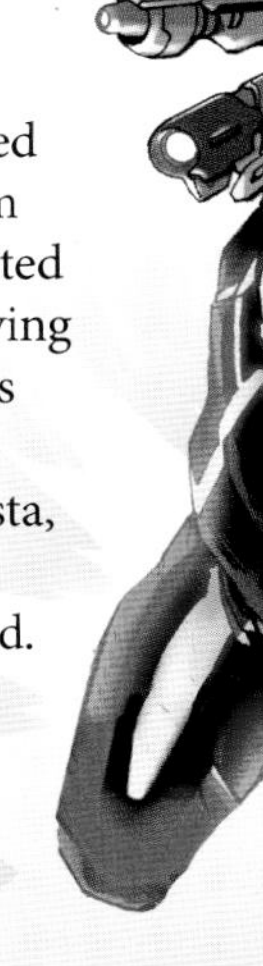

DATA FILE

REAL NAME X-51, alias Aaron Stack **OCCUPATION** Adventurer
BASE New York City
HEIGHT 6 ft **WEIGHT** 850 lbs **EYES** Red **HAIR** Black
FIRST APPEARANCE WITH AVENGERS *Avengers* #287 (January 1988)
POWERS As an android, X-51 has superhuman durability, endurance, speed, and strength. He also has several built-in instruments and weapons, and he can fly.

MARVEL BOY

The first in a long line of illustrious Marvel Boys, Robert Grayson was raised as an alien, but returned to Earth as a hero.

In the 1930s, German scientist Dr. Horace Grayson made contact with a colony of Eternals living on Uranus. They gave him plans to build a rocket, with which he escaped Nazi Germany with his infant son Robert and resettled with the Uranians. When Robert became an adult, the Uranians sent him back to Earth as a Super Hero to help pave the way for them to seize control of the planet.

He rebelled against this, instead joining the Agents of Atlas and becoming Marvel Boy. In modern times, he worked with the reunited Agents, who worked against Norman Osborn's Dark Avengers.

Grayson's developed inability to breathe Earth's air means he remains mostly on Uranus.

Quantum bands from the Uranian Eternals give Marvel Boy many of his powers.

DATA FILE

REAL NAME
Robert Grayson

OCCUPATION
Adventurer

BASE
Uranus, mobile

HEIGHT 5 ft 10 in

WEIGHT 170 lbs

EYES Blue

HAIR Blond

FIRST APPEARANCE WITH AVENGERS
Agents of Atlas #5 (July 2009)

POWERS
Robert wears a Uranian headband that gives him telepathic abilities. He also uses a set of quantum bands that grant him superhuman durability, endurance, and strength, and the ability to fire energy blasts and fly. He has a flying saucer that responds to his mental commands. After so much time on Uranus, he can no longer breathe Earth's atmosphere and so must wear a space suit while on Earth.

EXECUTIONER

This vicious Asgardian warrior had a soft side—spending his life pining for the Enchantress.

Born in Asgard, the child of a storm giant and an Asgardian goddess, Skurge earned his nickname "the Executioner" for his successes in the war against his father's people. Enamored with the evil Enchantress, he committed many horrible acts in the name of his love and battled the Avengers with her several times. However, he died a hero, fighting alongside Thor to rescue innocent souls from the world Hel.

Thick muscle and skin tissue increase the Executioner's strength and agility.

DATA FILE

REAL NAME Skurge **OCCUPATION** Giant-killer
BASE Asgard
HEIGHT 7 ft 2 in **WEIGHT** 1,100 lbs **EYES** Blue **HAIR** Black
FIRST APPEARANCE WITH AVENGERS *Avengers* #7 (August 1964)
POWERS As an immortal god of Asgard, Skurge had enhanced durability, endurance, speed, and strength. He was a gifted warrior, proficient in all kinds of weaponry, and he carried the enchanted Bloodaxe.

MARRINA

This amphibious alien became Namor's wife and part of Alpha Flight on Earth.

Millennia ago, the alien Plodex sent a ship of eggs to colonize Earth, but few of them survived. When Marrina hatched from one, she was imprinted with human DNA from a nearby fisherman's wife and took the form of a human infant. She later joined Alpha Flight and married Namor, but during a pregnancy she transformed into a leviathan, attacking the Avengers and forcing Namor to kill her. She has since returned to life.

Marrina's amphibious features include gills and webbed hands and feet.

DATA FILE

REAL NAME Marrina Smallwood **OCCUPATION** Adventurer
BASE Mobile
HEIGHT 6 ft **WEIGHT** 200 lbs **EYES** Black **HAIR** Green
FIRST APPEARANCE WITH AVENGERS *Avengers* #272 (October 1986)
POWERS Marrina has superhuman durability, endurance, and strength. She can breathe water as easily as air and can swim at superhuman speeds. She sometimes shifts into monstrous shapes as her alien nature requires.

PSYKLOP

After sleeping for millennia, this insectoid servant of ancient gods hoped to conquer Earth.

A member of an Insectoid race that predated humanity, Psyklop's ancient gods awakened him from hibernation and charged him with making a powerful sacrifice that would bring both them and his people back to retake the world. Psyklop chose the massive Hulk as the most appropriate sacrifice, but the Avengers foiled his initial attempt to capture him. Undeterred, Psyklop pursued the Hulk into the Microverse, where the Hulk and the Hulk's wife, Jarella, defeated him. For his failure, Psyklop was severely punished by his immortal masters and is now assumed dead.

DATA FILE

REAL NAME Psyklop **OCCUPATION** Servant of the Dark Gods
BASE Mobile
HEIGHT 8 ft **WEIGHT** 450 lbs **EYES** Red **HAIR** None
FIRST APPEARANCE WITH AVENGERS *Avengers* #88 (May 1971)
POWERS Psyklop had superhuman durability, endurance, speed, and strength. He could also fire energy blasts from his eye and hypnotize or delude people.

HYPERION

The last son of a destroyed planet, Hyperion has appeared in multiple dimensions.

Living on a doomed planet, Hyperion's Eternal parents sent their infant child to Earth to be raised by humans. In one world, he became a great hero and a founder of the Super Hero team Squadron Supreme.

From an alternate universe, a villainous counterpart of Hyperion appeared, working in the Grandmaster's villainous Squadron Sinister. The Avengers battled this form, but they also later met good Hyperion and his compatriots. The evil Hyperion joined the Avengers after his universe was destroyed.

DATA FILE

REAL NAME Marcus Milton **OCCUPATION** Adventurer
BASE Mobile (formerly Squadron City)
HEIGHT 6 ft 4 in **WEIGHT** 460 lbs **EYES** Blue **HAIR** Red
FIRST APPEARANCE WITH AVENGERS *Avengers* #69 (October 1969)
POWERS As an immortal Eternal, Hyperion has superhuman durability, endurance, healing, speed, and strength. He is nearly invulnerable and can also fly and fire energy blasts from his eyes. His body can absorb cosmic radiation.

CRYSTAL

A noble, exiled Inhuman, Crystal has used her elemental powers to aid Earth's heroes.

The younger sister of Medusa, Crystal is a member of Inhuman nobility. When Maximus forced the royal family from Attilan, she went to New York on Earth, where she fell in love with the Human Torch. She later married Quicksilver, in the first ever human-Inhuman marriage, and they had a baby girl named Luna. When the alien Brethren attacked the Inhumans, Crystal turned to the Avengers for help and soon after joined the team. In time, her marriage fell apart, and the Inhumans moved to Kree Space. Crystal chose a political alliance by marrying Ronan the Accuser as a means to merge the Inhumans and the Kree Empire. She remained committed to him even after the Inhumans returned to Earth.

As one of her elemental powers, Crystal can control fire.

DATA FILE

REAL NAME
Crystalia Amaquelin

OCCUPATION
Princess

BASE
Attilan

HEIGHT 5 ft 6 in

WEIGHT 110 lbs

EYES Green

HAIR Red

FIRST APPEARANCE WITH AVENGERS
Avengers #334 (July 1991)

POWERS
As an Inhuman, Crystal has superhuman durability, endurance, speed, and strength. She can also telekinetically control air, fire, earth, and water.

SERSI

One of the mighty Eternals, Sersi has inspired many myths over the years. As "Circe," she turned Odysseus's sailors to pigs. She was with Nero when he burned Rome, and worked with Merlin in the time of Camelot.

Although legends surrounding her name and powers travel before her, Sersi actually first met the Avengers when she invited them to a party she was hosting. This meeting also reacquainted her with her long-lost Eternals cousin, and then Avengers member, Starfox. In time, she would come to join the team herself, filling the gap her fellow Eternal, the Forgotten One, left on the roster.

With her powers as an enchantress, Sersi has played a major role in many key events, including the Eternals' struggle against the Deviants, and faced an attack by the villain Maestrom alongside the Avengers, including Starfox and the Wasp. At another time, and the influence of Proctor, she turned against the Avengers, but she managed to slay Proctor with his own version of the Black Knight's Ebony Blade and redeem herself. She later offered her services to Luke Cage's Heroes for Hire.

Having discovered that she prefers the quiet life of an ordinary person, and feeling damaged by her experiences—including having her memories of the Eternals wiped—Sersi has retired and become a party planner, despite many invitations to return to the Avengers.

Sersi often helped the Avengers take on cosmic-level trouble, using her powers to aid them.

Sersi uses cosmic energy to manipulate matter.

Sersi's war experiences have turned her from playful and flirtatious to angry and battle-thirsty.

Sersi fought alongside the Eternals, and has often felt torn between staying on Earth and returning to Olympia, their home.

ALLIES AND ENEMIES

At times far from her Eternals family, Sersi values the many friendships she formed during her time in the Avengers.

FRIEND

BLACK KNIGHT
Sersi loved the Black Knight and even left this universe to travel to an alternate world with him at her side.

FOE

PROCTOR
This alternate-universe Black Knight murdered Sersi's counterparts on many different Earths.

DATA FILE

REAL NAME Sersi **OCCUPATION** Adventurer
BASE New York City
HEIGHT 5 ft 9 in **WEIGHT** 140 lbs **EYES** Blue **HAIR** Black
FIRST APPEARANCE WITH AVENGERS *Avengers* #246 (August 1984)
POWERS As one of the immortal Eternals, Sersi has superhuman durability, endurance, healing, speed, and strength. She is also a master of sorcery, telepathy, and telekinesis, and she can fire energy blasts from her hands and eyes, fly, and teleport long distances.

TERMINUS

The Terminex built these alien robots to invade and destroy other planets.

When the Celestials wiped out the Terminex alien race, they were unaware that the Terminex had left behind them advanced robotic killing machines. A Terminus begins as a microbial robot that forms a larger creature as it merges with other Termini. The Fantastic Four defeated the first one on Earth, and the Avengers later fought a scientist named Jorro, who recreated a Terminus's armor and stole its atomic lance. They later defeated a combination of two Termini called the Ulterminus.

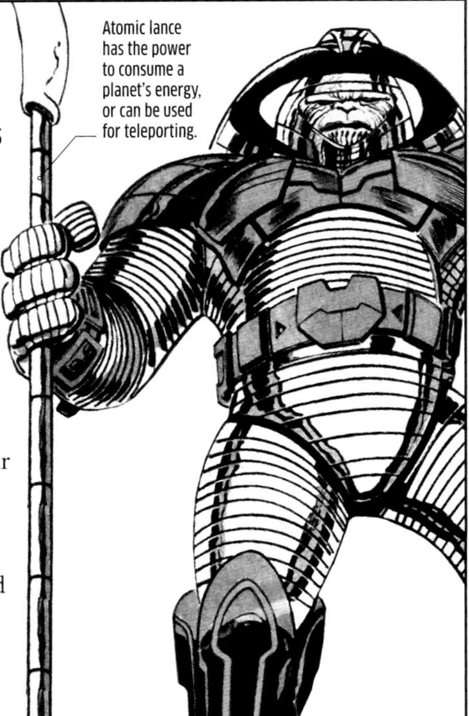

Atomic lance has the power to consume a planet's energy, or can be used for teleporting.

DATA FILE

REAL NAME Terminus **OCCUPATION** Destroyer of worlds
BASE Mobile
HEIGHT 150 ft **WEIGHT** Unrevealed **EYES** White **HAIR** None
FIRST APPEARANCE WITH AVENGERS *Avengers* #256 (July 1985)
POWERS The gigantic Termini are nearly invulnerable and have superhuman healing and strength. They can regenerate lost body parts, and they can fire energy blasts from their lances.

GENIS-VELL

The son of Captain Mar-Vell has worn many aliases.

After Captain Mar-Vell's death, his lover Elysius used Titanian technology to bear them a son, named Genis-Vell, and accelerate the boy's growth to adulthood. With his father's powerful wrist-worn Nega Bands, Genis adventured under the name Legacy. After Avenger Monica Rambeau (then Captain Marvel) gave him his father's title, Genis helped the Avengers as the new Captain Marvel. When Genis (aka Photon) was a member of the Thunderbolts, Baron Zemo killed him—supposedly to prevent the now unhinged Genis from destroying the universe.

The Kree-created Nega Bands give the wearer power beyond measure.

DATA FILE

REAL NAME Genis-Vell **OCCUPATION** Adventurer
BASE Mobile
HEIGHT 6 ft 2 in **WEIGHT** 210 lbs **EYES** Blue **HAIR** Silver
FIRST APPEARANCE WITH AVENGERS *Avengers Unplugged* #5 (June 1996)
POWERS Genis inherited his father's energy absorption and control powers, as well as his Nega Bands, and he had superhuman durability, endurance, speed, and strength. He could also fly, fire energy blasts, and open trans-dimensional shunts.

SUPREME INTELLIGENCE

This disembodied entity returned to rule the Kree Empire again and again.

The alien Kree traditionally merged the minds of their smartest citizens after death, to create the ultimate genius. This being was known as the Supreme Intelligence, or Supremor, and eventually became their warmongering leader.

Different teams of Avengers battled the Supreme Intelligence several times, until one incarnation seemed to succeed in executing it for its crimes. However, it actually survived and returned to lead the Kree again, although it recently perished for real with the destruction of the Kree homeworld.

The image of itself that Supremor chooses to project across space is large, green, and terrifying.

DATA FILE

REAL NAME Supremor **OCCUPATION** Ruler of the Kree Empire
BASE Kree-Lar, Hala
HEIGHT N/A **WEIGHT** N/A **EYES** Yellow **HAIR** Green
FIRST APPEARANCE WITH AVENGERS *Avengers* #89 (June 1971)
POWERS The Supreme Intelligence is a superhuman genius. It can project its mind into an artificial body when necessary and has the powers of telepathy, along with other psionic abilities.

VERANKE

A thorn in the Avengers' sides, Queen Veranke led the Skrulls' Earth invasion.

After the Skrull Empire was nearly destroyed, Veranke became the Skrull queen. She decided to make Earth the new Skrull homeworld and infiltrated the Avengers, replacing Spider-Woman in their ranks by kidnapping Jessica Drew and assuming her form. When ready, Veranke launched the Secret Invasion using an army of Skrull sleeper agents, but Norman Osborn killed her after the Avengers led the effort to foil her.

Veranke fooled many by taking on the form of Spider-Woman and leading her Skrull troops into battle.

DATA FILE

REAL NAME Veranke **OCCUPATION** Queen of the Skrulls
BASE Skrull Empire
HEIGHT Varies **WEIGHT** Varies **EYES** Vary **HAIR** Varies
FIRST APPEARANCE WITH AVENGERS *New Avengers* #1 (January 2005)
POWERS As a Skrull, Veranke can replicate other forms. When taking the form of Spider-Woman, for example, she gains all of Drew's powers. Other Skrull powers include superhuman durability, endurance, senses, speed, and strength. Veranke can fire energy blasts, secrete mood-altering pheromones, and fly.

Adam has the power to project energy blasts from his hands.

ADAM WARLOCK

An early member of the present-day Guardians of the Galaxy, this man wields the power of souls.

Adam was artificially created by a scientific cabal called the Enclave. Refusing to become a prototype for an army, he destroyed their lab and escaped. His mentor, the High Evolutionary, sent him to a new Counter-Earth to battle the Man-Beast, after which he acquired the name Adam Warlock. Back in his original dimension, Adam joined the Guardians, learned from Gamora about Thanos's plan to destroy the universe, and called on the Avengers for help. Together, they stopped Thanos from using the fabled Infinity Gauntlet. At his request, the Guardians killed Warlock when he transformed into an evil future version of himself called the Magus, but he has since returned.

Originally, Warlock worked with Thanos to defeat the Magus, but the two later became foes.

DATA FILE

REAL NAME
Adam Warlock

OCCUPATION
Adventurer, Savior of Worlds

BASE
Mobile

HEIGHT 6 ft 2 in

WEIGHT 240 lbs

EYES White

HAIR Blond

FIRST APPEARANCE WITH AVENGERS
Avengers #118 (December 1973)

POWERS
Adam can fly and survive in space. He has superhuman durability, endurance, healing, speed, and strength. He has cosmic awareness and can see the souls of others, and he wielded one of the Infinity Gems—the Soul Gem. As he evolved, he no longer needed the Soul Gem's power. He sometimes enters a cocoon state and emerges more powerful. He can now use quantum magic to manipulate matter, energy, and souls, and to teleport.

VICTOR MANCHA

This cyborg son of Ultron is working to become a hero.

When ex-criminal Marianella Mancha found Ultron's head in a dump, she took him home and helped to rebuild his body, hoping this might bring her good fortune. Seemingly as a reward for her assistance, Ultron built a teenaged cyborg son for her—using her DNA and his own technology to create Victor. Secretly, Ultron wanted the boy to join the Avengers and serve as his spy. But when a hero from an alternate future warned the Runaways about the evil force Victor would grow to become, the team found him and helped him break free from Ultron's influence, after Ultron killed his mother. With the Avengers, Victor then helped the Runaways. The Vision later recruited his little half-brother for the Avengers A.I., in whose company both feel at home.

Victor's mix of robotic and human parts has, on occasion, led to him being persecuted by Earth's general public.

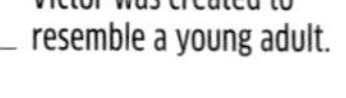

Victor was created to resemble a young adult.

DATA FILE

REAL NAME
Victor Mancha

OCCUPATION
Adventurer

BASE
New York City

HEIGHT 5 ft 8 in

WEIGHT 220 lbs

EYES Brown

HAIR Brown

FIRST APPEARANCE WITH AVENGERS
Runaways #9 (December 2005)

POWERS
Victor is a cyborg with superhuman durability, endurance, healing, intelligence, and strength. He can fly, fire energy bursts from his hands, and manipulate metals magnetically. He also features built-in weaponry and can generate force fields and network with computer systems.

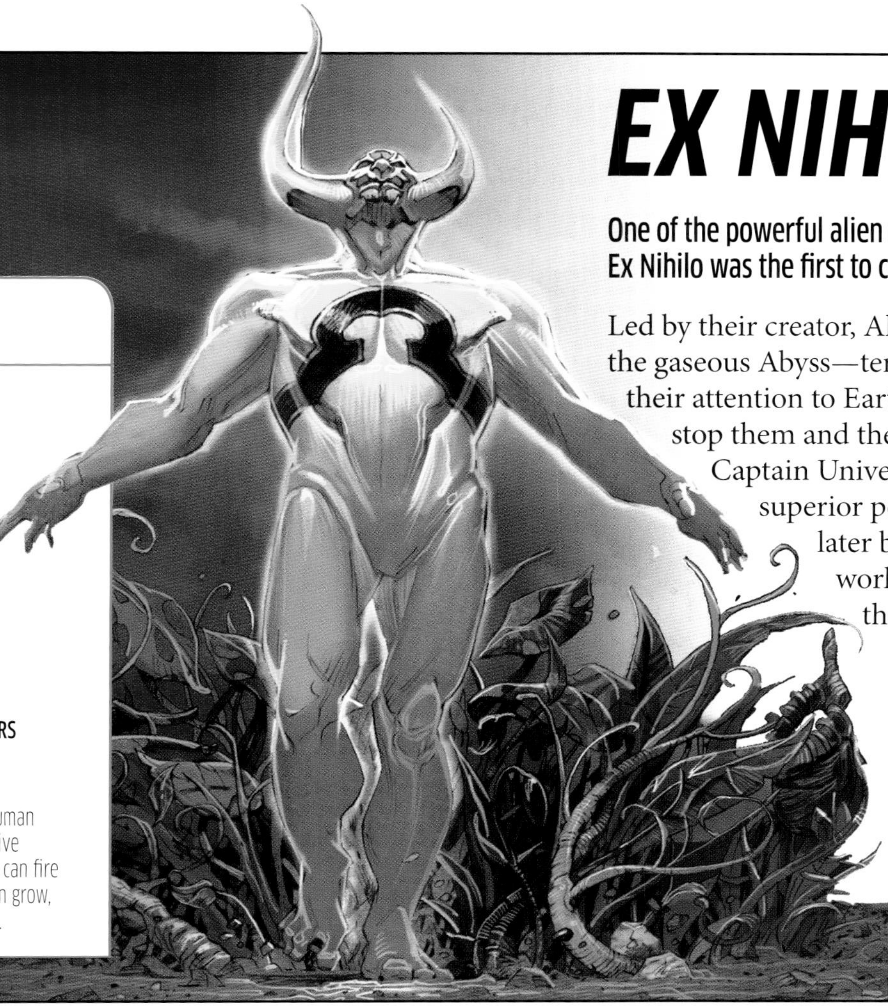

EX NIHILO

One of the powerful alien race of Gardeners, also called Ex Nihili, Ex Nihilo was the first to come to Earth and encounter the Avengers.

Led by their creator, Aleph, Ex Nihilo and his sister—the gaseous Abyss—terraformed Mars and then turned their attention to Earth. The Avengers were unable to stop them and their terraforming bombs, but when Captain Universe confronted them with her superior powers, they surrendered to her. They later became Avengers and helped save the world from the invasion of their creators, the Builders. While Abyss was the last of her kind, there were many other Gardeners, and they all joined forces with the Avengers to try to save the multiverse, sacrificing themselves to destroy one of the otherworldly Beyonders.

DATA FILE

REAL NAME
Ex Nihilo

OCCUPATION
Creator

BASE
Mars

HEIGHT 9 ft

WEIGHT 600 lbs

EYES Green

HAIR None

FIRST APPEARANCE WITH AVENGERS
Avengers #1 (February 2013)

POWERS
As a Gardener, Ex Nihilo has superhuman durability and strength. He can survive unprotected in space and can fly. He can fire energy blasts from his hands and can grow, evolve, and manipulate living things.

STRANGER

This alien arrived on Earth with one purpose: to destroy the superhumans.

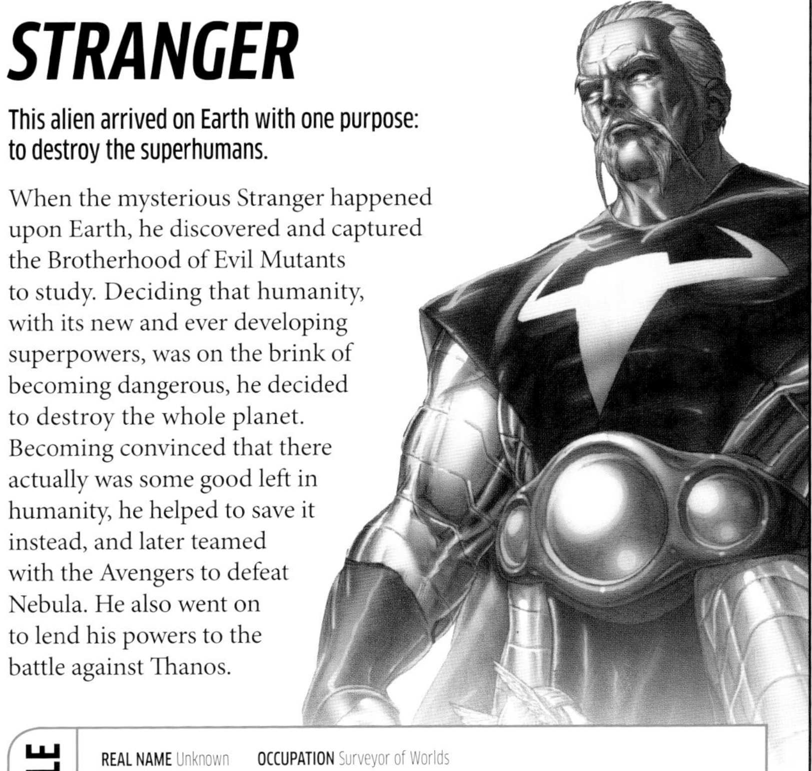

When the mysterious Stranger happened upon Earth, he discovered and captured the Brotherhood of Evil Mutants to study. Deciding that humanity, with its new and ever developing superpowers, was on the brink of becoming dangerous, he decided to destroy the whole planet. Becoming convinced that there actually was some good left in humanity, he helped to save it instead, and later teamed with the Avengers to defeat Nebula. He also went on to lend his powers to the battle against Thanos.

DATA FILE

REAL NAME Unknown **OCCUPATION** Surveyor of Worlds
BASE His personal, private Labworld
HEIGHT Varies **WEIGHT** Varies **EYES** Black **HAIR** White
FIRST APPEARANCE WITH AVENGERS *Avengers* #137 (July 1975)
POWERS The Stranger is immensely powerful. He wields cosmic and psionic power to fire energy blasts, manipulate matter at will, create force fields, alter his size, and levitate.

THOR GIRL

The young woman Tarene is the Designate—destined to raise people everywhere to a greater level of evolution.

Tarene designed her appearance and costume to remind others of Thor.

Created to elevate all life to a higher level, the Designate was the fulfillment of a prophesy made at the beginning of time, but Tarene found her powers diminished when Thanos destroyed her homeworld. With Thor's help, she defeated Thanos, became a version of Thor and named herself Thor Girl. She later sacrificed her powers to defeat Surtur, and after living a normal life on Earth for a while, joined the Avengers Initiative during the Civil War. Later, her skills with her hammer led her to being mistaken for one of the Worthy. With her cosmic powers restored, she has since left Earth.

DATA FILE

REAL NAME Tarene **OCCUPATION** Adventurer
BASE New York City
HEIGHT 5 ft 9 in **WEIGHT** 317 lbs **EYES** Blue **HAIR** Blonde
FIRST APPEARANCE WITH AVENGERS *Avengers: The Initiative* #1 (June 2007)
POWERS As the equivalent of an immortal Asgardian, Tarene has superhuman durability, endurance, speed, and strength. Her mystic hammer returns to her when thrown, allows her to fly, controls weather, and fires energy blasts. As the Designate, she also holds incredible cosmic powers.

HUMAN TORCH

The original hero blazed a trail for many later Super Heroes.

When Professor Phineas T. Horton Earth's first android, he did not expect the artificial man to burst into flame when exposed to air. Calling himself the Human Torch, Horton's invention became one of the first Super Heroes. The Torch joined the Invaders during World War II, during which time he killed Adolf Hitler. Immortus later split the Torch into two bodies, one of which became the Vision. The other joined the West Coast Avengers and later the Secret Avengers. During his career he adopted the name Jim Hammond.

DATA FILE

REAL NAME None, aka Jim Hammond **OCCUPATION** Adventurer; former police officer
BASE Mobile
HEIGHT 6 ft 3 in **WEIGHT** 350 lbs **EYES** Blue **HAIR** Blond
FIRST APPEARANCE WITH AVENGERS *Avengers* #71 (December 1969)
POWERS The Torch can generate and manipulate fire. He can increase and decrease its intensity around his body. The Torch can stay aflame for just over 16 hours. He is immune to heat and fire. When on fire, he can fly at speeds of up to 140 mph. As an android, he does not need food, water, or air to survive.

ARKON

The warrior-king came from a world that mixed high technology with a barbaric code of honor.

Arkon fought his way to the leadership of the mightiest nation on his homeworld of Polemachus. Arkon's scientists discovered that the rings surrounding their planet were disintegrating—which would eventually lead to its destruction. They believed the only way to save the planet was to blow up the Earth and use the resulting energy. Fortunately, the Avengers delayed Arkon long enough for Iron Man and Thor to revive Polemachus using their abilities. The Avengers would later help restore Arkon to the throne, following a coup.

DATA FILE

REAL NAME Arkon (the Magnificent) **OCCUPATION** Ruler (Imperion)
BASE Polemachus
HEIGHT 6 ft **WEIGHT** 400 lbs **EYES** Brown **HAIR** Brown
FIRST APPEARANCE WITH AVENGERS *Avengers* #75 (April 1970)
POWERS Arkon has superhuman agility, endurance, healing, speed, and strength. His skin and bones are denser than a human's, enabling him to withstand high-caliber bullets. Arkon is an expert warrior. He uses three kinds energy bolts that he carries in a quiver: The red and black bolts are explosive weapons, and the golden bolts open portals to other dimensions.

MEDUSA

The super-haired queen of the Inhumans is a dedicated ruler and formidable combatant.

Medusa is a member of the Inhumans' royal family. She fled Attilan (the Inhumans' home) after a revolt and lost her memory in a crash. The villainous Wizard made her part of his Frightful Four when he tried to battle the Fantastic Four, but she recovered her memory and joined the heroes instead.

Once she returned to Attilan, Medusa married her distant cousin, Black Bolt, and became the Inhumans' queen. Since her husband's voice is capable of great destruction, Medusa often interprets his silent wishes. She also rules their people wisely during Black Bolt's absences serving with the Avengers. Recently, along with She-Hulk, Medusa became one of the founding members of A-Force, the first all-female team of Avengers.

Medusa's hair is six feet long.

Medusa learned to communicate with Black Bolt via sign language, and their connection blossomed into love.

DATA FILE

REAL NAME
Medusalith Amaquelin Boltagon

OCCUPATION
Queen, royal interpreter

BASE
Attilan, Blue Area of the Moon

HEIGHT 5 ft 11 in

WEIGHT 130 lbs

EYES Green

HAIR Red

FIRST APPEARANCE WITH AVENGERS
Avengers #118 (December 1973)

POWERS
Medusa is an Inhuman with long, prehensile hair. Her locks are superstrong and she can control the growth, shape, and length of every single strand. Medusa can use her hair as a weapon, a whip, and a rope—she can even pick locks with it! Her power works even if her hair has been cut off. Being Inhuman, she exhibits enhanced strength, speed, stamina, and reflexes. Her time outside Attilan has strengthened her immune system compared to that of her fellow Inhumans.

LADY SIF

The greatest warrior-goddess of Asgard, fearless Sif is always focused on protecting her homeland.

Sif grew up alongside Thor and soon developed a soft spot for the Asgardian prince. When she was younger, she had long, golden-colored hair which a spiteful Loki cut off. It was later replaced with magical hair made from the blackness of night. Before Thor's exile to Midgard, he returned Sif's feelings and for a time the pair were pledged to be married.

In battle, Sif wields an enchanted sword given to her by Odin. She can also use it to cleave pathways between Asgard and Earth. Along with the other gods of Asgard, Sif died during Ragnarok. When she returned to life, Loki possessed her body and forced her spirit into the body of an elderly cancer patient. Fortunately, Thor was able to save Sif before the cancer patient died. Sif fought alongside Thor and the Avengers during the Siege of Asgard and again during Fear Itself.

DATA FILE

REAL NAME
Lady Sif

OCCUPATION
Warrior

BASE
Asgard

HEIGHT 6 ft 2 in

WEIGHT 425 lbs

EYES Blue

HAIR Black

FIRST APPEARANCE WITH AVENGERS
Avengers #105 (November 1972)

POWERS
Sif is an immortal goddess of Asgard with superhuman agility, durability, endurance, speed, and strength. Sif has regenerative healing powers and ages at a slow rate. Like other Asgardians, her body tissue is three times more dense than humans', making her heavier and stronger than she appears. She is an expert in hand-to-hand combat. She carries a sword and can teleport between Asgard and Earth.

ODIN

This one-eyed ruler of the Asgardian gods is a force to be reckoned with.

The All-Father of Asgard, Odin ruled for millennia before his apparent demise in battle with the demon, Surtur. Married to the goddess Frigga on Asgard, he fathered Balder and Angela. Odin later traveled to Earth (Midgard) to father a child, Thor, with the Earth Mother Gaea. Odin also adopted Loki after slaying the boy's father in battle. Although not always supportive of Thor's concern for Midgard, Odin fought alongside the Avengers during Fear Itself to end the plans of his evil brother Cul.

DATA FILE

REAL NAME Odin Borson **OCCUPATION** All-Father

BASE Asgard

HEIGHT 6 ft 9 in **WEIGHT** 650 lbs **EYES** Blue (one) **HAIR** White

FIRST APPEARANCE WITH AVENGERS *Avengers* #1 (September 1963)

POWERS Odin is an immortal god of Asgard with superhuman agility, durability, endurance, speed, and strength. He is an expert in hand-to-hand combat and with ancient weaponry. He is a powerful sorcerer with mastery of the Odinforce—this enables him to read minds, stop time, and cast foes into deep space. He can create impenetrable force fields. Once a year he must restore his powers via the Odinsleep.

ARES

The Olympian god of war had a fierce hatred of Hercules.

Son of Zeus and Hera, who ruled over the gods of Olympus, Ares was the half-brother of Hercules, whom he despised. Ares tried to take over Olympus many times, but his attempts were thwarted by Hercules and his allies. In recent years, he moved to Earth to raise his son Alexander. Struggling to be a good father, Ares accepted Tony Stark's invitation to join the Avengers after the Civil War. He later stayed with the Dark Avengers, but when he turned against its leader Norman Osborn, the Sentry killed him.

Ares wore a Spartan helmet in battle.

DATA FILE

REAL NAME Ares **OCCUPATION** God of war

BASE New York, Olympus

HEIGHT 6 ft 1 in **WEIGHT** 500 lbs **EYES** Brown **HAIR** Brown

FIRST APPEARANCE WITH AVENGERS *Avengers* #38 (March 1967)

POWERS Ares was an immortal god of Olympus with superhuman agility, durability, endurance, speed, and strength. He was an expert in all forms of combat and all kinds of weaponry. He healed quickly from wounds, although magical weapons, such as Thor's Mjolnir hammer, could cause him harm.

ALETA OGORD

The other half of Starhawk, Aleta became a key member of the 31st century Guardians of the Galaxy.

Born on Arcturus in the 31st century, Aleta married her adopted brother, Stakar. An accident merged the two of them together so that only one could exist in the real world at a time, while the other was trapped in Limbo. Together becoming Starkhawk, they became a member of the original Guardians of the Galaxy and traveled to modern times to help the Avengers defeat Korvac. Aleta was locked in a constant power struggle with her husband until they were eventually physically and emotionally separated, then divorced. However, so much time inhabiting the dual role of Starhawk has affected Aleta's mentality.

DATA FILE

REAL NAME Aleta Ogord **OCCUPATION** Adventurer
BASE Mobile
HEIGHT 6 ft **WEIGHT** 149 lbs **EYES** Gold **HAIR** Blonde
FIRST APPEARANCE WITH AVENGERS *Avengers* #168 (February 1978)
POWERS As an Arcturan, Aleta has superhuman durability, endurance, speed, and strength. She can turn light solid and manipulate it to create weaponry, shields, and energy blasts, as well as energy discs on which she can fly. She can also phase through matter.

PHOBOS

Raised on Earth, "Alex" is really Phobos, the son of the god of war.

Ares, the Olympian god of war, tried to raise his son Alex as a mortal, while living a "normal" life as a carpenter, away from Olympus. The villainous Chaos King, Amatsu-Mikaboshi, kidnapped Alex and trained him to kill, but with Zeus's help, Ares rescued the boy and made him forget the ordeal. Alex joined the Avengers and became a member of Nick Fury's Secret Warriors. While on a mission, Phobos was slain by the Japanese villain Gorgon, and was reunited with Ares in the afterlife.

DATA FILE

REAL NAME Alexander Aaron **OCCUPATION** God of fear; adventurer
BASE New York City
HEIGHT 5 ft 1 in **WEIGHT** 95 lbs **EYES** Blue **HAIR** Blond
FIRST APPEARANCE WITH AVENGERS *Mighty Avengers* #13 (July 2008)
POWERS As an Immortal god of Olympus, Alex had superhuman durability, endurance, speed, and strength. He could induce fear by looking into a target's eyes, and he had precognition skills.

BLACK BOLT

The ruler of the Inhumans' very voice can level mountains.

Born into the Inhumans' royal family, Blackagar's voice proved dangerous even as an infant, and he had to be isolated for his own safety. As an adult, he became ruler of the Inhumans and began a long rivalry with his insane younger brother, Maximus. After one coup, the Avengers helped restore him to his throne. Black Bolt married Medusa and had a daughter (Luna) and a son (Ahura).

He later joined the Illuminati to guide the Avengers in secret. He helped their efforts to stop the destructive incursions of Earths from other dimensions.

DATA FILE

REAL NAME Blackagar Boltagon **OCCUPATION** Ruler of the Inhumans
BASE Attilan
HEIGHT 6 ft 2 in **WEIGHT** 210 lbs **EYES** Blue **HAIR** Black
FIRST APPEARANCE WITH AVENGERS *Avengers* #95 (January 1972)
POWERS As an Inhuman, Black Bolt has superhuman durability, endurance, speed, and strength. He can also manipulate matter and energy, fly, and fire blasts of energy. His voice causes powerful shockwaves.

The tuning fork antenna Black Bolt wears on his forehead helps him to control his powers.

The members of the Inhuman royal family are Black Bolt's most loyal subjects.

As a member of the Illuminati, Black Bolt's influence extends far beyond the Inhumans.

ULTRA GIRL

According to ancient Kree writings, Tsu-Zana is the great hope for the future of the Kree race.

Born a human/Kree mutant, Suzy was raised in secret on Earth, unaware of her own powers until a Sentinel attacked her during a modeling shoot. She joined the New Warriors soon after. During the Civil War, she joined Captain America's Avengers. Afterward, she joined the Fifty-State Initiative, but she later returned to the New Warriors. Gaining her Super Hero name due to her enthusiastic use of the word "ultra" in interviews, Suzy Sherman is still available to the Avengers, and still chooses to call Earth her home.

For a while, Ultra Girl wore Ms. Marvel's costume, but she has since given it up.

DATA FILE

REAL NAME Tsu-Zana (better known as Suzy Sherman) **OCCUPATION** Former model; adventurer
BASE Mobile
HEIGHT 5 ft 6 in **WEIGHT** 233 lbs **EYES** Blue **HAIR** Blonde
FIRST APPEARANCE WITH AVENGERS *Civil War* #5 (January 2007)
POWERS Suzy has superhuman durability, endurance, healing, speed, and strength. She can also fly and see invisible energy auras around people.

ATTUMA

The would-be barbarian lord of Atlantis detests all of humanity.

As chief of a nomadic tribe of Atlanteans, Attuma sought to wrest the throne of the Sub-Mariner, Prince Namor from him many times. He also tried to attack the surface world, but the Avengers regularly foiled him. When Attuma finally managed to oust Namor, the Avengers fought to return the favor. He became Nerkkod, Breaker of Oceans with the power of a hammer located deep in the ocean.

Attuma was deemed worthy to wield the Hammer of Nerkkod.

DATA FILE

REAL NAME Attuma **OCCUPATION** Barbaric chief
BASE Mobile
HEIGHT 6 ft 8 in **WEIGHT** 410 lbs **EYES** Brown **HAIR** Black
FIRST APPEARANCE WITH AVENGERS *Avengers* #26 (March 1966)
POWERS As an Atlantean, Attuma his amphibious and has superhuman durability, endurance, speed, and strength. He is also an expert warrior.

HULKLING

Upon learning of his Kree-Skrull origins, Teddy chose to remain on Earth with the Young Avengers as Hulkling.

Teddy Altman grew up on Earth, unaware that his birth parents were Kree Captain Mar-Vell and the Skrull Princess Anelle, and didn't learn about his true heritage until the Super-Skrull came to kidnap him and take him back to the Skrull Empire. Instead believing that his powers were the result of being a mutant, he took the name Hulkling and became one of the first Young Avengers. Soon after, he started a relationship with fellow teammate Wiccan, with whom he later became engaged. Both Teddy and Wiccan were later made fully fledged Avengers, but after Wiccan left for a while to see if his mystical, reality-distorting powers had affected their relationship, Teddy joined a reformed version of the Young Avengers with Noh-Varr and Prodigy.

Teddy can give himself wings to fly.

DATA FILE

REAL NAME
Theodore "Teddy" Altman, Dorrek VIII

OCCUPATION
Adventurer, student

BASE
New York City

HEIGHT Varies

WEIGHT Varies

EYES Vary, usually blue

HAIR Varies, usually blond

FIRST APPEARANCE WITH AVENGERS
Young Avengers #1 (April 2005)

POWERS
Teddy has superhuman durability, endurance, healing and strength and can shape-shift at will—including giving himself the appropriate physical features, such as wings, to enable flight. His usual fighting appearance is that of a teenage version of the Hulk.

KEY STORYLINE SIEGE

SIEGE #1-4

JANUARY 2010–MAY 2010
WRITER: Brian Michael Bendis
PENCILER: Olivier Coipel **INKER:** Mark Morales **COLORIST:** Laura Martin **LETTERER:** Chris Eliopoulos **EDITOR:** Tom Brevoort

Marvel's heroes found themselves in a strange new world where Norman Osborn was at the helm of both the Avengers and S.H.I.E.L.D. With a Super Villain in charge, peace seemed unlikely.

The diabolical Norman Osborn had taken advantage of the events of the Skrull Invasion to engineer a new role for himself as leader of the entire U.S. defense system. Osborn created a team of ruthless Dark Avengers, and reshaped S.H.I.E.L.D. into the brutal force that was H.A.M.M.E.R. However, in a world of comic-book heroes, surely evil couldn't prevail for long. Creators Brian Michael Bendis and Olivier Coipel soon put an end to the Dark Reign of Osborn, which they themselves had helped devise. Unfortunately for the Super Heroes, the necessary catalyst for change was an all-out declaration of war against the realm of Asgard. Even worse, victory over the ruthless Norman Osborn would not be achieved without the sacrifice of many lives.

1 After being destroyed, the realm of Asgard has been rebuilt in the sky over Oklahoma, to the unhappiness of some. Norman Osborn sees the hovering gods as a threat to his power, and Earth-scorning Asgardian Loki wishes to restore Asgard to its former home. Together, they stage an explosion, for which Asgardian warrior Volstagg is blamed by the public.

2 Using the media uproar to justify his actions, Osborn orders a strike on Asgard—something completely unsanctioned by the U.S. President. Osborn recruits the Dark Avengers to his cause, overcoming their reluctance by promising them an out from his team, in return for one last mission. An angry Thor soon arrives to defend his birthplace, and Steve Rogers issues a call-to-arms to his fellow heroes to assemble once more.

3 As battle breaks out, the all-seeing Asgardian guardian Heimdall reveals the truth of Osborn's deception to Ares, one of the Dark Avengers. Ares confronts Osborn, but the supremely powerful Sentry comes to the evil leader's aid. A vicious fight ensues. To the horror of the surrounding heroes, Sentry literally tears Ares limb from limb.

4 As the battle progresses, it appears the tide is turning in favor of the true Avengers. Nick Fury and Tony Stark join Steve Rogers at the front of a heroic force, who are more than a match for Osborn's criminal crew and soon gain the official support of the U.S. President and government.

5 The heroes corner Osborn, and Rogers declares that the villain will face the full force of the American justice system. But, just when it appears the heroes will prevail, a bitter Osborn commands the Sentry to destroy Asgard. Thor's home and many of its resident gods are obliterated.

"FOR NOW AND FOREVER ANYONE WHO NEEDS TO KNOW WILL KNOW, ASGARD AND EARTH ARE ALLIES."
- THOR

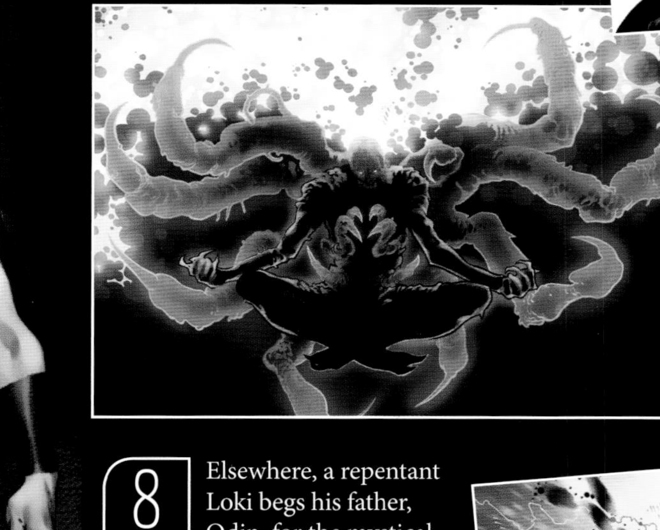

6 Osborn's mask is torn off, showing the world he is still the irredeemable Green Goblin. Ranting and raving, Osborn insists the Avengers have made a serious mistake. Even after a well-timed right hook from Spider-Man, Osborn insists the heroes face a greater threat than he.

7 At that moment, a bizarre demon appears in the sky. Ominously, Osborn tells the assembled heroes that the huge creature is called the Angel of Death, and that they will all be killed. He claims his actions have all been to protect the world from this fate.

8 Elsewhere, a repentant Loki begs his father, Odin, for the mystical Norn Stones to help repair the damage he has done. The stones drain the power of Osborn's gang, and boost the power of the Super Heroes. Then, in front of a horrified Thor, Loki sacrifices himself to help defeat the Angel of Death.

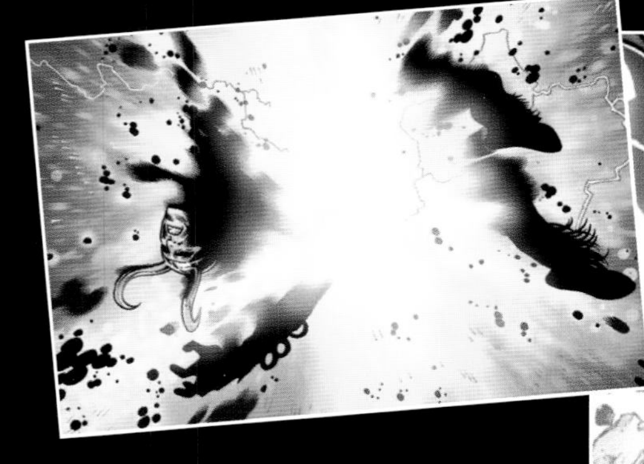

9 In the debris, the team find a dazed Robert Reynolds, aka the Sentry. He is appalled by his own actions and begs for the heroes to kill him. At first Thor refuses but, on realizing Reynolds is possessed by the Angel of Death, carries out the grisly act. The heroes then begin rebuilding the reputation of the Avengers' name, under the guidance of Steve Rogers.

KEY STORYLINE AVENGERS RELAUNCH

AVENGERS #1; THE NEW AVENGERS #1

JULY 2010–AUGUST 2010
WRITER: Brian Michael Bendis
PENCILERS: Stuart Immonen, John Romita Jr. **INKERS:** Wade von Grawbadger, Klaus Janson **COLORISTS:** Laura Martin, Dean White
LETTERERS: Chris Eliopoulos, Cory Petit **EDITORS:** Tom Brevoort, Joe Quesada

The heroes of the Marvel Universe were finally reunited in an Avengers team led by former Captain America, Steve Rogers.

Brian Michael Bendis had changed the dynamics of the Marvel Universe again with the release of *Siege*, a four-issue series he crafted alonside the pencils of talented artist Olivier Coipel. Within that series, Loki and Norman Osborn were defeated, and Bendis finally resolved tensions within the Super Hero community. Steve Rogers, the original Captain America, had returned from the seeming dead, and was put in charge of S.H.I.E.L.D.'s assets. He was determined to restart the legacy of the team he had been a part of for so many years, burying old grudges in the process. The result was a fourth incarnation of the *Avengers* ongoing series, accompanied by a second volume of *The New Avengers.*

1 Norman Osborn had taken S.H.I.E.L.D. and molded it into the corrupt H.A.M.M.E.R. But when he fell during the Siege of Asgard, Steve Rogers became America's Super Hero team leader. He decides to form two teams of Avengers who will not serve as agents of either S.H.I.E.L.D. or the supposedly defunct H.A.M.M.E.R.

2 For his main team, Steve recruits Thor, Spider-Man, Wolverine, current Captain America Bucky Barnes, Iron Man, Hawkeye, and Spider-Woman. This is a powerful starting point for Rogers, operating out of Avengers Towers in New York City.

3 But just as Steve Rogers announces that Maria Hill will be running the team, the Avengers are interrupted by the arrival of their old enemy, Kang the Conqueror. Kang comes armed with a doomsday device that is designed by a future version of Iron Man, further complicating things.

4 Kang warns the Avengers of a future where their own children are on the verge of destroying the universe. But as Kang returns to that future, it seems nothing he said can be true and it is revealed that he is working for someone just as dangerous—a future version of Hulk.

5 Meanwhile, Luke Cage is having a hard time accepting Steve Rogers' planned path for the Avengers. Rogers is conducting a Super Hero mixer of sorts, with many of his prospective recruits in attendance.

6 Rogers offers Cage his own team of New Avengers and Tony Stark sells Cage Avengers Mansion to use as a headquarters for the bargain price of one dollar. The team would have no ties to the U.S. government, and Cage is free to run his group however he sees fit.

"OUR PRESIDENT ASKED ME WHAT THE WORLD NEEDS NOW... I TOLD HIM THE WORLD NEEDS WHAT IT ALWAYS NEEDS. HEROES."

– STEVE ROGERS

7 As Cage's team members prepare to settle in to the Mansion, they are surprised to find Norman Osborn's former right-hand woman, Victoria Hand, inside and armed with a sophisticated rifle. Before Cage can attack her, she hands him a note from Steve Rogers that declares that she is assigned to them to help facilitate Cage's New Avengers' work.

8 As things settle down, Luke Cage has his recruits all share a meal, officially declaring them the New Avengers. Their original roster includes Wolverine, Mockingbird, Iron Fist, the Thing, Spider-Man, Hawkeye, Ms. Marvel, and Luke's wife, Jessica Jones.

9 Luke Cage's group don't have long to adjust before they must face a new threat. In their first test as a team, they are invaded by magical forces that grow Luke Cage to a monstrous size, beginning an adventure that involves Dr. Strange, Dr. Voodoo, and Damian Hellstrom.

KEY STORYLINE AGE OF ULTRON

AVENGERS #12.1; *AGE OF ULTRON* #1–10

JUNE 2011 AND MAY 2013–JUNE 2013
WRITER: Brian Michael Bendis
PENCILERS: Butch Guice, Bryan Hitch, Alex Maleev, David Marquez, Carlos Pacheco, Brandon Peterson, Joe Quesada **INKERS:** Roger Bonet, Butch Guice, Alex Maleev, David Marquez, Roger Martinez, Paul Neary, Tom Palmer, Brandon Peterson, Joe Quesada **COLORISTS:** Richard Isanove, Paul Mounts, Jose Villarrubia **LETTERER:** Cory Petit
EDITORS: Axel Alonso, Tom Brevoort, John Denning, Lauren Sankovitch, Jake Thomas

In the Ultron event to end all Ultron events, the Avengers faced off with perhaps their most powerful foe in a blockbuster time traveling epic.

Ultron, the rogue artificial intelligence given life by founding team member Hank Pym, had been a thorn in the Avengers' side for decades. So when writer Brian Michael Bendis and various talented artists—and even Marvel Chief Creative Officer Joe Quesada—got to work on the ten-part *Age of Ultron* series starring the infamous villain, they decided to follow in the footsteps of the fondly remembered X-Men event "Age of Apocalypse," and depict an entire new universe at the mercy of Ultron. With a title later utilized for the second big budget Avengers movie, *Age of Ultron* was another blockbuster smash for Marvel.

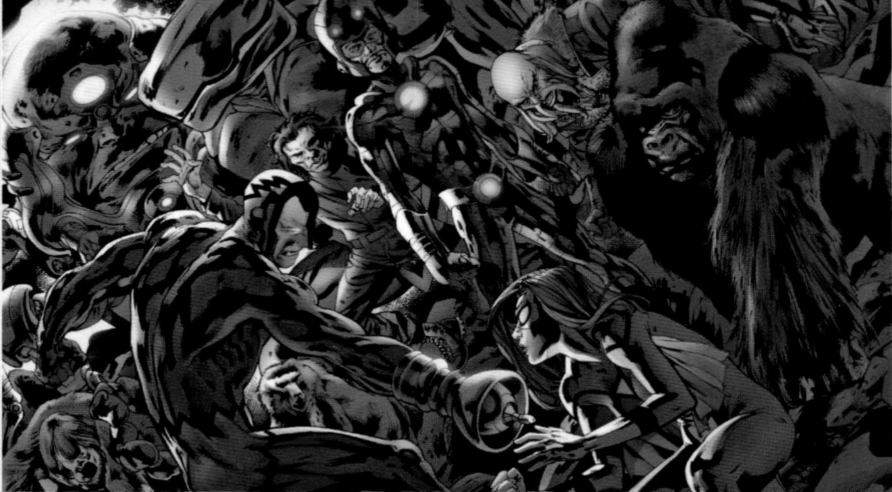

1 When Spider-Woman encounters a group of Super Villain scientists calling themselves the Intelligencia, the villains unwittingly unleash the artificial intelligence known as Ultron on the world before the Avengers could stop them. Soon, the entire Earth becomes a very, very dark place.

2 Ultron takes over, seemingly ruling the world from an enormous ship hovering over New York City. A member of an underground rebellion refusing to play by the villain's rules, Hawkeye keeps up the good fight, saving Spider-Man from a handful of Super Villains who plan on trading the hero to Ultron in exchange for their own freedom to operate.

3 Hawkeye takes Peter Parker underground, to where the rest of the Avengers can be found hiding. While the Avengers are concerned that Hawkeye could have compromised their location to save Spider-Man's life, the Avengers soon happily accept Peter into their ranks.

5 With their plan having failed and Cage mortally injured as a result, the Avengers head to the Savage Land to regroup. There they meet up with a faction of other heroes, as well as Nick Fury. Fury has devised a new plan that will utilize Dr. Doom's time platform to confront Ultron in the future.

4 Upon hearing Spider-Man's story, Captain America is inspired into action. He sends Luke Cage and She-Hulk into Ultron's spaceship stronghold under the pretense of bargaining with the android. However, She-Hulk is killed during the meeting, while Cage learns that Ultron is in fact ruling from the future, using the Vision as a

6 Nick Fury, along with Captain America, Iron Man, Quicksilver, Red Hulk, Storm, Black Widow, and Quake, journey to Ultron's future domain. Despite their best efforts there, they are overwhelmed and massacred by Ultron's forces.

"EVERYTHING THAT HAS EVER HAPPENED, HAS TO HAPPEN. EVERYTHING BUT THE PART WHERE ULTRON MOPS THE WORLD WITH US."

– WOLVERINE

7 Meanwhile, Wolverine doesn't buy Fury's plan. He realizes that the only way to defeat Ultron is to travel into the past and kill Hank Pym before he builds Ultron in the first place. Accompanied by the Invisible Woman, Wolverine does just that.

8 Wolverine returns to the present, only to discover an unfamiliar world where the Defenders lose a deadly battle to Morgan Le Fay's armies. Realizing killing Pym had not worked, Wolverine time travels once more—this time to stop his past self from killing Pym, and to instead instruct Pym to create a failsafe to stop Ultron.

9 In their new present, Hank Pym is warned by his past self of a way to defeat Ultron. Pym had not retained this knowledge due to a mind wipe after Wolverine's intervention. So when the Avengers confront Ultron, Pym only has to trigger a hidden virus in the robot's system. When Wolverine and Invisible Woman return home, the world is Ultron-free, even if the space-time continuum might have been injured in the process.

KEY STORYLINE

ORIGINAL SIN

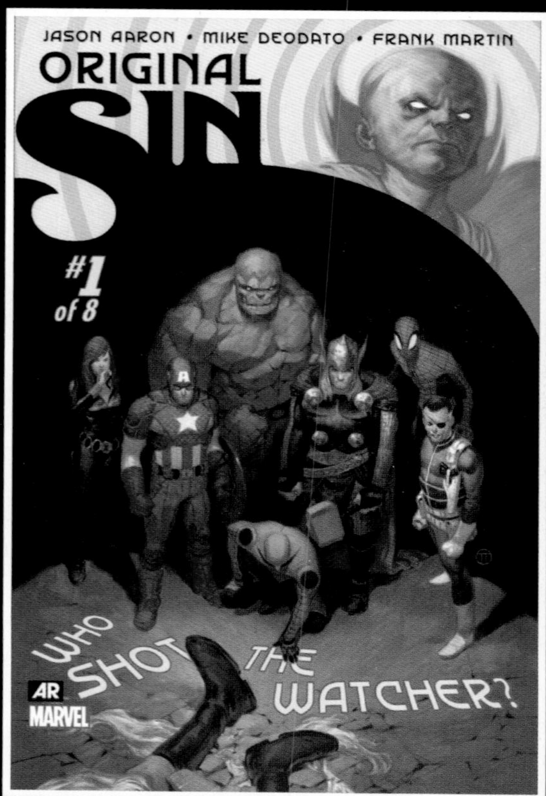

ORIGINAL SIN #0–8

JUNE 2014–OCTOBER 2014
WRITERS: Jason Aaron, Mark Waid
PENCILERS: Jim Cheung, Mike Deodato, Paco Medina **INKERS:** Jim Cheung, Mike Deodato, Dave Melkis, Mark Morales, Guillermo Ortego, Juan Vlasco **COLORISTS:** Frank Martin, Justin Ponsor **LETTERER:** Chris Eliopoulos **EDITORS:** Axel Alonso, Tom Brevoort, Will Moss

The ramifications of this nine-part story arc were far-reaching, altering the status quo for several prominent characters, including Nick Fury.

Writer Jason Aaron had quickly risen in the ranks of Marvel's scribes to become a firm fan favorite. As such, he helmed *Original Sin*, an eight-issue series that was graced with a prelude #0 issue by fellow writer Mark Waid and artists Jim Cheung and Paco Medina. Handling the art for the rest of the *Original Sin* series was another fan favorite, Mike Deodato Jr., whose work on titles including *The Incredible Hulk* and *Thunderbolts* showed his ability to apply mood and shadow to the characters of the Marvel Universe. In a storyline where Nick Fury revealed his clandestine past and appeared not to be the person everyone thought he was, mood and shadow would certainly play a big factor in the summer blockbuster series that promised to change the world of the Avengers forever.

1 As Nick Fury enjoys lunch with old friends Wolverine, Black Widow, and Captain America, the group learn of a seemingly impossible murder. Uatu, the legendary cosmic being called the Watcher, has been killed in his home. And what's worse, someone has stolen his eyes.

2 In reaction, a mysterious man sends Black Panther, Ant-Man, and the White Queen to a monster's graveyard at the center of the Earth, as well as sending Dr. Strange and the Punisher to an otherworldly realm. The Winter Soldier, Gamora, and Moon Knight are also assigned to an investigation—one that will lead them into space.

3 Meanwhile, a villain called the Orb has teamed with two other criminals, Dr. Midas and the Exterminatrix. Though no one knows how they obtained it, the villains have in their possession one of the Watcher's eyes. The trio, and the precious eye, are soon tracked down by the Avengers.

4 When he is confronted by the heroes, the Orb unleashes the power of the Watcher's eye on them. Suddenly, a wealth of secrets is revealed: among them, the Hulk realizes he needs to settle a score with Iron Man, and Thor discovers he has a sister. Despite the revelations and the chaos that ensues, Nick Fury manages to take the Orb hostage.

5 When Black Panther, Moon Knight, and Dr. Strange's separate teams all follow trails back to a satellite that is the source of their mystery boss's broadcast, they discover that Nick Fury is not who he has appeared to be for all these years. Fury reveals he is actually an old man, operating many Life Model Decoys (androids that can mimic a living person) of his younger self in his place.

6 Fury has assembled these heroes with a purpose. Years ago, he had been given a clandestine job protecting humanity from extraterrestrial threats. His covert mission saw him assassinate aliens who planned to harm his planet, something he did on a smaller scale in his day job as Director of S.H.I.E.L.D.

"SOMEONE WAS MURDERED. ALL I CARE ABOUT IS THE TRUTH."
- CAPTAIN AMERICA

7 Fury has brought these selected men and women together so they can replace him. But before he can discuss his job any further with his recruits, the Avengers storm his stronghold. The recruits soon discover that it was Fury himself who killed the Watcher, after Uatu had been attacked by the Orb and his allies.

8 Nick Fury had killed Uatu when the Watcher refused to name his attackers. Fury knew the secrets stored in Uatu's eyes were too important to be made public, so he took the remaining eye in order to discover (and stop) the villains who took the other. After Fury confronts Dr. Midas and does battle, at the apparent cost of his own life, the Winter Soldier steps up to take on Fury's role as Earth's protector.

9 But Nick Fury hasn't died. As punishment for killing Uatu, Fury is forced to fill the Watcher's role. He becomes the Unseen, a watcher cursed to observe but never interfere in the events of the world he has spent his life trying to protect.

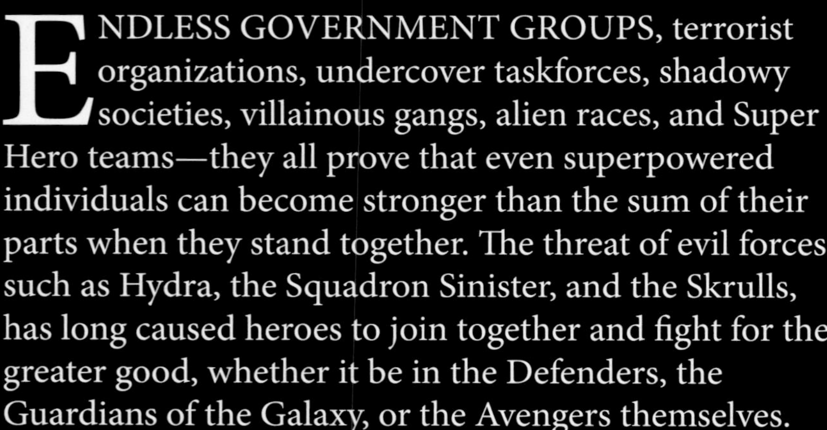

ENDLESS GOVERNMENT GROUPS, terrorist organizations, undercover taskforces, shadowy societies, villainous gangs, alien races, and Super Hero teams—they all prove that even superpowered individuals can become stronger than the sum of their parts when they stand together. The threat of evil forces such as Hydra, the Squadron Sinister, and the Skrulls, has long caused heroes to join together and fight for the greater good, whether it be in the Defenders, the Guardians of the Galaxy, or the Avengers themselves.

SHOULDER TO SHOULDER

WITHOUT THE AVENGERS, the universe would have been destroyed many times over by any number of invading aliens, would-be despots, and corrupt organizations. This team is truly made up of Earth's mightiest heroes—an astonishing collection of individuals willing to sacrifice their own safety for the sake of others. The original Avengers created a legacy of teamwork, honor, and justice that has remained through its many incarnations.

Thor, Ant-Man, the Hulk, Iron Man, and Wasp were brought together by chance, but they soon realized the value of their new Super Hero team and formalized their alliance with a catchy moniker. The original Avengers would soon learn the ropes, while besting villain after villain.

THE AVENGERS

SAY HELLO TO EARTH'S **MIGHTIEST** HEROES!

Global threats are ever changing, and so, too, are the heroes who combat them. The Avengers of today hardly resemble their "founding fathers," but have adapted to suit the shifting world—and even the universe—around them.

When Iron Man, Thor, Wasp, Ant-Man, and the Hulk banded together after quashing a plan cooked up by Thor's nefarious brother Loki, they had no idea what they had put in motion. While they felt they were simply creating a club of Super Heroes who excelled when by each other's sides, in reality they were creating an institution that would define the course of human history.

The Avengers have become an organization with many offshoots. They have spread out into secret strike forces, teams comprised of only teenagers, and branches based on opposite sides of America. They have faced countless teams of Super Villains and alien invasions, and, on more than one occasion, have even been forced to right reality when the entire universe changed around them. Whether led by Captain America, Iron Man, Wasp, or any other valued member, the Avengers have remained a much-needed force for justice. For years, the team has been there to defend the unprotected and avenge the innocent. And the Avengers show no indication of stopping now.

The original Avengers were soon joined by the iconic World War II hero, Captain America.

In one of their most recent incarnations, the Avengers featured Sam Wilson as the new Captain America, a female Thor, and Iron Man in striking white armor.

TEAM INCARNATIONS

Geniuses, gods, robots, mutants, and warlocks: The Avengers have welcomed them all into their ranks at one point or another. With a packed history and dozens of roster changes, the Avengers' membership reads like a who's who of the very biggest and brightest Super Heroes.

TEETHING

THE FOUNDERS
Iron Man, Ant-Man, Wasp, Thor, and the Hulk all came together to form the Avengers, but the team wasn't cemented until Cap became their leader.

FORMER CRIMINALS
The Avengers displayed an open-minded attitude when they welcomed ex-cons Hawkeye, Scarlet Witch, and Quicksilver into the fold.

AVENGING VISIONS
Black Panther joined the team along with the Vision and Black Knight—both of whom were originally mistaken for enemies.

GROWTH

THE NEW ICONS
The Avengers soon added Ms. Marvel, Falcon, Wonder Man, and the former X-Man Beast to the team, as well as Moondragon and Hellcat.

FANTASTIC FIVE
In a new era, the Fantastic Four's Mr. Fantastic and the Invisible Woman united with Steve Rogers, Thor, and the Forgotten One.

THE MINORS
When lesser-known heroes Stingray, Sersi, and Quasar joined the Avengers, their deeds were just as valiant as their counterparts.

RETURN

HEROES RETURN
Having been trapped in a pocket dimension, the original Avengers returned to their own world, joined by new members Justice and Firestar.

WORLD TRUST
Designated a world power by the United Nations, the Avengers team welcomed new faces like Lionheart to join its shifting roster.

NEW AVENGERS
Cap thanked fate when a new team of Avengers was drawn together, six months after an unbalanced Scarlet Witch caused the team to break up.

UPHEAVAL

SECRET AVENGERS
The events of the Superhuman Civil War forced the Avengers into hiding, yet they fought on in an unofficial capacity, with Steve Rogers as leader.

THE HEROIC AGE
After Norman Osborn's failed attempt to corrupt the country, the President sanctioned a restored Avengers team, with Rogers at the helm.

STORM FRONT
Returning to the Captain America name after a hiatus, Steve Rogers added power to his Avengers team, enlisting former X-Men member, Storm.

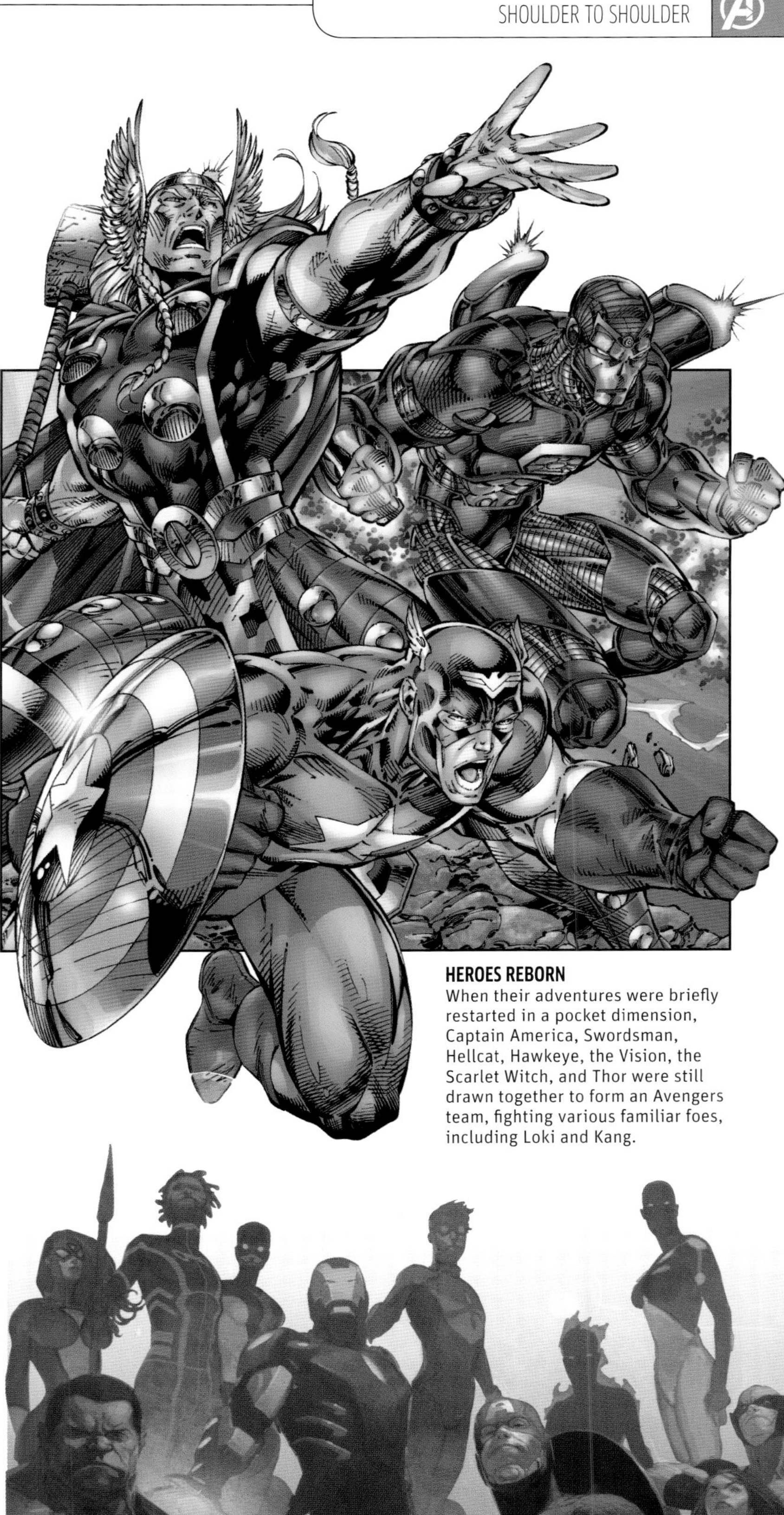

HEROES REBORN
When their adventures were briefly restarted in a pocket dimension, Captain America, Swordsman, Hellcat, Hawkeye, the Vision, the Scarlet Witch, and Thor were still drawn together to form an Avengers team, fighting various familiar foes, including Loki and Kang.

A BROADENING UNIVERSE
With the threat of events such as the Superhuman Civil War, the Secret Invasion, and Norman Osborn's rule long in the past, the Avengers decided to expand to a global level—and beyond!

AVENGERS NO MORE

In their time of crisis, the Avengers were supported by heroes including Daredevil, Black Panther, Moon Knight, and the Thing. A mix of former and future members, they all sensed the risk posed by Scarlet Witch.

Perhaps one of the most trying times in the Avengers' long and storied history was when one of their own attacked the heroes she had previously considered family.

The Scarlet Witch had been mentally unstable for quite some time. A mutant who attributed her magical abilities to "hex powers," Scarlet Witch had created two children with her magic—but they were a figment of her imagination. Unable to tell reality from the world inside her disturbed mind, she began lashing out at her fellow Avengers members, convinced they were trying to take her sons away from her. To that end, she used her powers to stage what seemed to be attacks on Avengers Mansion by a horde of Ultron robots and an Kree armada, threatened the recovery of former alcoholic Iron Man, and turned her fellow Avenger She-Hulk from a rational hero into a fierce, rampaging monster. Scarlet Witch was eventually taken into custody by her father, Magneto. Although the events had been constructs of Scarlet Witch's mind, the consequences were very real. With longtime members like the Vision and Hawkeye fallen in battle, and Avengers Mansion destroyed, it seemed that the age of the Avengers was finally over.

HULKING OUT

During Scarlet Witch's attack on Avengers Mansion, powerhouse She-Hulk suddenly lost control, attacking her own teammates and literally ripping the Vision in two. Scarlet Witch had used her hex powers to send the steady She-Hulk into a rage more familiar to her cousin, Bruce Banner. She-Hulk was finally subdued by the timely arrival of Iron Man.

AVENGERS RETURN!

After being formally disassembled, the Avengers faced some tumultuous years of infighting, clandestine operations, and participation in a global Civil War. The sight of Norman Osborn as their leader seemed the final straw. Fortunately, they soon returned as the public heroes the world needed.

Norman Osborn, the villain known for his murderous career as the Green Goblin, had wormed his way into the most powerful position in the country: head of S.H.I.E.L.D., later called H.A.M.M.E.R. However, Osborn's reign of terror ended after he overstepped his legal bounds and the Avengers finally brought him to justice. A grateful nation placed Steve Rogers into the position of top cop, and the former Captain America brought the Avengers back into the light with him.

Mending relationships that had been shattered since the Superhuman Civil War, Rogers created several Avengers teams—a flagship team helmed by Iron Man and Thor, a team of New Avengers led by Luke Cage, and an underground group of Secret Avengers, whose missions Roger participated in directly. The Avengers had once again returned to greatness, and it was the original Captain America who had taken them there.

While the rift in the friendship between Steve Rogers and Iron Man had been drastic during the Superhuman Civil War, the two finally put politics aside for the benefit of the common good, and Iron Man was one of the first recruits for Steve's premier Avengers team.

Steve Rogers chose Iron Man, Thor, Hawkeye, Spider-Man, Wolverine, Spider-Woman, and the current Captain America, Bucky Barnes, as his main team of Avengers. They were soon joined by Protector and Red Hulk.

WEST COAST AVENGERS

When many of Earth's greatest heroes were summoned to a planet called Battleworld during the first Secret Wars, other heroes stepped up to fill the void in the Avengers' roster on Earth. But when the iconic crime-fighters returned home, suddenly there were too many Avengers. Rather than fire any of them, the then chairman of the Avengers, Vision, decided to create a second team instead, headed up by Hawkeye.

Hawkeye recruited Tigra and Mockingbird, among others, into the West Coast Avengers. His wife, Mockingbird, proved to be one of the great motivating forces behind the California-based team.

DATA FILE

TEAM NAME
West Coast Avengers

FIRST APPEARANCE
West Coast Avengers #1 (September 1984)

MEMBERS AND THEIR ABILITIES
Hawkeye—master archer; Mockingbird—martial arts ace; Tigra—feline ability; Wonder Man—ionic energy; Iron Man (James Rhodes/Tony Stark)—high intellect, armor; the Thing—superhuman strength; Moon Knight—weapons expert; Henry Pym—genius scientist; Firebird—radiates heat; the Wasp—size change, sting; Mantis—mental powers; Scarlet Witch—chaos magic; Vision—sensory powers; U.S. Agent—superhuman power; Human Torch (Jim Hammond)—emits heat; Quicksilver—superhuman speed; Machine Man—robot; Spider-Woman—superhuman powers; Living Lightning—sentient electrical form; Darkhawk—superhuman strength; Moira Brandon (honorary member).

HAWKEYE'S A-LIST LINEUP

Setting up shop at an elaborate compound on the West Coast, Hawkeye collected an impressive lineup of Avengers to protect everything west of the Rockies.

Hawkeye's first act as leader was to recruit his love interest and crime-fighting partner, S.H.I.E.L.D. agent Mockingbird. But as a longtime Avenger, he understood that they'd need much more brute strength than a pair of non-powered heroes could provide. That soon came in the form of Tigra, Iron Man, and Wonder Man. The heroes faced some teething problems, with Hawkeye unsuccessful at recruiting local vigilante the Shroud, and Iron Man failing to reveal he was in fact James Rhodes, not Tony Stark. Nevertheless, they soon formed a team mighty enough to defeat their first true foes—the thief known as the Blank and his ally, the heavy-hitting Graviton.

Key members of the West Coast Avengers team included (from left to right): Iron Man, Tigra, Wonder Man, Hawkeye, and Mockingbird.

When Hawkeye first enlisted Iron Man to serve on his team, he had no idea that the man he was hiring wasn't his old friend, but Iron Man's replacement, James Rhodes.

THE DEATH OF MOCKINGBIRD

In a dramatic event that would eventually lead to the end of the West Coast Avengers team, longtime member Mockingbird fell during battle.

SOUL GAUNTLET

Avengers: West Coast #100 (November 1993)

When the villain Satannish kidnapped Mockingbird, Hawkeye vowed to save her. Aided by Scarlet Witch, U.S. Agent, War Machine, and Spider-Woman, Hawkeye traveled to Satannish's dimension, only to be caught in a battle between Satannish and the demon Mephisto. While the other Avengers escaped, Mockingbird was killed.

Hawkeye believed for a long time that Mephisto had murdered his wife, Mockingbird. However, the couple would later be reunited.

TEAM INCARNATIONS

Over time, the West Coast Avengers would change their team's moniker to Avengers West Coast, and also evolved their roster. While they didn't undergo quite as many shake-ups as their parent team, the West Coast Avengers still had their fair share of members coming and going.

THE DEBUT TEAM
Hawkeye, Mockingbird, Tigra, Wonder Man, and Iron Man (James Rhodes, later replaced by Tony Stark) formed the original cast.

CHANGING THINGS
Known for his longstanding membership of the Fantastic Four, the Thing joined the Avengers' California-based team for a short tenure.

OLD FRIENDS
Two of the Avengers' most established and esteemed members—Scarlet Witch and the Vision—headed out to the West Coast.

WEB DESIGNER
A loyal and faithful ally, the second Spider-Woman (later dubbed Madame Web) was another recruit to the West Coast Avengers.

AVENGERS TERMINATED

After the traumatic death of Mockingbird, the West Coast Avengers' luck eventually ran out when the android Vision decided to terminate the West Coast branch.

AVENGERS WEST COAST ARE FINISHED

Avengers: West Coast #102 (January 1994)

The Vision giveth, and the Vision taketh away. That was the feeling amongst the remaining members of the Avengers' West Coast branch when the android led a vote to disband their team. Through a final vote placed by Iron Man, the branch was officially shut down. However, Iron Man then promptly quit the Avengers altogether, as did the rest of the West Coast team. They formed a new group of California-based Super Heroes named Force Works, determined to carry on the work of the West Coast Avengers.

GUARDIANS OF THE GALAXY

THE TEAM KNOWN as the Guardians of the Galaxy was formed to fulfil a vital mission—taking a proactive stance in galactic affairs and protecting Earth and the Milky Way. It is now made up of two groups, one team in the far future, and one fighting alongside the present-day Avengers. Both teams are ragtag bags of misfits, regarded by many as good-for-nothing wastrels and criminals, but united by their reformed, heroic hearts.

Peter Quill (front left) pulled together a roster including (clockwise from back left) Groot, Agent Venom (Eugene "Flash" Thompson), Rocket Racoon, Drax, Captain Marvel and Gamora.

GUARDIANS OF EARTH

Just like the original, 31st-century gang, the present era Guardians of the Galaxy were formed from necessity, to fight threats that others could not deal with, and to defend the otherwise helpless.

After facing down the cosmic danger presented by both Annihilus and the Phalanx, an adventurer named Star-Lord organized a new Super Hero squad. Star-Lord, otherwise known as Peter Quill, recruited a fearless team of defenders from far-flung corners of the galaxy. Alongside main players Drax the Destroyer, Gamora, Groot, and Rocket Racoon, Quill would later team up with the Avengers in order to defeat the nefarious Thanos.

Not immune from disagreements, in part due to the big personalities within the group, the Guardians of the Galaxy have weathered many storms and are still on call for emergencies, with the Avengers or on their own.

The Guardians have fought, and killed, Thanos more than once, but he is often resurrected by Death.

DATA FILE

TEAM NAME Guardians of the Galaxy

FIRST AVENGERS APPEARANCE
Avengers #167 (January 1978)

MEMBERS AND THEIR ABILITIES
Starhawk—generates light; Charlie-27—genetically-engineered human; Yondu—Centaurian, expert archer; Martinex—right hand emits heat, left hand emits cold; Vance Astro (Major Victory)—blasts psychic energy, uses Cap's shield; Nikki—talented acrobat; Aleta Ogord—manipulates cosmic energy; Firelord (honorary)—manipulates cosmic energy, Replica—shape-shifting Skrull; Yellowjacket (Rita DeMara)—size change, stingers; Star-Lord—human/Spartoi hybrid, peak human ability; Gamora—expert combatant; Rocket Raccoon—expert combatant; Groot—Flora Colossus with immense strength; Drax the Destroyer—superhuman ability; Quasar (Phyla-Vell)—Quantum bands enable increased speed; Adam Warlock—quantum magic ability; Mantis—telepathic powers, astral projection; Bug—insect physiology, superhuman ability; Jack Flag—Hyde formula yields superhuman strength; Moondragon—martial artist, telekinetic power; Iron Man—business genius, armor gives superhuman ability; Angela—daughter of Odin, superhuman strength; Agent Venom—symbiotic costume enables superhuman ability; Captain Marvel (Carol Danvers) (Avengers liason)—superhuman ability, energy absorption.

IRON SPACEMAN

After taking down Thanos with the Guardians of the Galaxy, Iron Man mentioned how jealous he was of Star-Lord's lifestyle beyond the stars, and how he wished that he too could explore the vastness of space. Star-Lord extended an invitation for Iron Man to join him—one the hero later accepted when he needed to escape his problems for a bit.

TARGET: LONDON

Guardians Of The Galaxy #1 (March 2013)

Happily space-bound, Iron Man had hoped to be able to get away from Earth for a while, but instead found himself heading back in a hurry in order to protect it from an alien invasion. The Emperor of Spartax had tried to warn his son, Peter Quill, to stay away from Earth in a double-cross maneuver that revealed his own hand in the affairs. Having sent a galactic broadcast ordering everyone in the vicinity to abandon Earth, he had planned for an easy takeover, but reckoned without his son and the Guardians. Unable to contact the rest of the Avengers, the Fantastic Four, or any other kind of backup due to the disabled communications systems, the team ended up saving the planet in their own unique and spontaneous style, with the help of Iron Man.

Iron Man wore a new suit equipped for space travel when teaming with the Guardians.

The invading forces made London, England, their first port of call.

BACK *TO THE* FAR FUTURE

The original Guardians of the Galaxy are a Super Hero team based in the 31st century. So when these Guardians first traveled to their past and met the Avengers, Earth's Mightiest Heroes were a bit taken aback by the futuristic warriors.

The Avengers met the Guardians of the Galaxy during an epic struggle against the cyborg Korvac.

Nick Fury was the first to discover the Guardians' arrival. When the Guardians' spacecraft appeared near S.H.I.E.L.D.'s satellite, Fury called in the Avengers to investigate. Beast met the heroes before the rest of his team, attacking them after they referred to him as a "space monkey." However, soon the two groups became allies, and the Avengers agreed to help the Guardians locate the reason these future Super Heroes came to the present in the first place: the villain Korvac.

The futuristic Guardians had originally formed with four members: Vance Astro from Earth, Charlie-27 from Jupiter, Martinex from Pluto, and Yondu from Centauri IV. However, when they met the Avengers they had been joined by key members Starhawk, Starhawk's wife Aleta, and Nikki from Mercury. Vance at times assumed the identities of Major Victory and Marvel Boy, and led his squad on many missions. In another time, Vance was discovered encased in ice and suffering from amnesia by none other than Peter Quill. It was this encounter that inspired Quill to name his own, newly formed, team the Guardians of the Galaxy.

TEAM INCARNATIONS

The future incarnation of the Guardians of the Galaxy wasn't the last that the Avengers would meet. Instead, due to their time-traveling adventures, it was only the first!

31ST CENTURY
The original team was given honorary Avengers status after traveling to the present time.

PRESENT ERA
Iron Man temporarily joined Star-Lord, Groot, Gamora, Drax, and Rocket Racoon on their adventures.

AVENGERS CROSSOVER
To maintain a strong link with the Avengers, Agent Venom and Captain Marvel joined the Quill's Guardians.

SECRET AVENGERS

A former West Coast Avenger, Moon Knight was one of Steve Rogers' original picks for the Secret Avengers.

No longer calling himself Captain America, Rogers went unmasked and by his given name when leading this clandestine team.

When Steve Rogers was given total control over the Avengers as America's top cop, he soon realized the need for a strike force that valued stealth above all else. So, Rogers created the Secret Avengers—a covert team with the ability to take on missions that the high-profile Avengers roster couldn't publicly address.

Steve Rogers was tired of the spotlight, but happy to lead a shadow ops team such as the Secret Avengers. Rogers played to the strengths of his individual team members, enlisting them for their knowledge and power.

DATA FILE

TEAM NAME
Secret Avengers

FIRST APPEARANCE
Secret Avengers #1 (May 2010)

MEMBERS AND THEIR ABILITIES
Steve Rogers–master combatant; Moon Knight–weapons expert; Beast–genius mutant; Nova–vast energy source; Black Widow–superhuman ability; War Machine–armor, superhuman strength; Sharon Carter–expert combatant; Ant Man III–size change; Valkyrie–superhuman ability; Shang Chi (auxiliary member)–martial arts expert; Prince of Orphans (aux.)–becomes green mist; Hawkeye–master archer; Captain Britain–power from interdimensional energy; Giant-Man–size change; Phil Coulson–espionage abilities; Human Torch (Jim Hammond)–emits heat; Venom–symbiotic costume; Thor (aux.)–superhuman strength; Vision (aux.)–superhuman powers; Ms. Marvel (aux.)–superhuman ability; Protector (aux.); Nick Fury, Jr.–infinity formula; Mockingbird–martial arts ace; Hulk–superhuman strength; Taskmaster–photographic reflexes; Iron Patriot/War Machine–armor, superhuman ability; Spider-Woman–superhuman ability; M.O.D.O.K.–high intellect.

STEVE'S SECRET SUPER SQUAD

Captain America's rebellion of heroes during the Civil War had been dubbed the Secret Avengers. Later, when organizing his own undercover Avengers strike force team, Rogers saw the opportunity to employ the name once again.

When given control of the Avengers franchise, Steve Rogers handpicked a new Avengers team, and allowed Luke Cage to choose a team of New Avengers. While those teams had most crises covered, Rogers still worried about the threats that he had yet to learn about. Consequently, Rogers recruited a team of Secret Avengers, a covert group meant to assess and deal with these secret issues before they became worldwide problems. Rogers' original team faced many missions, from traveling to Mars to track down the origins of a mysterious relic, to facing John Steele, America's first super-soldier working with the Secret Avengers' biggest threat, the Shadow Council. Rogers would later return to his position as Captain America, but the Secret Avengers continued, under various leaders.

S.H.I.E.L.D. RUNNING THE SHOW

S.H.I.E.L.D. alumnae Black Widow and Spider-Woman spearheaded a new Secret Avengers strike force team—one with government funding and non-stop action.

Black Widow and Spider-Woman were excellent recruits for a new Secret Avengers team. Both had a history of training in stealth, espionage, and covert combat.

SAVE THE EMPIRE

Secret Avengers #1 (May 2014)

The most recent incarnation of the Secret Avengers began after the Avengers and S.H.I.E.L.D. had formed an alliance to work together in order to destroy serious threats to the world. S.H.I.E.L.D. director Maria Hill assembled a black ops team to handle the sensitive problems that the Avengers could not address publicly, recruiting Black Widow and Spider-Woman, alongside S.H.I.E.L.D. agents including Nick Fury Jr. and Phil Coulson. Hill decided against recruiting Hawkeye, due to his reputation for being headstrong. However, when circumstances led him into the wrong place at the wrong time—specifically a Russian spa—Hawkeye found himself recruited against his will to help the Secret Avengers deal with a cybiote known as the Fury on a secret space station.

TEAM INCARNATIONS

Set up as a strike force that employed people whose powers fit the mission at hand, the Secret Avengers went through many roster changes.

THE ORIGINALS
Rogers' first team included Black Widow, Beast, Valkyrie, Eric O'Grady, Nova, Sharon Carter, and Moon Knight.

HAWKEYE'S TEAM
Rogers soon recruited old ally Hawkeye as head of the Secret Avengers and new members, including Captain Britain.

S.H.I.E.L.D.'S AVENGERS
This incarnation, led by Nick Fury, Jr., recruited Mockingbird, Taskmaster, and, briefly, the Hulk.

SECRET AGENTS
S.H.I.E.L.D.'s Secret Avengers were mainly agents without superpowers, with the exception of Spider-Woman.

S.H.I.E.L.D. kept strict tabs on its Secret Avengers. Nick Fury Jr. wasn't forthcoming with his Super Hero teammates, and wasn't above betraying them for the sake of the mission at hand.

KEEPING SECRETS

S.H.I.E.L.D. wanted its own Secret Avengers, but the government organization wasn't above keeping secrets from its own team members.

During her tenure as director of S.H.I.E.L.D, Daisy Johnson had agent Phil Coulson recruit Hawkeye and Black Widow to a new S.H.I.E.L.D. Secret Avengers strike force team. Reluctant to tie themselves to an organized bureaucratic team, the pair initially refused. They were even less keen when Coulson revealed they would be required to implant nanotechnology into their bodies, so S.H.I.E.L.D. could erase their memories at will. It was only once Coulson revealed a secret, personal objective of the new team, that the two heroes signed up for service. Johnson soon explained that not only could their memories be wiped, all knowledge of the team and missions would categorically be removed when they were not actively serving. This secretive way of working was justified as necessary to ensure no confidential information would be disclosed in case of kidnap, torture, or betrayal. The pair soon began working with Nick Fury, Jr., son of the former S.H.I.E.L.D. director Nick Fury and an ex-army ranger. Unbeknownst to Hawkeye and Black Widow, their S.H.I.E.L.D colleagues were also using the technology to keep mission details secret from them.

As the new head of S.H.I.E.L.D., Iron Man organized the Fifty-State Initiative so that heroes were held accountable for their actions.

FIFTY-STATE INITIATIVE

The Gauntlet served as the superhuman drill instructor for the newest batch of young would-be Avengers.

IN THE MESSY AFTERMATH of the Superhuman Civil War, Iron Man emerged the true victor. With every hero now forced to register his or her identity with the government, Tony Stark began an initiative that saw an Avengers team created for every state: the Fifty-State Initiative. Many heroes refused to register, but the majority of the U.S. vigilantes went on the government's payroll.

CAMP HAMMOND RECRUITS

Among those who registered with the government were many novice Super Heroes. Camp Hammond was created to help train these crime-fighters and mold them into seasoned professionals.

One of the most important facets of the Fifty-State Initiative was the establishment of Camp Hammond, a training facility located in Connecticut. Built in the city of Stamford—the location of a devastating explosion that had inspired the government to develop the Superhuman Registration Act in the first place—Camp Hammond was controversial from the start. Nevertheless, young, inexperienced heroes began registering themselves, knowing that they had to be trained at Hammond in order to achieve the legal status needed to fight crime.

DIFFICULT **LESSONS** *TO* **LEARN**

The learning curve was a steep one for the new recruits of the Initiative, and many were left wondering if the sacrifices were worth the stature.

DATA FILE

TEAM NAME
The Fifty-State Initiative

FIRST APPEARANCE
Civil War #5 (January 2007)

TEAMS AND THEIR BASE OF OPERATIONS
The Mighty Avengers (New York); Great Lakes Initiative (Wisconsin); Force Works (Iowa); Freedom Force (Washington D.C.); Desert Stars (Arizona); the Order (California); Rangers (Texas); Spaceknights (Illinois); the Women Warriors (Delaware); Action Pack (Kentucky); Earth Force (Washington State); Psionex (Maryland); Liberteens (Pennsylvania); the Battalion (Arkansas); the Command (Florida); the Calvary (Georgia); Mavericks (New Mexico); the Called (Utah); the Garrison (Vermont); Point Men (Hawaii); Harvesters (Kansas); Forces of Nature (Oregon); Thunderbolts (Colorado); Defenders (New Jersey); Fantastic Four (New York); Heavy Hitters (Nevada); U-Foes (North Carolina).

UNHAPPY ACCIDENTS

Avengers: The Initiative #1 (June 2007)

Under the supervision of Iron Man's longtime trusted ally War Machine, and staffed by other veteran Super Heroes including Yellowjacket (Hank Pym) and Justice, Camp Hammond served as the perfect testing grounds for recruits often handpicked by established crime-fighters. Justice recruited a young man named Michael van Patrick—who called himself MVP—who seemed to be a fast-rising star among the teenage heroes. However, the rest of the students soon learned how dangerous their line of work really was when a training exercise involving Trauma, Armory, and Cloud 9, went wrong, causing MVP to be struck in the head and killed.

Believing he had saved his fellow student Cloud 9, MVP was struck and killed by a stray blast from fellow Initiative recruit Armory.

Camp Hammond trainees would often accompany a supervisor into real combat, as was the case when War Machine took a team to fight a Hydra Terror-Carrier in Texas.

TEAM INCARNATIONS

50 full teams served as members of the Fifty-State Initiative program, with more waiting in the wings as they trained at Camp Hammond.

THE GAUNTLET
Tasked with training new heroes, the Gauntlet was recruited by Henry Peter Gyrich while serving in Iraq.

FIRST CLASS
Rage and Slapstick were two trainees, despite Rage's past experience with the New Warriors and the Avengers.

NEW RECRUITS
Batwing, Butterball, Annex, Gorilla Girl, Sunstreak, and Prodigy were later recruits, trained by the Taskmaster.

U-FOES
When Norman Osborn took over the Initiative, he formed teams of villains like North Carolina's U-Foes.

SHADOW INITIATIVE

There was more to this government organization than met the eye.

Henry Peter Gyrich, a longtime associate of the Avengers with a tainted record, was determined to bolster the ranks of the Fifty-State Initiative, even if he had to cross moral lines to do so. With the help of former Nazi scientist Baron Von Blitzschlag, Gyrich used MVP's genetic material to create clones. These would serve as Scarlet Spiders, part of a black ops team named the Shadow Initiative, controlled only by Gyrich. Working in secret, this team faced threats that the government wished to keep hidden from the public. When these unethical and secretive dealings were exposed, it helped lead to the dissolution of the Fifty-State Initiative.

AVENGERS ACADEMY

The first class of Avengers Academy (from left to right): Hazmat, Striker, Finesse, Mettle, Veil, and Reptil (front).

AFTER THE DISSOLUTION of the Fifty-State Initiative, a safe, controlled environment was needed to train the upcoming generation of Super Heroes. Avengers Academy was created, with the goal of establishing the heroes of tomorrow.

AVENGERS IN TRAINING

Six young would-be heroes were handpicked by Hank Pym and his fellow professors to enroll in the Avengers Academy, not because they had potential to be heroes, but because they showed signs of becoming Super Villains.

When Norman Osborn, also known as the villainous Green Goblin, became the Director of H.A.M.M.E.R., he took over Tony Stark's Fifty-State Initiative and began recruiting, and sometimes forcibly altering, a new breed of superhumans. But Osborn finally fell from grace after a misguided attack on Thor's birthplace, Asgard, and Hank Pym and other heroes took over his program. They decided to recruit six of his most dangerous young superhumans in an attempt to guide them toward a heroic future. These powerful protégés struggled with this path at times, but with the help of a rotating roster of Avengers staff members, they began to progress in the Academy.

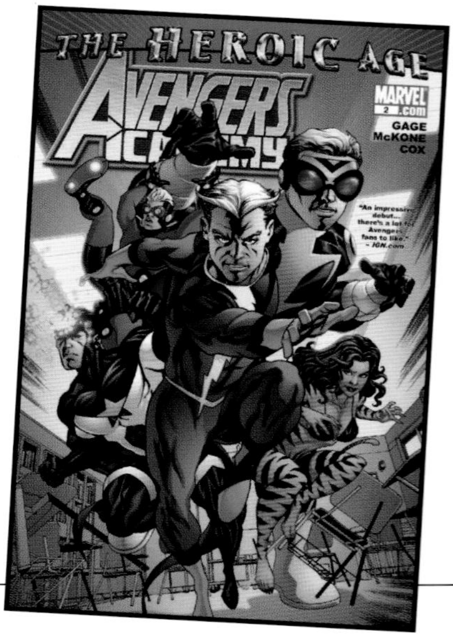

Academy faculty members included: (clockwise from top) Hank Pym, Tigra, Justice, Speedball, and Quicksilver (center).

DATA FILE

TEAM NAME Avengers Academy

FIRST AVENGERS APPEARANCE *Avengers Academy* #1 (August 2010)

MEMBERS AND THEIR ABILITIES

Students Veil—gaseous form; Reptil—prehistoric animal form; Hazmat—emits radiation; Striker—electrokinesis; Finesse—accelerated learning powers; Mettle—iridium body; Lightspeed—acceleration; White Tiger V—has Amulets of Power; X-23—Wolverine clone; Butterball—invulnerability; Batwing—bat-like powers; Hollow—razor-sharp claws; Hybrid—symbiotic costume; Juston Seyfert—creator of robot Sentinel; Thunderstrike II—superhuman ability; Loa—permeates solid matter; Lyra—superhuman strength; Machine Teen—android; Power Man III— superhuman strength; Ricochet—mutant, superhuman ability; Rocket Racer—rocket-powered accessories; Spider-Girl—spider-like powers; Turbo—torpedo armor; Wiz Kid—mutant computer genius.

Faculty Giant-Man (Hank Pym)—genius scientist, size change; Justice—telekinesis; Tigra—feline ability; Speedball—energy projection; Quicksilver—superhuman speed; Jocasta—robot with superhuman abilties; Hawkeye—master archer.

GROWING PAINS

Life in the Avengers Academy proved a juggling act between training, fighting Super Villains, and some regular high-school drama.

ARCADE FIRE

Avengers Academy Giant-Size #1 (July 2011)

With a free day of no classes on their hands, Reptil, Veil, Finesse, and Striker were walking through New York City's Bryant Park when they caught a glimpse of Young Allies members Firestar and Spider-Girl swooping overhead. Soon, a normal day of goofing off was interrupted when the team, along with Spider-Girl, Toro, and Firestar, was kidnapped by Arcade. While Arcade placed all of their friends in death traps, Spider-Girl and Reptil were forced to participate in his twisted games in order to save them. In the end, however, the teens managed to foil Arcade's plan, and Reptil gave the villain a knockout punch.

Several of the Young Allies, including Spider-Girl and Firestar, had plenty of experience in battling villains to share with the students from the Avengers Academy.

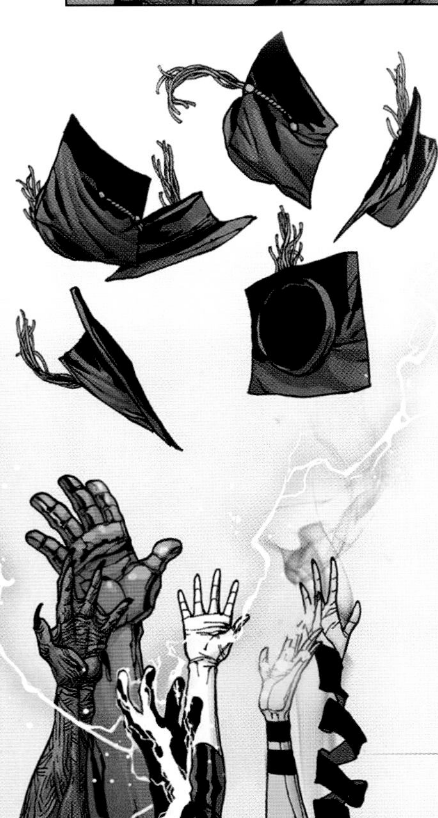

COMMENCEMENT

Avengers Academy #39 (January 2013)

When Giant-Man told the original members of the Avengers Academy that they were all now Avengers Third Grade, they thought they were being demoted. But in reality, the label was a promotion, the equivalent of progressing to a sophomore year in a standard high school. If they continued along their current path, their next step would be Second Grade, then First Grade, then full Avengers. It was an honor, and one the young teens happily accepted.

TEAM INCARNATIONS

After starting out with a small class of trainee heroes, the Avengers Academy went on to gain new students over time.

ADULT ACADEMY
The original six members temporarily had their minds put into the bodies of adult versions of themselves.

EXPANSION
After the events dubbed "Fear Itself," Lightspeed and White Tiger joined the expanding Academy.

SUSPENDED
The Academy is briefly closed to ensure student safety, after it was attacked by a possessed Emma Frost.

LIFE ON *CAMPUS*

Dubbed Infinite Avengers Mansion, the campus at the Avengers Academy was almost as spectacular as its Super Hero students.

The Avengers Academy housed a dramatic lobby that showcased vintage images of the Avengers in action. In addition, there was an impressive training room, where the students could learn from their normal professors as well as from guest teachers including Captain America and Iron Fist. Dorms were located on campus, as was the World Communications Room that was equipped with state-of-the-art computers housing valuable Avengers files. Following the destruction of its first campus, the Academy was relocated to the former headquarters of the West Coast Avengers in California. A much larger site, this new compound allowed the Academy to significantly expand its student body.

GREAT LAKES AVENGERS

Dinah Soar was the only GLA member capable of flight, and her ability to emit high frequencies could calm Mr. Immortal when his anger had gotten out of control.

THERE WERE AVENGERS on the East Coast and Avengers on the West Coast, but none protecting the northern United States. At least not until a new group popped up in Milwaukee, Wisconsin, calling themselves the Great Lakes Avengers (GLA).

Doorman's teleportation abilities came in very useful when he joined the GLA.

GREETINGS FROM THE GREAT LAKES

The formation of the Great Lakes Avengers was, like the team itself, out of the ordinary. Assembling in response to an advert in a newspaper, these eccentric adventurers were eager Avengers.

Craig Hollis had a childhood history of surviving accidents that should have killed him. As an adult, he decided to use these powers as the crime-fighting Mr. Immortal. After placing an advertisment in a newspaper calling for fellow aspiring heroes, Mr. Immortal recruited the size-shifting supermodel Big Bertha, master of Origami-fu Flatman, teleporter Doorman, and the unintelligible Dinah Soar. The Great Lakes Avengers were born.

Angry that this bizarre group of Milwaukee-based upstarts would use the Avengers name without permission, Hawkeye and his wife Mockingbird flew to meet the GLA. Surprisingly impressed with what they saw, the couple decided to stay on with the team and train them.

Craig Hollis became Mr. Immortal, after several failed suicide bids.

Hawkeye had faith in this band of misfits, aiming to train them to the same standard as his former West Coast colleagues.

Big Bertha had two drastically different body types—as her large heroic form and as the slender supermodel Ashley Crawford.

While Hawkeye joked that "Flatman" should have a partner named "Ribbon," the hero nevertheless proved to be quite capable with his stretching powers.

DATA FILE

TEAM NAME Great Lakes Avengers, Great Lakes Champions, Great Lakes Initiative, Great Lakes Defenders, Great Lakes X-Men, and the Lightning Rods.

FIRST APPEARANCE *The West Coast Avengers* #46 (July 1989)

MEMBERS AND THEIR ABILITIES Mr. Immortal—Death-defying; Doorman—Darkforce portal; Big Bertha—body transformation; Dinah Soar—flight, hypersonic voice; Flatman—stretchy body; Hawkeye—expert archer; Mockingbird—martial arts ace; Squirrel Girl—prehensile tail; Grasshopper—insectoid abilities; Deadpool—accelerated healing factor; Gravity—manipulates gravity; Leather Boy (accidental member)—no special powers or abilities, responded to a personal ad in a newspaper.

The GLA benefitted from being trained by established heroes Hawkeye and Mockingbird, although the new heroes weren't always taken seriously by the rest of the Super Hero community. Nevertheless, the team faced a series of threats including Maelstrom, A.I.M., and Asbestos Man. Another success came when Flatman won a Super Hero poker contest, prompting to a brief name change to the Great Lakes Champions.

Hawkeye and Mockingbird took it upon themselves to lead the team of oddball heroes.

THE **END** OF THE GREAT LAKES AVENGERS?

When the Avengers disassembled thanks to the Scarlet Witch's machinations, would the GLA be up to standing in their place?

Although Mr. Immortal's death-defying abilities allowed him to withstand the worst of Maelstrom's energy blasts, his long-time love, Dinah Soar, was not so fortunate.

GLA: MISASSEMBLED

Great Lakes Avengers: Misassembled #1-4 (June 2005 - September 2005)

Mr. Immortal knew what he was doing was futile. The GLA would always be seen as a third-tier team. But just when he was about to give up on his Super Hero dream altogether, the Avengers dramatically disbanded. Thinking it was the GLA's chance at the big time, Mr. Immortal was distraught when their first foray against the Super Villain Maelstrom resulted in the death of his love, Dinah Soar. After overcoming his depression, however, Mr. Immortal was able to later trick Maelstrom into committing suicide, earning his revenge.

TEAM INCARNATIONS

Miraculously, the GLA team kept up the fight for justice, despite the odds stacked against them. Just like the regular Avengers, their roster added a few new heroes to the mix over time.

THE FOUNDING FIVE
Bankrolled by Big Bertha's supermodel earnings, the Great Lakes Avengers protected the northern United States and the Midwest.

GREAT LAKES X-MEN (GLX)
Already a team of mutants, the GLA took a cue from the X-Men to become the GLX, in an attempt to breathe new life into their own franchise.

ADDING A HEAVYWEIGHT
Having previously refused membership, Gravity was forced to join the Great Lakes Initiative when assigned to duty there by Norman Osborn.

THE GREAT LAKES **INITIATIVE**

During the Fifty-State Initiative, the Great Lakes Avengers continued in an all-new form, this time with the moniker Great Lakes Initiative.

In the wake of the Superhuman Civil War, the Fifty-State Initiative was created to ensure a Super Hero team in every one of America's fifty states. Willing participants, the Great Lakes team re-emerged as the Great Lakes Initiative charged with protecting Wisconsin, with members including Doorman, Mr. Immortal, Big Bertha, Flatman, Squirrel Girl, and Grasshopper. During the Skrull invasion, almost every Super Hero team on the planet was infiltrated by the alien race, including the GLI in the form of a Skrull posing as Grasshopper. When the team found there was an imposter in their midst, they confronted the Skrull with aid from Gravity.

The Skrull invasion caused chaos, but that didn't stop Flatman from trying to convince the young hero Gravity to join the Great Lakes team.

DARK AVENGERS

AFTER THE EVENTS of the "Secret Invasion," the world was looking for a hero to replace Iron Man as the head of S.H.I.E.L.D. That "hero" was the former Super Villain Norman Osborn, and with him came the ascendance of the Dark Avengers—a team formed of crooks masquerading as iconic, trusted characters.

DARK BEGINNINGS

While corrupt to the core, Norman Osborn managed to fool the world into thinking him a hero. But every hero needs an entourage, and Osborn soon adopted the name Iron Patriot and recruited his own team of Avengers.

Norman Osborn had killed the Skrull queen, the ruler of an invading alien force. The queen's death was witnessed by the same public that believed Iron Man had failed them. In the aftermath of the attack, Osborn was promoted to the head of S.H.I.E.L.D., and quickly changed the organization's title to H.A.M.M.E.R. But the former Green Goblin wasn't done insulting the Super Hero community yet. His next step was to don the mantle of the Iron Patriot and recruit a team comprised mostly of Super Villains to masquerade as the Avengers. These Dark Avengers would be his personal henchmen, helping Osborn maintain his position as the world's most powerful man, while publicly appearing to be Earth's Mightiest Heroes.

A known associate of Osborn's in the Thunderbolts, Moonstone adopted the guise of Ms. Marvel in the Dark Avengers.

Norman capitalized on the reputation of two American icons—Iron Man and Captain America—to create his role as the Iron Patriot.

The public had no idea that the heroes they were cheering were hardened criminals and murderers.

DATA FILE

TEAM NAME
Dark Avengers

FIRST AVENGERS APPEARANCE
Dark Avengers #1 (March 2009)

MEMBERS AND THEIR ABILITIES
Iron Patriot (Norman Osborn)—genius intellect, skilled combatant; Ms. Marvel (Moonstone)—superhuman ability, including speed; Ares—superhuman ability, master combatant, Sentry—chemically-enhanced superhuman ability; Captain Marvel (Noh-Varr)—superhuman ability; Wolverine (Daken)—mutant with superhuman ability; Hawkeye (Bullseye)—expert marksman; Spider-Man (Venom Mac Gargan)—wears black symbiote costume replicating Spider-Man's abilities; Hawkeye (Trickshot)—expert marksman; Scarlet Witch (Toxic Doxie)—genius intellect, genetically enhanced physiology; Spider-Man (Decapitator)—superhuman ability, four sets of limbs; Thor (Ragnarok)—superhuman strength, durability; Hulk (Skaar)—immense strength; Ms. Marvel (Superia)—genius intellect, superhuman ability; Wolverine (Gorgon)—mutant with genius intellect, superhuman ability; Luke Cage—superhuman ability; U.S. Agent—military combatant; Victoria Hand—advanced espionage.

DOOM AND GLOOM

The Dark Avengers were forced to do more than mug for the cameras when they went to the aid of Norman Osborn's associate, the nefarious Dr. Doom.

Dr. Doom's magical expertise helped him deal with Morgana's attack, with a little help from Iron Patriot.

DARK ASSEMBLY

Dark Avengers #1-4 (March 2009 - June 2009)

While Norman Osborn presented a heroic face in public, in private he was working with the Cabal, a group of powerful underworld figures. One of the members of that team was Super Villain Victor von Doom. When Doom returned to his home of Latveria only to be attacked by Morgan le Fay, Osborn was forced to fly his team of Dark Avengers to Latveria to come to Doom's aid. In what could have been a public relations nightmare for the new team, Osborn nevertheless stopped Morgana's attack when he and Doom managed to banish her to the year 1,000,000 B.C.E.

TEAM INCARNATIONS

While the Dark Avengers began with Norman Osborn, their legacy would last longer than the career of the Iron Patriot.

THE ORIGINALS
The first Dark Avengers included Moonstone as Ms. Marvel, Daken as Wolverine, and Venom as Spider-Man.

TAKE TWO
After escaping jail, Osborn organized a new team with Toxic Doxie as the Scarlet Witch and Ragnarok as Thor.

THIRD TIME'S A CHARM
With Osborn back in jail, Luke Cage briefly led the Dark Avengers, utilizing the recruits as a force for good.

As a S.H.I.E.L.D. operative, Victoria Hand had never failed to advocate a hard-line approach to foes. Norman Osborn recognized this by making her deputy director of H.A.M.M.E.R.

OSBORN'S SIEGE OF ASGARD

The Iron Patriot's reign neared its end when he overstepped his bounds by attacking the mystical land of Asgard.

Osborn's call to arms included a military strike backed by the able might of his entire Dark Avengers team.

Norman Osborn had let his power get to his head, and had gradually become less careful when balancing his criminal agenda with his duties as the head of H.A.M.M.E.R. When the home of the Norse Gods, Asgard, was relocated to Earth, Osborn viewed this floating metropolis as a threat.

He plotted with his ally Loki to cause an incident that would give H.A.M.M.E.R. just cause to invade the mystical land. Osborn then had his Dark Avengers invade Asgard in an unsanctioned attack, meeting resistance from both the gods and the Super Hero community alike. The Avengers, the Young Avengers, and the Secret Warriors sped to the aid of the Asgardians, but they were unable to save Asgard itself, which was destroyed by the Sentry. Osborn's actions ultimately led to his defeat at the hands of Captain America, and the revelation of his evil intentions. Steve Rogers took over control of Osborn's operations, and the real Avengers once again took their rightful place in the public eye.

Not too happy to see their names dragged through the proverbial mud, the true Avengers jumped at the chance to put Osborn's corrupt team in their place.

MASTERS OF EVIL

ORIGINALLY FORMED by an old foe of Captain America's—Baron Zemo—the Masters of Evil was an ever-changing roster of the worst villains the universe had to offer.

FOUNDER: BARON ZEMO

The Masters of Evil was the first Super Villain team the Avengers ever faced. Each member had a score to settle with one of the Avengers, and helped begin a group that would be a thorn in the Avengers' sides for years to come.

Decades ago, when Baron Zemo caused the wreck that "killed" Bucky Barnes and Captain America, he thought he was rid of the heroic duo forever. When Captain America was found floating in a block of ice by the Avengers and resuscitated, Zemo was furious and immediately began plotting the Avengers' downfall. Employing a former foe of Hank Pym known as the Black Knight, an enemy of Iron Man called the Melter, and a villain named Radioactive Man who had tussled with Thor in the past, Zemo united his Masters of Evil. The Masters caused chaos in New York City by spraying a powerful adhesive everywhere, trapping Cap and Pym. The Avengers found a solution to rescue them, with the help of the jailed villain Paste-Pot Pete. The Masters were defeated by the Avengers for the moment, but the villains would return on many future occasions with increasingly sophisticated plots.

When the mighty Avengers met Zemo and his Masters of Evil, they recognized many old enemies.

DATA FILE

TEAM NAME Masters of Evil

FIRST AVENGERS APPEARANCE *Avengers* #6 (July 1964)

MEMBERS Baron Zemo; Black Knight II; Radioactive Man; the Melter; Enchantress; Executioner; Wonder Man; Ultron; Klaw; Whirlwind; Egghead; Moonstone; Tiger Shark; Scorpion; Beetle; Shocker; Baron Helmut Zemo; Absorbing Man; Titania; Blackout; Fixer; Goliath; Grey Gargoyle; Mr. Hyde; Screaming Mimi; Wrecker; Bulldozer; Piledriver; Thunderball; Yellowjacket (Rita DeMara); Dr. Octopus; Gargantua; Jackhammer; Oddball; Powderkeg; Puff Adder; Crimson Cowl; Aqueduct; Bison; Blackwing; Boomerang; Cardinal; Constrictor; Cyclone III; Dragonfly; Eel II; Flying Tiger; Icemaster; Joystick; Lodestone; Man-Ape; Man-Killer; Quicksand; Scorcher; Shatterfist; Shockwave; Slyde; Sunstroke; Supercharger; Black Mamba; Gypsy Moth; Hydro-Man; Machinesmith; Max Fury; Bi-Beast; Black Talon; Brothers Grimm; Carrion III; Crossfire; Damion Hellstrom; Diablo; Firebrand III; Griffin; Killer Shrike; Lady Stilt-Man; Lascivious; Letha; Madame Masque; Madcap; Pink Pearl; Princess Python II; Ringer II; Scarecrow; Squid; Taskmaster; Vengeance (Kowalski); Vector; Vapor; Ironclad; X-Ray; Whiplash (Anton Vanko); Lightmaster.

THE MASTERS TRIUMPHANT

In one of the Masters of Evil's greatest hours—the siege at Avengers Mansion—the Super Villains used every advantage they could find to take over the heroes' headquarters.

UNDER SIEGE

Avengers #270–277 (August 1986 - February 1987)

Wanting to prove himself an even bigger threat than his father before him, Baron Helmut Zemo organized the largest line up of the Masters of Evil up to that point. After stacking the odds in his favor by enlisting an impressive roster, Zemo utilized the direct approach and simply stormed the Avengers Mansion. He and his crew seized the Mansion, briefly holding Captain America and the Black Knight captive, but were ultimately defeated when the Avengers rallied and took out them out one by one.

For a brief moment, Baron Zemo's Masters of Evil had indeed won the day.

MASTERS OF DISGUISE

Baron Zemo's planned to play the long game in one particular attempt for power. He gathered a new Masters of Evil team, who would trick the entire world into believing that they were really heroes.

The world thought the Avengers were dead, but in fact they had been transported to a pocket dimension during a battle with an entity named Onslaught. While they would later return to Earth, in the meantime, the world needed heroes. So when a new team called the Thunderbolts appeared, the public welcomed their apparent saviors.

However, the team was in fact the Masters of Evil in disguise. Baron Zemo called himself Citizen V, Goliath disguised himself as Atlas, the Beetle wore the guise of Mach-1, Screaming Mimi was named Songbird, Moonstone was called Meteorite, and the Fixer took the codename Techno. They carried out a number of heroic missions, and the deception became so successful that even some of the Super Villains began to rethink their evil ways. The addition of Jolt—a new member unaware of the team's original motives—further altered the group's dynamic. When the Avengers returned to Earth, Zemo revealed the Thunderbolts' true nature, only to be turned upon by his own team.

Zemo's plan was for the Thunderbolts to worm their way past society's defenses.

TEAM INCARNATIONS

The Masters of Evil has never been short of villains with a grudge against the Avengers. Each incarnation was hopeful of defeating their foes once and for all.

THE ORIGINALS
Baron Zemo's Masters of Evil had three other members: Radioactive Man, the Melter, and the Black Knight.

REDUX
The second incarnation saw Enchantress and Executioner sign up, followed later by Wonder Man.

UNITED BY ULTRON
Thanks to Ultron-5, the Masters returned with some veterans, plus new members Whirlwind and Klaw.

EGGHEAD'S ELITE
Egghead formed his own Masters of Evil comprising Tiger Shark, Moonstone, Scorpion, and Whirlwind.

NEW ZEMO, NEW TEAM
The Wrecking Crew and Blackout joined Baron Helmut Zemo as he sought to avenge his father.

DOC OCK'S TEAM
Dr. Octopus led a new Masters of Evil team in order to steal the Avengers' advanced technology.

THE THUNDERBOLTS
Zemo hid his Masters of Evil in plain sight when the team masqueraded as heroes named the Thunderbolts.

CRIMSON COWL'S MASTERS
When the Crimson Cowl's Masters of Evil debuted they were confronted by Zemo's team the Thunderbolts.

THE MASTERS' SECRET
A synthetic Nick Fury named Max Fury formed his own Masters of Evil, including Taskmaster and Vengeance.

MASTERS OF LIGHT
A foe of Spider-Man, Lightmaster, set a group of Masters of Evil against fellow foe Dr. Octopus.

SQUADRON SUPREME

ON A FAMILIAR world, far from the universe inhabited by the Avengers, a team of Super Heroes named the Squadron Supreme helped guide their planet as they saw fit. The Squadron worked hard to protect their home from evil, danger, and corruption.

When satisfied that the Squadron were truly heroes, the Avengers joined them to defeat Brain-Child—the first joint mission of many for the two teams.

THE STORY OF THE SQUADRON SUPREME

With Hyperion, Nighthawk, Dr. Spectrum and Power Princess at the helm, the Squadron Supreme served in the parallel reality of Earth-712, also known as Earth-S.

When Avengers including Goliath (Clint Barton), Quicksilver, the Scarlet Witch, and the Vision were accidentally sent to an alternate dimension, they encountered the Squadron Supreme. Mistaking these heroes for the near-identical group of villains on their own Earth (Earth-616) named the Squadron Sinister, the Avengers fought the Squadron before learning of the team's heroic nature. They then teamed up with them to battle against the Brain-Child.

Shape uses his shape-shifting ability to elongate, stretch, and enlarge different parts of his body at will.

Dr. Spectrum's multi-colored suit reflects his ability to produce colored lights.

Hyperion, together with Power Princess and Nighthawk, founded the Squadron Supreme.

DATA FILE

TEAM NAME Squadron Supreme

FIRST APPEARANCE *Avengers* #85 (February 1971)

MEMBERS AND THEIR ABILITIES Hyperion—superhuman intellect; Dr. Spectrum—holds power prism; Nighthawk (Kyle Richmond)—nocturnal superhuman abilities; Power Princess—superhuman abilities; Amphibian—breathes underwater; Lady Lark—sonic powers; Whizzer—hyper speed; Tom Thumb—science genius; Blue Eagle—winged suit; Golden Archer—expert bowman; Nuke—transforms nuclear energy; Arcanna/Moonglow—sorceress; Ape-X—super intellect; Lamprey—absorbs energy; Shape—shape-shifter; Dr. Decibel—surgeon; Quagmire—emits Darkforce; Foxfire—transmits bioluminescent energy; Haywire—emits tanglewire; Redstone—superhuman abilities; Inertia—controls kinetic energy; Skymax—shape-shifter; Nighthawk (Neal Richmond)—extensive combat skills and weapons knowledge.

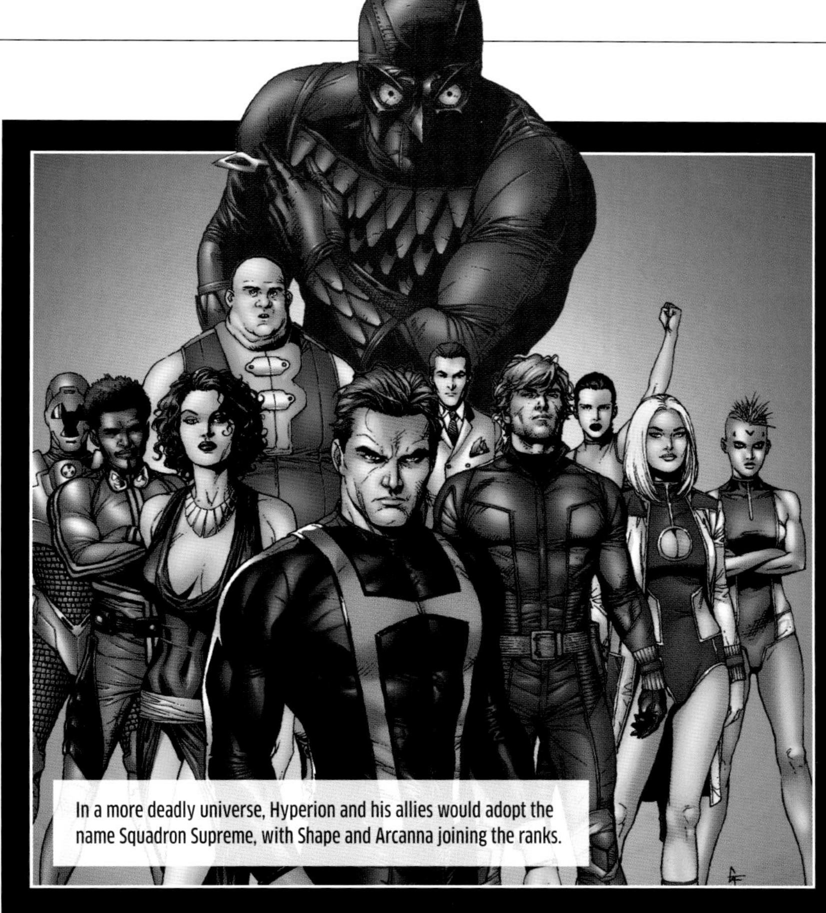

In a more deadly universe, Hyperion and his allies would adopt the name Squadron Supreme, with Shape and Arcanna joining the ranks.

SUPREME **POWER**

On yet another alternate world called Earth-31916, a grittier and more violent incarnation of the Squadron Supreme emerged.

On this world, when the young Eternal Hyperion's crashed rocketship was found, he was not adopted by human parents as happened in other dimensions, but taken away by the government to be raised in a controlled environment. He would later rebel against his "caretakers," and become a darker and more jaded version of Hyperion.

Meanwhile, Corporal Joe Ledger's hand was merged with an energy source in Hyperion's rocket, giving him powers and causing him to adopt the name of Dr. Spectrum; an extremely violent vigilante calling himself Nighthawk had began fighting crime; and a young super-speedster called the Blur became a popular public figure. Joined by the female Amphibian, whose mother had witnessed the descent of Hyperion's original rocket all those years ago, and Zarda, a wondrous woman almost as mighty as Hyperion himself, the group soon formed a squadron possessing almost supreme power.

TROUBLE IN DOUBLE **DIMENSIONS!**

Thor would have to contend with two Hyperions when the hero from the Squadron Supreme clashed with the villain from the almost-identical group from Earth-616 calling itself the Squadron Sinister.

CRISIS ON TWIN EARTHS

The Mighty Thor #280 (February 1979)

Traveling to Earth-616 via a portal, Hyperion of the Squadron Supreme sought out the Avengers with the hope of using them in a film about his life. However, by chance, the Hyperion of the Squadron Sinister was nearby at the time and leapt through the portal into the heroic Hyperion's "Other-Earth." With no luck recruiting the Avengers to his cause, Hyperion returned to his dimension with Thor, only to be ambushed by the evil Hyperion, forcing Thor and the Squadron Supreme to work together to bring the evil Hyperion to justice.

Before fighting the Squadron Sinister's Hyperion, Thor also clashed with the heroic Hyperion from the Squadron Supreme, who was a bit hot tempered and eager to show off his might.

TEAM INCARNATIONS

There have been many incarnations of the Squadron Supreme over the years, from noble heroes to corporate pawns. The team continually expanded, adding ever-familiar crime-fighting characters to its roster.

EARLY TEAM
Hyperion, Dr. Spectrum, Nighthawk, Lady Lark, and the Golden Archer were formative team members.

CLASSIC ROSTER
When the team began to take a proactive role in their world, characters like Nuke and Arcanna joined.

SQUADRON RETURNS
After the events dubbed "Heroes Return," Haywire and Moonglow were again among the team's ranks.

S.H.I.E.L.D.

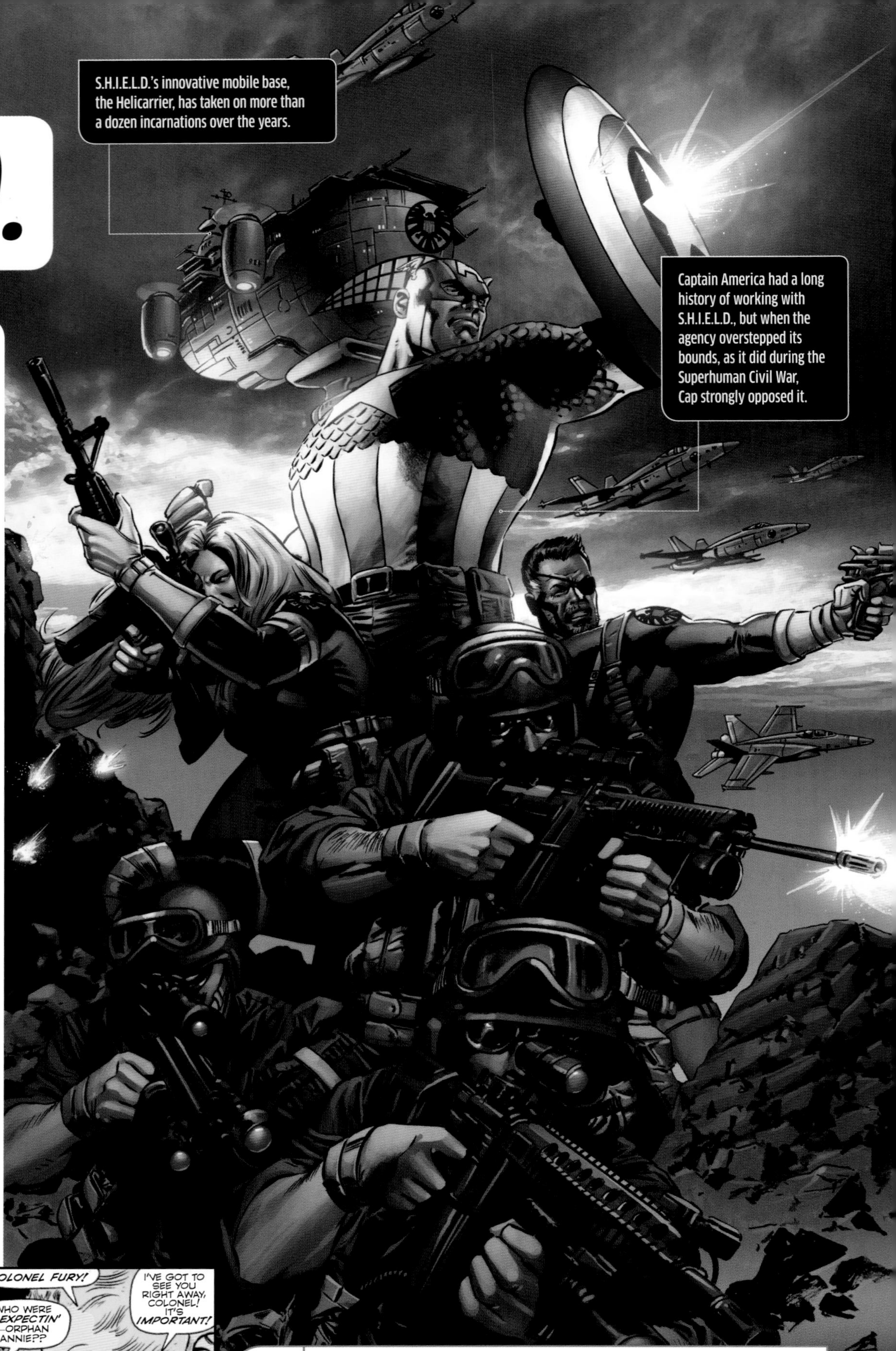

S.H.I.E.L.D.'s innovative mobile base, the Helicarrier, has taken on more than a dozen incarnations over the years.

Captain America had a long history of working with S.H.I.E.L.D., but when the agency overstepped its bounds, as it did during the Superhuman Civil War, Cap strongly opposed it.

IN A WORLD as dangerous as the one inhabited by the Avengers, a peacekeeping force needs to be ready for anything. S.H.I.E.L.D. is that agency. It has protected Earth and beyond from threats such as Hydra and A.I.M., as well as from despotic Super Villains and mutants.

WHAT'S IN A **NAME?**

As times have changed, so has S.H.I.E.L.D.'s famous acronym. Originally the Supreme Headquarters International Espionage Law-Enforcement Division, its moniker has been through many permutations on its way to the current name: Strategic Homeland Intervention, Enforcement, and Logistics Division.

Although in many minds S.H.I.E.L.D. is intrinsically tied to longtime Director Colonel Nick Fury, it was actually formed without his knowledge by an individual whose identity is still classified. But when Fury was brought in to serve as the organization's Director after his predecessor's assassination, Nick's dreams were realized. He was just the man to lead this super spy agency, especially against the nefarious forces of the terrorist organization, Hydra. Armed with a flying Helicarrier, as well as dozens of Life Model Decoys (LMDs) to serve as realistic doubles of himself, Fury truly unlocked S.H.I.E.L.D.'s full potential as a protective force.

Nick Fury first met Captain America during World War II, and teamed with him many times after the creation of the Avengers

DATA FILE

TEAM NAME S.H.I.E.L.D.

FIRST AVENGERS APPEARANCE *Avengers* #19 (August 1965)

MEMBERS AND THEIR ABILITIES Thousands of agents spread across the globe, including: Commander Abigail Brand—flame generation; Black Widow—superhuman ability; Diamondback—Olympic-level gymnast; Dum-Dum Dugan—expert combatant; Druid—monster DNA gives magical powers; Human Torch—emits heat energy; Spider-Woman—spider-like ability; Invisible Woman—invisibility, force field generation; Jemma Simmons—biologist; Phil Coulson—expert in espionage; Captain Marvel—superhuman ability; Hawkeye—master archer; Maria Hill—expert in espionage.

TEAM DIRECTORS

S.H.I.E.L.D. employs thousands of agents, and they all fall under the command of the Director.

NICK FURY
The longest-serving Director, Nick Fury knew the ins and outs of the spy game better than any agent alive.

MARIA HILL
As Fury's successor, no-nonsense Maria Hill tried to make up for Fury's mistakes during his "Secret War."

IRON MAN
As leader, Tony Stark started the Fifty-State Initiative and created his own red and gold Helicarrier.

STEVE ROGERS
Rogers took his role as Director very seriously, considering it part of his patriotic duty.

NORMAN OSBORN
Under Osborn's corrupt leadership, S.H.I.E.L.D. morphed into the nefarious H.A.M.M.E.R.

QUAKE
Appointed by Steve Rogers, Daisy Johnson served as Director before Maria Hill reclaimed the title.

SAVING THE **WORLD**

The Avengers and S.H.I.E.L.D. have shared a close working relationship more often than not, due to the fact that both organizations have Earth's safety as their main interest.

THE SECRET WAR

Secret War #1-5 (April 2004 - December 2005)

With near absolute power over S.H.I.E.L.D. forces and a gritty determination to succeed, it was only a matter of time before Nick Fury overstepped his bounds, even if it was for a noble cause. When he discovered that the country of Latveria was supplying Super Villains with advanced weaponry, Fury launched a Super Hero strike force to intercede, even though he did not have the authority to do so. When a huge group of Super Villains struck back at New York City, Fury's "Secret War" was discovered, and he was removed from his position.

Fury knew his "Secret War" could possibly cost him his job, but he couldn't allow Latveria's actions to go without a proper response.

S.W.O.R.D.'s headquarters were in a space station called the Peak, and run by Special Agent Abigail Brand.

S.W.O.R.D.

Secret Invasion #1 (June 2008)

One of S.H.I.E.L.D.'s recent factions was called S.W.O.R.D., the Sentient World Observation and Response Department. Tasked with keeping the planet safe from alien threats, S.W.O.R.D. was hit hardest during the invasion by the Skrulls. Some of the Avengers were initially wary of S.W.O.R.D.'s boss, Abigail Brand, due to her muddied history at S.H.I.E.L.D. But when Avenger and S.W.O.R.D. member Beast vouched for Brand, the two teams found a way to work together, and confront the threat.

THE **HELICARRIER**

Whilst operational, S.H.I.E.L.D.'s most impressive piece of technology also served as its roving home base, evolving in response to the threat being faced.

Designed by the genius of Tony Stark, S.H.I.E.L.D.'s Helicarrier had always been an essential part of the organization's operations, offering secure and mobile headquarters for Nick Fury to battle the forces of Hydra and other terrorist sects. Outfitted with sophisticated weaponry and communication technology, the huge Helicarrier also housed living quarters and holding cells. Designed to stay aloft for most of its lifespan, the Helicarrier could be accessed by various aircraft, including Fury's flying car.

H.A.M.M.E.R.

Norman Osborn's corrupt version of S.H.I.E.L.D. bears an appropriately brutal name.

Norman Osborn, the former Green Goblin, had tricked America into believing that he was one of the good guys. After killing the Skrulls' queen during their invasion of Earth, Osborn had become a national hero. Osborn was put in charge of S.H.I.E.L.D.'s assets, and changed its name to H.A.M.M.E.R. Deputy director Victoria Hand was charged with developing an actual name to fit the theatrical acronym, but if she did, it has remained classified information. Using his influence to create his own Dark Avengers and corrupt the entire government, Osborn was finally ousted and imprisoned when his true colors began to show. He would later escape and form a new incarnation of H.A.M.M.E.R, uniting Hydra and A.I.M. agents to his cause.

Osborn led H.A.M.M.E.R. as the Iron Patriot.

DATA FILE

TEAM NAME H.A.M.M.E.R.

FIRST AVENGERS APPEARANCE *Secret Invasion* #8 (January 2009)

MEMBERS AND THEIR ABILITIES

Director Norman Osborn (Iron Patriot)—genius intellect, skilled combatant.

Agents Thousands of agents spread across the globe, including: Victoria Hand—expert in espionage, master tactician; Sentry—invulnerability, superhuman ability; Ares—immortal warrior, superhuman powers; Headsman—wears strength-enhancing power-pack; Ghost—electronics and computers genius; Superia—genius intellect, superhuman ability; the Gorgon —genius mutant, superhuman ability.

HYDRA

Hydra is a terrorist organization that has proven itself an enduring foil for S.H.I.E.L.D.

The main reason S.H.I.E.L.D. was created was to combat the terrorist efforts of the equally clandestine organization known as Hydra. Although suspected to have originated millennia ago, Hydra reemerged in earnest in connection with Nazi forces during World War II. Hydra's aim was to gain world domination through subversive and violent means. With its menacing motto of "cut off a limb and two more shall take its place," Hydra has been a constant threat to the safety of the world ever since. At one point, Hydra merged with H.A.M.M.E.R. loyalists and A.I.M. terrorists under Norman Osborn's leadership. But when Osborn was defeated by the Avengers, Hydra's longtime leader, Madame Hydra aka Venom, stepped back up to reclaim her rightful role as the organization's head.

Distinctive Hydra logo is an octopus with a skull head.

Viper is skilled in many forms of weaponry, including whips, guns, and knives.

A squad of Hydra agents in their traditional green uniforms follow Viper.

DATA FILE

TEAM NAME
Hydra

FIRST AVENGERS APPEARANCE
Avengers #19 (August 1965)

MEMBERS AND THEIR ABILITIES
Thousands of agents spread across the globe, including: Viper—extensive knowledge of venoms, toxins, and poisons; Dreadnought—robot with advanced weaponry; Horst Eisel—vest enables superhuman-strength; Doctor Locke—medical expert; Hydra Four (including: Bowman—expert archer; Tactical Force—powerful armor; Hammer—carries mighty hammer; Militant—carries indestructible shield).

SQUADRON SINISTER

The Squadron Sinister is the power equivalent of the Squadron Supreme, but without a moral compass.

When Kang and the Grandmaster decided to play a game of sorts, the Avengers were trapped in the middle as unwilling pawns. With the Avengers forced to represent Kang, the Grandmaster gathered four individuals to serve as his own players, molding them into his own corrupted version of Super Heroes. He based the mock heroes on a team called the Squadron Supreme who existed in a parallel universe. He pit his Squadron Sinister against the Avengers, only to see the Avengers triumph. The Squadron Sinister later returned to battle the Defenders, although their member Nighthawk abandoned his own team to join the Defenders' heroic effort.

DATA FILE

TEAM NAME Squadron Sinister

FIRST AVENGERS APPEARANCE *Avengers* #69 (October 1969)

MEMBERS AND THEIR ABILITIES Hyperion (Zhib-Ran)—an eternal with cosmic energy, superhuman ability; Doctor Spectrum (Kenji Obatu)—host of power prism, energy manipulation; Nighthawk (Kyle Richmond)—nocturnal superhuman ability; Whizzer (James Sanders)—superhuman ability, incredible speed; Doctor Spectrum (Alice Nugent)—host of power prism, energy manipulation.

ILLUMINATI

The aim of this secret society, formed of many influential minds, is to protect all mankind.

The week after the Kree/Skrull War, Iron Man called a meeting in Wakanda with Dr. Strange, Professor X, Mr. Fantastic, Black Bolt, Namor, and Black Panther. While Iron Man wanted to form a large team, uniting the Avengers, X-Men, Fantastic Four, and more, the rest of the group thought that concept was too big. Instead, they settled on the idea of meeting privately as the Illuminati in order to build transparency among their groups. Black Panther refused the initial invitation to participate, believing the Illuminati to be rather elitist, but would later join them. The group have attempted to find solutions for issues from the Infinity Gems to the problem of the Hulk recently destroying Las Vegas!

DATA FILE

TEAM NAME
Illuminati

FIRST AVENGERS APPEARANCE
New Avengers #7 (July 2005)

MEMBERS AND THEIR ABILITIES
Iron Man—genius businessman, wears iron armor; Professor X—mutant with telepathic powers; Black Bolt—inhuman with devastating voice, superhuman powers; Mr. Fantastic—body shape change; Dr. Strange—knowledge of sorcery; Namor—mutant who can survive under water; Medusa—superstrong hair used as weapon; Captain America—expert combatant; Black Panther—immense athleticism; Beast—genius mutant scientist, superhuman strength; Captain Britain—interdimensional travel, superhuman ability; Amadeus Cho—genius with computer-like mind; Hulk—superhuman strength; Yellowjacket (Hank Pym)—science genius with size reduction abilties.

The Illuminati featured the most respected figures in the universe including (clockwise from top): Mr. Fantastic, Dr. Strange, Black Bolt, Namor, Iron Man, and Professor X.

SONS OF THE SERPENT

The Sons of the Serpent were a hate group—snakes in the grass who repeatedly struck at the Avengers.

The Avengers first learned of this racist group when Black Widow witnessed one of their rallies. Vowing to rid America of all they saw as foreigners, the Sons of the Serpent hid their identities and obeyed their ranting leader, the Supreme Serpent. Not herself an Avenger at the time, Black Widow asked Hawkeye and the rest of the team to help her destroy the Sons. While the Avengers brought down the original incarnation, the group would rear its ugly head several more times.

The Sons cloaked their faces to avoid prosecution for their racist actions.

DATA FILE

TEAM NAME Sons of the Serpent

FIRST AVENGERS APPEARANCE *Avengers* #32 (September 1966)

MEMBERS AND THEIR ABILITIES Hundreds of clandestine agents, including: General Chen—leader; Animus (Hate-Monger)—emotional Jean Claude Pennysworth—stave used for firing energy bolts; Montague Hale; Dan Dunn; Simmons.

SHADOW COUNCIL

This organization works in the darkness, serving an otherwordly force with mysterious motives.

In 1865, a Confederate soldier named Aloysius Thorndrake discovered the existence of a dark entity called the Abyss. Deciding to serve this power, Thorndrake created the Shadow Council. This secret organization would later recruit a synthetic clone of Nick Fury, named Max Fury, to its cause. When the Shadow Council was noticed by Steve Rogers, the Shadow Council became the main adversary of the Secret Avengers.

Nick Fury's evil double, Max was like Nick only in appearance.

DATA FILE

TEAM NAME Shadow Council

FIRST AVENGERS APPEARANCE *Secret Avengers* #1 (July 2010)

MEMBERS AND THEIR ABILITIES Hundreds, if not thousands of agents spread across the globe and beyond, including: John Steele—American soldier with superhuman ability; Arnim Zola 4.2.3.—human mind in robot body, genius intellect.

LEGION OF THE UNLIVING

When the threats of the past returned once again, they formed the eerie Legion of the Unliving.

First brought back to life by Immortus (at the time, an unwitting pawn of Kang), the Legion of the Unliving was a macabre assemblage of famous faces plucked from various eras of the time stream. Forced to do Kang's bidding, this original team battled the Avengers in a mysterious ancient castle.

The Grandmaster would later assemble another version of the Legion of the Unliving by manipulating the power of Death herself. Later, Immortus would once again summon the departed to face the West Coast Avengers, a feat mimicked a few more times by the Avengers' villain, Grim Reaper.

The original Human Torch, Jim Hammond

Fiction turned reality, Frankenstein's monster

DATA FILE

TEAM NAME
Legion of the Unliving

FIRST AVENGERS APPEARANCE
Avengers #131 (January 1975)

MEMBERS AND THEIR ABILITIES
Frankenstein's monster—superhuman strength; Wonder Man—ionic powers; Baron Heinrich Zemo—science genius; Midnight—martial artist; the Ghost (Flying Dutchman)—metal claws, eyepatch fires blasts; Baron Blood—vampire; Green Goblin (Barton Hamilton)—pyschotherapist; Red Guardian—pilot, athlete; Terrax the Tamer—mutant; Black Knight II—science genius; Grim Reaper—magic powers; Iron Man 2020—technological genius;
Left Winger and Right Winger—soldiers with superhuman ability; Toro—creates fiery energy; Amenhotep—ancient vampire; Nebulon—energy manipulation; Necrodamus—sorcerer, Thunderstrike—enchanted hammer; Oort the Living Comet; Dracula; Swordsman; Dr. Druid; Hellcat; Hyperion; Bucky Barnes; Nighthawk; Count Nefaria; Inferno; Mockingbird; Human Torch (Jim Hammond); Captain Mar-Vell; Death Adder; Drax the Destroyer; Star-Stalker; Korvac; Executioner; Black Knight (Sir Percy).

AVENGERS A.I.

Dealing with advanced artificial intelligence requires a specialist team. Who better to combat a digital threat than a team of artificially intelligent heroes, led by none other than the father of A.I. technology, Hank Pym?

In an alternate future timeline, the android Ultron, created by Hank Pym, had conquered the world. In order to defeat him, Pym had been forced to collaborate with his past self, and craft an A.I. that could rapidly replicate itself in order to destroy the Ultron of the future. The world seemed safe from A.I. threats, but not for long.

The urgency with which Pym had created the A.I. program meant he had not had time to instate fail-safes or consider potential risks. So, when Pym's self-replicating A.I. began calling itself Dimitrios and started attacking military intelligence targets, S.H.I.E.L.D. Division Chief Monica Chang called in Pym and together they gathered a team to stop the human-hating android. The team included Pym, the Vision, one of Dr. Doom's Doombots reprogrammed to obey Pym's commands, and Ultron's "son," Victor Mancha. They were soon joined by a mysterious A.I. named Alexis with no access to her memory storage.

Together Avengers A.I. worked to stop Dimitrios destroying all organic life, despite many personal obstacles. Victor was seemingly killed, Pym had to deal with his guilt and grief, and the Vision was forced to choose between the Avengers and an A.I. world of which he felt a part.

Dimitrios took great pleasure in stealing one of Tony Stark's Iron Man suits to use as a physical form, believing Stark to be a tyrant working to enslave technology.

Monica Chang serves as the team's S.H.I.E.L.D. liaison.

Ultron's creator, Henry Pym

Victor Mancha wields electromagnetic energy.

The Vision upgrades before joining the team.

Doombot still states his intent for world domination, but under Pym's control he uses his strength for good.

Alexis is revealed to be one of the first generation of A.I.s from Pym's program—known as the Protector.

DATA FILE

TEAM NAME Avengers A.I.

FIRST AVENGERS APPEARANCE *Avengers A.I.* #1 (September 2013)

MEMBERS AND THEIR ABILITIES Monica Chang—military expert; Hank Pym—science genius, creator of Ultron; the Vision—android with superhuman ability; Doombot—robot, shoots lightning, jet-pack enables flight; Victor Mancha—cyborg with superhuman intelligence and ability, projects electricity; Jocasta—robot with superhuman intelligence and ability; Alexis (the Protector)—robot, one of the Six, an early A.I. charged with protecting both organic and digital life.

NEW WARRIORS

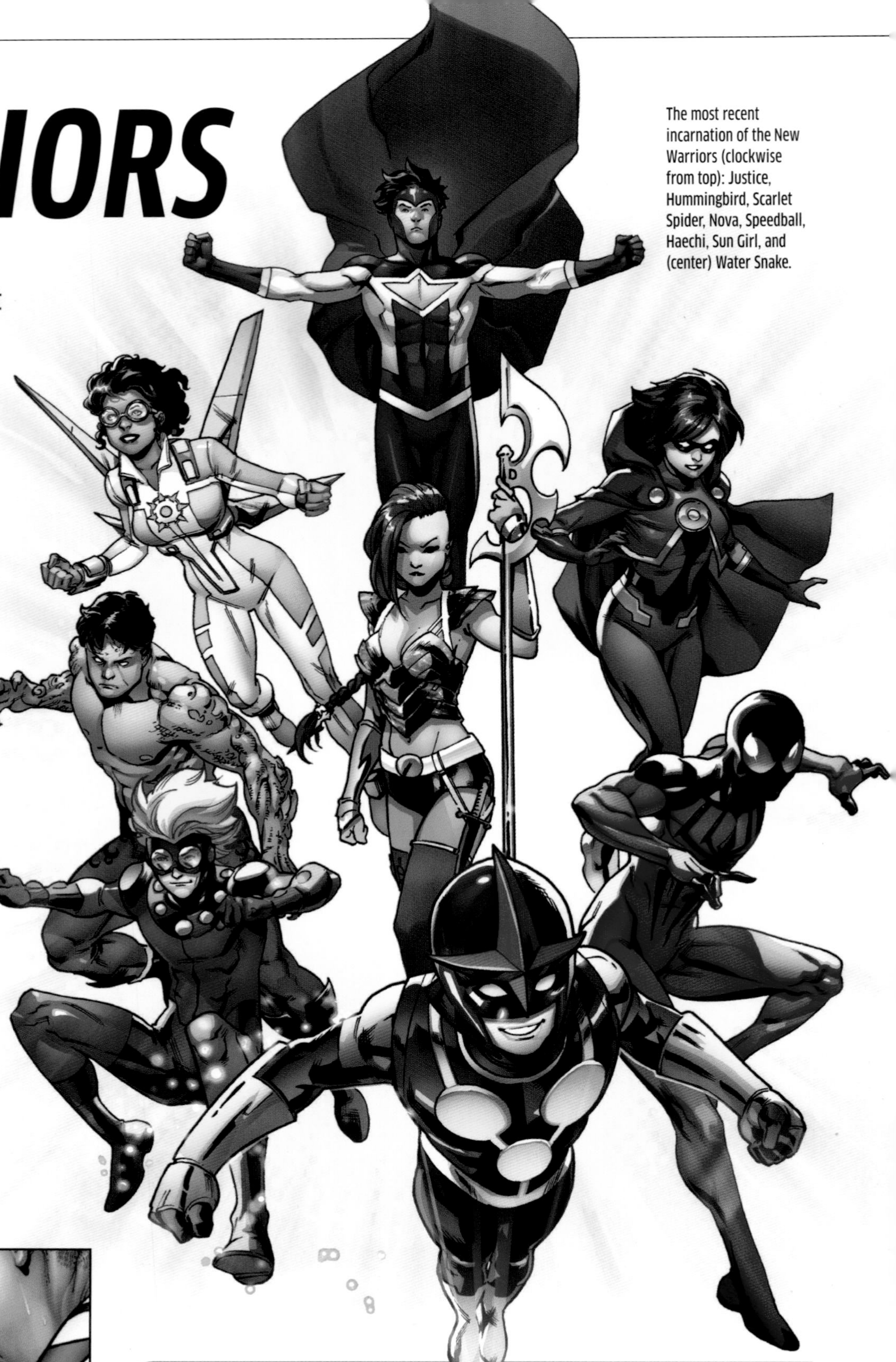

The most recent incarnation of the New Warriors (clockwise from top): Justice, Hummingbird, Scarlet Spider, Nova, Speedball, Haechi, Sun Girl, and (center) Water Snake.

Originally formed as a team of teen heroes, the New Warriors have seen several incarnations, even overcoming their involvement in the accident that prompted the Superhuman Civil War.

Dwayne Taylor was a martial arts expert who was inspired to become a vigilante after witnessing the murder of his parents as a child. Calling himself Night Thrasher, Taylor began gathering together young heroes, including Kid Nova, Firestar, and Marvel Boy to join a team based on the structure of the Fantastic Four. He saw himself as the Reed Richards of the group—in combining intellect and leadership. When Taylor and his new associates found themselves facing the rampaging behemoth Terrax, they joined forces with Speedball and Namorita to end the threat.

After Terrax was seemingly killed, the young heroes were met by the Avengers Captain America, She-Hulk, and Quasar. Influenced by the established team, Night Thrasher decided to unite all the young heroes under the banner of the New Warriors.

The team would undergo several roster changes over the years, even disbanding and reforming several times. At one point, the group took part in a reality TV show, fighting against a Super Villain team including Nitro. When Nitro exploded, hundreds were killed, prompting calls for Super Hero registration, and leading to the Civil War. After fighting alongside Captain America's anti-registration forces during the War, the New Warriors joined the Fifty-State Initiative. The most recent incarnation of the New Warriors formed to face the threat posed by the Evolutionaries.

The New Warriors were often more worried about their TV show ratings than the reality of dangerous situations. So much so that they neglected to prevent an explosion that resulted in the death of civilians.

DATA FILE

TEAM NAME New Warriors

FIRST AVENGERS APPEARANCE *Avengers* #341 (November 1991)

MEMBERS AND THEIR ABILITIES Night Thrasher–martial arts master; Firestar–generates heat; Namorita–amphibious; Nova–energy source; Speedball–kinetic energy; Justice–telekinetic powers; Silhouette–teleporting ability; Rage–superhuman ability; Darkhawk–armor enables flight; Hindsight Lad–expert strategist; Bandit–emits electrical charge; Powerpax–controls gravity; Speedball–kinetic energy; Scarlet Spider (Ben Reilly)–Spider-Man clone; Helix–reactive adaptoid; Slapstick–invulnerability; Ultragirl–mutant/Kree hybrid; Debrii–magnetic; Wondra–power suit; Blackwing (Barnell Bohusk)–power suit, flight; Tempest–suit generates fire and ice; Ripcord–pheromone control; Longstrike–armor, lengthens limbs; Renascence–aerokinesis; Scarlet Spider (Michael Van Patrick)–enhanced physiology; Nova (Sam Alexander)–helmet, cosmic awareness, flight; Scarlet Spider (Kaine)–Spider-Man clone; Haechi–energy absorption; Hummingbird–telepathy, empathy; Phaser; Aegis; Bolt; Microbe; Decibel; Skybolt; Sun Girl; Water Snake, Timeslip; Turbo.

U-FOES

The U-Foes (left to right): Ironclad, Vapor, Vector, and X-Ray.

Originally enemies of the Hulk, the U-Foes have also caused trouble for the whole Avengers team over the years.

A millionaire with a greed for power, Simon Utrecht was inspired by the story of the Fantastic Four, and decided to see if history could repeat itself. Alongside pilot Michael Steel, and sibling specialists Ann Darnell and James Darnell, he traveled via spaceship into the same cosmic ray belt around Earth that gave the Fantastic Four their amazing powers. The four did indeed gain powers, and became the U-Foes, fighting the Hulk many times, before becoming a short-lived addition to the Avenger's Fifty-State Initiative, thanks to the influence of fellow Super Villain, Norman Osborn.

DATA FILE

TEAM NAME
U-Foes

FIRST AVENGERS APPEARANCE
Avengers #304 (June 1989)

MEMBERS AND THEIR ABILITIES

Founder Vector (Simon Utrecht)—powers of telekinesis and the ability to fly

Other Members
Vapor—changes into gas; X-Ray—living energy field; Ironclad—formed of organic metal, superhuman strength.

Soviet Super Soldiers (left to right): Ursa Major, Red Guardian, Crimson Dynamo, and Darkstar.

SOVIET SUPER SOLDIERS

These comrades were the Soviets's answer to American Super Soldiers.

In the superhuman arms race, the Soviet Super Soldiers were created to balance the scales with American teams such as the Avengers and Fantastic Four. Organized by Professor Phobos, the team originally clashed with the Hulk and would later face the Avengers and the X-Men. A similar group would later serve under the name the Winter Guard.

DATA FILE

TEAM NAME Soviet Super Soldiers

FIRST AVENGERS APPEARANCE *The X-Men Vs. The Avengers* #1 (April 1987)

MEMBERS AND THEIR ABILITIES Ursa Major—transforms into bear, superhuman strength; Vanguard—mutant, possesses force field; Darkstar—Darkforce manipulation; Crimson Dynamo—armor gives superhuman strength; Titanium Man—mutant genius, power armor; Blind Faith—hypnotic control; Fantasia—accomplished at magic and illusion; Perun—Russian god, superhuman abilities; Red Guardian—superb athlete, pilot; Sputnik/Vostok—android capable of flight, enhanced strength; Sibercat—mutant with feline-like ability; Stencil—telepathic; Synthesizer—light, electromagnetic, and sonic generation.

YOUNG MASTERS

The Young Masters are the heirs apparent to the notorious Masters of Evil.

When they first appeared on the scene, led by Coat of Arms, the Young Masters claimed the title the Young Avengers. But when the true teen heroes learned of their imitators' exploits and dark backgrounds, they confronted these new vigilantes. They allowed them to try out for their team rather than impersonate it, however, the youngsters decided they'd be better off as masters of their own destiny.

Clockwise from top: Enchantress, Egghead, Executioner, Melter, Big Zero, Coat of Arms.

DATA FILE

TEAM NAME Young Masters, (informally) New Young Avengers

FIRST AVENGERS APPEARANCE *Dark Reign: Young Avengers* #1 (July 2009)

MEMBERS AND THEIR ABILITIES Egghead—android with ability to fly; Executioner—weapons expert; Big Zero—change size, Melter—ability to melt solid matter; Enchantress—magical powers; Coat of Arms—wears coat with two extra pairs of arms, good combatant; Mako—Atlantean with amphibious ability; Radioactive Kid—melts and mutates flesh on contact, wears hazmat suit; Black Knight V—expert swordsman.

SKRULLS

An alien race able to shape-change at will, the Skrulls have proven a dangerous threat to all of humanity, and have menaced nearly every hero on Earth, from the Fantastic Four to the Avengers.

The Skrulls are an ancient people who share common traits with both reptiles and mammals. Millions of years ago, when the Skrulls were still evolving, a race of genetic manipulators called the Celestials landed on their planet, Skrullos. They experimented on the Skrulls, and gifted them with the ability to rapidly mutate, or shape-change. This ability was useful when the Skrulls were locked in a longstanding war with another ancient alien race, the Kree.

The Skrulls's first journey to Earth brought them into conflict with the Fantastic Four. On that occasion, the Skrulls sought to impersonate and incriminate the Fantastic Four in order to have Earthlings hunt down and destroy the team, clearing the way for a Skrull invasion. But thanks to Mr. Fantastic, that plot was quickly foiled and the Skrull leaders left to rethink their methods.

The Avengers first encountered the Skrulls during the Kree/Skrull War, but that conflict would only be the first of many times the Avengers were forced to battle these deceptive aliens. In their biggest takeover attempt, the Skrulls waged a full-scale "Secret Invasion" that saw genetically manipulated Skrulls utilize superpowers. Able to infiltrate nearly every facet of superhuman culture, the Skrulls were nevertheless defeated, and their queen, Veranke, was shot and killed by Norman Osborn.

Captain America was no stranger to battling Skrulls.

Hawkeye's mind was manipulated when a Skrull impersonated his former love, Mockingbird.

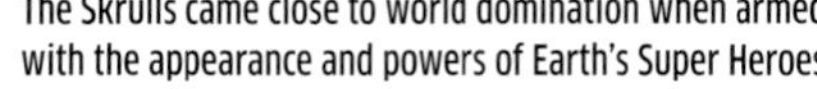

The Skrulls came close to world domination when armed with the appearance and powers of Earth's Super Heroes.

During the Avengers's involvement in the Kree/Skrull War, Captain Marvel was taken captive by the Skrulls.

DATA FILE

TEAM NAME Skrulls

FIRST AVENGERS APPEARANCE *Avengers* #91 (August 1971)

MEMBERS AND THEIR ABILITIES An entire alien race—shape-shift to take on the appearance of host bodies or to create weapons; size and color change; flight; voice, and sound mimicry; undetectable by technological, mental, or other sensory forms of detection. Individuals have the ability to utilize the powers of current host, whereas Queen Veranke has detailed knowledge of Skrull prophecies.

INHUMANS

Close allies of the Avengers, the Inhumans are a genetically altered ancient race.

When the alien race known as the Kree came to Earth 25,000 years ago, their genetic experimentation on the planet's primitive people gave birth to a new race of advanced beings known as the Inhumans. Living isolated from the rest of Earth's people, the Inhumans soon developed and utilized the mutagenic Terrigen Mists that gave their race superpowers. The Avengers first learned of the Inhuman people when they met a member of its royal family, Triton, and helped him locate his missing ruler, Black Bolt. The Inhumans would go on to build a strong association with the Avengers, even allowing one of their own, Crystal, to serve on the team.

Black Bolt was leader of the Inhumans and went on to rule the Kree Empire.

Attilan is the ancestral home of the Inhumans, far more technologically advanced than other cities of its era.

DATA FILE

TEAM NAME
Inhumans

FIRST AVENGERS APPEARANCE
Avengers #90 (July 1971)

MEMBERS AND THEIR ABILITIES
Black Bolt—devastating voice, superhuman abilities; Medusa—super strong hair; Crystal—superhuman abilities, element manipulation; Triton—aquatic physiology; Lockjaw—a giant dog with superhuman strength, teleporting power; Karnak—enhanced strength; Gorgon—superhuman ability; Maximus the Mad—genius intellect, mind control, enhanced strength; recently increased population on Earth—various unidentified powers.

DATA FILE

TEAM NAME
Kree

FIRST AVENGERS APPEARANCE
Avengers #89 (June 1971)

MEMBERS AND THEIR ABILITIES
An entire alien race, with superhuman speed, strength, and stamina, including: Captain Marvel—cosmic awareness, superhuman ability; Ronan the Accuser—genius intellect, cybernetically-enhanced power; Protector (Noh-Varr)—warrior from an alternate universe, with superhuman abilities.

A regular ally of the Avengers, Captain Marvel was a valuable teammate thanks to his intensive Kree military training.

KREE

An ancient alien race, the Kree often head to war with rival space-faring civilizations.

Native to the planet Hala, the Kree began an alien civilization that reached far into the universe, stretching all the way to Earth. The Super Hero community at large didn't discover the existence of the Kree until one of its members, Ronan the Accuser, paid a visit to the Fantastic Four. He was ready to carry out a sentence passed against the Fantastic Four for destroying a Kree outpost, but was ultimately defeated. Later, the Avengers would become allies with Kree ex-patriot Captain Marvel when he approached them during the legendary Kree/Skrull War. And later still, they would induct another former Kree citizen into their ranks as an Avenger: From an alternate universe, Noh-Varr would go on to become known as the Protector.

ASGARDIAN GODS

Thor's family has had a hand in the adventures of the Avengers since that team's formation.

The Avengers originally formed due to the machinations of Thor's half brother, the mischievous Loki. However, this pair of rival siblings are only two of the many gods from Norse mythology that roam the mystical land of Asgard. Chief among the Asgardian Gods is Odin, the realm's regular ruler. His wife, Frigga, normally rules by his side as they protect their land from mystical creatures like Frost Giants, as well as wider cosmic threats. Originally only accessible by the mystical Rainbow Bridge, Asgard was later redubbed Asgardia when the realm and its rulers were relocated to Oklahoma, USA.

DATA FILE

TEAM NAME Asgardian Gods

FIRST AVENGERS APPEARANCE *Avengers* #1 (September 1963)

MEMBERS AND THEIR ABILITIES Odin–king of Asgard, superior superhuman abilities; Thor–God of Thunder, son of Odin, armed with Mjolnir hammer, superhuman ability; Heimdall–Asgardian warrior, avatar projection, superhuman ability; Frigga–wife of Odin, magical ability; Loki–adopted son of Odin, self-proclaimed God of Mischief, superhuman ability; Sif–sister of Heimdall, ability to teleport, superhuman ability; Enchantress–sorcerer, superhuman ability; Karnilla–sorcerer, superhuman ability; Valkyrie–superhuman ability, ability to teleport; Hela–Goddess of Death, astral projection, superhuman ability.

WARRIORS THREE

Thor's loyal companions, the Warriors Three are noble and skilled fighters.

Every hero needs an entourage from time to time, and to Thor, the Warriors Three have been just that. Eccentric characters all, the Warriors Three is made up of Volstagg, Fandral, and Hogun. Recently, when Volstagg was caught in a battle with the U-Foes, Norman Osborn sent an unsanctioned attack directed towards the then Earth-bound Asgard. The battle that ensued was fierce, but with the combined might of the Avengers and the Warriors Three, Osborn was defeated.

Clockwise from top: Volstagg, Fandral, and Hogun.

DATA FILE

TEAM NAME Warriors Three

FIRST AVENGERS APPEARANCE *Avengers* #249 (November 1984)

MEMBERS AND THEIR ABILITIES Hogun the Grim–superhuman ability, excellent horseman; Volstagg the Voluminous–expert combatant, superhuman strength; Fandral the Dashing–skilled swordsman, superhuman ability.

TIME KEEPERS

The custodians of time itself, the Time Keepers' agenda is known to them alone.

Three beings created at the end of the known time cycle, the Time Keepers serve as guardians of the timestream. Intent on preserving their own existence, they charged Immortus with guarding a portion of the timestream and destroying those they believed to be threats. These perceived threats included the Avengers and "nexus beings," such as Scarlet Witch, with the power to alter the timestream. The Avengers have foiled the Time Keepers' attempts to radically control the timestream many times.

The Time Keepers avoid physical combat but can summon energy blasts and shields when needed.

DATA FILE

TEAM NAME Time Keepers

FIRST AVENGERS APPEARANCE *West Coast Avengers* #61 (August 1990)

MEMBERS AND THEIR ABILITIES

Creator the Oracle of Siwa/He Who Remains–last director of the Time Variance Authority.

Members Ast, Vort, Zanth–semi-humanoids with great power to manipulate time and its effect, time travel, force field creation).

SERPENT SOCIETY

A team of snake-themed villains, the Serpent Society has often faced the Avengers.

Inspired by a former team of snake-themed villains called the Serpent Squad, the villain known as the Sidewinder created a criminal organization called the Serpent Society. Not all snake-like villains were keen on the idea, however. In fact, Constrictor rejected Sidewinder's invitation, and informed the Avengers about the Society.

Nevertheless, the Serpent Society survived to continue its criminal deeds, despite regular conflicts with heroes such as Captain America. In the days leading up to the war between the Avengers and X-Men, a mutant named Hope Summers foiled an attempted bank robbery by a number of members.

DATA FILE

TEAM NAME
Serpent Society

FIRST AVENGERS APPEARANCE
Captain America #310 (October 1985)

MEMBERS AND THEIR ABILITIES
Sidewinder–cloak with teleporting powers; Anaconda–bioengineered limb elongation, amphibian physiology; Asp–venom bolts and secretions; Black Mamba–hypnosis, Darkforce manipulation; Bushmaster–quadriplegic with bionic arms, cybernetic tail; Cobra–elasticity, constrictor; Cottonmouth–dislocating bionic jaw; Princess Python–snake dancer; Diamondback–arsenal of diamonds tipped with venom, narcotics, or explosives; Death Adder–bionic tail, amphibious, venomous claws; Black Racer–superhuman speed; Rattler–sonic shockwaves from bionic tail; Bruiser–ability to focus hard punch; Puff Adder–mutant, size change; Rock Python–durable skin, 'snake eggs' release steel strips; Boomslang–strong arm, arsenal of snake -shaped sickles; Coachwhip–skilled use of whips Copperhead–suit of chainmail, grappling hook; Fer-de-Lance–poison-covered talons; Slither–constrictor, superhuman strength; Viper–toxin knowledge; Sidewinder III; Death Adder II.

Many of the villains in the Society have powers related to snake-like physiology, something reflected in their reptilian costumes.

LETHAL LEGION

United by the Grim Reaper, the Lethal Legion is a group of villains with a fierce hatred of the Avengers.

Organized by the Grim Reaper, the Lethal Legion comprised those of his fellow Super Villains who had previously lost battles to the Avengers. Unfortunately, uniting didn't seem to help their cause. The Avengers's first battle with the Legion followed an attempt by Legion member Man-Ape to kidnap the Black Panther. Since that original battle, the Lethal Legion has been reformed many times over, and led by others in addition to the Grim Reaper. Villains such as Count Nefaria, Satannish, and the Porcupine have all taken the helm, only to be beaten by the Avengers on each attempt.

The original Lethal Legion featured Grim Reaper, Man-Ape, Power Man, Swordsman, and Living Laser.

DATA FILE

TEAM NAME
Lethal Legion

FIRST APPEARANCE WITH AVENGERS
Avengers #78 (July 1970)

MEMBERS AND THEIR ABILITIES
Grim Reaper–magic ability; Power Man (Atlas)–superhuman strength and durability; Whirlwind–mutant; Count Nefaria–energy projection, superhuman abilities; Black Talon (Samuel Barone)–voodoo magic; Nekra–voodoo magic; Ultron-12–humanoid robot; Attuma–Atlantean, amphibious; Batroc–accomplished unarmed combatant; Beetle–mechanic, cyber armor; Grey Gargoyle–transmutates into stone; Black Tiger–martial arts expert; Kurr'fri–humanoid lizard; Wonder Man–ionic energy; Sabretooth–unbreakable skeleton; Thundra–chain weapon; Trapster–gun fires adhesive; Unicorn–laser eye; Wrecker–crowbar; Zyklon–ability to fly, advanced strength; Axe of Violence–right hand replaced by double-bladed ax; Coldsteel–body armor; Cyana–poisonous touch; Absorbing Man–duplicates upon touch; Swordsman; Man-Ape; Piledriver; Porcupine; Mr. Hyde; Tiger Shark; Radioactive Man; Gorilla-Man II; Hangman II; Living Laser.

ZODIAC

A criminal organization that included Nick Fury's brother Jake as one of its twelve founding members, the astrologically named Zodiac proved to be a powerful match for the Avengers.

Upon learning that three high-ranking New York officials had disappeared, Captain America called an emergency meeting of the Avengers. During the meeting, the Avengers compared notes with Dum Dum Dugan of S.H.I.E.L.D. and learned that the sign of the villain Scorpio had been discovered in each of the victims' homes. Scorpio was a formidable villain, and one Nick Fury had faced on a few occasions. However, the Avengers wouldn't get the chance to hunt down the villain, as Scorpio soon took over their transceiver, exploding the device. The explosion knocked out the Avengers, and when they finally regained consciousness, they found they had been taken captive by Scorpio.

After Scorpio introduced the Avengers to the rest of the Zodiac—his partners in crime, all named after astrological signs—the heroes managed to escape from their bonds with the help of an army of ants summoned by Yellowjacket (Hank Pym). They soon discovered that Nick Fury had infiltrated Zodiac by masquerading as Scorpio after finding out that the villain was his own brother, Jake. During the ensuing battle, Aries brandished the Zodiac Key, keeping the Avengers at bay.

The Zodiac escaped this first encounter, only to return to plague the Avengers time and time again. Many more incarnations of the Zodiac would rise in the future, including a recent team backed by Titanian Eternal, Thanos.

Armed with the powerful Zodiac Key, Scorpio would have posed a serious threat to the Avengers, had he not been Nick Fury in disguise, attempting to infiltrate his brother's team.

Gemini's two-tone costume reflected his twin-based powers.

Taurus proved to be as bull-headed as his namesake.

Pisces wore an aquatic-themed costume.

DATA FILE

TEAM NAME Zodiac

FIRST AVENGERS APPEARANCE *Avengers* #72 (January 1970)

MEMBERS AND THEIR ABILITIES Aries—horns used for ramming opponents; Scorpio—genius intellect, bearer of Zodiac Key, superhuman strength; Taurus—carried Star Blazer gun, horns used for charging; Pisces—skilled underwater combatant; Leo—claws; Gemini—Joshua Link could mentally control and use his twin brother's mind and body; Capricorn—extendable, controllable horns; Virgo—good combatant; Cancer—prosthetic pincers for gripping; Libra—blind, psychic, martial artist; Sagittarius—professional criminal; Aquarius—later incarnations could blast water and electricity.

THE DEFENDERS

When Dr. Strange recruited the Hulk and Namor to fight the powerful foe Yandroth, the three realized the potential of an occasional alliance. The Defenders were formed, but rejected the idea of being considered a team.

After adding members Silver Surfer and Valkyrie to their regular lineup, the Defenders only had a few missions under their collective belts before they ran up against perhaps their greatest challenge: the Avengers.

Villainous Loki was up to his old tricks again. This time teaming up with Dr. Strange's foe Dormammu, Loki planned to destroy Earth with the use of a fabled weapon called the Evil Eye that could bring the entire planet to Dormammu's dimension. To that end, the pair tricked the Defenders into finding the fragments of the Evil Eye. However, when the trickster god realized that Dormammu would use that power to destroy Asgard as well, Loki informed the Avengers that the Defenders were hunting for the pieces of the Evil Eye for sinister means—thereby pitting the two teams against each other. Fortunately, the heroes discovered the deception and ended the threat. After this rather bumpy start, the Defenders continued on in various incarnations, fighting evil in their own maverick way.

DATA FILE

TEAM NAME The Defenders

FIRST AVENGERS APPEARANCE *Avengers* #116 (December 1977)

NOTABLE MEMBERS Hulk, Namor, Dr. Strange, Clea, Silver Surfer, Valkyrie, Namorita, Hawkeye, Hank Pym, Red Guardian (Tania Belinsky), Ms. Marvel, Spider-Man, Goliath (Bill Foster), Captain Marvel, Falcon, Hercules, Iron Fist, Moondragon, Beast, Captain America, Scarlet Witch, Wolverine, Darkhawk, Spider-Woman II, Punisher, Thunderstrike, War Machine, Dr. Druid, Luke Cage, Deadpool, U.S. Agent, Drax the Destroyer, She-Hulk, Red She-Hulk, Ant-Man II, Nick Fury, Misty Knight, Dr. Annabelle Riggs, Elsa Bloodstone, Ren Kimura, Nova (Frankie Raye), Moonstar, Hellcat, Quasar, Nova, and Hippolyta.

During the so-called Avengers/Defenders War, Iron Man fought Hawkeye, a former Avenger turned Defender.

FEARLESS DEFENDERS

The Defenders name was revived when longtime member Valkyrie came to the rescue of bionic private detective Misty Knight and her archeologist friend Dr. Annabelle Riggs who were under attack by undead Asgardians. Valkyrie soon learned that the chaos was her fault for not assembling a team of heroines to fill the void of the vanished Valkyrior.

Misty Knight was one of eight women chosen to fight beside Valkyrie.

WINTER GUARD

A new team for a new era, the Winter Guard picked up where the Soviet Super Soldiers left off.

As Russia's answer to the Avengers, the Winter Guard had met the American heroes as allies and adversaries alike. It was often difficult to see where the Winter Guard's allegiance rested. While it would aid Iron Man against Mandarin's forces, the team would later impede Iron Man's investigation into the Red Hulk. Tragedy would later strike the Winter Guard when it was tracking down the Avengers' villains known as the Intelligencia in Promyshlennyi, Russia. The team burst into the villains' supposed hideout, only to fall victim to a new weapon called the Zero Cannon. After a blast from the device sent the heroes into space, the members of the Winter Guard were presumed to be dead.

Clockwise from top: Ursa Major, Darkstar, Red Guardian, Crimson Dynamo.

DATA FILE

TEAM NAME
Winter Guard

FIRST AVENGERS APPEARANCE
Iron Man #9 (October 1998)

MEMBERS AND THEIR ABILITIES
Ursa Major–transforms into humanoid bear, superhuman ability; Fantasma–illusionist, ability to fly; Powersurge–radioactive, fires energy blasts, light flashes; Sibercat–mutant with cat-like abilities; Steel Guardian–carries circular shield, good combatant; Vanguard–mutant, force field repels electromagnetic and kinetic energy; Vostok–android capable of flight, enhanced strength; various incarnations of: Red Guardian–superb athlete, pilot; Crimson Dynamo–armor gives superhuman strength; Darkstar–Darkforce manipulation.

AGENTS OF ATLAS

The exploits of this team of adventurers date back decades.

In a battle against the master of time known as Immortus, several members of the Avengers traveled to a temporal imbalance in California in 1959. There, they met another heroic team called the Avengers. Made up of 3-D Man, Gorilla-Man, Human Robot, Venus, and Marvel Boy, the team actually existed in a different timeline. This team would later re-emerge in the present day as the Agents of Atlas.

DATA FILE

TEAM NAME Agents of Atlas

FIRST AVENGERS APPEARANCE *Avengers Forever* #4 (March 1999)

MEMBERS AND THEIR ABILITIES Gorilla-Man–immortal, strength of mountain gorilla, weapons expert; Jimmy Woo–secret agent, head of Atlas Foundation; M-11 (Human Robot)–possesses telescopic limbs, bulletproof frame, projects electric forcefields; the Uranian (Marvel Boy)–wears spacesuit that recreates Uranian atsmosphere, headband enables telepathy; Namora–human/Atlantean physiology, amphibious, superhuman ability; Venus–siren physiology, amphibious, manipulative voice, immortal, strong swimmer, shape-shifter; 3-D Man–enhanced human ability, 1950s NASA flight suit bonded to skin.

INTELLIGENCIA

Representing the best minds evil had to offer, this team wanted world domination.

The Intelligencia are a villainous group intent on gaining knowledge, and through it, power. Led by the aptly named Leader, the group planned to kidnap the world's smartest heroes, including Bruce Banner and Hank Pym. They first battled the Avengers when Spider-Woman found their hideout and they took her captive. While the Avengers rescued their teammate, the Intelligencia accidentally let loose Ultron during the chaotic battle.

DATA FILE

TEAM NAME Intelligencia

FIRST AVENGERS APPEARANCE *Avengers* #12.1 (June 2011)

MEMBERS AND THEIR ABILITIES Leader–enhanced mental powers, high intellect, exceptional memory, weapons knowledge; Mad Thinker–technological genius, analytical and mathematical mind; Red Ghost–science genius, ability to become intangible; Wizard–science genius, illusionist, electrical gauntlets, possesses anti-gravity devices; M.O.D.O.K.–super intelligence, telekinetic powers, generates force fields, uses hoverchair with missiles and lasers; Dr. Doom– polymath, science genius, strong mental powers; armor enables superhuman ability; Egghead–genius intellect, weapons designer.

SECRET WARRIORS

During the Skrulls's "Secret Invasion," Nick Fury formed his own strike force, consisting of a group of unlikely heroes, all with strong familial ties to the world of superhumans.

Nick Fury's Secret Warriors represented a new generation of heroes, including a young boy, all significantly off the grid enough to be overlooked by the invading Skrulls.

When a threat emerges that challenged world security, Nick Fury was always one of the first to know. And despite being ousted from S.H.I.E.L.D. after overstepping his bounds during his "Secret War," Fury still kept his ear to the ground and attempted to keep one step ahead of Earth's enemies.

After encountering a Skrull months before the aliens' total "Secret Invasion," Fury contacted his loyal operative Quake, who began to recruit prospective heroes from Fury's "Caterpillar File." Hoping to turn these novice superpowered individuals into "butterflies," Quake gathered the children and grandchildren of various former heroes. Fury then unleashed his new strike force when the Skrulls invaded Times Square. Often known as "Team White," the group has since fought evil in the form of Hydra, Leviathon, Norman Osborn, and others. It was later discovered that Fury was secretly running multiple teams of operatives.

No stranger to conducting impromptu Super Hero boot camps, Nick Fury was a natural leader and the perfect person to whip an inexperienced group of recruits into shape. The superpowered trainees were about to become part of Fury's Secret Warriors.

DATA FILE

TEAM NAME Secret Warriors

FIRST AVENGERS APPEARANCE *Mighty Avengers* #13 (July 2008)

MEMBERS AND THEIR ABILITIES Nick Fury—military and martial arts expert, delayed ageing; Quake—ability to generate powerful vibrations, expert combatant; Phobos—10-year-old son of Olympic god Ares, ability to cause fear in others, precognition; Hellfire—uses Hellfire chain as weapon; Druid—sorcerer, ability to project force fields and teleport; Slingshot—superhuman speed, transports back to where she started running; Stonewall—superhuman strength and durability, can absorb properties of elements; Manifold—mutant with ability to teleport himself and others.

RUNAWAYS

When a group of teenagers discovered that their parents were secretly a Super Villain team, they became the last thing their parents wanted them to be: a Super Hero team.

Every year, Alex Wilder's parents invited the same five couples over for a party, and every year, Alex was forced to hang out with the children of those couples, even though he knew very little about them. However, on the year that Alex turned sixteen, he and the other kids stumbled upon a discovery that would change their lives forever. They learned that their parents were all part of a Super Villain team called the Pride.

After discovering their parents' dark secret, the teens became the Runaways, using either their superpowers, genius, or their parents' technology for good rather than evil. While on the run, they each adopted a codename, learned to work together, and eventually ended the threat of the Pride. Soon, the Runaways were discovered by Captain America and the Avengers, and their recent ordeal was made public. Rather than be entered into the child welfare system, the young heroes once again decided to live on the run.

During the Superhuman Civil War, the Runaways were helped by the Young Avengers, members of Captain America's rebellion, when the Runaways were targeted by S.H.I.E.L.D. Soon, the two teams also came under attack by a mind-controlled Marvel Boy (Noh-Varr), whom they ultimately overcame.

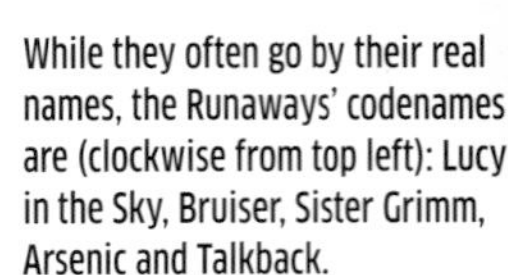

While they often go by their real names, the Runaways' codenames are (clockwise from top left): Lucy in the Sky, Bruiser, Sister Grimm, Arsenic and Talkback.

DATA FILE

TEAM NAME
Runaways

FIRST AVENGERS APPEARANCE
Civil War: Young Avengers & Runaways #1 (September 2006)

MEMBERS AND THEIR ABILITIES
Alex Wilder—gifted intellect, natural leader, strategist; Nico Minoru (Sister Grimm)—magical Staff of One emerges from her chest, lost arm replaced by magical gauntlet; Molly Hayes (Bruiser)—second-generation mutant, superhuman strength, eyes glow pink; Victor Mancha—cyborg, ability to manipulate magnetic fields; Karolina Dean (Lucy in the Sky)—ability to manipulate solar energy, flight; Xavin—shape-shifting Skrull, switches between genders; Gertrude Yorkes (Arsenic)—telepathic and empathetic link to Old Lace, her dinosaur; Old Lace—genetically-engineered deinonychus from 87th century with telepathic and empathetic link to Gertrude and Chase; Chase Stein (Talkback)—telepathic and empathetic link to Old Lace, wore 'fistigons'—weaponized gloves; Klara Prast—mutant, ability to communicate with plants and manipulate their growth; Topher (brief member)—vampire with superhuman ability.

The Runaways and the Young Avengers helped free Marvel Boy from his brainwashing. He would go on to later join the Young Avengers' ranks.

The Runaways and Young Avengers made such a good team, they joined forces again during the events of the Skrulls' "Secret Invasion."

YOUNG AVENGERS

Despite starting out as novice knock-offs of the world's greatest Super Hero team, the Young Avengers soon earned the title they appropriated.

When the Young Avengers first appeared, the Avengers didn't know what to think of this young team created in their image and using their team name. They soon learned that the Young Avengers were actually organized by Iron Lad, a time-traveling young version of Avengers adversary, Kang the Conqueror. While Iron Lad was forced to return to his own time, the Young Avengers remained and became a mainstay on the Super Hero scene, adopting new members as they saw fit. The heroes occasionally teamed up with the Runaways and went on to fight valiantly during the Superhuman Civil War, as well as against new enemies including the Young Masters.

The founding Young Avengers team (from left to right): Iron Lad, Hulkling, Patriot, and Asgardian (Wiccan).

DATA FILE

TEAM NAME Young Avengers
FIRST AVENGERS APPEARANCE *Young Avengers* #1 (April 2005)
MEMBERS AND THEIR ABILITIES Iron Lad–responsive armor, superhuman ability, flight; Patriot–given grandfather's blood containing Super Soldier Serum; Wiccan – manipulates magic force, teleports; Hulkling–Kree/Skrull hybrid, superhuman strength, shape-shifter; Stature–Pym Particles enable size change; Hawkeye (Kate Bishop)–quick reflexes, master archer; Vision–shape-shifter, time travel; Speed –mutant, supersonic speed; Miss America II–flight, superhuman strength; Loki–superhuman ability; Prodigy II–mutant, ability to acquire knowledge; Marvel Boy–Kree, superhuman ability.

YOUNG ALLIES

An informal hero team, the Young Allies have yet to prove the staying power of their namesake.

During World War II, Captain America's sidekick, Bucky Barnes, teamed with El Toro and a few other scrappy youngsters to form the Young Allies and fight serious threats such as Hitler and the Red Skull. Decades later, a Bucky from an alternate reality—a girl calling herself Nomad—united with several likeminded teenagers to create an informal alliance as the new Young Allies. Aided by former Avenger Firestar and other heroes including a new Toro, Spider-Girl, and Gravity, Nomad helped battle a group of young Super Villains, calling themselves the Bastards of Evil. The Young Allies later joined forces with a few members of the Avengers Academy to thwart the latest scheme by the genius Super Villain known as Arcade.

Spider-Girl's grappling hooks help her cling to buildings and can be used as a whip-like weapon.

DATA FILE

TEAM NAME Young Allies
FIRST AVENGERS APPEARANCE *Avengers Academy: Giant-Size* #1 (July 2011)
MEMBERS AND THEIR ABILITIES Spider-Girl (Anya Corazon)–spider-like ability, superhuman strength; Firestar–mutant, generates microwave energy; Gravity–controls own gravity; Nomad (Rebecca "Rikki" Barnes)–trained S.H.I.E.L.D. agent; El Toro–superhuman strength, horns; Toro (Thomas Raymond)–ability to self-ignite, can fly at speeds of 150 mph.

TEEN BRIGADE

Teenager and Hulk sidekick Rick Jones decided to organize a team of superpowered youths into the Teen Brigade, in order to help the world via radio broadcasts.

Just as Rick Jones had unwittingly triggered the Hulk's creation, so too would he help form the Avengers. When Loki framed Hulk as a criminal, Rick Jones sent a monumental radio broadcast to the Fantastic Four that Loki diverted instead to the soon-to-be founders of the Avengers.

DATA FILE

TEAM NAME Teen Brigade

FIRST AVENGERS APPEARANCE *Avengers* #1 (September 1963)

MEMBERS AND THEIR ABILITIES Rick Jones—ability to tap into Destiny Force; physical transformation enables superhuman ability; Angel Salvadore—mutant with insectoid physiology; In-Betweener—power to alter reality on cosmic scale; Miss America II—ability to fly, invulnerable, superhuman strength; Ultimate Nullifier—possesses ray guns; Beak—mutant with avian physiology, ability to fly, long-range sight; other members include: Willie, Ted, Les, Mike Armstrong, Bill Bishop, Tom Smith, Charlie, K.C. Ritter, Specs, Wheels, Rider, Candy Barr, and many unnamed agents.

FORCE WORKS

When the West Coast Avengers disbanded, Iron Man went on to set up Force Works.

Frustrated with the state of the Avengers and how the West Coast team was viewed as an undervalued asset, Tony Stark set up Force Works. This was a more proactive team comprised of former West Coast Avengers and a few new faces, who fought heavy-hitting foes including Iron Man's archenemy, the Mandarin. Their work was fated to be shortlived and they disbanded following leadership issues, but they later restarted as part of the Fifty-State Initiative.

DATA FILE

TEAM NAME Force Works

FIRST AVENGERS APPEARANCE *Avengers: West Coast* #102 (January 1994)

MEMBERS AND THEIR ABILITIES Iron Man—business genius, armor gives superhuman ability; Spider-Woman II—superhuman ability, psionic power used to create webs; Scarlet Witch—sorcerer, taps into mystic energy to alter reality; U.S. Agent—superhuman strength, stamina, agility, endurance; Century—ability to teleport; Moonraker—ability to alter time, skilled combatant; Cybermancer—specially-armored suit can create force fields and weapons; War Machine—former soldier, wears amor similar to Iron Man's; Wonder Man—superhuman ability, invulnerability, ionic powers.

Kitty Pryde's longtime friend Lockheed is a capable hero in his own right.

PET AVENGERS

When certain missions require a less-than-human touch, the Pet Avengers are immediately on the case.

In search of the six fabled Infinity Gems, Mr. Fantastic visited Attilan, the home of the Inhumans. But when the Inhumans' dog Lockjaw discovered the Mind Gem, the telepathic, superpowered pet decided he would locate the remaining powerful jewels himself. Recruiting Speedball's pet cat Hairball, the mutant Kitty Pryde's dragon, Lockheed, Falcon's bird, Redwing, Ka-Zar's sabertooth tiger, Zabu, Aunt May Parker's dog, Ms. Lion, and the amphibian Throg who possessed the power of Thor, Lockjaw formed the Pet Avengers. After securing the Infinity Gems and battling Thanos along the way, the team even had time to befriend the US President's dog, Bo Obama.

DATA FILE

TEAM NAME
Pet Avengers

FIRST AVENGERS APPEARANCE
Lockjaw and the Pet Avengers #1 (July 2009)

MEMBERS AND THEIR ABILITIES
All members are telepathically linked through the power of the Mind Gem. Members include: Lockjaw—dog with ability to read minds and teleport himself and up to twelve others, immense size and weight; Lockheed—dragon with ability to breathe fire and fly; Zabu—Smilodon physiology, cat-like ability, claws and two saber teeth; Redwing—falcon; Ms. Lion—male dog belonging to Spider-Man's aunt; Hairball—ability to create kinetic energy field around himself; Throg—human transformed into frog by gypsy curse, ability to communicate with humans, uses Frogjolnir hammer to give him superhuman ability akin to that of Thor; Bo Obama—final Infinity Gem located on Bo's collar.

A-FORCE

A-Force assemble! On the island nation of Arcadia, a team of female Super Heroes known as A-Force, are charged with protecting their world from a whole host of threats.

With an collection of mutant, Inhuman, and enhanced human superpowers, A-Force pose a fierce threat to their foes.

One of the many Battleworld lands, Arcadia is a dominion led by its many female Super Heroes. At the heart of this society is A-Force, a heroic team dedicated to defending its land against evil forces. Despite its core roster of She-Hulk, Medusa, Dazzler, Captain Marvel, Nico Minoru, and the mysterious newcomer Singularity, A-Force has drawn on the wider Arcadian population on many occasions to fill its ranks. The regal Medusa, the optimistic Dazzler, the emotional Nico, and the fearless Carol Danvers may not have always seen eye to eye. As leader, no-nonsense She-Hulk has struggled at times to ease these tensions, but when situations turn against the heroes, their differences have been put aside in favor of teamwork, and the greater good.

A pocket universe that developed self-consciousness during the Secret Wars, Singularity was so-named by her A-Force teammates. With their guidance, Singularity discovered what it was to be human, to be gendered, and, ultimately, to be a hero.

DATA FILE

TEAM NAME A-Force

FIRST AVENGERS APPEARANCE *A-Force* #1 (May 2015)

MEMBERS AND THEIR ABILITIES She-Hulk–superhuman strength, speed, reflexes, and stamina; Dazzler–ability to transform sound energy into light, creating blinding or disorienting light beams, excellent athlete; Medusa–long red hair with immense strength and elasticity, ability to animate her hair to act as a weapon or tool; Nico Minoru–magical abilities, spellcasting using Staff of One; Captain Marvel–superhuman strength, flight, expert markman, pilot, espionage agent; Singularity–a pocket universe with the ability to travel between worlds and dimensions.

SECRET WARS When two Earths from two separate dimensions faced each other in a fight for survival, it turned hero against hero, Avenger against Avenger. The mighty heroes of both Earths were forced to battle in order to save their respective homes, in a multiverse where worlds were being destroyed all around them. Not only were the heroes required to stretch the very limits of their powers in combat, they soon discovered that all their efforts may have been in vain—their separate worlds were no more.

INDEX

Main entries are **in bold**

N

O

P

Q

R

S

W

X

Y

Z

ACKNOWLEDGMENTS

DK WOULD LIKE TO THANK:
Matt Forbeck, Matt Manning, Dan Wallace, Alan Cowsill, and Glenn Dakin for their writing; Mike McKone for the cover art and Rod Reis for the colors; Jeff Youngquist, Brian Overton, Sarah Brunstad, and David Gabriel at Marvel; Chelsea Alon, Shihoh Tilley, and Krista Wong at Disney; Ralph Macchio for the foreword; Marcus Scudamore and Martin Stiff at Amazing15; Pamela Afram, Hannah Dolan, Tori Kosara, Helen Murray, Lauren Nesworthy, and Kathryn Hill for extra editorial help; Marc Richards and Nathan Martin for extra design assistance; Vanessa Bird for the index.